POSTMODERNISM,

or,

The Cultural Logic of Late Capitalism

POSTMODERNISM,

or,

The Cultural Logic of Late Capitalism

◆

FREDRIC JAMESON

VERSO

London · New York

First published in the UK by Verso 1991
and in the United States by Duke University Press
First printing in paperback 1992
Second printing in paperback 1993
© 1991 Duke University Press
All rights reserved

Verso
UK: 6 Meard Street, London W1V 3HR
USA: 29 West 35th Street, New York, NY 10001-2291

Verso is the imprint of New Left Books

British Library Cataloging in Publication Data
Jameson, Fredric
Postmodernism, or, The cultural logic of late capitalism.
1. Culture. Postmodernism.
I. Title
306

ISBN 0-86091-314-7
ISBN 0-86091-537-9

Printed by the The Cromwell Press,
Trowbridge, Wiltshire.
on acid free paper

A number of chapters, or parts of chapters, of this book
have appeared in previous publications, sometimes in an
earlier form. Chapter 1. 1984, "Postmodernism, Or, The
Cultural Logic of Late Capitalism." *New Left Review*, no.
146 (July–August): 59–92. Chapter 2. 1984, "The Politics
of Theory: Ideological Positions in the Debate." *New
German Critique*, no. 53 (Fall): 53–65. Chapter 4. 1990,
"Spatial Equivalents: Postmodernist Architecture and the
World System," *The States of Theory*, ed. David Carroll
(Columbia University Press): 125–48. Chapter 6. 1988,
"Postmodernism and Utopia. *Institute of Contemporary
Art* publication (Boston) (March): 11–32. Chapter 8. 1990,
'Postmodernism and the Market," in *The Retreat of the
Intellectuals: Socialist Register 1990*, ed. Ralph Miliband
and Leo Panitch (London: Merlin): 95–110. Chapter 9.
1989, "Nostalgia for the Present." *SAQ* 38, no. 2 (Spring):
517–37.

For Mitchell Lawrence

Contents

Introduction

It is safest to grasp the concept of the postmodern as an attempt to think the present historically in an age that has forgotten how to think historically in the first place. In that case, it either "expresses" some deeper irrepressible historical impulse (in however distorted a fashion) or effectively "represses" and diverts it, depending on the side of the ambiguity you happen to favor. Postmodernism, postmodern consciousness, may then amount to not much more than theorizing its own condition of possibility, which consists primarily in the sheer enumeration of changes and modifications. Modernism also thought compulsively about the New and tried to watch its coming into being (inventing for that purpose the registering and inscription devices akin to historical time-lapse photography), but the postmodern looks for breaks, for events rather than new worlds, for the telltale instant after which it is no longer the same; for the "When-it-all-changed," as Gibson puts it,[1] or, better still, for shifts and irrevocable changes in the *representation* of things and of the way they change. The moderns were interested in what was likely to come of such changes and their general tendency: they thought about the thing itself, substantively, in Utopian or essential fashion. Postmodernism is more formal in that sense, and more "distracted," as Benjamin might put it; it only clocks the variations themselves, and knows only too well that the contents are just more images. In modernism, as I will try to show later on, some residual zones of "nature" or "being," of the old, the older, the archaic, still subsist; culture can still do something to that nature and work at transforming that "referent." Postmodernism is what you have when the modernization process is complete and nature is gone for good. It is a more fully human world than the older one, but one in which "culture" has become a veritable "second nature." Indeed, what happened to culture may well be one of the more important clues for tracking the postmodern: an immense dilation of its sphere (the sphere of commodities), an immense and historically original acculturation of the Real, a quantum leap in what Benjamin still called the "aestheticization" of reality (he thought it meant fascism, but we know it's only fun: a prodigious exhilaration with the new order of things, a commodity rush, our "representations" of things tending to arouse an enthusiasm and a mood swing not necessarily inspired by the things themselves). So, in postmodern culture, "culture" has become a product in its own right; the market has become a substitute for itself and fully as much a commodity as any of the items it includes within itself: modernism was still minimally and tendentially the critique of the commodity and the effort to make it transcend itself. Postmodernism is the consumption of sheer commodification as a process. The "life-style" of the superstate therefore stands in relationship to Marx's "fetishism" of commodities as the most advanced monotheisms to primitive animisms or the most rudimentary idol worship; indeed, any sophisticated theory of the postmodern ought to bear something of the same relationship to Horkheimer and Adorno's old "Culture Industry" concept as MTV or fractal ads bear to fifties television series.

"Theory" has meanwhile itself also changed and offers its own kind of clue to the mystery. Indeed, one of the more striking features of the postmodern is the way in which, in it, a whole range of tendential analyses of hitherto very different kinds—economic forecasts, marketing studies, culture critiques, new therapies, the (generally official) jeremiad about drugs or permissiveness, reviews of art shows or national film festivals, religious "revivals" or cults—have all coalesced into a new discursive genre, which we might as well call "postmodernism theory," and which demands some attention in its own right. It is clearly a class which is a member of its own class, and I would not want to have to decide whether the following chapters are inquiries into the nature of such "postmodernism theory" or mere examples of it.

I have tried to prevent my own account of postmodernism—which stages a series of semiautonomous and relatively independent traits or features—from conflating back into the one uniquely privileged symptom of a loss of historicity, something that by itself could scarcely connote the presence of the postmodernism in any unerring fashion, as witness peasants, aesthetes, children, liberal economists, or analytic philosophers. But it is hard to discuss "postmodernism theory" in any

general way without having recourse to the matter of historical deaf-
ness, an exasperating condition (provided you are aware of it) that determines a series of spasmodic and intermittent, but desperate, attempts at
recuperation. Postmodernism theory is one of those attempts: the effort
to take the temperature of the age without instruments and in a situation in which we are not even sure there is so coherent a thing as an
"age," or zeitgeist or "system" or "current situation" any longer.
Postmodernism theory is then dialectical at least insofar as it has the
wit to seize on that very uncertainty as its first clue and to hold to its
Ariadne's thread on its way through what may not turn out to be a labyrinth at all, but a gulag or perhaps a shopping mall. An enormous Claes
Oldenburg thermometer, however, as long as a whole city block, might
serve as some mysterious symptom of the process, fallen without warning from the sky like a meteorite.

For I take it as axiomatic that "modernist history" is the first casualty
and mysterious absence of the postmodernism period (this is essentially Achille Bonito-Oliva's version of postmodernism theory):[2] in art,
at least, the notion of progress and telos remained alive and well up to
very recent times indeed, in its most authentic, least stupid and caricatural, form, in which each genuinely new work unexpectedly but logically outtrumped its predecessor (not "linear history" this, but rather
Shklovsky's "knight's gambit," the action at distance, the quantum leap
to the undeveloped or underdeveloped square). Dialectical history, to be
sure, affirmed that all history worked this way, on its left foot, as it were,
progressing, as Henri Lefebvre once put it, by way of catastrophe and
disaster; but fewer ears heard that than believed the modernist aesthetic
paradigm, which was on the point of being confirmed as a virtual religious doxa when it unexpectedly vanished without a trace. ("We went
out one morning and the Thermometer was gone!")

This seems to me a more interesting and plausible story than Lyotard's
related one about the end of "master narratives" (eschatalogical sche-
mata that were never really narratives in the first place, although I
may also have been incautious enough to use the expression from time
to time). But it now tells us at least two things about postmodernism
theory.

First, the theory seems necessarily imperfect or impure:[3] in the present case, owing to the "contradiction" whereby Oliva's (or Lyotard's)
perception of everything significant about the disappearance of master
narratives has itself to be couched in narrative form. Whether, as with
Gödel's proof, one can demonstrate the logical impossibility of any inter-

nally self-coherent theory of the postmodern—an antifoundationalism that really eschews all foundations altogether, a nonessentialism without the last shred of an essence in it—is a speculative question; its empirical answer is that none have so far appeared, all replicating within themselves a mimesis of their own title in the way in which they are parasitory on another system (most often on modernism itself), whose residual traces and unconsciously reproduced values and attitudes then become a precious index to the failure of a whole new culture to come to birth. Despite the delirium of some of its celebrants and apologists (whose euphoria, however, is an interesting historical symptom in its own right), a truly new culture could only emerge through the collective struggle to create a new social system. The constitutive impurity of all postmodernism theory, then (like capital itself, it must be at internal distance from itself, must include the foreign body of alien content), confirms the insight of a periodization that must be insisted on over and over again, namely, that postmodernism is not the cultural dominant of a wholly new social order (the rumor about which, under the name of "postindustrial society," ran through the media a few years ago), but only the reflex and the concomitant of yet another systemic modification of capitalism itself. No wonder, then, that shreds of its older avatars—of realism, even, fully as much as of modernism—live on, to be rewrapped in the luxurious trappings of their putative successor.

But this unforeseeable return of narrative as the narrative of the end of narratives, this return of history in the midst of the prognosis of the demise of historical telos, suggests a second feature of postmodernism theory which requires attention, namely, the way in which virtually any observation about the present can be mobilized in the very search for the present itself and pressed into service as a symptom and an index of the deeper logic of the postmodern, which imperceptibly turns into its own theory and the theory of itself. How could it be otherwise where there no longer exists any such "deeper logic" for the surface to manifest and where the symptom has become its own disease (and vice versa, no doubt)? But the frenzy whereby virtually anything in the present is appealed to for testimony as to the latter's uniqueness and radical difference from earlier moments of human time does indeed strike one sometimes as harboring a pathology distinctively autoreferential, as though our utter forgetfulness of the past exhausted itself in the vacant but mesmerized contemplation of a schizophrenic present that is incomparable virtually by definition.

However, as will be demonstrated later on, the decision as to whether one faces a break or a continuity—whether the present is to be seen as a historical originality or as the simple prolongation of more of the same under different sheep's clothing—is not an empirically justifiable or philosophically arguable one, since it is itself the inaugural narrative act that grounds the perception and interpretation of the events to be narrated. In what follows—but for pragmatic reasons I will disclose at the proper time—I have pretended to believe that the postmodern is as unusual as it thinks it is, and that it constitutes a cultural and experiential break worth exploring in greater detail.

Nor is this a merely or basely self-fulfilling procedure; or rather, it may well be that, but such procedures are by no means as frequent occurrences and possibilities as their formula suggests (they thereby themselves, predictably enough, become historical objects of study). For the name itself—postmodernism—has crystallized a host of hitherto independent developments which, thus named, prove to have contained the thing itself in embryo and now step forward richly to document its multiple genealogies. It thus turns out that it is not only in love, cratylism, and botany that the supreme act of nomination wields a material impact and, like lightning striking from the superstructure back to the base, fuses its unlikely materials into a gleaming lump or lava surface. The appeal to experience, otherwise so doubtful and untrustworthy —even though it does really seem as if any number of things had changed, perhaps for good!—now recovers a certain authority as what, in retrospect, the new name allowed you to think you felt, because you now have something to call it that other people seem to acknowledge by themselves using the word. The success story of the word *postmodernism* demands to be written, no doubt in best-seller format; such lexical neoevents, in which the coinage of a neologism has all the reality impact of a corporate merger, are among the novelties of media society which require not merely study but the establishment of a whole new media-lexicological subdiscipline. Why we needed the word *postmodernism* so long without knowing it, why a truly motley crew of strange bedfellows ran to embrace it the moment it appeared, are mysteries that will remain unclarified until we have been able to grasp the philosophical and social function of the concept, something impossible, in its turn, until we are somehow able to grasp the deeper identity between the two. In the present instance it seems clear that a range of competing formulations ("poststructuralism," "postindustrial society," this or that McLuhanite nomenclature) were unsatisfactory insofar as they were too rigidly specified and marked by their area of provenance (philosophy, economics, and the media, respectively); however suggestive, therefore, they could not occupy the mediatory position within the various specialized dimensions of postcontemporary life that was required. "Postmodern," however, seems to have been able to welcome in the appropriate areas of daily life or the quotidian; its cultural resonance, appropriately vaster than the merely aesthetic or artistic,[4] distracts suitably from the economic while allowing newer economic materials and innovations (in marketing and advertising, for example, but also in business organization) to be recatalogued under the new heading. Nor is the matter of recataloguing and transcoding without its own special kind of significance: the active function—the ethics and the politics—of such neologisms lies in the new work they propose of rewriting all the familiar things in new terms and thus proposing modifications, new ideal perspectives, a reshuffling of canonical feelings and values; if "postmodernism" corresponds to what Raymond Williams meant by his fundamental cultural category, a "structure of feeling" (and one that has become "hegemonic" at that, to use another of Williams's crucial categories), then it can only enjoy that status by dint of profound collective self-transformation, a reworking and rewriting of an older system. That ensures novelty and gives intellectuals and ideologues fresh and socially useful tasks: something also marked by the new term, with its vague, ominous or exhilarating, promise to get rid of whatever you found confining, unsatisfying, or boring about the modern, modernism, or modernity (however you understand those words): in other words, a very modest or mild apocalypse, the merest sea breeze (that has the additional advantage of having already taken place). But this prodigious rewriting operation—which can lead to whole new perspectives on subjectivity as well as on the object world—has the additional result, already touched on above, that everything is grist for its mill and that analyses like the one proposed here are easily reabsorbed into the project as a set of usefully unfamiliar transcoding rubrics.

The fundamental ideological task of the new concept, however, must remain that of coordinating new forms of practice and social and mental habits (this is finally what I take Williams to have had in mind by the notion of a "structure of feeling") with the new forms of economic production and organization thrown up by the modification of capitalism —the new global division of labor—in recent years. It is a relatively small and local version of what I elsewhere tried to generalize as "cultural revolution" on the scale of the mode of production itself;[5] in the same way the interrelationship of culture and the economic here is not a one-way street but a continuous reciprocal interaction and feedback loop. But just as (for Weber) new inner-directed and more ascetic religious values gradually produced "new people" capable of thriving in the delayed gratification of the emergent "modern" labor process, so also the "postmodern" is to be seen as the production of postmodern people capable of functioning in a very peculiar socioeconomic world indeed, one whose structure and objective features and requirements—if we had a proper account of them—would constitute the situation to which "postmodernism" is a response and would give us something a little more decisive than mere postmodernism theory. I have not done that here, of course, and it should be added that "culture," in the sense of what cleaves almost too close to the skin of the economic to be stripped off and inspected in its own right, is itself a postmodern development not unlike Magritte's shoe-foot. Unfortunately, therefore, the infrastructural description I seem to be calling for here is necessarily itself already cultural and a version of postmodernism theory in advance.

I have reprinted my program analysis of the postmodern ("The Cultural Logic of Late Capitalism") without significant modifications, since the attention it received at the time (1984) lends it the additional interest of a historical document; other features of the postmodern that have seemed to impose themselves since then are discussed in the conclusion. I have also not modified the sequel, which has been widely reprinted and which offers a *combinatoire* of positions on the postmodern, for and against, since while a great many more positions have been taken since then, the lineup remains essentially the same. The more fundamental modification in the situation today involves those who were once able to avoid using the word, out of principle; not many of them are left.

The remainder of this volume turns essentially on four themes: interpretation, Utopia, survivals of the modern, and "returns of the repressed" of historicity, none of which were present in these forms in my original essay. The problem of interpretation is raised by the nature of the new textuality itself, which, when mainly visual, seems to leave no room for interpretation of the older kind, or, when mainly temporal in its "total flow," leaves no time for it either. The exhibits here are the videotext as such and also the *nouveau roman* (the last significant innovation in the novel, about which I will also argue that, within the new reconfiguration of the "fine arts" in postmodernism, it is no longer a very significant form or marker); on the other hand, video can lay some claim to being postmodernism's most distinctive new medium, a medium which, at its best, is a whole new form in itself.

Utopia is a spatial matter that might be thought to know a potential change in fortunes in so spatialized a culture as the postmodern; but if this last is as dehistoricized and dehistoricizing as I sometimes claim here, the synaptic chain that might lead the Utopian impulse to expression becomes harder to localize. Utopian representations knew an extraordinary revival in the 1960s; if postmodernism is the substitute for the sixties and the compensation for their political failure, the question of Utopia would seem to be a crucial test of what is left of our capacity to imagine change at all. Such, at least, is the question addressed here to one of the most interesting (and least characteristic) buildings of the postmodern period, Frank Gehry's house in Santa Monica, California; it is also addressed, around and behind the visual, as it were, to contemporary photography and installation art. At any rate, *Utopian*, in First World postmodernism, has become a powerful (left) political word rather than its opposite.

But if Michael Speaks is right, and there is no pure postmodernism as such, then the residual traces of modernism must be seen in another light, less as anachronisms than as necessary failures that inscribe the particular postmodern project back into its context, while at the same time reopening the question of the modern itself for reexamination. That reexamination will not be undertaken here; but the residuality of the modern and its values—most notably irony (in Venturi or DeMan) or the questions of totality and representation—offer the occasion for working out one of the assertions of my initial essay that most troubled some readers; namely, the notion that what was variously called "poststructuralism" or even simply "theory" was also a subvariety of the postmodern, or at least proves to be that in hindsight. Theory—I here prefer the more cumbersome formula "theoretical discourse"—has seemed unique, if not privileged, among the postmodern arts and genres in its occasional capacity to defy the gravity of the zeitgeist and to produce schools, movements, and even avant-gardes where they are no longer supposed to exist. Two very lengthy and disproportionate chapters examine two of the most successful American theoretical avant-gardes, deconstruction and the New Historicism, for traces of their modernity and postmodernity alike. But Simon's old "new novel" could also be the object of this kind of discrimination, which will not take us very far unless—for the urge to classify objects once and for all in the modern, or the postmodern, or even Jencks's "late modern" or other "transitional" categories—we build a model of the contradictions all these categories stage within the text itself.

In any case, this book is not a survey of the "postmodern," nor even an introduction to it (always supposing such a thing was possible in the first place); nor are any of its textual exhibits characteristic of the postmodern or prime *examples* of it, "illustrations" of its principal features. That has something to do with the qualities of the characteristic, the exemplary, and the illustrative; but it has more to do with the nature of postmodern texts themselves, which is to say, the nature of a *text* in the first place, since that is a postmodern category and phenomenon which has replaced the older one of a "work." Indeed, in one of those extraordinary postmodern mutations where the apocalyptic suddenly turns into the decorative (or at least diminishes abruptly into "something you have around the home"), Hegel's legendary "end of art"—the premonitory concept that signaled modernism's supreme anti- or transaesthetic vocation to be more than art (or religion either, or even "philosophy" in some narrower sense)—now modestly simmers down into the "end of the work of art" and the arrival of the text. But this throws the chicken coops of criticism into commotion fully as much as it stirs those of "creation": the fundamental disparity and incommensurability between *text* and *work* means that to select sample texts and, by analysis, to make them bear the universalizing weight of a representative particular, turns them imperceptibly back into that older thing, the work, which is not supposed to exist in the postmodern. This is, as it were, the Heisenberg principle of postmodernism, and the most difficult representational problem for any commentator to come to terms with, save via the endless slide show, "total flow" prolonged into the infinite.

The same holds true for my penultimate chapter, on some recent films and some recent representations of history of a new and allegorical type. The word *nostalgia* in my title, however, does not mean what I normally want to make it mean, and I will therefore exceptionally (other objections being dealt with at some length in the concluding section) comment in advance on an expression, "nostalgia film," about which I have some misunderstandings to regret. I don't remember any longer whether I am responsible for this term, which still seems to me indispensable, provided you understand that the fashion-plate, historicist films it designates are in no way to be grasped as passionate expressions of that older longing once called nostalgia but rather quite the opposite; they are a depersonalized visual curiosity and a "return of the repressed" of the twenties and thirties "without affect" (in another place I try to term it "nostalgia-deco"). But one can no more alter a term like this retroactively than substitute some altogether different word for postmodernism itself.

The "total flow" of associative conclusions then takes up, in passing, some of the other inveterate but more serious objections to or misunderstandings of my positions and also comments on politics, demography, nominalism, media and the image, and other topics which ought to figure in any self-respecting book on the subject. In particular I have tried to remedy what (rightly) struck some readers as a crucial missing component of the program essay, namely, the absence of any discussion of "agency," or the lack of what I prefer to call, following old Plekhanov, any "social equivalent" for this seemingly disembodied cultural logic.

Agency, however, raises the issue of the other unit of my title, "late capitalism," about which something further needs to be said. In particular, people have begun to notice that it functions as a sign of some kind and seems to carry a burden of intent and consequences not clear to the noninitiate.[6] It is not my favorite slogan, and I try to vary it with the appropriate synonyms ("multinational capitalism," "spectacle or image society," "media capitalism," "the world system," even "postmodernism" itself); but as the Right has also spotted what evidently seems to them a dangerous new concept and way of speaking (even though some of the economic diagnoses overlap their own, and a term like *postindustrial society* certainly has a family likeness), this particular terrain of ideological struggle, which unfortunately one rarely chooses oneself, seems a solid one and worth defending.

As far as I can see, the general use of the term *late capitalism* originated with the Frankfurt School;[7] it is everywhere in Adorno and Horkheimer, sometimes varied with their own synonyms (for example, "administered society"), which make it clear that a very different conception was involved, of a more Weberian type, which, derived essentially from Grossman and Pollock, stressed two essential features: (1) a tendential web of bureaucratic control (in its more nightmarish forms, a Foucault-like grid *avant la lettre*), and (2) the interpenetration of government and big business ("state capitalism") such that Nazism and the New Deal are related systems (and some form of socialism, benign or Stalinist, also seems on the agenda).

As widely used today, the term *late capitalism* has very different overtones from these. No one particularly notices the expansion of the state sector and bureaucratization any longer: it seems a simple, "natural" fact of life. What marks the development of the new concept over the older one (which was still roughly consistent with Lenin's notion of a "monopoly stage" of capitalism) is not merely an emphasis on the emergence of new forms of business organization (multinationals, transna-

tionals) beyond the monopoly stage but, above all, the vision of a world
capitalist system fundamentally distinct from the older imperialism,
which was little more than a rivalry between the various colonial powers. The scholastic, I am tempted to say theological, debates on whether
the various notions of "late capitalism" are really consistent with Marxism itself (despite Marx's own repeated evocation, in the *Grundrisse*, of
the "world market" as the ultimate horizon of capitalism)[8] turn on this
matter of internationalization and how it is to be described (and in particular whether the component of "dependency theory" or of Waller-
stein's "world system" theory is a production model, based on social
classes). In spite of these theoretical uncertainties, it seems fair to say
that today we have some rough idea of this new system (called "late
capitalism" in order to mark its continuity with what preceded it rather
than the break, rupture, and mutation that concepts like "postindustrial
society" wished to underscore). Besides the forms of transnational business mentioned above, its features include the new international division of labor, a vertiginous new dynamic in international banking and
the stock exchanges (including the enormous Second and Third World
debt), new forms of media interrelationship (very much including transportation systems such as containerization), computers and automation,
the flight of production to advanced Third World areas, along with all
the more familiar social consequences, including the crisis of traditional
labor, the emergence of yuppies, and gentrification on a now-global scale.

In periodizing a phenomenon of this kind, we have to complicate the
model with all kinds of supplementary epicycles. It is necessary to distinguish between the gradual setting in place of the various (often unrelated) preconditions for the new structure and the "moment" (not exactly
chronological) when they all jell and combine into a functional system.
This moment is itself less a matter of chronology than it is of a well-
nigh Freudian *Nachträglichkeit*, or retroactivity: people become aware
of the dynamics of some new system, in which they are themselves
seized, only later on and gradually. Nor is that dawning collective consciousness of a new system (deduced itself intermittently in a fragmentary way from various unrelated crisis symptoms such as factory closings
or higher interest rates) exactly the same as the coming into being of
fresh cultural forms of expression (Raymond Williams's "structures of
feeling" do finally strike one as a very odd way to have to characterize
postmodernism culturally). That the various preconditions for a new
"structure of feeling" also preexist their moment of combination and
crystallization into a relatively hegemonic style everyone acknowledges;

but that prehistory is not in synch with the economic one. Thus Mandel suggests that the basic new technological prerequisites of the new "long wave" of capitalism's third stage (here called "late capitalism") were available by the end of World War II, which also had the effect of reorganizing international relations, decolonizing the colonies, and laying the groundwork for the emergence of a new economic world system. Culturally, however, the precondition is to be found (apart from a wide variety of aberrant modernist "experiments" which are then restructured in the form of predecessors) in the enormous social and psychological transformations of the 1960s, which swept so much of tradition away on the level of *mentalités*. Thus the economic preparation of postmodernism or late capitalism began in the 1950s, after the wartime shortages of consumer goods and spare parts had been made up, and new products and new technologies (not least those of the media) could be pioneered. On the other hand, the psychic *habitus* of the new age demands the absolute break, strengthened by a generational rupture, achieved more properly in the 1960s (it being understood that economic development does not then pause for *that*, but very much continues along its own level and according to its own logic). If you prefer a now somewhat antiquated language, the distinction is very much the one Althusser used to harp on between a Hegelian "essential cross section" of the present (or *coupe d'essence*), where a culture critique wants to find a single principle of the "postmodern" inherent in the most varied and ramified features of social life, and that Althusserian "structure in dominance" in which the various levels entertain a semiautonomy over against each other, run at different rates of speed, develop unevenly, and yet conspire to produce a totality. Add to this the unavoidable representational problem that there is no "late capitalism in general" but only this or that specific national form of the thing, and non-North American readers will inevitably deplore the Americanocentrism of my own particular account, which is justified only to the degree that it was the brief "American century" (1945–73) that constituted the hothouse, or forcing ground, of the new system, while the development of the cultural forms of postmodernism may be said to be the first specifically North American global style.

Meanwhile, it is my sense that both levels in question, infrastructure and superstructures—the economic system and the cultural "structure of feeling"—somehow crystallized in the great shock of the crises of 1973 (the oil crisis, the end of the international gold standard, for all intents and purposes the end of the great wave of "wars of national liberation" and the beginning of the end of traditional communism), which, now that the dust clouds have rolled away, disclose the existence, already in place, of a strange new landscape: the landscape the essays in this book try to describe (along with an increasing number of other probes and hypothetical accounts).[9]

This matter of periodization is not, however, altogether alien to the signals given off by the expression "late capitalism," which is by now clearly identified as a kind of leftist logo which is ideologically and politically booby-trapped, so that the very act of using it constitutes tacit agreement about a whole range of essentially Marxian social and economic propositions the other side may be far from wanting to endorse. *Capitalism* was itself always a funny word in this sense: just using the word—otherwise a neutral enough designation for an economic and social system on whose properties all sides agree—seemed to position you in a vaguely critical, suspicious, if not outright socialist stance: only committed right-wing ideologues and full-throated market apologists also use it with the same relish.

"Late capitalism" still does some of that, but with a difference: its qualifier in particular rarely means anything so silly as the ultimate senescence, breakdown, and death of the system as such (a temporal vision that would rather seem to belong to modernism than postmodernism). What "late" generally conveys is rather the sense that something has changed, that things are different, that we have gone through a transformation of the life world which is somehow decisive but incomparable with the older convulsions of modernization and industrialization, less perceptible and dramatic, somehow, but more permanent precisely because more thoroughgoing and all-pervasive.[10]

That means that the expression *late capitalism* carries the other, cultural half of my title within it as well; not only is it something like a literal translation of the other expression, *postmodernism*, its temporal index seems already to direct attention to changes in the quotidian and on the cultural level as such. To say that my two terms, the *cultural* and the *economic*, thereby collapse back into one another and say the same thing, in an eclipse of the distinction between base and superstructure that has itself often struck people as significantly characteristic of postmodernism in the first place, is also to suggest that the base, in the third stage of capitalism, generates its superstructures with a new kind of dynamic. And this may also be what (rightly) worries the unconverted about the term; it seems to obligate you in advance to talk about cultural phenomena at least in business terms if not in those of political economy.

As for *postmodernism* itself, I have not tried to systematize a usage or to impose any conveniently coherent thumbnail meaning, for the concept is not merely contested, it is also internally conflicted and contradictory. I will argue that, for good or ill, we cannot *not* use it. But my argument should also be taken to imply that every time it is used, we are under the obligation to rehearse those inner contradictions and to stage those representational inconsistencies and dilemmas; we have to work all that through every time around. *Postmodernism* is not something we can settle once and for all and then use with a clear conscience. The concept, if there is one, has to come at the end, and not at the beginning, of our discussions of it. Those are the conditions—the *only* ones, I think, that prevent the mischief of premature clarification—under which this term can productively continue to be used.

The materials assembled in the present volume constitute the third and last section of the penultimate subdivision of a larger project entitled *The Poetics of Social Forms.*

Durham, April 1990

The Cultural Logic of

Late Capitalism

The last few years have been marked by an inverted millenarianism in which premonitions of the future, catastrophic or redemptive, have been replaced by senses of the end of this or that (the end of ideology, art, or social class; the "crisis" of Leninism, social democracy, or the welfare state, etc., etc.); taken together, all of these perhaps constitute what is increasingly called postmodernism. The case for its existence depends on the hypothesis of some radical break or *coupure*, generally traced back to the end of the 1950s or the early 1960s.

As the word itself suggests, this break is most often related to notions of the waning or extinction of the hundred-year-old modern movement (or to its ideological or aesthetic repudiation). Thus abstract expressionism in painting, existentialism in philosophy, the final forms of representation in the novel, the films of the great *auteurs*, or the modernist school of poetry (as institutionalized and canonized in the works of Wallace Stevens) all are now seen as the final, extraordinary flowering of a high-modernist impulse which is spent and exhausted with them. The enumeration of what follows, then, at once becomes empirical, chaotic, and heterogeneous: Andy Warhol and pop art, but also photorealism, and beyond it, the "new expressionism"; the moment, in music, of John Cage, but also the synthesis of classical and "popular" styles found in composers like Phil Glass and Terry Riley, and also punk and new wave rock (the Beatles and the Stones now standing as the high-modernist moment of that more recent and rapidly evolving tradition); in film, Godard, post-Godard, and experimental cinema and video, but also a whole new type of commercial film (about which more below); Burroughs, Pynchon, or Ishmael Reed, on the one hand, and the French *nouveau roman* and its succession, on the other, along with alarming new kinds of literary criticism based on some new aesthetic of textuality or *écriture* . . . The list might be extended indefinitely; but does it imply any more fundamental change or break than the periodic style and fashion changes determined by an older high-modernist imperative of stylistic innovation?

It is in the realm of architecture, however, that modifications in aesthetic production are most dramatically visible, and that their theoretical problems have been most centrally raised and articulated; it was indeed from architectural debates that my own conception of postmodernism—as it will be outlined in the following pages—initially began to emerge. More decisively than in the other arts or media, postmodernist positions in architecture have been inseparable from an implacable critique of architectural high modernism and of Frank Lloyd Wright or the so-called international style (Le Corbusier, Mies, etc), where formal criticism and analysis (of the high-modernist transformation of the building into a virtual sculpture, or monumental "duck," as Robert Venturi puts it)[1] are at one with reconsiderations on the level of urbanism and of the aesthetic institution. High modernism is thus credited with the destruction of the fabric of the traditional city and its older neighborhood culture (by way of the radical disjunction of the new Utopian high-modernist building from its surrounding context), while the prophetic elitism and authoritarianism of the modern movement are remorselessly identified in the imperious gesture of the charismatic Master.

Postmodernism in architecture will then logically enough stage itself as a kind of aesthetic populism, as the very title of Venturi's influential manifesto, *Learning from Las Vegas*, suggests. However we may ultimately wish to evaluate this populist rhetoric,[2] it has at least the merit of drawing our attention to one fundamental feature of all the postmodernisms enumerated above: namely, the effacement in them of the older (essentially high-modernist) frontier between high culture and so-called mass or commercial culture, and the emergence of new kinds of texts infused with the forms, categories, and contents of that very culture industry so passionately denounced by all the ideologues of the modern, from Leavis and the American New Criticism all the way to Adorno and the Frankfurt School. The postmodernisms have, in fact, been fascinated precisely by this whole "degraded" landscape of schlock and kitsch, of TV series and *Reader's Digest* culture, of advertising and motels, of the late show and the grade-B Hollywood film, of so-called paraliterature, with its airport paperback categories of the gothic and the romance, the popular biography, the murder mystery, and the science fiction or fantasy novel: materials they no longer simply "quote," as a Joyce or a Mahler might have done, but incorporate into their very substance.

Nor should the break in question be thought of as a purely cultural affair: indeed, theories of the postmodern—whether celebratory or couched in the language of moral revulsion and denunciation—bear a strong family resemblance to all those more ambitious sociological generalizations which, at much the same time, bring us the news of the arrival and inauguration of a whole new type of society, most famously baptized "postindustrial society" (Daniel Bell) but often also designated consumer society, media society, information society, electronic society or high tech, and the like. Such theories have the obvious ideological mission of demonstrating, to their own relief, that the new social formation in question no longer obeys the laws of classical capitalism, namely, the primacy of industrial production and the omnipresence of class struggle. The Marxist tradition has therefore resisted them with vehemence, with the signal exception of the economist Ernest Mandel, whose book *Late Capitalism* sets out not merely to anatomize the historic originality of this new society (which he sees as a third stage or moment in the evolution of capital) but also to demonstrate that it is, if anything, a purer stage of capitalism than any of the moments that preceded it. I will return to this argument later; suffice it for the moment to anticipate a point that will be argued in chapter 2, namely, that every position on postmodernism in culture—whether apologia or stigmatization—is also at one and the same time, and *necessarily*, an implicitly or explicitly political stance on the nature of multinational capitalism today.

A last preliminary word on method: what follows is not to be read as stylistic description, as the account of one cultural style or movement among others. I have rather meant to offer a periodizing hypothesis, and that at a moment in which the very conception of historical periodization has come to seem most problematical indeed. I have argued elsewhere that all isolated or discrete cultural analysis always involves a buried or repressed theory of historical periodization; in any case, the conception of the "genealogy" largely lays to rest traditional theoretical worries about so-called linear history, theories of "stages," and teleological historiography. In the present context, however, lengthier theoretical discussion of such (very real) issues can perhaps be replaced by a few substantive remarks.

One of the concerns frequently aroused by periodizing hypotheses is that these tend to obliterate difference and to project an idea of the historical period as massive homogeneity (bounded on either side by inexplicable chronological metamorphoses and punctuation marks). This is, however, precisely why it seems to me essential to grasp postmodernism not as a style but rather as a cultural dominant: a conception which allows for the presence and coexistence of a range of very different, yet subordinate, features.

Consider, for example, the powerful alternative position that postmodernism is itself little more than one more stage of modernism proper (if not, indeed, of the even older romanticism); it may indeed be conceded that all the features of postmodernism I am about to enumerate can be detected, full-blown, in this or that preceding modernism (including such astonishing genealogical precursors as Gertrude Stein, Raymond Roussel, or Marcel Duchamp, who may be considered outright postmodernists, avant la lettre). What has not been taken into account by this view, however, is the social position of the older modernism, or better still, its passionate repudiation by an older Victorian and post-Victorian bourgeoisie for whom its forms and ethos are received as being variously ugly, dissonant, obscure, scandalous, immoral, subversive, and generally "antisocial." It will be argued here, however, that a mutation in the sphere of culture has rendered such attitudes archaic. Not only are Picasso and Joyce no longer ugly; they now strike us, on the whole, as rather "realistic," and this is the result of a canonization and academic institutionalization of the modern movement generally that can be traced to the late 1950s. This is surely one of the most plausible explanations for the emergence of postmodernism itself, since the younger generation of the 1960s will now confront the formerly oppositional modern movement as a set of dead classics, which "weigh like a nightmare on the brains of the living," as Marx once said in a different context.

As for the postmodern revolt against all that, however, it must equally be stressed that its own offensive features—from obscurity and sexually explicit material to psychological squalor and overt expressions of social and political defiance, which transcend anything that might have been imagined at the most extreme moments of high modernism—no longer scandalize anyone and are not only received with the greatest complacency but have themselves become institutionalized and are at one with the official or public culture of Western society.

What has happened is that aesthetic production today has become integrated into commodity production generally: the frantic economic urgency of producing fresh waves of ever more novel-seeming goods (from clothing to airplanes), at ever greater rates of turnover, now assigns an increasingly essential structural function and position to aesthetic innovation and experimentation. Such economic necessities then find recognition in the varied kinds of institutional support available for the newer art, from foundations and grants to museums and other forms of patronage. Of all the arts, architecture is the closest constitutively to the economic, with which, in the form of commissions and land values, it has a virtually unmediated relationship. It will therefore not be surprising to find the extraordinary flowering of the new postmodern architecture grounded in the patronage of multinational business, whose expansion and development is strictly contemporaneous with it. Later I will suggest that these two new phenomena have an even deeper dialectical interrelationship than the simple one-to-one financing of this or that individual project. Yet this is the point at which I must remind the reader of the obvious; namely, that this whole global, yet American, postmodern culture is the internal and superstructural expression of a whole new wave of American military and economic domination throughout the world: in this sense, as throughout class history, the underside of culture is blood, torture, death, and terror.

The first point to be made about the conception of periodization in dominance, therefore, is that even if all the constitutive features of postmodernism were identical with and coterminous to those of an older modernism—a position I feel to be demonstrably erroneous but which only an even lengthier analysis of modernism proper could dispel—the two phenomena would still remain utterly distinct in their meaning and social function, owing to the very different positioning of postmodernism in the economic system of late capital and, beyond that, to the transformation of the very sphere of culture in contemporary society.

This point will be further discussed at the conclusion of this book. I must now briefly address a different kind of objection to periodization, a concern about its possible obliteration of heterogeneity, one most often expressed by the Left. And it is certain that there is a strange quasi-Sartrean irony—a "winner loses" logic—which tends to surround any effort to describe a "system," a totalizing dynamic, as these are detected in the movement of contemporary society. What happens is that the more powerful the vision of some increasingly total system or logic —the Foucault of the prisons book is the obvious example—the more powerless the reader comes to feel. Insofar as the theorist wins, therefore, by constructing an increasingly closed and terrifying machine, to that very degree he loses, since the critical capacity of his work is thereby paralyzed, and the impulses of negation and revolt, not to speak of those of social transformation, are increasingly perceived as vain and trivial in the face of the model itself.

I have felt, however, that it was only in the light of some conception of a dominant cultural logic or hegemonic norm that genuine difference could be measured and assessed. I am very far from feeling that all cultural production today is "postmodern" in the broad sense I will be conferring on this term. The postmodern is, however, the force field in which very different kinds of cultural impulses—what Raymond Williams has usefully termed "residual" and "emergent" forms of cultural production—must make their way. If we do not achieve some general sense of a cultural dominant, then we fall back into a view of present history as sheer heterogeneity, random difference, a coexistence of a host of distinct forces whose effectivity is undecidable. At any rate, this has been the political spirit in which the following analysis was devised: to project some conception of a new systematic cultural norm and its reproduction in order to reflect more adequately on the most effective forms of any radical cultural politics today.

The exposition will take up in turn the following constitutive features of the postmodern: a new depthlessness, which finds its prolongation both in contemporary "theory" and in a whole new culture of the image or the simulacrum; a consequent weakening of historicity, both in our relationship to public History and in the new forms of our private temporality, whose "schizophrenic" structure (following Lacan) will determine new types of syntax or syntagmatic relationships in the more temporal arts; a whole new type of emotional ground tone—what I will call "intensities"—which can best be grasped by a return to older theories of the sublime; the deep constitutive relationships of all this to a whole new technology, which is itself a figure for a whole new economic world system; and, after a brief account of postmodernist mutations in the lived experience of built space itself, some reflections on the mission of political art in the bewildering new world space of late or multinational capital.

I

We will begin with one of the canonical works of high modernism in visual art, Van Gogh's well-known painting of the peasant shoes, an example which, as you can imagine, has not been innocently or randomly chosen. I want to propose two ways of reading this painting, both of which in some fashion reconstruct the reception of the work in a two-stage or double-level process.

I first want to suggest that if this copiously reproduced image is not to sink to the level of sheer decoration, it requires us to reconstruct some initial situation out of which the finished work emerges. Unless that situation—which has vanished into the past—is somehow mentally restored, the painting will remain an inert object, a reified end product impossible to grasp as a symbolic act in its own right, as praxis and as production.

This last term suggests that one way of reconstructing the initial situation to which the work is somehow a response is by stressing the raw materials, the initial content, which it confronts and reworks, transforms, and appropriates. In Van Gogh that content, those initial raw materials, are, I will suggest, to be grasped simply as the whole object world of agricultural misery, of stark rural poverty, and the whole rudimentary human world of backbreaking peasant toil, a world reduced to its most brutal and menaced, primitive and marginalized state.

Fruit trees in this world are ancient and exhausted sticks coming out of poor soil; the people of the village are worn down to their skulls, caricatures of some ultimate grotesque typology of basic human feature types. How is it, then, that in Van Gogh such things as apple trees explode into a hallucinatory surface of color, while his village stereotypes are suddenly and garishly overlaid with hues of red and green? I will briefly suggest, in this first interpretative option, that the willed and violent transformation of a drab peasant object world into the most glorious materialization of pure color in oil paint is to be seen as a Utopian gesture, an act of compensation which ends up producing a whole new Utopian realm of the senses, or at least of that supreme sense—sight, the visual, the eye—which it now reconstitutes for us as a semiautonomous space in its own right, a part of some new division of labor in the body of capital, some new fragmentation of the emergent sensorium which replicates the specializations and divisions of capitalist life at the same time that it seeks in precisely such fragmentation a desperate Utopian compensation for them.

There is, to be sure, a second reading of Van Gogh which can hardly be ignored when we gaze at this particular painting, and that is Heidegger's central analysis in *Der Ursprung des Kunstwerkes*, which is organized around the idea that the work of art emerges within the gap between Earth and World, or what I would prefer to translate as the meaningless materiality of the body and nature and the meaning endowment of history and of the social. We will return to that particular gap or rift later on; suffice it here to recall some of the famous phrases that model the process whereby these henceforth illustrious peasant shoes slowly re-create about themselves the whole missing object world which was once their lived context. "In them," says Heidegger, "there vibrates the silent call of the earth, its quiet gift of ripening corn and its enigmatic self-refusal in the fallow desolation of the wintry field." "This equipment," he goes on, "belongs to the *earth*, and it is protected in the *world* of the peasant woman. . . . Van Gogh's painting is the disclosure of what the equipment, the pair of peasant shoes, *is* in truth. . . . This entity emerges into the unconcealment of its being,"[3] by way of the mediation of the work of art, which draws the whole absent world and earth into revelation around itself, along with the heavy tread of the peasant woman, the loneliness of the field path, the hut in the clearing, the worn and broken instruments of labor in the furrows and at the hearth. Heidegger's account needs to be completed by insistence on the renewed materiality of the work, on the transformation of one form of materiality —the earth itself and its paths and physical objects—into that other materiality of oil paint affirmed and foregrounded in its own right and for its own visual pleasures, but nonetheless it has a satisfying plausibility.

At any rate, both readings may be described as *hermeneutical*, in the sense in which the work in its inert, objectal form is taken as a clue or a symptom for some vaster reality which replaces it as its ultimate truth. Now we need to look at some shoes of a different kind, and it is pleasant to be able to draw for such an image on the recent work of the central figure in contemporary visual art. Andy Warhol's *Diamond Dust Shoes* evidently no longer speaks to us with any of the immediacy of Van Gogh's footgear; indeed, I am tempted to say that it does not really speak to us at all. Nothing in this painting organizes even a minimal place for the viewer, who confronts it at the turning of a museum corridor or gallery with all the contingency of some inexplicable natural object. On the level of the content, we have to do with what are now far more clearly fetishes, in both the Freudian and the Marxian senses (Derrida remarks, somewhere, about the Heideggerian *Paar Bauernschuhe*, that the Van Gogh footgear are a heterosexual pair, which allows neither for perversion nor for fetishization). Here, however, we have a random collection of dead objects hanging together on the canvas like so many turnips, as shorn of their earlier life world as the pile of shoes left over from Auschwitz or the remainders and tokens of some incomprehensible and tragic fire in a packed dance hall. There is therefore in Warhol no way to complete the hermeneutic gesture and restore to these oddments that whole larger lived context of the dance hall or the ball, the world of jetset fashion or glamour magazines. Yet this is even more paradoxical in the light of biographical information: Warhol began his artistic career as a commercial illustrator for shoe fashions and a designer of display windows in which various pumps and slippers figured prominently. Indeed, one is tempted to raise here—far too prematurely—one of the central issues about postmodernism itself and its possible political dimensions: Andy Warhol's work in fact turns centrally around commodification, and the great billboard images of the Coca-Cola bottle or the Campbell's soup can, which explicitly foreground the commodity fetishism of a transition to late capital, *ought* to be powerful and critical political statements. If they are not that, then one would surely want to know why, and one would want to begin to wonder a little more seriously about the possibilities of political or critical art in the postmodern period of late capital.

But there are some other significant differences between the high-modernist and the postmodernist moment, between the shoes of Van Gogh and the shoes of Andy Warhol, on which we must now very briefly dwell. The first and most evident is the emergence of a new kind of flatness or depthlessness, a new kind of superficiality in the most literal sense, perhaps the supreme formal feature of all the postmodernisms to which we will have occasion to return in a number of other contexts.

Then we must surely come to terms with the role of photography and the photographic negative in contemporary art of this kind; and it is this, indeed, which confers its deathly quality to the Warhol image, whose glacéd X-ray elegance mortifies the reified eye of the viewer in a way that would seem to have nothing to do with death or the death obsession or the death anxiety on the level of content. It is indeed as though we had here to do with the inversion of Van Gogh's Utopian gesture: in the earlier work a stricken world is by some Nietzschean fiat and act of the will transformed into the stridency of Utopian color. Here, on the contrary, it is as though the external and colored surface of things —debased and contaminated in advance by their assimilation to glossy advertising images—has been stripped away to reveal the deathly black-and-white substratum of the photographic negative with subtends them. Although this kind of death of the world of appearance becomes thematized in certain of Warhol's pieces, most notably the traffic accidents or the electric chair series, this is not, I think, a matter of content any longer but of some more fundamental mutation both in the object world itself—now become a set of texts or simulacra—and in the disposition of the subject.

All of which brings me to a third feature to be developed here, what I will call the waning of affect in postmodern culture. Of course, it would be inaccurate to suggest that all affect, all feeling or emotion, all subjectivity, has vanished from the newer image. Indeed, there is a kind of return of the repressed in *Diamond Dust Shoes*, a strange, compensatory, decorative exhilaration, explicitly designated by the title itself, which is, of course, the glitter of gold dust, the spangling of gilt sand that seals the surface of the painting and yet continues to glint at us. Think, however, of Rimbaud's magical flowers "that look back at you," or of the august premonitory eye flashes of Rilke's archaic Greek torso which warn the bourgeois subject to change his life; nothing of that sort here in the gratuitous frivolity of this final decorative overlay. In an interesting review of the Italian version of this essay,[4] Remo Ceserani expands this foot fetishism into a fourfold image which adds to the gaping "modernist" expressivity of the Van Gogh-Heidegger shoes the "realist" pathos of Walker Evans and James Agee (strange that pathos should thus require a team!); while what looked like a random assortment of yesteryear's fashions in Warhol takes on, in Magritte, the carnal reality of the human member itself, now more phantasmic than the leather it is printed on. Magritte, unique among the surrealists, survived the sea change from the modern to its sequel, becoming in the process something of a postmodern emblem: the uncanny, Lacanian foreclusion, without expression. The ideal schizophrenic, indeed, is easy enough to please provided only an eternal present is thrust before the eyes, which gaze with equal fascination on an old shoe or the tenaciously growing organic mystery of the human toenail. Ceserani thereby deserves a semiotic cube of his own:

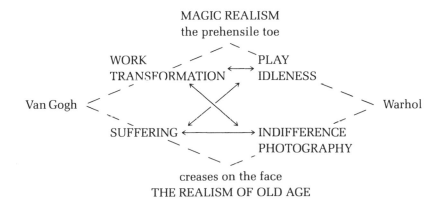

MAGIC REALISM
the prehensile toe

WORK   PLAY
TRANSFORMATION   IDLENESS

Van Gogh   Warhol

SUFFERING ⟷ INDIFFERENCE
PHOTOGRAPHY

creases on the face
THE REALISM OF OLD AGE

Vincent Van Gogh, "A Pair of Boots"

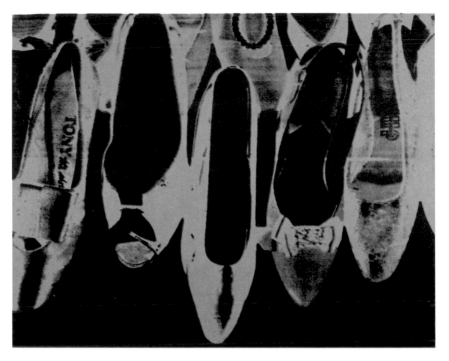

Andy Warhol, "Diamond Dust Shoes"

René Magritte, "Le modèle rouge"

Edvard Munch, "The Scream"

The Westin Bonaventure, interior (Portman)

Oliver Wasow, "#146"

Frank Gehry House, Santa Monica, California

Diego Rivera, "Man at the Crossroads"

Walker Evans, "Floyd Burroughs' Work Shoes"

The waning of affect is, however, perhaps best initially approached by way of the human figure, and it is obvious that what we have said about the commodification of objects holds as strongly for Warhol's human subjects: stars—like Marilyn Monroe—who are themselves commodified and transformed into their own images. And here too a certain brutal return to the older period of high modernism offers a dramatic shorthand parable of the transformation in question. Edward Munch's painting *The Scream* is, of course, a canonical expression of the great modernist thematics of alienation, anomie, solitude, social fragmentation, and isolation, a virtually programmatic emblem of what used to be called the age of anxiety. It will here be read as an embodiment not merely of the expression of that kind of affect but, even more, as a virtual deconstruction of the very aesthetic of expression itself, which seems to have dominated much of what we call high modernism but to have vanished away—for both practical and theoretical reasons—in the world of the postmodern. The very concept of expression presupposes indeed some separation within the subject, and along with that a whole metaphysics of the inside and outside, of the wordless pain within the monad and the moment in which, often cathartically, that "emotion" is then projected out and externalized, as gesture or cry, as desperate communication and the outward dramatization of inward feeling.

This is perhaps the moment to say something about contemporary theory, which has, among other things, been committed to the mission of criticizing and discrediting this very hermeneutic model of the inside and the outside and of stigmatizing such models as ideological and metaphysical. But what is today called contemporary theory—or better still, theoretical discourse—is also, I want to argue, itself very precisely a postmodernist phenomenon. It would therefore be inconsistent to defend the truth of its theoretical insights in a situation in which the very concept of "truth" itself is part of the metaphysical baggage which poststructuralism seeks to abandon. What we can at least suggest is that the poststructuralist critique of the hermeneutic, of what I will shortly call the depth model, is useful for us as a very significant symptom of the very postmodernist culture which is our subject here.

Overhastily, we can say that besides the hermeneutic model of inside and outside which Munch's painting develops, at least four other fundamental depth models have generally been repudiated in contemporary theory: (1) the dialectical one of essence and appearance (along with a whole range of concepts of ideology or false consciousness which tend to accompany it); (2) the Freudian model of latent and manifest, or of repression (which is, of course, the target of Michel Foucault's programmatic and symptomatic pamphlet *La Volonté de savoir* [*The history of Sexuality*]); (3) the existential model of authenticity and inauthenticity whose heroic or tragic thematics are closely related to that other great opposition between alienation and disalienation, itself equally a casualty of the poststructural or postmodern period; and (4) most recently, the great semiotic opposition between signifier and signified, which was itself rapidly unraveled and deconstructed during its brief heyday in the 1960s and 1970s. What replaces these various depth models is for the most part a conception of practices, discourses, and textual play, whose new syntagmatic structures we will examine later on; let it suffice now to observe that here too depth is replaced by surface, or by multiple surfaces (what if often called intertextuality is in that sense no longer a matter of depth).

Nor is this depthlessness merely metaphorical: it can be experienced physically and "literally" by anyone who, mounting what used to be Raymond Chandler's Bunker Hill from the great Chicano markets on Broadway and Fourth Street in downtown Los Angeles, suddenly confronts the great free-standing wall of Wells Fargo Court (Skidmore,

Wells Fargo Court (Skidmore, Owings and Merrill)

Owings and Merrill)—a surface which seems to be unsupported by any volume, or whose putative volume (rectangular? trapezoidal?) is ocularly quite undecidable. This great sheet of windows, with its gravity-defying two-dimensionality, momentarily transforms the solid ground on which we stand into the contents of a stereopticon, pasteboard shapes profiling themselves here and there around us. The visual effect is the same from all sides: as fateful as the great monolith in Stanley Kubrick's *2001* which confronts its viewers like an enigmatic destiny, a call to evolutionary mutation. If this new multinational downtown effectively abolished the older ruined city fabric which is violently replaced, cannot something similar be said about the way in which this strange new surface in its own peremptory way renders our older systems of perception of the city somehow archaic and aimless, without offering another in their place?

Returning now for one last moment to Munch's painting, it seems evident that *The Scream* subtly but elaborately disconnects its own aesthetic of expression, all the while remaining imprisoned within it. Its gestural content already underscores its own failure, since the realm of the sonorous, the cry, the raw vibrations of the human throat, are incompatible with its medium (something underscored within the work by the homunculus's lack of ears). Yet the absent scream returns, as it were, in a dialectic of loops and spirals, circling ever more closely toward that even more absent experience of atrocious solitude and anxiety which the scream was itself to "express." Such loops inscribe themselves on the painted surface in the form of those great concentric circles in which sonorous vibration becomes ultimately visible, as on the surface of a sheet of water, in an infinite regress which fans out from the sufferer to become the very geography of a universe in which pain itself now speaks and vibrates through the material sunset and landscape. The visible world now becomes the wall of the monad on which this "scream running through nature" (Munch's words)[5] is recorded and transcribed: one thinks of that character of Lautréamont who, growing up inside a sealed and silent membrane, ruptures it with his own scream on catching sight of the monstrousness of the deity and thereby rejoins the world of sound and suffering.

All of which suggests some more general historical hypothesis: namely, that concepts such as anxiety and alienation (and the experiences to which they correspond, as in *The Scream*) are no longer appropriate in the world of the postmodern. The great Warhol figures—Marilyn herself or Edie Sedgewick—the notorious cases of burnout and self-destruction of the ending 1960s, and the great dominant experiences of drugs and schizophrenia, would seem to have little enough in common any more either with the hysterics and neurotics of Freud's own day or with those canonical experiences of radical isolation and solitude, anomie, private revolt, Van Gogh-type madness, which dominated the period of high modernism. This shift in the dynamics of cultural pathology can be characterized as one in which the alienation of the subject is displaced by the latter's fragmentation.

Such terms inevitably recall one of the more fashionable themes in contemporary theory, that of the "death" of the subject itself—the end of the autonomous bourgeois monad or ego or individual—and the accompanying stress, whether as some new moral ideal or as empirical description, on the *decentering* of that formerly centered subject or psyche. (Of the two possible formulations of this notion—the historicist one, that a once-existing centered subject, in the period of classical capitalism and the nuclear family, has today in the world of organizational bureaucracy dissolved; and the more radical poststructuralist position, for which such a subject never existed in the first place but constituted something like an ideological mirage—I obviously incline toward the former; the latter must in any case take into account something like a "reality of the appearance.")

We must however add that the problem of expression is itself closely linked to some conception of the subject as a monadlike container, within which things felt are then expressed by projection outward. What we must now stress, however, is the degree to which the high-modernist conception of a unique *style*, along with the accompanying collective ideals of an artistic or political vanguard or avant-garde, themselves stand or fall along with that older notion (or experience) of the so-called centered subject.

Here too Munch's painting stands as a complex reflection on this complicated situation: it shows us that expression requires the category of the individual monad, but it also shows us the heavy price to be paid for that precondition, dramatizing the unhappy paradox that when you constitute your individual subjectivity as a self-sufficient field and a closed realm, you thereby shut yourself off from everything else and condemn yourself to the mindless solitude of the monad, buried alive and condemned to a prison cell without egress.

Postmodernism presumably signals the end of this dilemma, which it replaces with a new one. The end of the bourgeois ego, or monad, no doubt brings with it the end of the psychopathologies of that ego—what I have been calling the waning of affect. But it means the end of much more—the end, for example, of style, in the sense of the unique and the personal, the end of the distinctive individual brush stroke (as symbolized by the emergent primacy of mechanical reproduction). As for expression and feelings or emotions, the liberation, in contemporary society, from the older *anomie* of the centered subject may also mean not merely a liberation from anxiety but a liberation from every other kind of feeling as well, since there is no longer a self present to do the feeling. This is not to say that the cultural products of the postmodern era are utterly devoid of feeling, but rather that such feelings—which it may be better and more accurate, following J.-F. Lyotard, to call "intensities"—are now free-floating and impersonal and tend to be dominated by a peculiar kind of euphoria, a matter to which we will want to return later on.

The waning of affect, however, might also have been characterized, in the narrower context of literary criticism, as the waning of the great high modernist thematics of time and temporality, the elegiac mysteries of durée and memory (something to be understood fully as much as a category of the literary criticism associated with high modernism as with the works themselves). We have often been told, however, that we now inhabit the synchronic rather than the diachronic, and I think it is at least empirically arguable that our daily life, our psychic experience, our cultural languages, are today dominated by categories of space rather than by categories of time, as in the preceding period of high modernism.[6]

II

The disappearance of the individual subject, along with its formal consequence, the increasing unavailability of the personal style, engender the well-nigh universal practice today of what may be called pastiche. This concept, which we owe to Thomas Mann (in Doktor Faustus), who owed it in turn to Adorno's great work on the two paths of advanced musical experimentation (Schoenberg's innovative planification and Stravinsky's irrational eclecticism), is to be sharply distinguished from the more readily received idea of parody.

To be sure, parody found a fertile area in the idiosyncracies of the moderns and their "inimitable" styles: the Faulknerian long sentence, for example, with its breathless gerundives; Lawrentian nature imagery punctuated by testy colloquialism; Wallace Stevens's inveterate hypostasis of nonsubstantive parts of speech ("the intricate evasions of as"); the fateful (but finally predictable) swoops in Mahler from high orchestral pathos into village accordion sentiment; Heidegger's meditative-solemn practice of the false etymology as a mode of "proof" . . . All these strike one as somehow characteristic, insofar as they ostentatiously deviate from a norm which then reasserts itself, in a not necessarily unfriendly way, by a systematic mimicry of their willful eccentricities.

Yet in the dialectical leap from quantity to quality, the explosion of modern literature into a host of distinct private styles and mannerisms has been followed by a linguistic fragmentation of social life itself to the point where the norm itself is eclipsed: reduced to a neutral and reified media speech (far enough from the Utopian aspirations of the inventors of Esperanto or Basic English), which itself then becomes but one more idiolect among many. Modernist styles thereby become postmodernist codes. And that the stupendous proliferation of social codes today into professional and disciplinary jargons (but also into the badges of affirmation of ethnic, gender, race, religious, and class-factional adhesion) is also a political phenomenon, the problem of micropolitics sufficiently demonstrates. If the ideas of a ruling class were once the dominant (or hegemonic) ideology of bourgeois society, the advanced capitalist countries today are now a field of stylistic and discursive heterogeneity without a norm. Faceless masters continue to inflect the economic strategies which constrain our existences, but they no longer need to impose their speech (or are henceforth unable to); and the postliteracy of the late capitalist world reflects not only the absence of any great collective project but also the unavailability of the older national language itself.

In this situation parody finds itself without a vocation; it has lived, and that strange new thing pastiche slowly comes to take its place. Pastiche is, like parody, the imitation of a peculiar or unique, idiosyncratic style, the wearing of a linguistic mask, speech in a dead language. But it is a neutral practice of such mimicry, without any of parody's ulterior motives, amputated of the satiric impulse, devoid of laughter and of any conviction that alongside the abnormal tongue you have momentarily borrowed, some healthy linguistic normality still exists. Pastiche is thus blank parody, a statue with blind eyeballs: it is to parody what that other interesting and historically original modern thing, the practice of a kind of blank irony, is to what Wayne Booth calls the "stable ironies" of the eighteenth century.

It would therefore begin to seem that Adorno's prophetic diagnosis has been realized, albeit in a negative way: not Schönberg (the sterility of whose achieved system he already glimpsed) but Stravinsky is the true precursor of postmodern cultural production. For with the collapse of the high-modernist ideology of style—what is as unique and unmistakable as your own fingerprints, as incomparable as your own body (the very source, for an early Roland Barthes, of stylistic invention and innovation)—the producers of culture have nowhere to turn but to the past: the imitation of dead styles, speech through all the masks and voices stored up in the imaginary museum of a now global culture.

This situation evidently determines what the architecture historians call "historicism," namely, the random cannibalization of all the styles of the past, the play of random stylistic allusion, and in general what Henri Lefebvre has called the increasing primacy of the "neo." This omnipresence of pastiche is not incompatible with a certain humor, however, nor is it innocent of all passion: it is at the least compatible with addiction—with a whole historically original consumers' appetite for a world transformed into sheer images of itself and for pseudo-events and "spectacles" (the term of the situationists). It is for such objects that we may reserve Plato's conception of the "simulacrum," the identical copy for which no original has ever existed. Appropriately enough, the culture of the simulacrum comes to life in a society where exchange value has been generalized to the point at which the very memory of use value is effaced, a society of which Guy Debord has observed, in an extraordinary phrase, that in it "the image has become the final form of commodity reification" (*The Society of the Spectacle*).

The new spatial logic of the simulacrum can now be expected to have a momentous effect on what used to be historical time. The past is thereby itself modified: what was once, in the historical novel as Lukács defines it, the organic genealogy of the bourgeois collective project —what is still, for the redemptive historiography of an E. P. Thompson or of American "oral history," for the resurrection of the dead of anonymous and silenced generations, the retrospective dimension indispensable to any vital reorientation of our collective future—has meanwhile itself become a vast collection of images, a multitudinous photographic simulacrum. Guy Debord's powerful slogan is now even more apt for the "prehistory" of a society bereft of all historicity, one whose own putative past is little more than a set of dusty spectacles. In faithful conformity to poststructuralist linguistic theory, the past as "referent" finds itself gradually bracketed, and then effaced altogether, leaving us with nothing but texts.

Yet it should not be thought that this process is accompanied by indifference: on the contrary, the remarkable current intensification of an addiction to the photographic image is itself a tangible symptom of an omnipresent, omnivorous, and well-nigh libidinal historicism. As I have already observed, the architects use this (exceedingly polysemous) word for the complacent eclecticism of postmodern architecture, which randomly and without principle but with gusto cannibalizes all the architectural styles of the past and combines them in overstimulating ensembles. Nostalgia does not strike one as an altogether satisfactory word for such fascination (particularly when one thinks of the pain of a properly modernist nostalgia with a past beyond all but aesthetic retrieval), yet it directs our attention to what is a culturally far more generalized manifestation of the process in commercial art and taste, namely the so-called nostalgia film (or what the French call *la mode rétro*).

Nostalgia films restructure the whole issue of pastiche and project it onto a collective and social level, where the desperate attempt to appropriate a missing past is now refracted through the iron law of fashion change and the emergent ideology of the generation. The inaugural film of this new aesthetic discourse, George Lucas's *American Graffiti* (1973), set out to recapture, as so many films have attempted since, the henceforth mesmerizing lost reality of the Eisenhower era; and one tends to feel, that for Americans at least, the 1950s remain the privileged lost object of desire[7] — not merely the stability and prosperity of a pax Americana but also the first naïve innocence of the countercultural impulses of early rock and roll and youth gangs (Coppola's *Rumble Fish* will then be the contemporary dirge that laments their passing, itself, however, still contradictorily filmed in genuine nostalgia film style). With this initial breakthrough, other generational periods open up for aesthetic colonization: as witness the stylistic recuperation of the American and the Italian 1930s, in Polanski's *Chinatown* and Bertolucci's *Il Conformista*, respectively. More interesting, and more problematical, are the ultimate attempts, through this new discourse, to lay siege either to our own present and immediate past or to a more distant history that escapes individual existential memory.

Faced with these ultimate objects — our social, historical, and existential present, and the past as "referent" — the incompatibility of a postmodernist "nostalgia" art language with genuine historicity becomes dramatically apparent. The contradiction propels this mode, however, into complex and interesting new formal inventiveness; it being understood that the nostalgia film was never a matter of some old-fashioned "representation" of historical content, but instead approached the "past" through stylistic connotation, conveying "pastness" by the glossy qualities of the image, and "1930s-ness" or "1950s-ness" by the attributes of fashion (in that following the prescription of the Barthes of *Mythologies*, who saw connotation as the purveying of imaginary and stereotypical idealities: "Sinité," for example, as some Disney-EPCOT "concept" of China).

The insensible colonization of the present by the nostalgia mode can be observed in Lawrence Kasdan's elegant film *Body Heat*, a distant "affluent society" remake of James M. Cain's *Double Indemnity*, set in a contemporary Florida small town a few hours' drive from Miami. The word *remake* is, however, anachronistic to the degree to which our awareness of the preexistence of other versions (previous films of the novel as well as the novel itself) is now a constitutive and essential part of the film's structure: we are now, in other words, in "intertextuality" as a deliberate, built-in feature of the aesthetic effect and as the operator of a new connotation of "pastness" and pseudohistorical depth, in which the history of aesthetic styles displaces "real" history.

Yet from the outset a whole battery of aesthetic signs begin to distance the officially contemporary image from us in time: the art deco scripting of the credits, for example, serves at once to program the spectator to the appropriate "nostalgia" mode of reception (art deco quotation has much the same function in contemporary architecture, as in Toronto's remarkable Eaton Centre).[8] Meanwhile, a somewhat different play of connotations is activated by complex (but purely formal) allusions to the institution of the star system itself. The protagonist, William Hurt, is one of a new generation of film "stars" whose status is markedly distinct from that of the preceding generation of male superstars, such as Steve McQueen or Jack Nicholson (or even, more distantly, Brando), let alone of earlier moments in the evolution of the institution of the star. The immediately preceding generation projected their various roles through and by way of their well-known off-screen personalities, which often connoted rebellion and nonconformism. The latest generation of starring actors continues to assure the conventional functions of stardom (most notably sexuality) but in the utter absence of "personality" in the older sense, and with something of the anonymity of character acting (which in actors like Hurt reaches virtuoso proportions, yet of a very different kind than the virtuosity of the older Brando or Olivier). This "death of the subject" in the institution of the star now, however, opens up the possibility of a play of historical allusions to much older roles—in this case to those associated with Clark Gable—so that the very style of the acting can now also serve as a "connotator" of the past.

Finally, the setting has been strategically framed, with great ingenuity, to eschew most of the signals that normally convey the contemporaneity of the United States in its multinational era: the small-town setting allows the camera to elude the high-rise landscape of the 1970s and 1980s (even though a key episode in the narrative involves the fatal destruction of older buildings by land speculators), while the object world of the present day — artifacts and appliances, whose styling would at once serve to date the image — is elaborately edited out. Everything in the film, therefore, conspires to blur its official contemporaneity and make it possible for the viewer to receive the narrative as though it were set in some eternal thirties, beyond real historical time. This approach to the present by way of the art language of the simulacrum, or of the pastiche of the stereotypical past, endows present reality and the openness of present history with the spell and distance of a glossy mirage. Yet this mesmerizing new aesthetic mode itself emerged as an elaborated symptom of the waning of our historicity, of our lived possibility of experiencing history in some active way. It cannot therefore be said to produce this strange occultation of the present by its own formal power, but rather merely to demonstrate, through these inner contradictions, the enormity of a situation in which we seem increasingly incapable of fashioning representations of our own current experience.

As for "real history" itself — the traditional object, however it may be defined, of what used to be the historical novel — it will be more revealing now to turn back to that older form and medium and to read its postmodern fate in the work of one of the few serious and innovative leftist novelists at work in the United States today, whose books are nourished with history in the more traditional sense and seem, so far, to stake out successive generational moments in the "epic" of American history, between which they alternate. E. L. Doctorow's *Ragtime* gives itself officially as a panorama of the first two decades of the century (like *World's Fair*); his most recent novel, *Billy Bathgate*, like *Loon Lake* addresses the thirties and the Great Depression, while *The Book of Daniel* holds up before us, in painful juxtaposition, the two great moments of the Old Left and the New Left, of thirties and forties communism and the radicalism of the 1960s (even his early western may be said to fit into this scheme and to designate in a less articulated and formally self-conscious way the end of the frontier of the late nineteenth century).

The Book of Daniel is not the only one of these five major historical novels to establish an explicit narrative link between the reader's and the writer's present and the older historical reality that is the subject of the work; the astonishing last page of *Loon Lake*, which I will not disclose, also does this in a very different way; it is a matter of some interest to note that the first version of *Ragtime*[9] positions us explicitly in our own present, in the novelist's house in New Rochelle, New York, which at once becomes the scene of its own (imaginary) past in the

1900s. This detail has been suppressed from the published text, symbolically cutting its moorings and freeing the novel to float in some new world of past historical time whose relationship to us is problematical indeed. The authenticity of the gesture, however, may be measured by the evident existential fact of life that there no longer does seem to be any organic relationship between the American history we learn from schoolbooks and the lived experience of the current multinational, high-rise, stagflated city of the newspapers and of our own everyday life.

A crisis in historicity, however, inscribes itself symptomatically in several other curious formal features within this text. Its official subject is the transition from a pre-World War I radical and working-class politics (the great strikes) to the technological invention and new commodity production of the 1920s (the rise of Hollywood and of the image as commodity): the interpolated version of Kleist's *Michael Kohlhaas*, the strange, tragic episode of the black protagonist's revolt, may be thought of as a moment related to this process. That *Ragtime* has political content and even something like a political "meaning" seems in any case obvious and has been expertly articulated by Linda Hutcheon in terms of

> its three paralleled families: the Anglo-American establishment one and the marginal immigrant European and American black ones. The novel's action disperses the center of the first and moves the margins into the multiple "centers" of the narrative, in a formal allegory of the social demographics of urban America. In addition, there is an extended critique of American democratic ideals through the presentation of class conflict rooted in capitalist property and moneyed power. The black Coalhouse, the white Houdini, the immigrant Tateh are all working class, and because of this—not in spite of it—all can therefore work to create new aesthetic forms (ragtime, vaudeville, movies).[10]

But this does everything but the essential, lending the novel an admirable thematic coherence few readers can have experienced in parsing the lines of a verbal object held too close to the eyes to fall into these perspectives. Hutcheon is, of course, absolutely right, and this is what the novel would have meant had it not been a postmodern artifact. For one thing, the objects of representation, ostensibly narrative characters, are incommensurable and, as it were, of incomparable substances, like oil and water—Houdini being a *historical* figure, Tateh a *fictional* one, and Coalhouse an *intertextual* one—something very difficult for an interpretive comparison of this kind to register. Meanwhile, the theme attributed to the novel also demands a somewhat different kind of scrutiny, since it can be rephrased into a classic version of the Left's "experience of defeat" in the twentieth century, namely, the proposition that the depolitization of the workers' movement is attributable to the media or culture generally (what she here calls "new aesthetic forms"). This is, indeed, in my opinion, something like the elegiac backdrop, if not the meaning, of *Ragtime*, and perhaps of Doctorow's work in general; but then we need another way of describing the novel as something like an unconscious expression and associative exploration of this left doxa, this historical opinion or quasi-vision in the mind's eye of "objective spirit." What such a description would want to register is the paradox that a seemingly realistic novel like *Ragtime* is in reality a nonrepresentational work that combines fantasy signifiers from a variety of ideologemes in a kind of hologram.

My point, however, is not some hypothesis as to the thematic coherence of this decentered narrative but rather just the opposite, namely, the way in which the kind of reading this novel imposes makes it virtually impossible for us to reach and thematize those official "subjects" which float above the text but cannot be integrated into our reading of the sentences. In that sense, the novel not only resists interpretation, it is organized systematically and formally to short-circuit an older type of social and historical interpretation which it perpetually holds out and withdraws. When we remember that the theoretical critique and repudiation of interpretation as such is a fundamental component of poststructuralist theory, it is difficult not to conclude that Doctorow has somehow deliberately built this very tension, this very contradiction, into the flow of his sentences.

The book is crowded with real historical figures—from Teddy Roosevelt to Emma Goldman, from Harry K. Thaw and Stanford White to J. Pierpont Morgan and Henry Ford, not to mention the more central role of Houdini—who interact with a fictive family, simply designated as Father, Mother, Older Brother, and so forth. All historical novels, beginning with those of Sir Walter Scott himself, no doubt in one way or another involve a mobilization of previous historical knowledge generally acquired through the schoolbook history manuals devised for whatever legitimizing purpose by this or that national tradition—thereafter instituting a narrative dialectic between what we already "know" about The Pretender, say, and what he is then seen to be concretely in the pages of the novel. But Doctorow's procedure seems much more extreme than this; and I would argue that the designation of both types of characters—historical names and capitalized family roles—operates powerfully and systematically to reify all these characters and to make it impossible for us to receive their representation without the prior interception of already acquired knowledge or doxa—something which lends the text an extraordinary sense of déjà vu and a peculiar familiarity one is tempted to associate with Freud's "return of the repressed" in "The Uncanny" rather than with any solid historiographic formation on the reader's part.

Meanwhile, the sentences in which all this is happening have their own specificity, allowing us more concretely to distinguish the moderns' elaboration of a personal style from this new kind of linguistic innovation, which is no longer personal at all but has its family kinship rather with what Barthes long ago called "white writing." In this particular novel, Doctorow has imposed upon himself a rigorous principle of selection in which only simple declarative sentences (predominantly mobilized by the verb "to be") are received. The effect is, however, not really one of the condescending simplification and symbolic carefulness of children's literature, but rather something more disturbing, the sense of some profound subterranean violence done to American English, which cannot, however, be detected empirically in any of the perfectly grammatical sentences with which this work is formed. Yet other more visible technical "innovations" may supply a clue to what is happening in the language of *Ragtime*: it is, for example, well known that the source of many of the characteristic effects of Camus's novel *The Stranger* can be traced back to that author's willful decision to substitute, throughout, the French tense of the *passé composé* for the other past tenses more normally employed in narration in that language.[11] I suggest that it is as if something of that sort were at work here: *as though* Doctorow had set out systematically to produce the effect or the equivalent, in his language, of a verbal past tense we do not possess in English, namely, the French preterite (or *passé simple*), whose "perfective" movement, as Émile Benveniste taught us, serves to separate events from the present of enunciation and to transform the stream of time and action into so many finished, complete, and isolated punctual event objects which find themselves sundered from any present situation (even that of the act of story telling or enunciation).

E. L. Doctorow is the epic poet of the disappearance of the American radical past, of the suppression of older traditions and moments of the American radical tradition: no one with left sympathies can read these splendid novels without a poignant distress that is an authentic way of confronting our own current political dilemmas in the present. What is culturally interesting, however, is that he has had to convey this great theme formally (since the waning of the content is very precisely his subject) and, more than that, has had to elaborate his work by way of that very cultural logic of the postmodern which is itself the mark and symptom of his dilemma. *Loon Lake* much more obviously deploys the strategies of the pastiche (most notably in its reinvention of Dos Passos); but *Ragtime* remains the most peculiar and stunning monument to the aesthetic situation engendered by the disappearance of the historical referent. This historical novel can no longer set out to represent the historical past; it can only "represent" our ideas and stereotypes about that past (which thereby at once becomes "pop history"). Cultural production is thereby driven back inside a mental space which is no longer that of the old monadic subject but rather that of some degraded collective "objective spirit": it can no longer gaze directly on some putative real world, at some reconstruction of a past history which was once itself a present; rather, as in Plato's cave, it must trace our mental images of that past upon its confining walls. If there is any realism left here, it is a "realism" that is meant to derive from the shock of grasping that confinement and of slowly becoming aware of a new and original historical situation in which we are condemned to seek History by way of our own pop images and simulacra of that history, which itself remains forever out of reach.

III

The crisis in historicity now dictates a return, in a new way, to the question of temporal organization in general in the postmodern force field, and indeed, to the problem of the form that time, temporality, and the syntagmatic will be able to take in a culture increasingly dominated by space and spatial logic. If, indeed, the subject has lost its capacity actively to extend its pro-tensions and re-tensions across the temporal manifold and to organize its past and future into coherent experience, it becomes difficult enough to see how the cultural productions of such a subject could result in anything but "heaps of fragments" and in a practice of the randomly heterogeneous and fragmentary and the aleatory. These are, however, very precisely some of the privileged terms in which postmodernist cultural production has been analyzed (and even defended, by its own apologists). They are, however, still privative features; the more substantive formulations bear such names as textuality, écriture, or schizophrenic writing, and it is to these that we must now briefly turn.

I have found Lacan's account of schizophrenia useful here not because I have any way of knowing whether it has clinical accuracy but chiefly because—as description rather than diagnosis—it seems to me to offer a suggestive aesthetic model.[12] I am obviously very far from thinking that any of the most significant postmodernist artists—Cage, Ashbery, Sollers, Robert Wilson, Ishmael Reed, Michael Snow, Warhol, or even Beckett himself—are schizophrenics in any clinical sense. Nor is the point some culture-and-personality diagnosis of our society and its art, as in psychologizing and moralizing culture critiques of the type of Christopher Lasch's influential *The Culture of Narcissism*, from which I am concerned to distance the spirit and the methodology of the present remarks: there are, one would think, far more damaging things to be said about our social system than are available through the use of psychological categories.

Very briefly, Lacan describes schizophrenia as a breakdown in the signifying chain, that is, the interlocking syntagmatic series of signifiers which constitutes an utterance or a meaning. I must omit the familial or more orthodox psychoanalytic background to this situation, which Lacan transcodes into language by describing the Oedipal rivalry in terms not so much of the biological individual who is your rival for the mother's attention but rather of what he calls the Name-of-the-Father, paternal authority now considered as a linguistic function.[13] His conception of the signifying chain essentially presupposes one of the basic principles (and one of the great discoveries) of Saussurean structuralism, namely, the proposition that meaning is not a one-to-one relationship between signifier and signified, between the materiality of language, between a word or a name, and its referent or concept. Meaning on the new view is generated by the movement from signifier to signifier. What we generally call the signified—the meaning or conceptual content of an utterance—is now rather to be seen as a meaning-effect, as that objective mirage of signification generated and projected by the relationship of signifiers among themselves. When that relationship breaks down, when the links of the signifying chain snap, then we have schizophrenia in the form of a rubble of distinct and unrelated signifiers. The connection between this kind of linguistic malfunction and the psyche of the schizophrenic may then be grasped by way of a twofold proposition: first, that personal identity is itself the effect of a certain temporal unification of past and future with one's present; and, second, that such active temporal unification is itself a function of language, or better still of the sentence, as it moves along its hermeneutic circle through time. If we are unable to unify the past, present, and future of the sentence, then we are similarly unable to unify the past, present, and future of our own biographical experience or psychic life. With the breakdown of the signifying chain, therefore, the schizophrenic is reduced to an experience of pure material signifiers, or, in other words, a series of pure and unrelated presents in time. We will want to ask questions about the aesthetic or cultural results of such a situation in a moment; let us first see what it feels like:

> I remember very well the day it happened. We were staying in the country and I had gone for a walk alone as I did now and then. Suddenly, as I was passing the school, I heard a German song; the children were having a singing lesson. I stopped to listen, and at that instant a strange feeling came over me, a feeling hard to analyze but akin to something I was to know too well later—a disturbing sense of unreality. It seemed to me that I no longer recognized the school, it had become as large as a barracks; the singing children were prisoners, compelled to sing. It was as though the school and the children's song were set apart from the rest of the world. At the same time my eye encountered a field of wheat whose limits I could not see. The yellow vastness, dazzling in the sun, bound up with the song of the children imprisoned in the smooth stone school-barracks, filled me with such anxiety that I broke into sobs. I ran home to our garden and began to play "to make things seem as they usually were," that is, to return to reality. It was the first appearance of those elements which were always present in later sensations of unreality: illimitable vastness, brilliant light, and the gloss and smoothness of material things.[14]

In our present context, this experience suggests the following: first, the breakdown of temporality suddenly releases this present of time from all the activities and intentionalities that might focus it and make it a space of praxis; thereby isolated, that present suddenly engulfs the subject with undescribable vividness, a materiality of perception properly overwhelming, which effectively dramatizes the power of the material —or better still, the literal—signifier in isolation. This present of the world or material signifier comes before the subject with heightened intensity, bearing a mysterious charge of affect, here described in the negative terms of anxiety and loss of reality, but which one could just as well imagine in the positive terms of euphoria, a high, an intoxicatory or hallucinogenic intensity.

What happens in textuality or schizophrenic art is strikingly illuminated by such clinical accounts, although in the cultural text, the isolated signifier is no longer an enigmatic state of the world or an incomprehensible yet mesmerizing fragment of language but rather something closer to a sentence in free-standing isolation. Think, for example, of the experience of John Cage's music, in which a cluster of material sounds (on the prepared piano, for example) is followed by a silence so intolerable that you cannot imagine another sonorous chord coming into existence and cannot imagine remembering the previous one well enough to make any connection with it if it does. Some of Beckett's narratives are also of this order, most notably *Watt*, where a primacy of the present sentence in time ruthlessly disintegrates the narrative fabric that attempts to reform around it. My example, however, will be a less somber one, a text by a younger San Francisco poet whose group or school—so-called Language Poetry or the New Sentence—seem to have adopted schizophrenic fragmentation as their fundamental aesthetic.

China

We live on the third world from the sun. Number three. Nobody tells us what to do.

The people who taught us to count were being very kind.

It's always time to leave.

If it rains, you either have your umbrella or you don't.

The wind blows your hat off.

The sun rises also.

I'd rather the stars didn't describe us to each other; I'd rather we do it for ourselves.

Run in front of your shadow.

A sister who points to the sky at least once a decade is a good sister.

The landscape is motorized.

The train takes you where it goes.

Bridges among water.

Folks straggling along vast stretches of concrete, heading into the plane.

Don't forget what your hat and shoes will look like when you are nowhere to be found.

Even the words floating in air make blue shadows.

If it tastes good we eat it.

The leaves are falling. Point things out.

Pick up the right things.

Hey guess what? What? I've learned how to talk. Great.

The person whose head was incomplete burst into tears.

As it fell, what could the doll do? Nothing.

Go to sleep.

You look great in shorts. And the flag looks great too.

Everyone enjoyed the explosions.

Time to wake up.

But better get used to dreams.

—Bob Perelman[15]

Many things could be said about this interesting exercise in discontinuities; not the least paradoxical is the reemergence here across these disjoined sentences of some more unified global meaning. Indeed, insofar as this is in some curious and secret way a political poem, it does seem to capture something of the excitement of the immense, unfinished social experiment of the New China—unparalleled in world history —the unexpected emergence, between the two superpowers, of "number three," the freshness of a whole new object world produced by human beings in some new control over their collective destiny; the signal event, above all, of a collectivity which has become a new "subject of history" and which, after the long subjection of feudalism and imperialism, again speaks in its own voice, for itself, as though for the first time.

But I mainly wanted to show the way in which what I have been calling schizophrenic disjunction or *écriture*, when it becomes generalized as a cultural style, ceases to entertain a necessary relationship to the morbid content we associate with terms like schizophrenia and becomes available for more joyous intensities, for precisely that euphoria which we saw displacing the older affects of anxiety and alienation.

Consider, for example, Jean-Paul Sartre's account of a similar tendency in Flaubert:

His sentence [Sartre tells us about Flaubert] closes in on the object, seizes it, immobilizes it, and breaks its back, wraps itself around it, changes into stone and petrifies its object along with itself. It is blind and deaf, bloodless, not a breath of life; a deep silence separates it from the sentence which follows; it falls into the void, eternally, and drags its prey down into that infinite fall. Any reality, once described, is struck off the inventory.[16]

I am tempted to see this reading as a kind of optical illusion (or photographic enlargement) of an unwittingly genealogical type, in which certain latent or subordinate, properly postmodernist, features of Flaubert's style are anachronistically foregrounded. However, it affords an interesting lesson in periodization and in the dialectical restructuring of cultural dominants and subordinates. For these features, in Flaubert, were symptoms and strategies in that whole posthumous life and resentment of praxis which is denounced (with increasing sympathy) throughout the three thousand pages of Sartre's *Family Idiot*. When such features become themselves the cultural norm, they shed all such forms of negative affect and become available for other, more decorative uses.

But we have not yet fully exhausted the structural secrets of Perelman's poem, which turns out to have little enough to do with that referent called China. The author has, in fact, related how, strolling through Chinatown, he came across a book of photographs whose idiogrammatic captions remained a dead letter to him (or perhaps, one should say, a material signifier). The sentences of the poem in question are then Perelman's own captions to those pictures, their referents another image, another absent text; and the unity of the poem is no longer to be found within its language but outside itself, in the bound unity of another, absent book. There is here a striking parallel to the dynamics of so-called photorealism, which looked like a return to representation and figuration after the long hegemony of the aesthetics of abstraction until it became clear that their objects were not to be found in the "real world" either but were themselves photographs of that real world, this last now transformed into images, of which the "realism" of the photorealist painting is now the simulacrum.

This account of schizophrenia and temporal organization might, however, have been formulated in a different way, which brings us back to Heidegger's notion of a gap or rift between Earth and World, albeit in a fashion that is sharply incompatible with the tone and high seriousness of his own philosophy. I would like to characterize the postmodernist experience of form with what will seem, I hope, a paradoxical slogan: namely, the proposition that "difference relates." Our own recent criticism, from Macherey on, has been concerned to stress the heterogeneity and profound discontinuities of the work of art, no longer unified or organic, but now a virtual grab bag or lumber room of disjoined subsystems and random raw materials and impulses of all kinds. The former work of art, in other words, has now turned out to be a text, whose reading proceeds by differentiation rather than by unification. Theories of difference, however, have tended to stress disjunction to the point at which the materials of the text, including its words and sentences, tend to fall apart into random and inert passivity, into a set of elements which entertain separations from one another.

In the most interesting postmodernist works, however, one can detect a more positive conception of relationship, which restores its proper tension to the notion of difference itself. This new mode of relationship through difference may sometimes be an achieved new and original way of thinking and perceiving; more often it takes the form of an impossible imperative to achieve that new mutation in what can perhaps no longer be called consciousness. I believe that the most striking emblem of this new mode of thinking relationships can be found in the work of Nam June Paik, whose stacked or scattered television screens, positioned at intervals within lush vegetation, or winking down at us from a ceiling of strange new video stars, recapitulate over and over again prearranged sequences or loops of images which return at dyssynchronous moments on the various screens. The older aesthetic is then practiced by viewers, who, bewildered by this discontinuous variety, decided to concentrate on a single screen, as though the relatively worthless image sequence to be followed there had some organic value in its own right. The postmodernist viewer, however, is called upon to do the impossible, namely, to see all the screens at once, in their radical and random difference; such a viewer is asked to follow the evolutionary mutation of David Bowie in *The Man Who Fell to Earth* (who watches fifty-seven television screens simultaneously) and to rise somehow to a level at which the vivid perception of radical difference is in and of itself a new mode of grasping what used to be called relationship: something for which the word *collage* is still only a very feeble name.

Duane Hanson, "Museum Guard"

IV

Now we need to complete this exploratory account of postmodernist space and time with a final analysis of that euphoria or those intensities which seem so often to characterize the newer cultural experience. Let us reemphasize the enormity of a transition which leaves behind it the desolation of Hopper's buildings or the stark Midwest syntax of Sheeler's forms, replacing them with the extraordinary surfaces of the photorealist cityscape, where even the automobile wrecks gleam with some new hal-

Duane Hanson, "Tourist II"

lucinatory splendor. The exhilaration of these new surfaces is all the more paradoxical in that their essential content—the city itself—has deteriorated or disintegrated to a degree surely still inconceivable in the early years of the twentieth century, let alone in the previous era. How urban squalor can be a delight to the eyes when expressed in commodification, and how an unparalleled quantum leap in the alienation of daily life in the city can now be experienced in the form of a strange new hallucinatory exhilaration—these are some of the questions that confront us in this moment of our inquiry. Nor should the human figure be exempted from investigation, although it seems clear that for the newer aesthetic the representation of space itself has come to be felt as incompatible with the representation of the body: a kind of aesthetic division of labor far more pronounced than in any of the earlier generic conceptions of landscape, and a most ominous symptom indeed. The privileged space of the newer art is radically antianthropomorphic, as in the empty bathrooms of Doug Bond's work. The ultimate contemporary fetishization of the human body, however, takes a very different direction in the statues of Duane Hanson: what I have already called the simulacrum, whose peculiar function lies in what Sartre would have called the *derealization* of the whole surrounding world of everyday reality. Your moment of doubt and hesitation as to the breath and warmth of these polyester figures, in order words, tends to return upon the real human beings moving about you in the museum and to transform them also for the briefest instant into so many dead and flesh-colored simulacra in their own right. The world thereby momentarily loses its depth and threatens to become a glossy skin, a stereoscopic illusion, a rush of filmic images without density. But is this now a terrifying or an exhilarating experience?

It has proved fruitful to think of such experiences in terms of what Susan Sontag, in an influential statement, isolated as "camp." I propose a somewhat different cross-light on it, drawing on the equally fashionable current theme of the "sublime," as it has been rediscovered in the works of Edmund Burke and Kant; or perhaps one might want to yoke the two notions together in the form of something like a camp or "hysterical" sublime. The sublime was for Burke an experience bordering on terror, the fitful glimpse, in astonishment, stupor, and awe, of what was so enormous as to crush human life altogether: a description then refined by Kant to include the question of representation itself, so that the object of the sublime becomes not only a matter of sheer power and of the physical incommensurability of the human organism with Nature but also of the limits of figuration and the incapacity of the human mind to give representation to such enormous forces. Such forces Burke, in his historical moment at the dawn of the modern bourgeois state, was only able to conceptualize in terms of the divine, while even Heidegger continues to entertain a phantasmatic relationship with some organic precapitalist peasant landscape and village society, which is the final form of the image of Nature in our own time.

Today, however, it may be possible to think all this in a different way, at the moment of a radical eclipse of Nature itself: Heidegger's "field path" is, after all, irredeemably and irrevocably destroyed by late capital, by the green revolution, by neocolonialism and the megalopolis, which runs its superhighways over the older fields and vacant lots and turns Heidegger's "house of being" into condominiums, if not the most miserable unheated, rat-infested tenement buildings. The *other* of our society is in that sense no longer Nature at all, as it was in precapitalist societies, but something else which we must now identify.

I am anxious that this other thing not overhastily be grasped as technology per se, since I will want to show that technology is here itself a figure for something else. Yet technology may well serve as adequate shorthand to designate that enormous properly human and anti-natural power of dead human labor stored up in our machinery—an alienated power, what Sartre calls the counterfinality of the practico-inert, which turns back on and against us in unrecognizable forms and seems to constitute the massive dystopian horizon of our collective as well as our individual praxis.

Technological development is however on the Marxist view the result of the development of capital rather than some ultimately determining instance in its own right. It will therefore be appropriate to distinguish several generations of machine power, several stages of technological revolution within capital itself. I here follow Ernest Mandel, who outlines three such fundamental breaks or quantum leaps in the evolution of machinery under capital:

> The fundamental revolutions in power technology—the technology of the production of motive machines by machines—thus appears as the determinant moment in revolutions of technology as a whole. Machine production of steam-driven motors since 1848; machine production of electric and combustion motors since the 90s of the 19th century; machine production of electronic and nuclear-powered apparatuses since the 40s of the 20th century —these are the three general revolutions in technology engendered by the capitalist mode of production since the "original" industrial revolution of the later 18th century.[17]

This periodization underscores the general thesis of Mandel's book *Late Capitalism*; namely, that there have been three fundamental moments in capitalism, each one marking a dialectical expansion over the previous stage. These are market capitalism, the monopoly stage or the stage of imperialism, and our own, wrongly called postindustrial, but what might better be termed multinational, capital. I have already pointed out that

Mandel's intervention in the postindustrial debate involves the proposition that late or multinational or consumer capitalism, far from being inconsistent with Marx's great nineteenth-century analysis, constitutes, on the contrary, the purest form of capital yet to have emerged, a prodigious expansion of capital into hitherto uncommodified areas. This purer capitalism of our own time thus eliminates the enclaves of precapitalist organization it had hitherto tolerated and exploited in a tributary way. One is tempted to speak in this connection of a new and historically original penetration and colonization of Nature and the Unconscious: that is, the destruction of precapitalist Third World agriculture by the Green Revolution, and the rise of the media and the advertising industry. At any rate, it will also have been clear that my own cultural periodization of the stages of realism, modernism, and postmodernism is both inspired and confirmed by Mandel's tripartite scheme.

We may therefore speak of our own period as the Third Machine Age; and it is at this point that we must reintroduce the problem of aesthetic representation already explicitly developed in Kant's earlier analysis of the sublime, since it would seem only logical that the relationship to and the representation of the machine could be expected to shift dialectically with each of these qualitatively different stages of technological development.

It is appropriate to recall the excitement of machinery in the moment of capital preceding our own, the exhilaration of futurism, most notably, and of Marinetti's celebration of the machine gun and the motorcar. These are still visible emblems, sculptural nodes of energy which give tangibility and figuration to the motive energies of that earlier moment of modernization. The prestige of these great streamlined shapes can be measured by their metaphorical presence in Le Corbusier's buildings, vast Utopian structures which ride like so many gigantic steamship liners upon the urban scenery of an older fallen earth.[18] Machinery exerts another kind of fascination in the works of artists like Picabia and Duchamp, whom we have no time to consider here; but let me mention, for completeness' sake, the ways in which revolutionary or communist artists of the 1930s also sought to reappropriate this excitement of machine energy for a Promethean reconstruction of human society as a whole, as in Fernand Léger and Diego Rivera.

It is immediately obvious that the technology of our own moment no longer possesses this same capacity for representation: not the turbine, nor even Sheeler's grain elevators or smokestacks, not the baroque elaboration of pipes and conveyor belts, nor even the streamlined profile of the railroad train—all vehicles of speed still concentrated at rest—but rather the computer, whose outer shell has no emblematic or visual power, or even the casings of the various media themselves, as with that home appliance called television which articulates nothing but rather implodes, carrying its flattened image surface within itself.

Such machines are indeed machines of reproduction rather than of production, and they make very different demands on our capacity for aesthetic representation than did the relatively mimetic idolatry of the older machinery of the futurist moment, of some older speed-and-energy sculpture. Here we have less to do with kinetic energy than with all kinds of new reproductive processes; and in the weaker productions of postmodernism the aesthetic embodiment of such processes often tends to slip back more comfortably into a mere thematic representation of content—into narratives which are *about* the processes of reproduction and include movie cameras, video, tape recorders, the whole technology of the production and reproduction of the simulacrum. (The shift from Antonioni's modernist *Blow-Up* to DePalma's postmodernist *Blow-out* is here paradigmatic.) When Japanese architects, for example, model a building on the decorative imitation of stacks of cassettes, then the solution is at best thematic and allusive, although often humorous.

Yet something else does tend to emerge in the most energetic postmodernist texts, and this is the sense that beyond all thematics or content the work seems somehow to tap the networks of the reproductive process and thereby to afford us some glimpse into a postmodern or technological sublime, whose power or authenticity is documented by the success of such works in evoking a whole new postmodern space in emergence around us. Architecture therefore remains in this sense the privileged aesthetic language; and the distorting and fragmenting reflections of one enormous glass surface to the other can be taken as paradigmatic of the central role of process and reproduction in postmodernist culture.

As I have said, however, I want to avoid the implication that technology is in any way the "ultimately determining instance" either of our present-day social life or of our cultural production: such a thesis is, of course, ultimately at one with the post-Marxist notion of a postindustrial society. Rather, I want to suggest that our faulty representations of some immense communicational and computer network are themselves but a distorted figuration of something even deeper, namely, the whole world system of a present-day multinational capitalism. The technology of contemporary society is therefore mesmerizing and fascinating not so much in its own right but because it seems to offer some privileged representational shorthand for grasping a network of power and control even more difficult for our minds and imaginations to grasp: the whole new decentered global network of the third stage of capital itself. This is a figural process presently best observed in a whole mode of contemporary entertainment literature—one is tempted to characterize it as "high-tech paranoia"—in which the circuits and networks of some putative global computer hookup are narratively mobilized by labyrinthine conspiracies of autonomous but deadly interlocking and competing information agencies in a complexity often beyond the capacity of the normal reading mind. Yet conspiracy theory (and its garish narrative manifestations) must be seen as a degraded attempt—through the figuration of advanced technology—to think the impossible totality of the contemporary world system. It is in terms of that enormous and threatening, yet only dimly perceivable, other reality of economic and social institutions that, in my opinion, the postmodern sublime can alone be adequately theorized.

Such narratives, which first tried to find expression through the generic structure of the spy novel, have only recently crystallized in a new type of science fiction, called *cyberpunk*, which is fully as much an expression of transnational corporate realities as it is of global paranoia itself: William Gibson's representational innovations, indeed, mark his work as an exceptional literary realization within a predominantly visual or aural postmodern production.

V

Now, before concluding, I want to sketch an analysis of a full-blown postmodern building—a work which is in many ways uncharacteristic of that postmodern architecture whose principal proponents are Robert Venturi, Charles Moore, Michael Graves, and, more recently, Frank Gehry, but which to my mind offers some very striking lessons about the originality of postmodernist space. Let me amplify the figure which has run through the preceding remarks and make it even more explicit: I am proposing the notion that we are here in the presence of something like a mutation in built space itself. My implication is that we ourselves, the human subjects who happen into this new space, have not kept pace with that evolution; there has been a mutation in the object unaccompanied as yet by any equivalent mutation in the subject. We do not yet possess the perceptual equipment to match this new hyperspace, as I will call it, in part because our perceptual habits were formed in that older kind of space I have called the space of high modernism. The newer architecture therefore—like many of the other cultural products I have evoked in the preceding remarks—stands as something like an imperative to grow new organs, to expand our sensorium and our body to some new, yet unimaginable, perhaps ultimately impossible, dimensions.

The building whose features I will very rapidly enumerate is the Westin Bonaventure Hotel, built in the new Los Angeles downtown by the architect and developer John Portman, whose other works include the various Hyatt Regencies, the Peachtree Center in Atlanta, and the Renaissance Center in Detroit. I have mentioned the populist aspect of the rhetorical defense of postmodernism against the elite (and Utopian) austerities of the great architectural modernisms: it is generally affirmed, in other words, that these newer buildings are popular works, on the one hand, and that they respect the vernacular of the American city fabric, on the other; that is to say, they no longer attempt, as did the masterworks and monuments of high modernism, to insert a different, a distinct, an elevated, a new Utopian language into the tawdry and commercial sign system of the surrounding city, but rather they seek to speak that very language, using its lexicon and syntax as that has been emblematically "learned from Las Vegas."

On the first of these counts Portman's Bonaventure fully confirms the claim: it is a popular building, visited with enthusiasm by locals and tourists alike (although Portman's other buildings are even more successful in this respect). The populist insertion into the city fabric is, however, another matter, and it is with this that we will begin. There are three entrances to the Bonaventure, one from Figueroa and the other two by way of elevated gardens on the other side of the hotel, which is built into the remaining slope of the former Bunker Hill. None of these is anything like the old hotel marquee, or the monumental porte cochere with which the sumptuous buildings of yesteryear were wont to stage your passage from city street to the interior. The entryways of the Bonaventure are, as it were, lateral and rather backdoor affairs: the gardens in the back admit you to the sixth floor of the towers, and even there you must walk down one flight to find the elevator by which you gain access to the lobby. Meanwhile, what one is still tempted to think of as the front entry, on Figueroa, admits you, baggage and all, onto the second-story shopping balcony, from which you must take an escalator down to the main registration desk. What I first want to suggest about these curiously unmarked ways in is that they seem to have been imposed by some new category of closure governing the inner space of the hotel

The Westin Bonaventure (Portman)

itself (and this over and above the material constraints under which Portman had to work). I believe that, with a certain number of other characteristic postmodern buildings, such as the Beaubourg in Paris or the Eaton Centre in Toronto, the Bonaventure aspires to being a total space, a complete world, a kind of miniature city; to this new total space, meanwhile, corresponds a new collective practice, a new mode in which individuals move and congregate, something like the practice of a new and historically original kind of hypercrowd. In this sense, then, ideally the minicity of Portman's Bonaventure ought not to have entrances at all, since the entryway is always the seam that links the building to the rest of the city that surrounds it: for it does not wish to be a part of the city but rather its equivalent and replacement or substitute. That

Le Corbusier, "Unite d'Habitation"

is obviously not possible, whence the downplaying of the entrance to its bare minimum.[19] But this disjunction from the surrounding city is different from that of the monuments of the International Style, in which the act of disjunction was violent, visible, and had a very real symbolic significance—as in Le Corbusier's great *pilotis*, whose gesture radically separates the new Utopian space of the modern from the degraded and fallen city fabric which it thereby explicitly repudiates (although the gamble of the modern was that this new Utopian space, in the virulence of its *novum*, would fan out and eventually transform its surroundings by the very power of its new spatial language). The Bonaventure, however, is content to "let the fallen city fabric continue to be in its being" (to parody Heidegger); no further effects, no larger protopolitical Utopian transformation, is either expected or desired.

This diagnosis is confirmed by the great reflective glass skin of the Bonaventure, whose function I will now interpret rather differently than I did a moment ago when I saw the phenomenon of reflection generally as developing a thematics of reproductive technology (the two readings are, however, not incompatible). Now one would want rather to stress the way in which the glass skin repels the city outside, a repulsion for which we have analogies in those reflector sunglasses which make it impossible for your interlocutor to see your own eyes and thereby achieve a certain aggressivity toward and power over the Other. In a similar way, the glass skin achieves a peculiar and placeless dissociation of the Bonaventure from its neighborhood: it is not even an exterior, inasmuch as when you seek to look at the hotel's outer walls you cannot see the hotel itself but only the distorted images of everything that surrounds it.

Now consider the escalators and elevators. Given their very real pleasures in Portman, particularly the latter, which the artist has termed "gigantic kinetic sculptures" and which certainly account for much of the spectacle and excitement of the hotel interior—particularly in the Hyatts, where like great Japanese lanterns or gondolas they ceaselessly rise and fall—given such a deliberate marking and foregrounding in their own right, I believe one has to see such "people movers" (Portman's own term, adapted from Disney) as somewhat more significant than mere functions and engineering components. We know in any case that recent architectural theory has begun to borrow from narrative analysis in other fields and to attempt to see our physical trajectories through such buildings as virtual narratives or stories, as dynamic paths and narrative paradigms which we as visitors are asked to fulfill and to complete with our own bodies and movements. In the Bonaventure, however, we find a dialectical heightening of this process: it seems to me that the escalators and elevators here henceforth replace movement but also, and above all, designate themselves as new reflexive signs and emblems of movement proper (something which will become evident when we come to the question of what remains of older forms of movement in this building, most notably walking itself). Here the narrative stroll has been underscored, symbolized, reified, and replaced by a transportation machine which becomes the allegorical signifier of that older promenade we are no longer allowed to conduct on our own: and this is a dialectical intensification of the autoreferentiality of all modern culture, which tends to turn upon itself and designate its own cultural production as its content.

I am more at a loss when it comes to conveying the thing itself, the experience of space you undergo when you step off such allegorical devices into the lobby or atrium, with its great central column surrounded by a miniature lake, the whole positioned between the four symmetrical residential towers with their elevators, and surrounded by rising balconies capped by a kind of greenhouse roof at the sixth level. I am tempted to say that such space makes it impossible for us to use the language of volume or volumes any longer, since these are impossible to seize. Hanging streamers indeed suffuse this empty space in such a way as to distract systematically and deliberately from whatever form it might be supposed to have, while a constant busyness gives the feeling that emptiness is here absolutely packed, that it is an element within which you yourself are immersed, without any of that distance that formerly enabled the perception of perspective or volume. You are in this hyperspace up to your eyes and your body; and if it seemed before that that suppression of depth I spoke of in postmodern painting or literature would necessarily be difficult to achieve in architecture itself, perhaps this bewildering immersion may now serve as the formal equivalent in the new medium.

Yet escalator and elevator are also in this context dialectical opposites; and we may suggest that the glorious movement of the elevator gondola is also a dialectical compensation for this filled space of the atrium — it gives us the chance at a radically different, but complementary, spatial experience: that of rapidly shooting up through the ceiling and outside, along one of the four symmetrical towers, with the referent, Los Angeles itself, spread out breathtakingly and even alarmingly before us. But even this vertical movement is contained: the elevator lifts you to one of those revolving cocktail lounges, in which, seated, you are again passively rotated about and offered a contemplative spectacle of the city itself, now transformed into its own images by the glass windows through which you view it.

We may conclude all this by returning to the central space of the lobby itself (with the passing observation that the hotel rooms are visibly marginalized: the corridors in the residential sections are low-ceilinged and dark, most depressingly functional, while one understands that the rooms are in the worst of taste). The descent is dramatic enough, plummeting back down through the roof to splash down in the lake. What happens when you get there is something else, which can only be characterized as milling confusion, something like the vengeance this space takes on those who still seek to walk through it. Given the absolute symmetry of the four towers, it is quite impossible to get your bearings in this lobby; recently, color coding and directional signals have been added in a pitiful and revealing, rather desperate, attempt to restore the coordinates of an older space. I will take as the most dramatic practical result of this spatial mutation the notorious dilemma of the shopkeepers on the various balconies: it has been obvious since the opening of the hotel in 1977 that nobody could ever find any of these stores, and even if you once located the appropriate boutique, you would be most unlikely to be as fortunate a second time; as a consequence, the commercial tenants are in despair and all the merchandise is marked down to bargain prices. When you recall that Portman is a businessman as well as an architect and a millionaire developer, an artist who is at one and the same time a capitalist in his own right, one cannot but feel that here too something of a "return of the repressed" is involved.

So I come finally to my principal point here, that this latest mutation in space—postmodern hyperspace—has finally succeeded in transcending the capacities of the individual human body to locate itself, to organize its immediate surroundings perceptually, and cognitively to map its position in a mappable external world. It may now be suggested that this alarming disjunction point between the body and its built environment—which is to the initial bewilderment of the older modernism as the velocities of spacecraft to those of the automobile—can itself stand as the symbol and analogon of that even sharper dilemma which is the incapacity of our minds, at least at present, to map the great global multinational and decentered communicational network in which we find ourselves caught as individual subjects.

But as I am anxious that Portman's space not be perceived as something either exceptional or seemingly marginalized and leisure-specialized on the order of Disneyland, I will conclude by juxtaposing this complacent and entertaining (although bewildering) leisure-time space with its analogue in a very different area, namely, the space of postmodern warfare, in particular as Michael Herr evokes it in *Dispatches*, his great book on the experience of Vietnam. The extraordinary linguistic innovations of this work may still be considered postmodern, in the eclectic way in which its language impersonally fuses a whole range of contemporary collective idiolects, most notably rock language and black language: but the fusion is dictated by problems of content. This first terrible postmodernist war cannot be told in any of the traditional paradigms of the war novel or movie—indeed, that breakdown of all previous narrative paradigms is, along with the breakdown of any shared language through which a veteran might convey such experience, among the principle subjects of the book and may be said to open up the place of a whole new reflexivity. Benjamin's account of Baudelaire, and of the emergence of modernism from a new experience of city technology which transcends all the older habits of bodily perception, is both singularly relevant and singularly antiquated in the light of this new and virtually unimaginable quantum leap in technological alienation:

> He was a moving-target-survivor subscriber, a true child of the war, because except for the rare times when you were pinned or stranded the system was geared to keep you mobile, if that was what you thought you wanted. As a technique for staying alive it seemed to make as much sense as anything, given naturally that you were there to begin with and wanted to see it close; it started out sound and straight but it formed a cone as it progressed, because the more you moved the more you saw, the more you saw the more besides death and mutilation you risked, and the more you risked of that the more you would have to let go of one day as a "survivor." Some of us moved around the war like crazy people until we couldn't see which way the run was taking us anymore, only the war all over its surface with occasional, unexpected penetration. As long as we could have choppers like taxis it took real exhaustion or depression near shock or a dozen pipes of opium to keep us even apparently quiet, we'd still be running around inside our skins like something was after us, ha ha, La Vida Loca. In the months after I got back the hundreds of helicopters I'd flown in began to draw together until they'd formed a collective meta-chopper, and in my mind it was the sexiest thing going; saver-destroyer, provider-waster, right hand – left hand, nimble, fluent, canny and human; hot steel, grease, jungle-saturated canvas webbing, sweat cooling and warming up again, cassette rock and roll in one ear and door-gun fire in the other, fuel, heat, vitality and death, death itself, hardly an intruder.[20]

In this new machine, which does not, like the older modernist machinery of the locomotive or the airplane, represent motion, but which can only be represented *in motion*, something of the mystery of the new postmodernist space is concentrated.

VI

The conception of postmodernism outlined here is a historical rather than a merely stylistic one. I cannot stress too greatly the radical distinction between a view for which the postmodern is one (optional) style among many others available and one which seeks to grasp it as the cultural dominant of the logic of late capitalism: the two approaches in fact generate two very different ways of conceptualizing the phenomenon as a whole: on the one hand, moral judgments (about which it is indifferent whether they are positive or negative), and, on the other, a genuinely dialectical attempt to think our present of time in History.

Of some positive moral evaluation of postmodernism little needs to be said: the complacent (yet delirious) camp-following celebration of this aesthetic new world (including its social and economic dimension, greeted with equal enthusiasm under the slogan of "postindustrial society") is surely unacceptable, although it may be somewhat less obvious that current fantasies about the salvational nature of high technology, from chips to robots—fantasies entertained not only by both left and right governments in distress but also by many intellectuals—are also essentially of a piece with more vulgar apologias for postmodernism.

But in that case it is only consequent to reject moralizing condemnations of the postmodern and of its essential triviality when juxtaposed against the Utopian "high seriousness" of the great modernisms: judgments one finds both on the Left and on the radical Right. And no doubt the logic of the simulacrum, with its transformation of older realities into television images, does more than merely replicate the logic of late capitalism; it reinforces and intensifies it. Meanwhile, for political groups which seek actively to intervene in history and to modify its otherwise passive momentum (whether with a view toward channeling it into a socialist transformation of society or diverting it into the regressive reestablishment of some simpler fantasy past), there cannot but be much that is deplorable and reprehensible in a cultural form of image addiction which, by transforming the past into visual mirages, stereotypes, or texts, effectively abolishes any practical sense of the future and of the collective project, thereby abandoning the thinking of future change to fantasies of sheer catastrophe and inexplicable cataclysm, from visions of "terrorism" on the social level to those of cancer on the personal. Yet if postmodernism is a historical phenomenon, then the attempt to conceptualize it in terms of moral or moralizing judgments must finally be identified as a category mistake. All of which becomes more obvious when we interrogate the position of the cultural critic and moralist; the latter, along with all the rest of us, is now so deeply immersed in postmodernist space, so deeply suffused and infected by its new cultural categories, that the luxury of the old-fashioned ideological critique, the indignant moral denunciation of the other, becomes unavailable.

The distinction I am proposing here knows one canonical form in Hegel's differentiation of the thinking of individual morality or moralizing (*Moralität*) from that whole very different realm of collective social values and practices (*Sittlichkeit*).[21] But it finds its definitive form in Marx's demonstration of the materialist dialectic, most notably in those classic pages of the *Manifesto* which teach the hard lesson of some more genuinely dialectical way to think historical development and change. The topic of the lesson is, of course, the historical development of capitalism itself and the deployment of a specific bourgeois culture. In a well-known passage Marx powerfully urges us to do the impossible, namely, to think this development positively *and* negatively all at once; to achieve, in other words, a type of thinking that would be capable of grasping the demonstrably baleful features of capitalism along with its extraordinary and liberating dynamism simultaneously within a single thought, and without attenuating any of the force of either judgment. We are somehow to lift our minds to a point at which it is possible to understand that capitalism is at one and the same time the best thing that has ever happened to the human race, and the worst. The lapse from this austere dialectical imperative into the more comfortable stance of the taking of moral positions is inveterate and all too human: still, the urgency of the subject demands that we make at least some effort to think the cultural evolution of late capitalism dialectically, as catastrophe and progress all together.

Such an effort suggests two immediate questions, with which we will conclude these reflections. Can we in fact identify some "moment of truth" within the more evident "moments of falsehood" of postmodern culture? And, even if we can do so, is there not something ultimately paralyzing in the dialectical view of historical development proposed above; does it not tend to demobilize us and to surrender us to passivity and helplessness by systematically obliterating possibilities of action under the impenetrable fog of historical inevitability? It is appropriate to discuss these two (related) issues in terms of current possibilities for some effective contemporary cultural politics and for the construction of a genuine political culture.

To focus the problem in this way is, of course, immediately to raise the more genuine issue of the fate of culture generally, and of the function of culture specifically, as one social level or instance, in the postmodern era. Everything in the previous discussion suggests that what we have been calling postmodernism is inseparable from, and unthinkable without the hypothesis of, some fundamental mutation of the sphere of culture in the world of late capitalism, which includes a momentous modification of its social function. Older discussions of the space, function, or sphere of culture (mostly notably Herbert Marcuse's classic essay "The Affirmative Character of Culture") have insisted on what a different language would call the "semiautonomy" of the cultural realm: its ghostly, yet Utopian, existence, for good or ill, above the practical world of the existent, whose mirror image it throws back in forms which vary from the legitimations of flattering resemblance to the contestatory indictments of critical satire or Utopian pain.

What we must now ask ourselves is whether it is not precisely this semiautonomy of the cultural sphere which has been destroyed by the logic of late capitalism. Yet to argue that culture is today no longer endowed with the relative autonomy it once enjoyed as one level among others in earlier moments of capitalism (let alone in precapitalist societies) is not necessarily to imply its disappearance or extinction. Quite the contrary; we must go on to affirm that the dissolution of an autonomous sphere of culture is rather to be imagined in terms of an explosion: a prodigious expansion of culture throughout the social realm, to the point at which everything in our social life—from economic value and state power to practices and to the very structure of the psyche itself —can be said to have become "cultural" in some original and yet untheorized sense. This proposition is, however, substantively quite consistent with the previous diagnosis of a society of the image or the simulacrum and a transformation of the "real" into so many pseudoevents.

It also suggests that some of our most cherished and time-honored radical conceptions about the nature of cultural politics may thereby find themselves outmoded. However distinct those conceptions—which range from slogans of negativity, opposition, and subversion to critique and reflexivity—may have been, they all shared a single, fundamentally spatial, presupposition, which may be resumed in the equally time-honored formula of "critical distance." No theory of cultural politics current on the Left today has been able to do without one notion or another of a certain minimal aesthetic distance, of the possibility of the positioning of the cultural act outside the massive Being of capital, from which to assault this last. What the burden of our preceding demonstration suggests, however, is that distance in general (including "critical distance" in particular) has very precisely been abolished in the new space of postmodernism. We are submerged in its henceforth filled and suffused volumes to the point where our now postmodern bodies are bereft of spatial coordinates and practically (let alone theoretically) incapable of distantiation; meanwhile, it has already been observed how the prodigious new expansion of multinational capital ends up penetrating and colonizing those very precapitalist enclaves (Nature and the Unconscious) which offered extraterritorial and Archimedean footholds for critical effectivity. The shorthand language of co-optation is for this reason omnipresent on the left, but would now seem to offer a most inadequate theoretical basis for understanding a situation in which we all, in one way or another, dimly feel that not only punctual and local countercultural forms of cultural resistance and guerrilla warfare but also even overtly political interventions like those of *The Clash* are all somehow secretly disarmed and reabsorbed by a system of which they themselves might well be considered a part, since they can achieve no distance from it.

What we must now affirm is that it is precisely this whole extraordinarily demoralizing and depressing original new global space which is the "moment of truth" of postmodernism. What has been called the postmodernist "sublime" is only the moment in which this content has become most explicit, has moved the closest to the surface of consciousness as a coherent new type of space in its own right—even though a certain figural concealment or disguise is still at work here, most notably in the high-tech thematics in which the new spatial content is still dramatized and articulated. Yet the earlier features of the postmodern which were enumerated above can all now be seen as themselves partial (yet constitutive) aspects of the same general spatial object.

The argument for a certain authenticity in these otherwise patently ideological productions depends on the prior proposition that what we have been calling postmodern (or multinational) space is not merely a cultural ideology or fantasy but has genuine historical (and socioeconomic) reality as a third great original expansion of capitalism around the globe (after the earlier expansions of the national market and the older imperialist system, which each had their own cultural specificity and generated new types of space appropriate to their dynamics). The distorted and unreflexive attempts of newer cultural production to explore and to express this new space must then also, in their own fashion, be considered as so many approaches to the representation of (a new) reality (to use a more antiquated language). As paradoxical as the terms may seem, they may thus, following a classic interpretive option, be read as peculiar new forms of realism (or at least of the mimesis of reality), while at the same time they can equally well be analyzed as so many attempts to distract and divert us from that reality or to disguise its contradictions and resolve them in the guise of various formal mystifications.

As for that reality itself, however—the as yet untheorized original space of some new "world system" of multinational or late capitalism, a space whose negative or baleful aspects are only too obvious—the dialectic requires us to hold equally to a positive or "progressive" evaluation of its emergence, as Marx did for the world market as the horizon of national economies, or as Lenin did for the older imperialist global network. For neither Marx nor Lenin was socialism a matter of returning to smaller (and thereby less repressive and comprehensive) systems of social organization; rather, the dimensions attained by capital in their own times were grasped as the promise, the framework, and the precondition for the achievement of some new and more comprehensive socialism. Is this not the case with the yet more global and totalizing space of the new world system, which demands the intervention and elaboration of an internationalism of a radically new type? The disastrous realignment of socialist revolution with the older nationalisms (not only in Southeast Asia), whose results have necessarily aroused much serious recent left reflection, can be adduced in support of this position.

But if all this is so, then at least one possible form of a new radical cultural politics becomes evident, with a final aesthetic proviso that must quickly be noted. Left cultural producers and theorists—particularly those formed by bourgeois cultural traditions issuing from romanticism and valorizing spontaneous, instinctive, or unconscious forms of "genius," but also for very obvious historical reasons such as Zhdanovism and the sorry consequences of political and party interventions in the arts—have often by reaction allowed themselves to be unduly intimidated by the repudiation, in bourgeois aesthetics and most notably in high modernism, of one of the age-old functions of art—the pedagogical and the didactic. The teaching function of art was, however, always stressed in classical times (even though it there mainly took the form of moral lessons), while the prodigious and still imperfectly understood work of Brecht reaffirms, in a new and formally innovative and original way, for the moment of modernism proper, a complex new conception of the relationship between culture and pedagogy. The cultural model I will propose similarly foregrounds the cognitive and pedagogical dimensions of political art and culture, dimensions stressed in very different ways by both Lukács and Brecht (for the distinct moments of realism and modernism, respectively).

We cannot, however, return to aesthetic practices elaborated on the basis of historical situations and dilemmas which are no longer ours. Meanwhile, the conception of space that has been developed here suggests that a model of political culture appropriate to our own situation will necessarily have to raise spatial issues as its fundamental organizing concern. I will therefore provisionally define the aesthetic of this new (and hypothetical) cultural form as an aesthetic of *cognitive mapping*.

In a classic work, *The Image of the City*, Kevin Lynch taught us that the alienated city is above all a space in which people are unable to map (in their minds) either their own positions or the urban totality in which they find themselves: grids such as those of Jersey City, in which none of the traditional markers (monuments, nodes, natural boundaries, built perspectives) obtain, are the most obvious examples. Disalienation in the traditional city, then, involves the practical reconquest of a sense of place and the construction or reconstruction of an articulated ensemble which can be retained in memory and which the individual subject can map and remap along the moments of mobile, alternative trajectories. Lynch's own work is limited by the deliberate restriction of his topic to the problems of city form as such; yet it becomes extraordinarily suggestive when projected outward onto some of the larger national and global spaces we have touched on here. Nor should it be too hastily assumed that his model—while it clearly raises very central issues of representation as such—is in any way easily vitiated by the conventional poststructural critiques of the "ideology of representation" or mimesis. The cognitive map is not exactly mimetic in that older sense; indeed, the theoretical issues it poses allow us to renew the analysis of representation on a higher and much more complex level.

There is, for one thing, a most interesting convergence between the empirical problems studied by Lynch in terms of city space and the great Althusserian (and Lacanian) redefinition of ideology as "the representation of the subject's *Imaginary* relationship to his or her *Real* conditions of existence."[22] Surely this is exactly what the cognitive map is called upon to do in the narrower framework of daily life in the physical city: to enable a situational representation on the part of the individual subject to that vaster and properly unrepresentable totality which is the ensemble of society's structures as a whole.

Yet Lynch's work also suggests a further line of development insofar as cartography itself constitutes its key mediatory instance. A return to the history of this science (which is also an art) shows us that Lynch's model does not yet, in fact, really correspond to what will become mapmaking. Lynch's subjects are rather clearly involved in precartographic operations whose results traditionally are described as itineraries rather than as maps: diagrams organized around the still subject-centered or existential journey of the traveler, along which various significant key features are marked—oases, mountain ranges, rivers, monuments, and the like. The most highly developed form of such diagrams is the nautical itinerary, the sea chart, or *portulans*, where coastal features are noted for the use of Mediterranean navigators who rarely venture out into the open sea.

Yet the compass at once introduces a new dimension into sea charts, a dimension that will utterly transform the problematic of the itinerary and allow us to pose the problem of a genuine cognitive mapping in a far more complex way. For the new instruments—compass, sextant, and theodolite—correspond not merely to new geographic and navigational problems (the difficult matter of determining longitude, particularly on the curving surface of the planet, as opposed to the simpler matter of latitude, which European navigators can still empirically determine by ocular inspection of the African coast); they also introduce a whole new coordinate: the relationship to the totality, particularly as it is mediated by the stars and by new operations like that of triangulation. At this point, cognitive mapping in the broader sense comes to require the coordination of existential data (the empirical position of the subject) with unlived, abstract conceptions of the geographic totality.

Finally, with the first globe (1490) and the invention of the Mercator projection at about the same time, yet a third dimension of cartography emerges, which at once involves what we would today call the nature of representational codes, the intrinsic structures of the various media, the intervention, into more naïve mimetic conceptions of mapping, of the whole new fundamental question of the languages of representation itself, in particular the unresolvable (well-nigh Heisenbergian) dilemma of the transfer of curved space to flat charts. At this point it becomes clear that there can be no true maps (at the same time it also becomes clear that there can be scientific progress, or better still, a dialectical advance, in the various historical moments of mapmaking).

Transcoding all this now into the very different problematic of the Althusserian definition of ideology, one would want to make two points. The first is that the Althusserian concept now allows us to rethink these specialized geographical and cartographic issues in terms of social space—in terms, for example, of social class and national or international context, in terms of the ways in which we all necessarily *also* cognitively map our individual social relationship to local, national, and international class realities. Yet to reformulate the problem in this way is also to come starkly up against those very difficulties in mapping which are posed in heightened and original ways by that very global space of the postmodernist or multinational moment which has been under discussion here. These are not merely theoretical issues; they have urgent practical political consequences, as is evident from the conventional feelings of First World subjects that existentially (or "empirically") they really do inhabit a "postindustrial society" from which traditional production has disappeared and in which social classes of the classical type no longer exist—a conviction which has immediate effects on political praxis.

The second point is that a return to the Lacanian underpinnings of Althusser's theory can afford some useful and suggestive methodological enrichments. Althusser's formulation remobilizes an older and henceforth classical Marxian distinction between science and ideology that is not without value for us even today. The existential—the positioning of the individual subject, the experience of daily life, the monadic "point of view" on the world to which we are necessarily, as biological subjects, restricted—is in Althusser's formula implicitly opposed to the realm of abstract knowledge, a realm which, as Lacan reminds us, is never positioned in or actualized by any concrete subject but rather by that structural void called *le sujet supposé savoir* (the subject supposed to know), a subject-place of knowledge. What is affirmed is not that we cannot know the world and its totality in some abstract or "scientific" way. Marxian "science" provides just such a way of knowing and conceptualizing the world abstractly, in the sense in which, for example, Mandel's great book offers a rich and elaborated *knowledge* of that global world system, of which it has never been said here that it was unknowable but merely that it was unrepresentable, which is a very different matter. The Althusserian formula, in other words, designates a gap, a rift, between existential experience and scientific knowledge. Ideology has then the function of somehow inventing a way of articulating those two distinct dimensions with each other. What a historicist view of this definition would want to add is that such coordination, the production of functioning and living ideologies, is distinct in different historical situations, and, above all, that there may be historical situations in which it is not possible at all—and this would seem to be our situation in the current crisis.

But the Lacanian system is threefold, and not dualistic. To the Marxian-Althusserian opposition of ideology and science correspond only two of Lacan's tripartite functions: the Imaginary and the Real, respectively.

Our digression on cartography, however, with its final revelation of a properly representational dialectic of the codes and capacities of individual languages or media, reminds us that what has until now been omitted was the dimension of the Lacanian Symbolic itself.

An aesthetic of cognitive mapping—a pedagogical political culture which seeks to endow the individual subject with some new heightened sense of its place in the global system—will necessarily have to respect this now enormously complex representational dialectic and invent radically new forms in order to do it justice. This is not then, clearly, a call for a return to some older kind of machinery, some older and more transparent national space, or some more traditional and reassuring perspectival or mimetic enclave: the new political art (if it is possible at all) will have to hold to the truth of postmodernism, that is to say, to its fundamental object—the world space of multinational capital—at the same time at which it achieves a breakthrough to some as yet unimaginable new mode of representing this last, in which we may again begin to grasp our positioning as individual and collective subjects and regain a capacity to act and struggle which is at present neutralized by our spatial as well as our social confusion. The political form of postmodernism, if there ever is any, will have as its vocation the invention and projection of a global cognitive mapping, on a social as well as a spatial scale.

2

Theories of the

Postmodern

The problem of postmodernism—
how its fundamental characteristics are to be described, whether it even
exists in the first place, whether the very *concept* is of any use, or is, on
the contrary, a mystification—this problem is at one and the same time
an aesthetic and a political one. The various positions that can logically
be taken on it, whatever terms they are couched in, can always be shown
to articulate visions of history in which the evaluation of the social
moment in which we live today is the object of an essentially political
affirmation or repudiation. Indeed, the very enabling premise of the
debate turns on an initial, strategic presupposition about our social
system: to grant some historic originality to a postmodernist culture is
also implicitly to affirm some radical structural difference between what
is sometimes called consumer society and earlier moments of the capitalism from which it emerged.

The various logical possibilities, however, are necessarily linked with
the taking of a position on that other issue inscribed in the very designation postmodernism itself, namely, the evaluation of what must now
be called high or classical modernism. Indeed, when we make some
initial inventory of the varied cultural artifacts that might plausibly be
characterized as postmodern, the temptation is strong to seek the "family resemblance" of such heterogeneous styles and products not in themselves but in some common high modernist impulse and aesthetic
against which they all, in one way or another, stand in reaction.

The architectural debates, however, the inaugural discussions of postmodernism as a style, have the merit of making the political resonance of
these seemingly aesthetic issues inescapable and allowing it to be detectable in the sometimes more coded or veiled discussions in the other
arts. On the whole, four general positions on postmodernism may be

disengaged from the variety of recent pronouncements on the subject; yet even this relatively neat scheme, or *combinatoire*, is further complicated by one's impression that each of these possibilities is susceptible of either a politically progressive or a politically reactionary expression (speaking now from a Marxist or more generally left perspective).

One can, for example, salute the arrival of postmodernism from an essentially antimodernist standpoint.[1] A somewhat earlier generation of theorists (most notably Ihab Hassan) seem already to have done something like this when they dealt with the postmodernist aesthetic in terms of a more properly poststructuralist thematics (the *Tel quel* attack on the ideology of representation, the Heideggerian or Derridean "end of Western metaphysics"), where what is often not yet called postmodernism (see the Utopian prophecy at the end of Foucault's *The Order of Things*) is saluted as the coming of a whole new way of thinking and being in the world. But since Hassan's celebration also includes a number of the more extreme monuments of high modernism (Joyce, Mallarmé), this would be a relatively more ambiguous stance were it not for the accompanying celebration of a new information high technology which marks the affinity between such evocations and the political thesis of a properly *postindustrial society*.

All of which is largely disambiguated in Tom Wolfe's *From Bauhaus to Our House*, an otherwise undistinguished book report on the recent architectural debates by a writer whose own New Journalism itself constitutes one of the varieties of postmodernism. What is interesting and symptomatic about this book, however, is the absence of any Utopian celebration of the postmodern and, far more striking, the passionate hatred of the modern that breathes through the otherwise obligatory camp sarcasm of the rhetoric; and this is not a new, but a dated and archaic passion. It is as though the original horror of the first middle-class spectators of the very emergence of the modern itself—the first Corbusiers, as white as the first freshly built cathedrals of the twelfth century, the first scandalous Picasso heads with two eyes on one profile like a flounder, the stunning "obscurity" of the first editions of *Ulysses* or *The Waste Land*—this disgust of the original philistines, Spiessbürger, bourgeois, or Main Street Babbitry, had suddenly come back to life, infusing the newer critiques of modernism with an ideologically very different spirit whose effect is, on the whole, to reawaken in the reader an equally archaic sympathy with the protopolitical, Utopian, anti-middle-class impulses of a now extinct high modernism itself. Wolfe's diatribe thus offers a textbook example of the way in which a reasoned and contemporary, theoretical repudiation of the modern—much of whose progressive force springs from a new sense of the urban and a now considerable experience of the destruction of older forms of communal and urban life in the name of a high modernist orthodoxy—can be handily reappropriated and pressed into the service of an explicitly reactionary cultural politics.

These positions—antimodern, propostmodern—then find their opposite number and structural inversion in a group of counterstatements whose aim is to discredit the shoddiness and irresponsibility of the postmodern in general by way of a reaffirmation of the authentic impulse of a high-modernist tradition still considered to be alive and vital. Hilton Kramer's twin manifestos in the inaugural issue of his journal, *The New Criterion*, articulate these views with force, contrasting the moral responsibility of the "masterpieces" and monuments of classical modernism with the fundamental irresponsibility and superficiality of a postmodernism associated with camp and the "facetiousness" of which Wolfe's style is a ripe and obvious example.

What is more paradoxical is that politically Wolfe and Kramer have much in common; and there would seem to be a certain inconsistency in the way in which Kramer must seek to eradicate from the "high seriousness" of the classics of the modern their fundamentally anti-middle-class stance and the protopolitical passion which informs the repudiation, by the great modernists, of Victorian taboos and family life, of commodification, and of the increasing asphyxiation of a desacralizing capitalism, from Ibsen to Lawrence, from Van Gogh to Jackson Pollack. Kramer's ingenious attempt to assimilate this ostensibly antibourgeois stance of the great modernists to a "loyal opposition" secretly nourished, by way of foundations and grants, by the bourgeoisie itself, while signally unconvincing, is surely itself enabled by the contradictions of the cultural politics of modernism proper, whose negations depend on the persistence of what they repudiate and entertain—when they do not (very rarely indeed, as in Brecht) attain some genuine political self-consciousness—a symbiotic relationship with capital.

It is, however, easier to understand Kramer's move here when the political project of *The New Criterion* is clarified; for the mission of the journal is clearly to eradicate the sixties itself and what remains of its legacy, to consign that whole period to the kind of oblivion which the fifties was able to devise for the thirties, or the twenties for the rich political culture of the pre-World War I era. *The New Criterion* therefore inscribes itself in the effort, ongoing and at work everywhere today, to construct some new conservative cultural counterrevolution, whose terms range from the aesthetic to the ultimate defense of the family and religion. It is therefore paradoxical that this essentially political project should explicitly deplore the omnipresence of politics in contemporary culture—an infection largely spread during the sixties but which Kramer holds responsible for the moral imbecility of the postmodernism of our own period.

The problem with the operation—an obviously indispensable one from the conservative viewpoint—is that for whatever reason, its paper-money rhetoric does not seem to have been backed by the solid gold of state power, as was the case with McCarthyism or during the period of the Palmer raids. The failure of the Vietnam War seems, at least for the moment, to have made the naked exercise of repressive power impossible[2] and to have endowed the sixties with a persistence in collective memory and experience that it was not given to the traditions of the thirties or the pre-World War I period to know. Kramer's "cultural revolution" therefore tends most often to lapse into a feeble and sentimental nostalgia for the fifties and the Eisenhower era.

In the light of what has been shown for an earlier set of positions on modernism and postmodernism, it will not be surprising that in spite of the openly conservative ideology of this second evaluation of the contemporary cultural scene, the latter can also be appropriated for what is surely a far more progressive line on the subject. We are indebted to Jürgen Habermas[3] for this dramatic reversal and rearticulation of what remains the affirmation of the supreme value of the modern and the repudiation of the theory and practice of postmodernism. For Habermas, however, the vice of postmodernism consists very centrally in its politically reactionary function, as the attempt everywhere to discredit a modernist impulse Habermas himself associates with the bourgeois Enlightenment and its still universalizing and Utopian spirit. With Adorno himself, Habermas seeks to rescue and recommemorate what both see as the essentially negative, critical, and Utopian power of the great high modernisms. On the other hand, his attempt to associate these last with the spirit of the eighteenth-century Enlightenment marks a decisive break indeed with Adorno and Horkheimer's somber *Dialectic of Enlightenment*, in which the scientific ethos of the philosophes is dramatized as a misguided will to power and domination over nature, and their desacralizing program as the first stage in the development of a sheerly instrumentalizing worldview which will lead straight to Auschwitz. This very striking divergence can be accounted for by Habermas's own vision of history, which seeks to maintain the promise of "liberalism" and the essentially Utopian content of the first, universalizing bourgeois ideology (equality, civil rights, humanitarianism, free speech, and open media) over against the failure of those ideals to be realized in the development of capitalism itself.

As for the aesthetic terms of the debate, however, it will not be adequate to respond to Habermas's resuscitation of the modern by some mere empirical certification of the latter's extinction. We need to take into account the possibility that the national situation in which Habermas thinks and writes is rather different from our own: McCarthyism and repression are, for one thing, realities in the Federal Republic of Germany today, and the intellectual intimidation of the Left and the silencing of a left culture (largely associated, by the West German Right, with "terrorism") has been on the whole a far more successful operation than elsewhere in the West.[4] The triumph of a new McCarthyism and of the culture of the Spiessbürger and the philistine suggests the possibility that in this particular national situation Habermas may well be right, and the older forms of high modernism may still retain something of the subversive power they have lost elsewhere. In that case, a postmodernism which seeks to enfeeble and undermine that power may well also merit his ideological diagnosis in a local way, even though the assessment remains ungeneralizable.

Both of the previous positions—antimodern/propostmodern, and promodern/antipostmodern—are characterized by an acceptance of the new term, which is tantamount to an agreement on the fundamental nature of some decisive break between the modern and the postmodern moments, however these last are evaluated. There remain, however, two final logical possibilities, both of which depend on the repudiation of any conception of such a historical break and which therefore, implicitly or explicitly, call into question the usefulness of the very category of postmodernism. As for the works associated with the latter, they will then be assimilated back into classical modernism proper, so that the "postmodern" becomes little more than the form taken by the authentically modern in our own period, and a mere dialectical intensification of the old modernist impulse toward innovation. (I must here omit yet another series of debates, largely academic, in which the very continuity of modernism as it is here reaffirmed is itself called into question by some vaster sense of the profound continuity of romanticism, from the late eighteenth century on, of which both the modern and the postmodern will be seen as mere organic stages.)

The two final positions on the subject thus logically prove to be a positive and negative assessment, respectively, of a postmodernism now assimilated back into the high-modernist tradition. Jean-François

Lyotard[5] thus proposes that his own vital commitment to the new and the emergent, to a contemporary or postcontemporary cultural production now widely characterized as "postmodern," be grasped as part and parcel of a reaffirmation of the authentic older high modernisms very much in Adorno's spirit. The ingenious twist, or swerve, in his own proposal involves the proposition that something called postmodernism does not *follow* high modernism proper, as the latter's waste product, but rather very precisely *precedes* and prepares it, so that the contemporary postmodernisms all around us may be seen as the promise of the return and the reinvention, the triumphant reappearance, of some new high modernism endowed with all its older power and with fresh life. This is a prophetic stance whose analyses turn on the antirepresentational thrust of modernism and postmodernism. Lyotard's aesthetic positions, however, cannot be adequately evaluated in aesthetic terms, since what informs them is an essentially social and political conception of a new social system beyond classical capitalism (our old friend "post-industrial society"): the vision of a regenerated modernism is, in that sense, inseparable from a certain prophetic faith in the possibilities and promise of the new society itself in full emergence.

The negative inversion of this position will then clearly involve an ideological repudiation of modernism of a type which might conceivably range from Lukács's older analysis of modernist forms as the replication of the reification of capitalist social life all the way to some of the more articulated critiques of high modernism of the present day. What distinguishes this final position from the antimodernisms already outlined above is, however, that it does not speak from the security of an affirmation of some new postmodernist culture but rather sees even the latter itself as a mere degeneration of the already stigmatized impulses of high modernism proper. This particular position, perhaps the bleakest of all and the most implacably negative, can be vividly confronted in the works of the Venetian architecture historian Manfredo Tafuri, whose extensive analyses[6] constitute a powerful indictment of what we have termed the "protopolitical" impulses in high modernism (the "Utopian" substitution of cultural politics for politics proper, the vocation to transform the world by transforming its forms, space, or language). Tafuri is, however, no less harsh in his anatomy of the negative, demystifying, "critical" vocation of the various modernisms, whose function he reads as a kind of Hegelian "ruse of History" whereby the instrumentalizing and desacralizing tendencies of capital itself are ultimately realized through just such demolition work by the thinkers and artists of the modern movement. Their "anticapitalism" therefore ends up laying the basis for the "total" bureaucratic organization and control of late capitalism, and it is only logical that Tafuri should conclude by positing the impossibility of any radical transformation of culture before a radical transformation of social relations themselves.

The political ambivalence demonstrated in the earlier two positions seems to me to be maintained here, but *within* the positions of both of these very complex thinkers. Unlike many of the previously mentioned theorists, Tafuri and Lyotard are both explicitly political figures with an overt commitment to the values of an older revolutionary tradition. It is clear, for example, that Lyotard's embattled endorsement of the supreme value of aesthetic innovation is to be understood as the figure for a certain kind of revolutionary stance, while Tafuri's whole conceptual framework is largely consistent with the classical Marxist tradition. Yet both are also, implicitly, and more openly at certain strategic moments, rewritable in terms of a post-Marxism which at length becomes indistinguishable from anti-Marxism proper. Lyotard has, for example, very frequently sought to distinguish his "revolutionary" aesthetic from the older ideals of political revolution, which he sees as either Stalinist or archaic and incompatible with the conditions of the new postindustrial social order; while Tafuri's apocalyptic notion of the total social revolution implies a conception of the "total system" of capitalism which, in a period of depolitization and reaction, is only too fatally destined for the kind of discouragement which has so often led Marxists to a renunciation of the political altogether (Horkheimer and Merleau-Ponty come to mind, along with many of the ex-Trotskyists of the thirties and forties and the ex-Maoists of the sixties and seventies).

The combination scheme outlined above can now be schematically represented as follows, the plus and minus signs designating the politically progressive or reactionary functions of the positions in question:

	ANTI-MODERNIST	PRO-MODERNIST
PRO-POSTMODERNIST	Wolfe − Jencks +	Lyotard { + −
ANTI-POSTMODERNIST	Tafuri { − +	Kramer − Habermas +

With these remarks we come full circle and can now return to the more positive potential political content of the first position in question, and in particular to the question of a certain *populist* impulse in postmodernism which it has been the merit of Charles Jencks (but also of Venturi and others) to have underscored—a question that will also allow us to deal a little more adequately with the absolute pessimism of Tafuri's Marxism itself. What must first be observed, however, is that most of the political positions which we have found to inform what is most often conducted as an aesthetic debate are in reality moralizing ones that seek to develop final judgments on the phenomenon of postmodernism, whether the latter is stigmatized as corrupt or, on the other hand, saluted as a culturally and aesthetically healthy and positive form of innovation. But a genuinely historical and dialectical analysis of such phenomena—particularly when it is a matter of a present of time and of history in which we ourselves exist and struggle—cannot afford the impoverished luxury of such absolute moralizing judgments: the dialectic is "beyond good and evil" in the sense of some easy taking of sides, whence the glacial and inhuman spirit of its historical vision (something that already disturbed contemporaries about Hegel's original system). The point is that we are *within* the culture of postmodernism to the point where its facile repudiation is as impossible as any equally facile celebration of it is complacent and corrupt. Ideological judgment on postmodernism today necessarily implies, one would think, a judgment on ourselves as well as on the artifacts in question; nor can an entire historical period, such as our own, be grasped in any adequate way by means of global moral judgments or their somewhat degraded equivalent, pop psychological diagnoses. On the classical Marxian view, the seeds of the future already exist within the present and must be conceptually disengaged from it, both through analysis and through political praxis (the workers of the Paris Commune, Marx once remarked in a striking phrase, "*have no ideals to realize*"; they merely sought to disengage emergent forms of new social relations from the older capitalist social relations in which the former had already begun to stir). In place of the temptation either to denounce the complacencies of postmodernism as some final symptom of decadence or to salute the new forms as the harbingers of a new technological and technocratic Utopia, it seems more appropriate to assess the new cultural production within the working hypothesis of a general modification of culture itself with the social restructuring of late capitalism as a system.[7]

As for emergence, however, Jencks's assertion that postmodern archi-

tecture distinguishes itself from that of high modernism through its populist priorities[8] may serve as the starting point for some more general
discussion. What is meant, in the specifically architectural context, is
that where the now more classical high-modernist space of a Corbusier
or a Wright sought to differentiate itself radically from the fallen city
fabric in which it appeared—its forms thus dependent on an act of
radical disjunction from its spatial context (the great *pilotis* dramatizing separation from the ground and safeguarding the novum of the new
space)—postmodernist buildings, on the contrary, celebrate their insertion into the heterogeneous fabric of the commercial strip and the motel
and fast-food landscape of the postsuperhighway American city. Meanwhile, a play of allusion and formal echoes ("historicism") secures the
kinship of these new art buildings with the surrounding commercial
icons and spaces, thereby renouncing the high-modernist claim to radical difference and innovation.

Whether this undoubtedly significant feature of the newer architecture is to be characterized as *populist* must remain an open question. It
would seem essential to distinguish the emergent forms of a new commercial culture—beginning with advertisements and spreading on to
formal *packaging* of all kinds, from products to buildings, and not
excluding artistic commodities such as television shows (the "logo")
and best-sellers and films—from the older kinds of folk and genuinely
"popular" culture which flourished when the older social classes of a
peasantry and an urban *artisanat* still existed and which, from the mid-
nineteenth century on, has gradually been colonized and extinguished
by commodification and the market system.

What can at least be admitted is the more universal presence of this
particular feature, which appears more unambiguously in the other arts
as an effacement of the older distinction between high and so-called
mass culture, a distinction on which modernism depended for its
specificity, its Utopian function consisting at least in part in the securing of a realm of authentic experience over against the surrounding environment of middle- and low-brow commercial culture. Indeed, it can be
argued that the emergence of high modernism is itself contemporaneous with the first great expansion of a recognizably mass culture (Zola
may be taken as the marker for the last coexistence of the art novel and
the best-seller within a single text).

It is this constitutive differentiation which now seems on the point of
disappearing: we have already mentioned the way in which, in music,
after Schönberg and even after Cage, the two antithetical traditions of

the "classical" and the "popular" once again begin to merge. In the visual arts the renewal of photography as a significant medium in its own right and also as the "plane of substance" in pop art or photorealism is a crucial symptom of the same process. At any rate, it becomes minimally obvious that the newer artists no longer "quote" the materials, the fragments and motifs, of a mass or popular culture, as Flaubert began to do; they somehow incorporate them to the point where many of our older critical and evaluative categories (founded precisely on the radical differentiation of modernist and mass culture) no longer seem functional.

But if this is the case, then it seems at least possible that what wears the mask and makes the gestures of "populism" in the various postmodernist apologias and manifestos is in reality a mere reflex and symptom of a (to be sure momentous) cultural mutation, in which what used to be stigmatized as mass or commercial culture is now received into the precincts of a new and enlarged cultural realm. In any case, one would expect a term drawn from the typology of political ideologies to undergo basic semantic readjustments when its initial referent (that Popular Front class coalition of workers, peasants, and petit bourgeois generally called "the people") has disappeared.

Perhaps, however, this is not so new a story after all: one remembers, indeed, Freud's delight at discovering an obscure tribal culture, which alone among the multitudinous traditions of dream analysis had managed to hit on the notion that all dreams had hidden sexual meanings —except for sexual dreams, which meant something else! So also it would seem in the postmodernist debate, and the depoliticized bureaucratic society to which it corresponds, where all seemingly cultural positions turn out to be symbolic forms of political moralizing, except for the single overtly political note, which suggests a slippage from politics back into culture again.

Here the usual objection—that the class includes itself and that the taxonomy fails to include any (sufficiently privileged) place from which to observe itself or to provide for its own theorization—has to be reckoned into the theory as a kind of bad reflexivity that eats its own tail without ever squaring the circle. Postmodernism theory seems indeed to be a ceaseless process of internal rollover in which the position of the observer is turned inside out and the tabulation recontinued on some larger scale. The postmodern thus invites us to indulge a somber mockery of historicity in general, wherein the effort at self-consciousness with which our own situation somehow completes the act of historical understanding, repeats itself drearily as in the worst kinds of dreams, and juxtaposes, to its own pertinent philosophical repudiation of the very concept of self-consciousness, a grotesque carnival of the latter's various replays. The reminder of this interminability is then staged in the form of the inescapability of the plus and minus signs that emerge from their local slots to bedevil the external observer and to insist cease-lessly on a moral judgment excluded in advance from the theory itself. The provisional act of prestidigitation whereby even this moral judg-ment is added to the list of pertinent features, by a theory momentarily able to get outside itself and to include its own external boundaries, scarcely lasts as long as it takes for the "theory" to re-form and serenely to become an example of what the closure it proposes and foretells is supposed to look like. Postmodernism theory can thus finally rise to the level of the system itself as well as its most intimate propagandas, which celebrate the innate freedom of an increasingly absolute self-reproduction.

These circumstances, which forestall in advance any foolproof theory of the postmodern that can be recommended unreservedly as a weapon let alone a litmus paper, demand some thoughts about an approximate proper use that does not lead us back into the self-indulgence of this or that infinite regress. In this particular new enchanted realm, however, the false problem may have become the only place of truth, so that reflection on the impossible matter of the nature of a political art in conditions that exclude it by definition may not be the worst way of marking time. Indeed, I imagine (and the pages to come may or may not confirm) that "postmodern political art" might turn out to be just that —not art in any older sense, but an interminable conjecture on how it could be possible in the first place.

As for the dualisms of the modern/postmodern, which are considera-bly more intolerable than most garden-variety dualisms, and thus are perhaps immunized in advance against the misuses of which such dual-ism are infallibly the mark as well as the instrument, it may be possible that the addition of a third term—absent from the present work, but mobilized elsewhere in a related one[9]—may serve to convert this revers-ible scheme for registering difference into a more productive and porta-ble historical schema. That third term—call it "realism" for the moment and for want of something better—acknowledges the emergence of the secular referent from the Englightenment purging of the sacred codes, at the same time that it accuses some first setting in place of the economic system itself, before both language and the market go on to know declen-sions of the second degree in the modern and imperialism. This new third term, then, earlier than the others, holds them together with whatever fourth terms are hypothesized for the various precapitalisms and affords a more abstract developmental paradigm that seems to recapitulate its chronology out of all chronological order, as in film, or rock music, or black literature, for example. What rescues the new schema from the aporias of the dualisms enumerated here then also offers a kind of intellectual training in leaving the dates out, a kind of ascesis of the diachronic in which we learn to postpone the final gratification of the chronological as a mode of understanding, a gratification that would in any case involve getting out of the system itself, of which, however, the two or three terms rehearsed here are the internal, infinitely substitutable elements.

As long as we cannot do that—and in the face of some justified reluctance to deploy a third term (itself as internally conflicted as the other two taken together)—only the following simple and hygienic recommendation can be proposed: namely, that the dualism be used in some sense against itself, like a lateral field of vision requiring you to fix an object you have no interest in. So it is that, rigorously conducted, an inquiry into this or that feature of the postmodern will end up telling us little of value about postmodernism itself, but against its own will and quite unintentionally a great deal about the modern proper, and perhaps the converse will also turn out to be true, even though the two were never to have been thought of as symmetrical opposites in the first place. An ever more rapid alternation between them can at the least help the celebratory posture or the old-fashioned fulminatory moralizing gesture from freezing into place.

3

Surrealism Without the

Unconscious

It has often been said that every age is dominated by a privileged form, or genre, which seems by its structure the fittest to express its secret truths; or perhaps, if you prefer a more contemporary way of thinking about it, which seems to offer the richest symptom of what Sartre would have called the "objective neurosis" of that particular time and place. Today, however, I think we would no longer look for such characteristic or symptomatic objects in the world and the language of forms or genres. Capitalism, and the modern age, is a period in which, with the extinction of the sacred and the "spiritual," the deep underlying materiality of all things has finally risen dripping and convulsive into the light of day; and it is clear that culture itself is one of those things whose fundamental materiality is now for us not merely evident but quite inescapable. This has, however, also been a historical lesson: it is because culture has *become* material that we are now in a position to understand that it always *was* material, or materialistic, in its structures and functions. We postcontemporary people have a word for that discovery — a word that has tended to displace the older language of genres and forms — and this is, of course, the word *medium*, and in particular its plural, *media*, a word which now conjoins three relatively distinct signals: that of an artistic mode or specific form of aesthetic production, that of a specific technology, generally organized around a central apparatus or machine; and that, finally, of a social institution. These three areas of meaning do not define a medium, or the media, but designate the distinct dimensions that must be addressed in order for such a definition to be completed or constructed. It should be evident that most traditional and modern aesthetic concepts — largely, but not exclusively, designed for literary texts — do not require this simultaneous attention to the multiple dimensions of the material, the social, and the aesthetic.

It is because we have had to learn that culture today is a matter of media that we have finally begun to get it through our heads that culture was always that, and that the older forms or genres, or indeed the older spiritual exercises and meditations, thoughts and expressions, were also in their very different ways media products. The intervention of the machine, the mechanization of culture, and the mediation of culture by the Consciousness Industry are now everywhere the case, and perhaps it might be interesting to explore the possibility that they were always the case throughout human history, and within even the radical difference of older, precapitalist modes of production.

Nonetheless, what is paradoxical about this displacement of literary terminology by an emergent mediatic conceptuality is that it takes place at the very moment in which the philosophical priority of language itself and of the various linguistic philosophies has become dominant and well-nigh universal. Thus, the written text loses its privileged and exemplary status at the very moment when the available conceptualities for analyzing the enormous variety of objects of study with which "reality" presents us (now all in their various ways designated as so many "texts") have become almost exclusively linguistic in orientation. Media analysis in linguistic or semiotic terms therefore may well appear to involve an imperializing enlargement of the domain of language to include nonverbal — visual or musical, bodily, spatial — phenomena; but it may equally well spell a critical and disruptive challenge to the very conceptual instruments which have been mobilized to complete this operation of assimilation.

As for the emergent priority of the media today, this is scarcely a new discovery. For some seventy years the cleverest prophets have warned us regularly that the dominant art form of the twentieth century was not literature at all — nor even painting or theater or the symphony — but rather the one new and historically unique art invented in the contemporary period, namely film; that is to say, the first distinctively mediatic art form. What is strange about this prognosis — whose unassailable validity has with time become a commonplace — is that it should have had so little practical effect. Indeed, literature, sometimes intelligently and opportunistically absorbing the techniques of film back into its own substance, remained throughout the modern period the ideologically dominant paradigm of the aesthetic and continued to hold open a space in which the richest varieties of innovation were pursued. Film, however, whatever its deeper consonance with twentieth-century realities, entertained a merely fitful relationship to the modern in that sense, owing, no doubt, to the two distinct lives or identities through which, successively (like Virginia Woolf's Orlando), it was destined to pass: the first, the silent period, in which some lateral fusion of the mass audience and the formal or modernist proved viable (in ways and resolutions we can no longer grasp, owing to our peculiar historical amnesia); the second, the sound period, then coming as the dominance of mass-cultural (and commercial) forms through which the medium must toil until again reinventing the forms of the modern in a new way in the great auteurs of the 1950s (Hitchcock, Bergman, Kurosawa, Fellini).

What this account suggests is that however helpful the declaration of the priority of film over literature in jolting us out of print culture and/or logocentrism, it remained an essentially *modernist* formulation, locked in a set of cultural values and categories which are in full post-modernism demonstrably antiquated and "historical." That film has today become postmodernist, or at least that certain films have, is obvious enough; but so have some forms of literary production. The argument turned, however, on the priority of these forms, that is, their capacity to serve as some supreme and privileged, symptomatic, index of the zeitgeist; to stand, using a more contemporary language, as the cultural *dominant* of a new social and economic conjuncture; to stand—now finally putting the most philosophically adequate face on the matter—as the richest allegorical and hermeneutic vehicles for some new description of the system itself. Film and literature no longer do that, although I will not belabor the largely circumstantial evidence of the increasing dependency of each on materials, forms, technology, and even thematics borrowed from the other art or medium I have in mind as the most likely candidate for cultural hegemony today.

The identity of that candidate is certainly no secret: it is clearly video, in its twin manifestations as commercial television and experimental video, or "video art." This is not a proposition one proves; rather, one seeks, as I will in the remainder of this chapter, to demonstrate the interest of presupposing it, and in particular the variety of new consequences that flow from assigning some new and more central priority to video processes.

One very significant feature of this presupposition must, however, be underscored at the outset, for it logically involves the radical and virtually a priori differentiation of film theory from whatever is to be proposed in the nature of a theory or even a description of video itself. The very richness of film theory today makes this decision and this warning unavoidable. If the experience of the movie screen and its mesmerizing images is distinct, and fundamentally different, from the experience of the television monitor—something that might be scientifically inferred by technical differences in their respective modes of encoding visual information but which could also be phenomenologically argued—then the very maturity and sophistication of film conceptualities will necessarily obscure the originality of its cousin, whose specific features demand to be reconstructed afresh and empty-handed, without imported and extrapolated categories. A parable can indeed be adduced here to support this methodological decision: discussing the hesitation Central European Jewish writers faced between writing in German and writing in Yiddish, Kafka once observed that these languages were too close to each other for any satisfactory translation from one into the other to be possible. Something like this, then, is what one would want to affirm about the relationship of the language of film theory to that of video theory, if indeed anything like this last exists in the first place.

Doubts on that score have frequently been raised, nowhere more dramatically than at an ambitious conference on the subject sponsored by *The Kitchen* in October 1980, at which a long line of dignitaries trooped to the podium only to complain that they couldn't understand why they had been invited, since they had no particular thoughts about television (which some of them admitted they watched), many then adding, as in afterthought, that only one halfway viable concept "produced" about television occurred to them, and that was Raymond Williams's idea of "whole flow."[1]

Perhaps these two remarks go together more intimately than we imagine: the blockage of fresh thinking before this solid little window against which we strike our heads being not unrelated to precisely that whole or total flow we observe through it.

For it seems plausible that in a situation of total flow, the contents of the screen streaming before us all day long without interruption (or where the interruptions—called *commercials*—are less intermissions than they are fleeting opportunities to visit the bathroom or throw a sandwich together), what used to be called "critical distance" seems to have become obsolete. Turning the television set off has little in common either with the intermission of a play or an opera or with the grand finale of a feature film, when the lights slowly come back on and memory begins its mysterious work. Indeed, if anything like critical distance is still possible in film, it is surely bound up with memory itself. But memory seems to play no role in television, commercial or otherwise (or, I am tempted to say, in postmodernism generally): nothing here haunts the mind or leaves its afterimages in the manner of the great moments of film (which do not necessarily happen, of course, in the "great" films). A description of the structural exclusion of memory, then, and of critical distance, might well lead on into the impossible, namely, a theory of video itself—how the thing blocks its own theorization becoming a theory in its own right.

My experience, however, is that you can't manage to think about things simply by deciding to, and that the mind's deeper currents often need to be surprised by indirection, sometimes, indeed, by treachery and ruse, as when you steer away from a goal in order to reach it more directly or look away from an object to register it more exactly. In that sense, thinking anything adequate about commercial television may well involve ignoring it and thinking about something else; in this instance, experimental video (or alternatively, that new form or genre called MTV, which I cannot deal with here). This is less a matter of mass versus elite culture than it is of controlled laboratory situations: what is so highly specialized as to seem aberrant and uncharacteristic in the world of daily life—hermetic poetry, for example—can often yield crucial information about the properties of an object of study (language, in that case), whose familiar everyday forms obscure it. Released from all conventional constraints, experimental video allows us to witness the full range of possibilities and potentialities of the medium in a way which illuminates its various more restricted uses, the latter being subsets and special cases of the former.

Even this approach to television via experimental video, however, needs to be estranged and displaced if the language of formal innovation and enlarged possibility leads us to expect a flowering and a multiplicity of new forms and visual languages: they exist, of course, and to a degree so bewildering in the short history of video art (sometimes dated from Nam June Paik's first experiments in 1963) that one is tempted to wonder whether any description or theory could ever encompass their variety. I have found it enlightening to come at this issue from a different direction, however, by raising the question of *boredom* as an aesthetic response and a phenomenological problem. In both the Freudian and the Marxist traditions (for the second, Lukács, but also Sartre's discussion of "stupidity" in Sartre's *Journal of the Phony War*), "boredom" is taken not so much as an objective property of things and works but rather as a response to the blockage of energies (whether those be grasped in terms of desire or of praxis). Boredom then becomes interesting as a reaction to situations of paralysis and also, no doubt, as defense mechanism or avoidance behavior. Even taken in the narrower realm of cultural reception, boredom with a particular kind of work or style or content can always be used productively as a precious symptom of our own existential, ideological, and cultural limits, an index of what has to be refused in the way of other people's cultural practices and their threat to our own rationalizations about the nature and value of art. Meanwhile, it is no great secret that in some of the most significant works of high modernism, what is boring can often be very interesting indeed, and vice versa: a combination which the reading of any hundred sentences by Raymond Roussel, say, will at once dramatize. We must therefore initially try to strip the concept of the *boring* (and its experience) of any axiological overtones and bracket the whole question of aesthetic value. It is a paradox one can get used to: if a boring text can also be good (or interesting, as we now put it), exciting texts, which incorporate diversion, distraction, temporal commodification, can also perhaps sometimes be "bad" (or "degraded," to use Frankfurt School language).

Imagine at any event a face on your television screen accompanied by an incomprehensible and never-ending stream of keenings and mutterings: the face remaining utterly without expression, unchanging throughout the course of the "work," and coming at length to seem some icon or floating immobile timeless mask. It is an experience to which you might be willing to submit out of curiosity for a few minutes. When, however, you begin to leaf through your program in distraction, only to discover that this particular videotext is twenty-one minutes long, then panic overcomes the mind and almost anything else seems preferable. But twenty-one minutes is not terribly long in other contexts (the immobility of the adept or religious mystic might offer some point of reference), and the nature of this particular form of aesthetic boredom becomes an interesting problem, particularly when we recall the difference between the viewing situation of video art and analogous experiences in experimental film (we can always shut the first one off, without sitting politely through a social and institutional ritual). As I have already suggested, however, we must avoid the easy conclusion that this tape or text is simply bad; one wants immediately to add, to forestall misconceptions, that there are many, many diverting and captivating videotexts of all kinds—but then one would also want to avoid the conclusion that those are simply better (or "good" in the axiological sense).

There then emerges a second possibility, a second explanatory temptation, which involves authorial intention. We may then conclude that the videomaker's choice was a deliberate and conscious one, and that therefore the twenty-one minutes of this tape are to be interpreted as provocation, as a calculated assault on the viewer, if not an act of outright aggressivity. In that case, our response was the right one: boredom and panic are appropriate reactions and a recognition of the meaning of that particular aesthetic act. Apart from the well-known aporias involved in concepts of literary intent and intention, the thematics of such aggressivity (aesthetic, class, gender, or whatever) are virtually impossible to reestablish on the basis of the isolated tape itself.

Perhaps, however, the problems of the motives of the individual subject can be elided by attention to the other type of mediation involved, namely, technology and the machine itself. We are told, for instance, that in the early days of photography, or rather, of the daguerrotype, subjects were obliged to sit in absolute immobility for periods of time which, although not long as the crow flies, could nonetheless be characterized as being *relatively* intolerable. One imagines the uncontrollable twitching of the facial muscles, for example, or the overwhelming urge to scratch or laugh. The first photographers therefore devised something on the order of the electric chair, in which the heads of their portrait subjects, from the lowliest and most banal generals all the way to Lincoln himself, were clamped in place and immobilized from the back for the obligatory five or ten minutes of the exposure. Roussel, whom I've already mentioned, is something like a literary equivalent of this process: his unimaginably detailed and minute description of objects—an absolutely infinite process without principle or thematic interest of any kind—forces the reader to work laboriously through one sentence after another, world without end. But it may now be appropriate to identify Roussel's peculiar experiments as a kind of anticipation of postmodernism within the older modernist period; at any rate, it seems at least arguable that aberrations and excesses which were marginal or subordinate in the modernist period become dominant in the systemic restructuration that can be observed in what we now call postmodernism. It is nevertheless clear that experimental video, whether we date it from the work of the ancestor Paik in the early 1960s or from the very floodtide of this new art which sets in in the mid 1970s, is rigorously coterminous with postmodernism itself as a historical period.

The machine on both sides, then; the machine as subject and object, alike and indifferently: the machine of the photographic apparatus peering across like a gun barrel at the subject, whose body is clamped into its mechanical correlative in some apparatus of registration/reception. The helpless spectators of video time are then as immobilized and mechanically integrated and neutralized as the older photographic subjects, who became, for a time, part of the technology of the medium. The living room, to be sure (or even the relaxed informality of the video museum), seems an unlikely place for this assimilation of human subjects to the technological: yet a voluntary attention is demanded by the total flow of the videotext in time which is scarcely relaxed at all, and rather different from the comfortable scanning of the movie screen, let alone of the cigar-smoking detachment of the Brechtian theatergoer. Interesting analyses (mostly from a Lacanian perspective) have been offered in recent film theory of the relationship between the mediation of the filmic machine and the construction of the viewer's subjectivity—at once depersonalized, and yet still powerfully motivated to reestablish the false homogeneities of the ego and of representation. I have the feeling that mechanical depersonalization (or decentering of the subject) goes even further in the new medium, where the auteurs themselves are dissolved along with the spectator (a point to which I will return shortly in another context).

Yet since video is a temporal art, the most paradoxical effects of this technological appropriation of subjectivity are observable in the experience of time itself. We all know, but always forget, that the fictive scenes and conversations on the movie screen radically foreshorten reality as the clock ticks and are never—owing to the now codified mysteries of the various techniques of film narrative—coterminous with the putative length of such moments in real life, or in "real time": something a filmmaker can always uncomfortably remind us of by returning occasionally to real time in this or that episode, which then threatens to project much the same intolerable discomfort we have ascribed to certain videotapes. Is it possible, then, that "fiction" is what is in question here and that it can be defined essentially as the construction of just such fictive and foreshortened temporalities (whether of film or reading), which are then substituted for a real time we are thereby enabled momentarily to forget? The question of fiction and the fictive would thereby find itself radically dissociated from questions of narrative and storytelling as such (although it would retain a key role and function in the practice of certain forms of narration): many of the confusions of the so-called representation debate (often assimilated to a debate about realism) are dispelled by just such an analytic distinction between fiction effects and their fictional temporalities, and narrative structures in general.

At any rate, in that case what one would want to affirm is that experimental video is *not* fictive in this sense, does not project fictive time, and does not work with fiction or fictions (although it may well work with narrative structures). This initial distinction then makes other ones possible, as well as interesting new problems. Film, for example, would clearly seem to approach this status of the nonfictive in its documentary form; but I suspect for various reasons that most documentary film (and documentary video) still projects a kind of residual fictionality—a kind of documentary constructed time—at the very heart of its aesthetic ideology and its sequential rhythms and effects. Meanwhile, alongside the nonfictional processes of experimental video, at least one form of video clearly does aspire to fictionality of a filmic type, and that is commercial television, whose specificities, whether one deplores or celebrates them, are also perhaps best approached by way of a description of experimental video. To characterize television series, dramas and the like, in other words, in terms of the imitation by this medium of other arts and media (most notably filmic narrative) probably dooms one to miss the most interesting feature of their production situation: namely, how, out of the rigorously nonfictive languages of video, commercial television manages to produce the simulacrum of fictive time.

As for temporality itself, it was for the modern movement conceived at best as an experience and at worst as a theme, even though the reality glimpsed by the first moderns of the nineteenth century (and designated by the word ennui is surely already this temporality of boredom we have identified in the video process, the ticking away of real time minute by minute, the dread underlying irrevocable reality of the meter running. Yet the involvement of the machine in all this allows us now perhaps to escape phenomenology and the rhetoric of consciousness and experience, and to confront this seemingly subjective temporality in a new and materialist way, a way which constitutes a new kind of materialism as well, one not of matter but of machinery. It is as though, rephrasing our initial discussion of the retroactive effect of new genres, the emergence of the machine itself (so central to Marx's organization of *Capital*) deconcealed in some unexpected way the produced materiality of human life and time. Indeed, alongside the various phenomenological accounts of temporality, and the philosophies and ideologies of time, we have also come to possess a whole range of historical studies of the social construction of time itself, of which the most influential no doubt remains E. P. Thompson's classic essay[2] on the effects of the introduction of the chronometer into the workplace. Real time in that sense is objective time; that is to say, the time of objects, a time subject to the measurements to which objects are subject. Measurable time becomes a reality on account of the emergence of measurement itself, that is, rationalization and reification in the closely related senses of Weber and Lukács; clock time presupposes a peculiar spatial machine—it is the time of a machine, or better still, the time of the machine itself.

I have tried to suggest that video is unique—and in that sense historically privileged or symptomatic—because it is the only art or medium in which this ultimate seam between space and time is the very locus of the form, and also because its machinery uniquely dominates and depersonalizes subject and object alike, transforming the former into a quasi-material registering apparatus for the machine time of the latter and of the video image or "total flow." If we are willing to entertain the hypothesis that capitalism can be periodized by the quantum leaps or technological mutations by which it responds to its deepest systemic crises, then it may become a little clearer why and how video—so closely related to the dominant computer and information technology of the late, or third, stage of capitalism—has a powerful claim for being the art form par excellence of late capitalism.

These propositions allow us to return to the concept of total flow itself and to grasp its relationship to the analysis of commercial (or fictive) television in a new way. Material or machine time punctuates the flow of commercial television by way of the cycles of hour and half-hour programming, shadowed as by a ghostly afterimage by the shorter rhythms of the commercials themselves. I have suggested that these regular and periodic breaks are very unlike the types of closure to be found in the other arts, even in film, yet they allow the simulation of such closures and thereby the production of a kind of imaginary fictive time. The simulacrum of the fictive seizes on such material punctuation much as a dream seizes on external bodily stimuli, to draw them back into itself and to convert them into the appearance of beginnings and endings; or, in other words, the illusion of an illusion, the second-degree simulation of what is already itself, in other art forms, some first-degree illusory fictiveness or temporality. But only a dialectical perspective, which posits presences and absences, appearances and realities, or essences, can reveal these constitutive processes: for a one-dimensional or positivistic semiotics, for example, which can only deal in the sheer presences and existent data of segments of commercial and experimental video alike, these two related yet dialectically distinct forms are reduced to cuts and lengths of an identical material to which identical instruments of analysis are then applied. Commercial television is not an autonomous object of study; it can only be grasped for what it is by positioning it dialectically over against that other signifying system which we have called experimental video, or video art.[3]

The hypothesis of some greater materiality of video as a medium suggests that its analogies are perhaps better sought for in other places than the obvious cross-referencing of commercial television or fiction or even documentary film. We need to explore the possibility that the most suggestive precursor of the new form may be found in animation or the animated cartoon, whose materialistic (and paradoxically nonfictive) specificity is at least twofold: involving, on the one hand, a constitutive match or fit between a musical language and a visual one (two fully elaborated systems which are no longer subordinate to one another as in fiction film), and, on the other, the palpably produced character of animation's images, which in their ceaseless metamorphosis now obey the "textual" laws of writing and drawing rather than the "realistic" ones of verisimilitude, the force of gravity, etc. Animation constituted the first great school to teach the reading of material signifiers (rather than the narrative apprenticeship of objects of representation—characters, actions, and the like). Yet in animation, as later in experimental video, the Lacanian overtones of this language of material signifiers is inescapably completed by the omnipresent force of human praxis itself; suggesting thereby an active materialism of production rather than a static or mechanical materialism of matter or materiality itself as some inert support.

As for total flow, meanwhile, it has significant methodological consequences for the analysis of experimental video, and in particular for the constitution of the object or unity of study such a medium presents. It is, of course, no accident that today, in full postmodernism, the older language of the "work"—the work of art, the masterwork—has everywhere largely been displaced by the rather different language of the "text," of texts and textuality—a language from which the achievement of organic or monumental form is strategically excluded. Everything can now be a text in that sense (daily life, the body, political representations), while objects that were formerly "works" can now be reread as immense ensembles or systems of texts of various kinds, superimposed on each other by way of the various intertextualities, successions of fragments, or, yet again, sheer process (henceforth called textual production or textualization). The autonomous work of art thereby—along with the old autonomous subject or ego—seems to have vanished, to have been volatilized.

Nowhere is this more materially demonstrable than with the "texts" of experimental video—a situation which, however, now confronts the analyst with some new and unusual problems characteristic in one way or another of all the postmodernisms, but even more acute here. If the old modernizing and monumental forms—the Book of the World, the "magic mountains" of the architectural modernisms, the central mythic opera cycle of a Bayreuth, the Museum itself as the center of all the possibilities of painting—if such totalizing ensembles are no longer the fundamental organizing frames for analysis and interpretation; if, in other words, there are no more masterpieces, let alone their canon, no more "great" books (and if even the concept of *good* books has become problematic)—if we find ourselves confronted henceforth with "texts," that is, with the ephemeral, with disposable works that wish to fold back immediately into the accumulating detritus of historical time—then it becomes difficult and even contradictory to organize an analysis and an interpretation around any single one of these fragments in flight. To select—even as an "example"—a single videotext, and to discuss it in isolation, is fatally to regenerate the illusion of the masterpiece or the canonical text and to reify the experience of total flow from which it was momentarily extracted. Video viewing indeed involves immersion in the total flow of the thing itself, preferably a kind of random succession of three or four hours of tapes at regular intervals. Indeed, video is in this sense (and owing to the commercialization of public television and cable) an urban phenomenon demanding video banks or museums in your neighborhood which can thus be visited with something of the institutional habits and relaxed informality with which we used to visit the theater or the opera house (or even the movie palace). What is quite out of the question is to look at a single "video work" all by itself; in that sense, one would want to say, there are no video masterpieces, there can never be a video canon, and even an auteur theory of video (where signatures are still evidently present) becomes very problematical indeed. The "interesting" text now has to stand out of an undifferentiated and random flow of other texts. Something like a Heisenberg principle of video analysis thereby emerges: analysts and readers are shackled to the examination of specific and individual texts, one after the other; or, if you prefer, they are condemned to a kind of linear *Darstellung* in which they have to talk about individual texts one at a time. But this very form of perception and criticism at once interferes with the reality of the thing perceived and intercepts it in mid-lightstream, distorting all the findings beyond recognition. The discussion, the indispensable prelim-

inary selection and isolation, of a single "text" then automatically transforms it back into a "work," turns the anonymous videomaker[4] back into
a named artist or auteur, and opens the way for the return of all those
features of an older modernist aesthetic which it was in the revolutionary nature of the newer medium to have precisely effaced and dispelled.

In spite of these qualifications and reservations, it does not seem possible to go further in this exploration of the possibilities of video without interrogating a concrete text. We will consider a twenty-nine-minute
"work" called *AlienNATION*, produced at the School of the Art Institute
of Chicago by Edward Rankus, John Manning, and Barbara Latham in
1979. For the reader this will evidently remain an imaginary text; but
the reader need not "imagine" that the spectator is in an altogether different situation. To describe, afterward, this stream of images of all kinds
is necessarily to violate the perpetual present of the image and to reorganize the few fragments that remain in the memory according to
schemes which probably reveal more about the reading mind than the
text itself: do we try to turn it back into a story of some kind? (A very
interesting book by Jacques Leenhardt and Pierre Józsa [*Lire la lecture*
(Paris: Le Sycamore, 1982)] shows this process at work even in the reading of "plotless novels"—the reader's memory creates "protagonists"
out of whole cloth, violates the reading experience in order to reassemble it into recognizable scenes and narrative sequences, and so forth.)
Or, at some more critically sophisticated level, do we at least try to sort
the material out into thematic blocks and rhythms and repunctuate it
with beginnings and endings, with graphs of rising and falling emotivity,
climaxes, dead passages, transitions, recapitulations, and the like? No
doubt; only the reconstruction of these overall formal movements turns
out differently every time we watch the tape. For one thing, twenty-nine
minutes in video is much longer than the equivalent temporal segment
of any feature film; nor is it excessive to speak of a genuine and a very
acute *contradiction* between the virtually druglike experience of the
present of the image in the videotape and any kind of textual memory
into which the successive presents might be inserted (even the return
and recognition of older images is, as it were, seized on the run, laterally and virtually too late for it to do us any good). If the contrast here
with the memory structures of Hollywood-type fiction films is stark and
obvious, one has the feeling—more difficult to document or to argue
—that the gap between this temporal experience and that of *experimental* film is no less great. These op art tricks and elaborate visual
montages in particular recall the classics of yesteryear such as *Ballet*

mechanique; but I have the impression that, above and beyond the difference in our institutional situation (art movie theater here, television monitor either at home or in a museum for the videotext), these experiences are very different ones, and in particular that the blocks of material in film are larger and more grossly and tangibly perceptible (even when they pass by rapidly), determining a more leisurely sense of combinations than can be the case with these attenuated visual data on the television screen.

One is therefore reduced to enumerating a few of these video materials, which are not themes (since for the most part they are material quotations from a quasi-commercial storehouse somewhere), but which certainly have none of the density of Bazinian mise-en-scène either, since even the segments which are not lifted from already existing sequences, but which have obviously been filmed explicitly for use in this tape, have a kind of shabbiness of low-grade color stock which marks them somehow as "fictional" and staged, as opposed to the manifest reality of the other images-in-the-world, the image objects. There is therefore a sense in which the word *collage* could still obtain for this juxtaposition of what one is tempted to call "natural" materials (the newly or directly filmed sequences) and artificial ones (the precooked image materials which have been "mixed" by the machine itself). What would be misleading is the ontological hierarchy of the older painterly collage: in this videotape the "natural" is worse and more degraded than the artificial, which itself no longer connotes the secure daily life of a new humanly constructed society (as in the objects of cubism) but rather the noise and jumbled signals, the unimaginable informational garbage, of the new media society.

First, a little existential joke about a "spot" of time, which is excised from a temporal "culture" that looks a little like a crepe; then experimental mice, voice-overed by various pseudoscientific reports and therapeutic programs (how to deal with stress, beauty care, hypnosis for weight loss, etc.); then science fiction footage (including monster music and camp dialogue), mostly drawn from a Japanese film, *Monster Zero* (1965). At this point the rush of image materials becomes too dense to enumerate: optical effects, children's blocks and erector sets, reproductions of classical paintings, as well as mannequins, advertising images, computer printouts, textbook illustrations of all kinds, cartoon figures rising and falling (including a wonderful Magritte hat slowly sinking into Lake Michigan); sheet lightning; a woman lying down and possibly under hypnosis (unless, as in a Robbe-Grillet novel, this is merely the

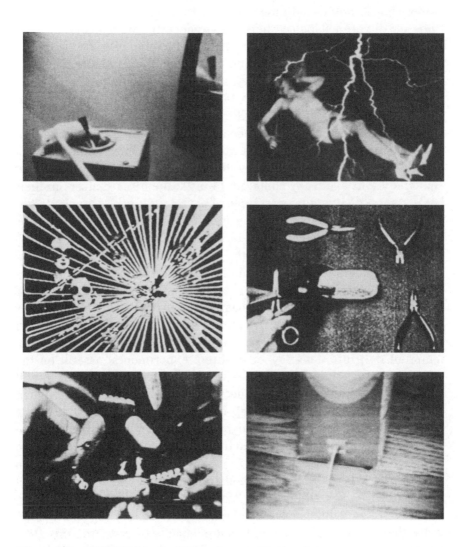

From *AlienNATION* (Rankus, Manning, and Latham)

photograph of a woman lying down and possibly under hypnosis); ultra-modern hotel or office building lobbies with escalators rising in all directions and at various angles; shots of a street corner with sparse traffic, a child on a big wheel and a few pedestrians carrying groceries; a haunting closeup of detritus and children's blocks on the lakeshore (in one of which the Magritte hat reappears, in real life: poised on stick in the sand); Beethoven sonatas, Holst's *Planets*, disco music, funeral parlor organs, outer space sound effects, the *Lawrence of Arabia* theme accompanying the arrival of flying saucers over the Chicago skyline; a grotesque sequence as well in which friable orange oblongs (that resemble Hostess Twinkies) are dissected with scalpels, squeezed by vises, and shattered by fists; a leaky container of milk; the disco dancers in their habitat; shots of alien planets; closeups of various kinds of brushstrokes; ads for 1950s kitchens; and many more. Sometimes these seem to be combined in longer sequences, as when the sheet lightning is over-charged with a whole series of opticals, advertisements, cartoon figures, movie music, and unrelated radio dialogue. Sometimes, as in the transition from a relatively pensive "classical music" accompaniment to the stridence of a mass-cultural beat, the principle of variation seems obvious and heavy-handed. Sometimes the accelerated flow of mixed images strikes one as modeling a certain unified temporal urgency, the tempo of delirium, let's say, or of direct experimental assault on the viewer-subject; while the whole is randomly punctuated with formal signals—the "prepare to disconnect" which is presumably designed to warn the viewer of impending closure, and the final shot of the beach, which borrows a more recognizably filmic connotative language —dispersal of an object world into fragments, but also the touching of a kind of limit or ultimate edge (as in the closing sequence of Fellini's *La Dolce Vita*). It is all, no doubt, an elaborate visual joke or hoax (if you were expecting something more "serious"): a student's training exercise, if you like; while such is the tempo of the history of experimental video that insiders or connoisseurs are capable of watching this 1979 production with a certain nostalgia and remembering that people did that kind of thing in those days but are now busy doing something else.

The most interesting questions posed by a videotext of this kind— and I hope it will be clear that the text *works*, whatever its value or its meaning: it can be seen again and again (at least partly on account of its informational overload, which the viewer will never be able to master) —remain questions of value and of interpretation, provided it is understood that it may be the absence of any possible response to those questions which is the historically interesting matter. But my attempt to tell or summarize this text makes it clear that even before we reach the interpretative question—"what does it mean?" or, to use its petit bourgeois version, "what is it supposed to represent?"—we have to confront the preliminary matters of form and reading. It is not evident that a spectator will ever reach a moment of knowledge and saturated memory from which a formal reading of this text in time slowly disengages itself: beginnings and thematic emergences, combinations and developments, resistances and struggles for dominance, partial resolutions, forms of closure leading on to one or another full stop. Could one establish such an overall chart of the work's formal time, even in a very crude and general way, our description would necessarily remain as empty and as abstract as the terminology of musical form, whose problems today, in aleatory and post-twelve-tone music, are analogous, even though the mathematical dimensions of sound and musical notation provide what look like more tangible solutions. My sense is, however, that even the few formal markers we have been able to isolate—the lakeshore, the building blocks, the "sense of an ending"—are deceptive; they are now no longer features or elements of a form but signs and traces of older forms. We must remember that those older forms are still included within the bits and pieces, the bricolated material, of this text: Beethoven's sonata is but one component of this bricolage, like a broken pipe retrieved and inserted in a sculpture or a torn piece of newspaper pasted onto a canvas. Yet within the musical segment of the older Beethoven work, "form" in the traditional sense persists and can be named—the "falling cadence," say, or the "reappearance of the first theme." The same can be said of the film clips of the Japanese monster movie: they include quotations of the SF form itself: "discovery," "menace," "attempted flight," and so forth (here the available formal terminology—in analogy to the musical nomenclature—would probably be restricted to Aristotle or to Propp and his successors, or to Eisenstein, virtually the only sources of a neutral language of the movement of narrative form). The question that suggests itself, then, is whether the formal properties within these quoted segments and pieces are anywhere transferred to the videotext itself, to the bricolage of which they are parts and components. But this is a question that must first be raised on the microlevel of individual episodes and moments. As for the larger formal properties of the text considered as a "work" and as temporal organization, the lakeshore image suggests that the strong form of an older temporal or musical closure is here present merely as a formal residue:

whatever in Fellini's ending still bore the traces of a mythic residue —the sea as some primordial element, as the place at which the human and the social confront the otherness of nature—is here already long since effaced and forgotten. That content has disappeared, leaving but a faint aftertrace of its original formal connotation, that is, of its syntactical function as closure. At this most attenuated point in the sign system the signifier has become little more than a dim memory of a former sign, and indeed, of the formal function of that now extinct sign.

The language of connotation which began to impose itself in the preceding paragraph would seem to impose a reexamination of the central elaboration of this concept, which we owe to Roland Barthes, who elaborated it, following Hjemslev, in his *Mythologies*, only in his later "textual" work to repudiate its implicit differentiation of first- and second-degree languages (denotation and connotation), which must have come to strike him as a replication of the old divisions between aesthetic and social, artistic free play and historical referentiality—divisions which essays like *Le Plaisir du texte* were concerned to evade or escape. No matter that the earlier theory (still enormously influential in media studies) ingeniously reversed the priorities of this opposition, assigning authenticity (and thereby aesthetic value) to the denotative value of the photographic image, and a guilty social or ideological functionality to its more "artificial" prolongation in advertising texts that take the original denotative text as their own new content, pressing already existent images into the service of some heightened play of degraded thoughts and commercial messages. Whatever the stakes and implications of this debate, it seems clear that Barthes's earlier, classical conception of how connotation functions can be suggestive for us here only if it is appropriately complicated, perhaps beyond all recognition. For the situation here is rather the inverse of the advertising one, where "purer" and somehow more material signs were appropriated and readapted to serve as vehicles for a whole range of ideological signals. Here, on the contrary, the ideological signals are already deeply embedded in the primary texts, which are already profoundly cultural and ideological: the Beethoven music already includes the connotator of "classical music" in general, the science fiction film already includes multiple political messages and anxieties (an American Cold War form readapted to Japanese antinuclear politics, and both then folding into the new cultural connotator of "camp"). But connotation is here—in a cultural sphere whose "products" have functions that largely transcend the narrowly commercial ones of advertising images (while no doubt still including some of those and surely replicating their structures in other ways)—a polysemic process in which a number of "messages" coexist. Thus the alternation of Beethoven and disco no doubt emits a class message—high versus popular or mass culture, privilege and education versus more popular and bodily forms of diversion—but is also continues to vehiculate the older content of some tragic gravity, the formal time sense of the sonata form itself, the "high seriousness" of the most rigorous bourgeois aesthetic in its grappling with time, contradiction, and death; which now finds itself opposed to the relentless temporal distraction of the big city commercial music of the postmodern age that fills time and space implacably to the point where the older "tragic" questions seem irrelevant. All these connotations are in play simultaneously. To the degree to which they appear easily reducible to some of the binary oppositions just mentioned (high and low culture), and to that degree alone, we are in the presence of a kind of "theme," which might at the outside limit be the occasion for an interpretive act and allow us to suggest that the videotext is "about" this particular opposition. We will return to such interpretive possibilities or options later on.

What must be excluded, however, is anything like a process of demystification at work in this particular videotext: all its materials are degraded in that sense, Beethoven no less than disco. And although, as we will shortly make clear, there is a very complex interaction at work here between various levels and components of the text, or various languages (image versus sound, music versus dialogue), the political use of one of these levels against another (as in Godard), the attempt somehow to purify the image by setting it off against the written or spoken, is here no longer on the agenda, if it is even still conceivable. This is something that can be clarified, I believe, if we think of the various quoted elements and components—the broken pieces of a whole range of primary texts in the contemporary cultural sphere—as so many logos, that is to say, as a new form of advertising language which is structurally and historically a good deal more advanced and complicated than any of the advertising images with which Barthes's earlier theories had to deal. A logo is something like the synthesis of an advertising image and a brand name; better still, it is a brand name which has been transformed into an image, a sign or emblem which carries the memory of a whole tradition of earlier advertisements within itself in a well-nigh intertextual way. Such logos can be visual or auditory and musical (as in the Pepsi theme): an enlargement which allows us to include the materials of the sound track under this category, along with the more immediately identifiable logo segments of the office escalators, the fashion mannequins, the psychological counseling clips, the street corner, the lakefront, *Monster Zero*, and so forth. "Logo" then signifies the transformation of each of these fragments into a kind of sign in its own right; yet it is not yet clear what such new signs might be signs of, since no product seems identifiable, nor even the range of generic products strictly designated by the logo in its original sense, as the badge of a diversified multinational corporation. Still, the term *generic* is itself suggestive if we conceive of its literary implications a little more broadly than the older, more static, tables of "genres," or fixed kinds. The generic cultural consumption projected by these fragments is more dynamic and demands some association with narrative (itself now grasped in the wider sense of a type of textual consumption). In that sense, the scientific experiments are narratives fully as much as *Lawrence of Arabia*; the vision of white-collar workers and bureaucrats mounting flights of escalators is no less a narrative vision than the science fiction film clips (or horror music); even the still photograph of sheet lightning suggests a multiple set of narrative frames (Ansel Adams, or the terror of the great storm, or the "logo" of the Remington-type western landscape, or the eighteenth-century sublime, or the answer of God to the rainmaking ceremony, or the beginning of the end of the world).

The matter grows more complicated, however, when we realize that none of these elements or new cultural signs or logos exists in isolation; the videotext itself is at virtually all moments a process of ceaseless, apparently random, interaction between them. This is clearly the structure which demands description and analysis, but it is a relationship between signs for which we have only the most approximate theoretical models. It is indeed a matter of apprehending a constant stream, or "total flow," of multiple materials, each of which can be seen as something like a shorthand signal for a distinct type of narrative or a specific narrative process. But our immediate questions will be synchronic rather than diachronic: how do these various narrative signals or logos intersect? Is one to imagine a mental compartmentalization in which each is received in isolation, or does the mind somehow establish connections of some kind; and in that case, how can we describe those connections? How are these materials wired into one another, if at all? Or do we merely confront a simultaneity of distinct streams of elements which the senses grasp all together like a kaleidoscope? The measure of our conceptual weakness here is that we are tempted to begin with the most unsatisfactory methodological decision—the Cartesian point of departure—in which we begin by reducing the phenomenon to its simplest form, namely, the interaction of two such elements or signals (whereas dialectical thinking asks us to begin with the most complex form, of which the simpler ones are considered derivatives).

Even in the case of two elements, however, suggestive theoretical models are few enough. The oldest one is, of course, the logical model of *subject* and *predicate*, which, divested of its propositional logic—with its statement sentences and truth claims—has in recent times been rewritten as a relationship between a *topic* and a *comment*. Literary theory has for the most part been obliged to confront this structure only in the analysis of metaphor, for which I. A. Richards's distinction between a *tenor* and a *vehicle* seems suggestive. The semiotics of Peirce, however, which seeks insistently to grasp the process of interpretation— or semiosis—in time, usefully rewrites all these distinctions in terms of an initial sign in relationship to which a second sign stands as an *interpretant*. Contemporary narrative theory, finally, with its operative distinction between the fable (the anecdote, the raw materials of the basic story) and the mise-en-scène itself, the way in which those materials are told or staged; in other words, their *focalization*.

What must be retained from these formulations is the way in which they pose two signs of equal nature and value, only to observe that in their moment of intersection a new hierarchy is at once established in which one sign becomes something like the material on which the other one works, or in which the first sign establishes a content and a center to which the second is annexed for auxiliary and subordinate functions (the priorities of the hierarchical relationship here seeming reversible). But the terminology and nomenclature of the traditional models do not register what surely becomes a fundamental property of the stream of signs in our video context: namely, that they change places; that no single sign ever retains priority as a topic of the operation; that the situation in which one sign functions as the interpretant of another is more than provisional, it is subject to change without notice; and in the ceaselessly rotating momentum with which we have to do here, our two signs occupy each other's positions in a bewildering and well-nigh permanent exchange. This is something like Benjaminian "distraction" raised to a new and historically original power: indeed, I am tempted to suggest that the formulation gives us at least one apt characterization of some properly postmodernist temporality, whose consequences now remain to be drawn.

For we have not yet sufficiently described the nature of the process whereby, even allowing for the perpetual displacements we have insisted on, one such element—or sign or logo—somehow "comments" on the other or serves as its "interpretant." The content of that process, however, was already implicit in the account of the logo itself, which was described as the signal or shorthand for a certain kind of narrative. The microscopic atomic or isotopic exchange under study here can therefore be nothing less than the capture of one narrative signal by another: the rewriting of one form of narrativization in terms of a different, momentarily more powerful one, the ceaseless renarrativization of already existent narrative elements by each other. Thus, to begin with the most obvious examples, there does not seem much doubt that images like the fashion model or mannequin sequences are strongly and crudely rewritten when they intersect with the force field of the science fiction movie and its various logos (visual, musical, verbal): at such moments the familiar human world of advertising and fashion becomes "estranged" (a concept to which we will return), and the contemporary department store becomes as peculiar and as chilling as any of the institutions of an alien society on a distant planet. In much the same way, something happens to the photograph of the recumbent woman subject when it is surcharged with the profile of sheet lightning: sub specie aeternitatis, perhaps? culture versus nature? at any event, the two signs cannot fail to enter into a relationship with each other in which the generic signals of one begin to predominate (it is, for example, somewhat more difficult to imagine how the image of the woman under hypnosis could begin to draw the lightning stroke into its thematic orbit). Finally, it seems evident that as the image of the mice and the associated texts of behavioral experiments and psychological and vocational counseling intersect, the combination yields predictable messages about the hidden programing and conditioning mechanisms of bureaucratic society. Yet these three forms of influence or renarrativization—generic estrangement, the opposition of nature and culture, and the pop psychological or "existential" culture critique—are only a few of the provisional effects in a much more complex repertoire of interactions which it would be tedious, if not impossible, to tabulate (others might, however, include the high and low cultural opposition described earlier, and also the most diachronic alternation between the shabby and "natural" directly filmed street scenes and the flow of stereotypical media materials into which they are inserted).

Questions of priority or unequal influence can now be raised in a new way, one which need not be limited to the evidently central matter of the relative priority of sound and image. The psychologists distinguish between auditory and visual forms of recognition, and the former being apparently more instantaneous and working by means of fully formed auditory or musical gestalts, while the latter is subject to an incremental exploration which may never crystallize into something appropriately "recognizable." We recognize a tune all at once, in other words, while the flying saucers which ought to allow us to identify the generic class of a film clip may remain the object of some vague geometric gaze which never bothers to slot them into their obvious cultural and connotational position. In that case, it is clear how auditory logos would tend to dominate and rewrite visual ones, rather than the other way round (although one would have liked to imagine some reciprocal "estrangement" of the science fiction music by the photographs of mannequins, for example, in which the former is turned back into late twentieth-century cultural junk of the same substance as these last).

Above and beyond this simplest case of the relative influence of signs from distinct senses and distinct media, there persists the more general problem of the relative weight of the various generic systems themselves in our culture: is science fiction a priori more powerful than the genre we call advertising, or than the discourse that offers images of bureaucratic society (the rat race, the office, the routine), or the computer print-out, or that unnamed "genre" of visuals we have called op art effects (which probably connote a good deal more than the new technology of graphics)? Godard's work seems to me to turn on this question, or at least to pose it explicitly in various local ways; some political video art—such as that of Martha Rosler—also plays with these unequal influences of cultural languages to problematize familiar cultural priorities. The videotext under consideration here, however, does not allow us to formulate such issues as problems, since its very formal logic—what we have called the ceaselessly rotating momentum of its provisional constellations of signs—depends on effacing them: a proposition and a hypothesis that will lead us on into those matters of interpretation and aesthetic value that we have postponed until this point.

The interpretive question—"what is the text or work *about*?"—generally encourages a thematic answer, as indeed in the obliging title of the present tape, *AlienNATION*. There it is and now we know: it is the alienation of a whole nation, or perhaps a new kind of nation organized around alienation itself. The concept of alienation had rigor when specifically used to articulate the various concrete privations of working-class life (as in Marx's Paris manuscripts); and it also had a specific function at a specific historical moment (the Khrushchev opening), which radicals in the East (Poland, Yugoslavia) and the West (Sartre) believed could inaugurate a new tradition in Marxist thinking and practice. It surely does not amount to much, however, as a general designation for (bourgeois) spiritual malaise. But this is not the only reason for the discontent one feels when, in the midst of splendid postmodernist performances like Laurie Anderson's *USA*, the repetition of the word *alienation* (as it were, whispered in passing to the public) made it difficult to avoid the conclusion that this was indeed what that also was supposed to be "about." Two virtually identical responses then follow: so that's what it was supposed to mean; so that's all it was supposed to mean. The problem is twofold: alienation is, first of all, not merely a *modernist* concept but also a modernist *experience* (something I cannot argue further here, except to say that "psychic fragmentation" is a better term for what ails us today, if we need a term for it). But the problem's second ramification is the decisive one: whatever such a meaning and its adequacy (qua meaning), one has the deeper feeling that "texts" like *USA* or *AlienNATION* ought not to have any "meaning" at all in that thematic sense. This is something everyone is free to verify, by self-observation and a little closer attention to precisely those moments in which we briefly feel that disillusionment I have described experiencing at the thematically explicit moments in *USA*. In effect, the points at which one can feel something similar during the Rankus-Manning-Latham videotape have already been enumerated in another context. They are very precisely those points at which the intersection of sign and interpretant seems to produce a fleeting message: high versus low culture, in the modern world we're all programmed like laboratory mice, nature versus culture, and so forth. The wisdom of the vernacular tells us that these "themes" are corny, as corny as alienation itself (but not old-fashioned enough to be camp). Yet it would be a mistake to simplify this interesting situation and reduce it to a question of the nature and quality, the intellectual substance, of the themes themselves; indeed, our preceding analysis has the makings of a much better explanation of such lapses.

We tried to show, indeed, that what characterizes this particular video process (or "experimental" total flow) is a ceaseless rotation of elements such that they change place at every moment, with the result that no single element can occupy the position of "interpretant" (or that of primary sign) for any length of time but must be dislodged in turn in the following instant (the filmic terminology of "frames" and "shots" does not seem appropriate for this kind of succession), falling to the subordinate position in its turn, where it will then be "interpreted" or narra-tivized by a radically different kind of logo or image content altogether. If this is an accurate account of the process, however, then it follows logically that anything which arrests or interrupts it will be sensed as an aesthetic flaw. The thematic moments we have complained about above are just such moments of interruption, of a kind of blockage in this process: at such points a provisional "narrativization"—the provi-sional dominance of one sign or logo over another, which it interprets and rewrites according to its own narrative logic—quickly spreads out over the sequence like a burn spot on the film, at that point "held" long enough to generate and emit a thematic message quite inconsistent with the textual logic of the thing itself. Such moments involve a pecu-liar form of reification, which we might characterize equally well as a *thematization*—a word the late Paul DeMan was fond of, using it to characterize the misreading of Derrida as a "philosopher" whose "phil-osophical system" was somehow "about" writing. Thematization is then the moment in which an element, a component, of a text is promoted to the status of official theme, at which point it becomes a candidate for that even higher honor, the work's "meaning." But such thematic reification is not necessarily a function of the philosophical or intellec-tual quality of the "theme" itself: whatever the philosophical interest and viability of the notion of the alienation of contemporary bureau-cratic life, its emergence here as a "theme" is registered as a flaw for what are essentially formal reasons. The proposition might be argued the other way around by identifying another possible lapse in our text as the excessive dependence on the "estrangement effects" of the Japan-ese SF film clips (repeated viewings, however, make it clear that they were not so frequent as one remembered). If so, we have here to do with a thematization of a narrative or generic type rather than a degradation via pop philosophy and stereotypical doxa.

We can now draw some unexpected consequences from this analysis, consequences that bear not only on the vexed question of interpretation in postmodernism but also on another matter, that of aesthetic value, which had been provisionally tabled at the outset of this discussion. If interpretation is understood, in the thematic way, as the disengagement of a fundamental theme or meaning, then it seems clear that the post-modernist text—of which we have taken the videotape in question to be a privileged exemplar—is from that perspective defined as a struc-ture or sign flow which resists meaning, whose fundamental inner logic is the exclusion of the emergence of themes as such in that sense, and

which therefore systematically sets out to short-circuit traditional interpretive temptations (something Susan Sontag prophetically intuited in
the appropriately titled *Against Interpretation*, at the very dawn of what
was not yet called the postmodern age). New criteria of aesthetic value
then unexpectedly emerge from this proposition: whatever a good, let
alone a great, videotext might be, it will be bad or flawed whenever
such interpretation proves possible, whenever the text slackly opens
up just such places and areas of thematization itself.

Thematic interpretation, however—the search for the "meaning" of
the work—is not the only conceivable hermeneutic operation to which
texts, including this one, can be subjected, and I want to describe two
other interpretive options before concluding. The first returns us to the
question of the referent in an unexpected fashion, by way of that other
set of component materials to which we have so far paid less attention
than to the quoted inscribed and recorded spools of canned cultural
junk which are here interwoven: those (characterized as "natural" materials) were the segments of directly shot footage, which, above and
beyond the lakeshore sequence, essentially fell into three groups. The
urban street crossing, to begin with, is a kind of degraded space, which
—distant, poor cousin in that to the astonishing concluding sequence
of Antonioni's *Eclipse*—begins faintly to project the abstraction of an
empty stage, a place of the Event, a bounded space in which something
may happen and before which one waits in formal expectation. In
Eclipse, of course, when the event fails to materialize and neither of the
lovers appears at the rendezvous, place—now forgotten—slowly finds
itself degraded back into space again, the reified space of the modern
city, quantified and measurable, in which land and earth are parceled
out into so many commodities and lots for sale. Here also nothing happens; only the very sense of the possibility of something happening and
of the faint emergence of the very category of the Event itself is unusual
in this particular tape (the menaced events and anxieties of the science
fiction clips are merely "images" of events or, if you prefer, spectacle
events without any temporality of their own).

The second sequence is that of the perforated milk carton, a sequence
which perpetuates and confirms the peculiar logic of the first one, since
here we have in some sense the pure event itself, about which there's
no point crying, the irrevocable. The finger must give up stopping the
breach, the milk must pour out across the table and over the edge, with
all the visual fascination of this starkly white substance. If this quite
wonderful image seems to me to revert even distantly to a more properly

filmic status, my own aberrant and strictly personal association of it with a famous scene in *The Manchurian Candidate* is no doubt also partially responsible.

As for the third segment, the wackiest and more pointless, I have already described the absurdity of a laboratory experiment conducted with hardware store tools on orange objects of indeterminate size which have something of the consistency of a Hostess Twinkie. What is scandalous and vaguely disturbing about this homemade bit of dada is its apparent lack of motivation: one tries, without any great satisfaction, to see it as an Ernie Kovacs parody of the laboratory animal sequence; in any case, nothing else in the tape echoes this particular mode or zaniness of "voice." All three groups of images, but in particular this autopsy of a Twinkie, reminds one vaguely of a strand of organic material which has been woven in among an organic texture, like the whale blubber in Joseph Beuys's sculpture.

Nonetheless, a first approach suggested itself to me on the level of unconscious anxiety, where the hole in the milk carton—following the assassination scene in *The Manchurian Candidate*, where the victim is surprised at a midnight snack in front of the open refrigerator door—is now explicitly read as a bullet hole. I have meanwhile neglected to supply another clue, namely, the computer-generated X that moves across the empty street crossing like the sights of a long-range rifle. It remained for an astute listener (at an earlier version of this paper) to make the connection and point out the henceforth obvious and unassailable: for the American media public, the combination of the two elements—milk and Twinkie—is too peculiar to be unmotivated. In fact, on November 27, 1978 (the year preceding the composition of this particular videotape), San Francisco Mayor George Moscone and City Supervisor Harvey Milk were shot to death by a former supervisor, who entered the unforgettable plea of not guilty by reason of insanity owing to the excessive consumption of Hostess Twinkies.

Here, then, at last, the referent itself is disclosed: the brute fact, the historical event, the real toad in this particular imaginary garden. To track such a reference down is surely to perform an act of interpretation or hermeneutic disclosure of a very different kind from that previously discussed: for if *AlienNATION* is "about" this, then such an expression can only have a sense quite distinct from its use in the proposition that the text was "about" alienation itself.

The problem of reference has been singularly displaced and stigmatized in the hegemony of the various poststructuralist discourses which characterizes the current moment (and along with it, anything that smacks of "reality," "representation," "realism," and the like—even the word *history* has an r in it); only Lacan has shamelessly continued to talk about "the Real" (defined, however, as an absence). The respectable philosophical solutions to the problem of an external real world independent of consciousness are all traditional ones, which means that however logically satisfying they may be (and none of them were ever really very satisfactory from a logical standpoint), they are not suitable candidates for participation in contemporary polemics. The hegemony of theories of textuality and textualization means, among other things, that your entry ticket to the public sphere in which these matters are debated is an agreement, tacit or otherwise, with the basic presuppositions of a general problem field, something traditional positions on these matters refuse in advance. My own feeling has been that historicism offers a peculiarly unexpected escape from this vicious circle or double bind.

To raise the issue, for example, of the fate of the "referent" in contemporary culture and thought is not the same thing as to assert some older theory of reference or to repudiate all the new theoretical problems in advance. On the contrary, such problems are retained and endorsed, with the proviso that they are not only interesting problems in their own right but also, at the same time, symptoms of a historical transformation.

In the immediate instance that concerns us here, I have argued for the presence and existence of what seems to me a palpable referent—namely, death and historical fact, which are ultimately not textualizable and tear through the tissues of textual elaboration, of combination and free play ("the Real," Lacan tells us, "is what resists symbolization absolutely"). I want to add at once that this is no particularly triumphant philosophical victory for some putative realism or other over the various textualizing worldviews. For the assertion of a buried referent—as in the present example—is a two-way street whose antithetical directions might emblematically be named "repression" and *Aufhebung*, or "sublation": the picture has no way of telling us whether we are looking at a rising or a setting sun. Does our discovery document the persistence and stubborn, all-informing gravitational charge of reference, or, on the contrary, does it show the tendential historical process whereby reference is systematically processed, dismantled, textualized, and volatilized, leaving little more than some indigestible remnant?

However this ambiguity is handled, there remains the matter of the structural logic of the tape itself, of which this particular directly filmed sequence is only a single strand among many, and a particularly minor one at that (although its properties attract a certain attention). Even if its referential value could be satisfactorily demonstrated, the logic of rotating conjunction and disjunction that has been described above clearly works to dissolve such a value, which cannot be tolerated any more than the emergence of individual themes. Nor is it clear how an axiological system could be developed in the name of which we might then affirm that these strange sequences are somehow better than the random and aimless "irresponsibility" of the collages of media stereotypes.

Yet another way of interpreting such a tape is conceivable, however — an interpretation that would seek to foreground the process of production itself rather than its putative messages, meanings, or content. On this reading some distant consonance might be invoked between the fantasies and anxieties aroused by the idea of assassination and the global system of media and reproductive technology. The structural analogy between the two seemingly unrelated spheres is secured in the collective unconscious by notions of conspiracy, while the historical juncture between the two was burned into historical memory by the Kennedy assassination itself, which can no longer be separated from its media coverage. The problem posed by such interpretation in terms of autoreferentiality is not its plausibility: one would want to defend the proposition that the deepest "subject" of all video art, and even of all postmodernism, is very precisely reproductive technology itself. The methodological difficulty lies rather in the way in which such a global "meaning" — even of some type and status newer than the interpretive meanings we have touched on above — once again dissolves the individual text into an even more disastrous indistinction than the total flow — individual work antinomy evoked above: if all videotexts simply designate the process of production/reproduction, then presumably they all turn out to be "the same" in a peculiarly unhelpful way.

I will not try to solve any of these problems; instead I will restage the approaches and perspectives of the historicism I have called for by way of a kind of myth I have found useful in characterizing the nature of contemporary (postmodernist) cultural production and also in positioning its various theoretical projections.

Once upon a time at the dawn of capitalism and middle-class society, there emerged something called the sign, which seemed to entertain unproblematical relations with its referent. This initial heyday of the sign—the moment of literal or referential language or of the unprob-lematic claims of so-called scientific discourse—came into being because of the corrosive dissolution of older forms of magical language by a force which I will call that of reification, a force whose logic is one of ruthless separation and disjunction, of specialization and rationaliza-tion, of a Taylorizing division of labor in all realms. Unfortunately, that force—which brought traditional reference into being—continued unre-mittingly, being the very logic of capital itself. Thus this first moment of decoding or of realism cannot long endure; by a dialectical reversal it then itself in turn becomes the object of the corrosive force of reification, which enters the realm of language to disjoin the sign from the referent. Such a disjunction does not completely abolish the referent, or the objec-tive world, or reality, which still continue to entertain a feeble existence on the horizon like a shrunken star or red dwarf. But its great distance from the sign now allows the latter to enter a moment of autonomy, of a relatively free-floating Utopian existence, as over against its former objects. This autonomy of culture, this semiautonomy of language, is the moment of modernism, and of a realm of the aesthetic which redou-bles the world without being altogether of it, thereby winning a certain negative or critical power, but also a certain otherworldly futility. Yet the force of reification, which was responsible for this new moment, does not stop there either: in another stage, heightened, a kind of rever-sal of quantity into quality, reification penetrates the sign itself and dis-joins the signifier from the signified. Now reference and reality disap-pear altogether, and even meaning—the signified—is problematized. We are left with that pure and random play of signifiers that we call postmodernism, which no longer produces monumental works of the modernist type but ceaselessly reshuffles the fragments of preexistent texts, the building blocks of older cultural and social production, in some new and heightened bricolage: metabooks which cannibalize other books, metatexts which collate bits of other texts—such is the logic of postmodernism in general, which finds one of its strongest and most original, authentic forms in the new art of experimental video.

4

Spatial Equivalents in the

World System

Postmodernism raises questions about the appetite for architecture which it then virtually at once redirects. Along with food, architecture may be thought to be a relatively late taste among North Americans, who know all about music and story telling, have been less interested in eloquence, and have sometimes painted small, dark, secret pictures for suspicious purposes, redolent of superstition or the occult. But until very recently they have not wanted —for good reason!—to think much about what they were eating; and as for built space, there too a protective narcosis has long reigned, a don't-want-to-see-it, don't-want-to-know-about-it attitude that may, on the whole, have been the most sensible relationship to develop with the older American city. (Postmodernism would then be the date on which all that changed.) The immediate postwar heritage of this virtually natural or biological species protection has been the diversion of such aesthetic instincts (a very doubtful thing to call them) into instant commodification—fast foods, on the one hand, and, on the other hand, the kitch interior decoration and furniture for which the United States is famous and which has been explained as a kind of security blanket — chintz of the first postwar domestic production—designed to ward off memories of the depression and its stark physical deprivations. But you can't start again from scratch; and everything after that—in the so-called postmodernism, long after the depression has been forgotten save as the pretext for Reagan's comparison of himself with FDR—has had to build on those unpromising commercial beginnings. As though it had studied under Hegel, therefore, the postmodern lifts up, and cancels, all that junk (*Aufhebung*), including the hamburger within the diremption of its gourmet meals and Las Vegas within the rainbow-flavor landscape of its psychedelic corporate monuments.

The appetite for architecture, however, is inconsistent with the older nothing-to-do-with-me with which the republic's various social classes used to negotiate their downtowns. It means the city, certainly, and it means the free-standing building, preferably blocks of stone, whose shape in space does you some good to see, if that is the right verb. What is in question here is the monumental; it does not need contemporary rhetorics of the body and its trajectories, nor is it basely visual in any of the color-coded postmodern senses. You don't have to walk up the grand staircase personally, but it is not some mannerist parabola, either, that you can miniaturize with a quick look and carry home in your pocket. As Heidegger and J. Pierpont Morgan have both been mentioned already, it is appropriate to say that the monumental lies in between them somewhere, Pittsburgh rather than the Parthenon, yet partaking of both by the Idea; and it is probably time in any case to say something positive about the neoclassical, which is what seems to be meant here, and which may also be the submerged, tacit opposite number in the combination scheme on which, so unexpectedly, a few years ago, the postmodern suddenly lit up. Like French cuisine, therefore, this appetite is a solid, bourgeois, nineteenth-century one, and it requires if not Paris itself, then at least a solid neoclassical city that still includes the formal category of the street-and-sidewalk that modernism was famously out to abolish, with no little success. Postmodernism, I think, went on to abolish something even more fundamental, namely, the distinction between the inside and the outside (all the modernists ever said about that was that the one ought to express the other, which suggests that no one had yet begun to doubt whether you needed to have either of them at all in the first place). The former streets then become so many aisles in a department store, which, if you think about it in Japanese fashion, becomes the model and the emblem, the secret inner structure and the concept, of the postmodern "city," already, appropriately enough, realized in certain sections of Tokyo.

The consequence is, however, that as spatially exciting as the new thing may be, it becomes ever more difficult in this urban landscape to order a high-class architectural meal of the older kind, even though you might like one (and in that sense the very real accomplishments of the postmodernist architects are comparable to late-night reefer munchies, substitutes rather than the thing itself). The appetite for architecture today, therefore—about which I am on record as agreeing that the postmodern certainly revived, if it did not outright reinvent it—must in reality be an appetite for something else.

I think it is an appetite for photography: what we want to consume today are not the buildings themselves, which you scarcely even recognize as you round the freeway. Downtown conditioned reflexes turn it drab before you remember its photo; the classic Southern California construction site tarnishes its image and imprints the usual provisionality, which is supposed to be a fine thing in a "text" but in space just another synonym for shoddiness. Actually, it is as though that "external reality," which we will be careful to refrain from characterizing as the referent, is the last refuge and sanctuary of black and white (as in black-and-white film): what we take for color in the outside real world is nothing but information on some inner computer program, retranslating the data and marking it with the appropriate hue, like the tinting of classical Hollywood movies. The real color comes when you look at the photographs, the glossy plates, in all their splendor. "Tout, au monde, existe pour aboutir au Livre." Well, at least the picture book! and many are the postmodern buildings that seem to have been designed for photography, where alone they flash into brilliant existence and actuality with all the phosphorescence of the high-tech orchestra on CD. Any return to the haptic and the tactile, like Venturi's conversion to respectability in the Gordon Wu Hall at Princeton, with its polished metals and genuinely solid banisters, seem to hearken back to Louis Kahn and the "late modern," when building materials were expensive and of the finest quality and people still wore suits and ties. It is like the transition from precious metals to the credit card: the "bad new things" are no less expensive, and you no less consume their very value, but (as will be suggested later on), it is the value of the photographic equipment you consume first and foremost, and not of its objects.

So perhaps postmodern architecture is the property of literary critics after all, and textual in more ways than one. The modernist way of doing all this would be to organize it around the individual styles and names, which are more distinctive than the individual works: the residual after-effects of modernism are as tangible in the methods works solicit as they are in the latter's structures, and not the least significant inquiry about the postmodern (it will also, in its fashion, be pursued in this chapter) consists in examining these residues and speculating as to their necessity.

On the other hand, there are residues that long predate the modern itself and come before us as something of an archaic "return of the repressed" within the postmodern.

It must be supposed, for instance, that fanlike collective forms are generally residual and inherited from previous modes of production that are more collective in nature than our own: thus Chinese cuisine and its synchronic interrelationships, or, in another area, what is now known as the Japanese team concept, but which evidently organizes groups of people in other areas than the factory proper. This leads to the presumption that monumental models of "totality," of an architectonic kind, are reconstructions of those residual fragments in the modern period. They do not, in other words, offer alternate, capitalist, "Western" forms of totality to these more archaic ones, since the logic of capitalism is dispersive and disjunctive in the first place and does not tend toward wholes of whatever kind. Where one finds these last in our mode of production, therefore, as in state power (or, in other words, the construction or reconstruction of a state bureaucracy), the effort may be seen as a reaction against dispersal and fragmentation and a reactive or second-degree form. The relaxation of the postmodern then determines not a return to older collective forms but a loosening of the modern constructions such that its elements and components—still identifiable and relatively undecomposed—float at a certain distance from each other in a miraculous stasis or suspension, which, like the constellations, is certain to come apart in the next minute. The most vivid pictorial representation of the process is surely to be found in the so-called historicism of the postmodern architects, and above all in their relationship to the classical language, whose various elements—architrave, column, arch, order, lintel, dormer, and dome—begin with the slow force of cosmological processes to flee each other in space, standing out from their former supports, as it were, in free levitation, and, as it were, endowed for a last brief moment with the glowing autonomy of the psychic signifier, as though their secondary syncategoremic function had become for an instant the Word itself, before being blown out into the dust of empty spaces. Such flotation was already present in surrealism, where Dali's late Christs hovered over the crosses they were nailed to, and Magritte's men with bowler hats slowly descended from the skies in the form of the raindrops that determined them to wear their bowler hats and carry their umbrellas in the first place. *The Interpretation of Dreams* was most often appealed to for motivation in the experience of weightlessness used to inscribe all these objects somehow together; that then endowed them with the depth of the psychic model or the unconscious, in ways quite alien to the postmodern and old-fashioned in its context. But in Charles Moore's Piazza d'Italia, and in many of his other buildings, the elements float loose under their own momentum, each

becoming a sign or logo for architecture itself, which is thereby, need-
less to say, consumed like a commodity—and with all the avid relish
that accompanies such consumption—in contrast to the role such elements were called upon to play, or most often repressed from playing, in
a modernism anxious to resist consumption and offer an experience
that could not be commodified.

Internal differentiation of this kind, therefore, as though the elements
and components of the work were held in solution by a kind of antigrav-
ity of the postmodern utterly different in spirit from the law of falling
bodies of the modern, which sought to agglomerate and combine by
attraction (Freud's Eros), would seem to be a fundamental symptom of
postmodern space. The other is, on the face of it, unrelated to this, for it
seems to imply a positive principle of relationship rather than this centrifugal movement, and rather suggests the way in which organisms react
to foreign bodies and seek to surround and neutralize them in a kind
of spatial quarantine or cordon sanitaire. Yet such elements are most
often extrinsic or extrasystemic merely by virtue of their belonging to
the past.

I will therefore borrow the architects' own term and call this second
procedure *wrapping*, it being understood that we are doing something
similar here, and that it would therefore be well to try to "produce its
concept" on a theoretical level also. Wrapping can be seen as a reaction
to the disintegration of that more traditional concept Hegel called
"ground," which passed into humanistic thought in the form named
"context," felt by its opponents to be basely "external" or "extrinsic,"
since it seemed to imply the double standard of two radically distinct
sets of thoughts and procedures (one for the text, the other—generally
imported from the outside, from history or sociology manuals—for
the context in question), and, in addition, to be always redolent of
some larger and even more intolerable conception of the social totality
to come. The problem then seemed to reorganize itself into a formal
one: what kind of relationships are we now to establish between these
two distinct sets of data or raw materials if the figure/ground relationship is excluded from the outset? "Intertextuality" was always an
exceedingly weak and formalistic solution to this problem, which wrapping solves much better, being first of all more frivolous (and thereby
instantly disposable), but also, and above all, because, unlike intertextuality, it retains the essential prerequisite of *priority* or even *hierarchy*
—the functional subordination of one element to another (sometimes
also even called "causality")—but makes that now reversible. What is

Andrey Tarkovsky, from *Nostalgia*, "The Russian house
inside the Italian cathedral"

wrapped can also be used as the wrapper; the wrapper can also be
wrapped in its turn.

Such effects can be proximately approached by way of older anticipations, such as Malraux's intuition[1] of a fictive work of art: he had in
mind the way in which photography creates hitherto unrealized art forms,
for example, magnifying the beaten gold of a piece of Scythian jewelry
into volumes reminiscent of the friezes on the Parthenon, transforming
decorative art into sculpture, and the provisional, mobile, minor products of nomads, into monumental and sedentary canonical "works." He
himself, being canonical and modernist in his views, did not succeed in
producing the concept of such transformations but only in adding the
anonymous Scythians (along with the grave painters of Fayoum) to the
"major" canon. Whether the operation could work in the other direction, and the great canonical forms be turned back into minor art, is
another, unanswered, question (Deleuze and Guattari try to do so with
that modern classic called Kafka).[2]

After the emergence of theoretical discourse, however, and along with the now virtually universal feeling that (everything being a text anyway) the former context is also really just a text in its own right, since we took it from another book, some version of Malraux's practice of the creation of fictional art forms comes into being by way of what used to look like quotation. (See, for instance, the photo from Andrey Tarkovsky's film *Nostalgia*.) It becomes ever clearer that in whatever criticism or *explication de texte*, but far more visibly in the more idiosyncratic practices of contemporary theory, one text is simply being wrapped in another, with the paradoxical effect that the first—a mere writing sample, a paragraph or illustrative sentence, a segment or moment torn out of its context—becomes affirmed as autonomous and as a kind of unity in its own right, like the devouring lions on Malraux's earrings. The new discourse works hard to assimilate the "primary text" (formerly called Literature) into its own substance, transcoding its elements, foregrounding all the echoes and analogies, sometimes even borrowing the stylistic features of the illustration in order to forge the neologisms, that is to say, the official terminology of the theoretical wrapper from them. And sometimes indeed the weaker classics melt away into their powerful theoretical spokespeople and end up as appendixes or extended footnotes to a named theoretician. More often, however, the lasting result is rather this secondary and not altogether intended one of loosening the primary unity, dissolving a work into a text, releasing the elements and setting them free for semiautonomous existence as information bits in the message-saturated space of late-capitalist media culture or "objective spirit." But in this case the movement can be reversible, as when writers like Samuel Delany drew the terminological fragments of theoretical discourse back into their own official "literary production" and leave them embedded there, like fossils in stratified remains or the outlines of some atomized body in a future Pompeii. "Fragments" in theoretical discourse are not, in any case, such pieces of a former work of art but rather the terms themselves, the neologisms, which, having become ideological logos, then spray out into the social world like so much shrapnel, passing into general usage and describing their parabola with diminishing force until they end up lodging in this or that immovable obstacle which may, of course, end up simply being the media in its own right.

What is also perpetuated by the strategy of the wrapper and the wrapped is the suggestion (implicitly the most explicit message of the "concept" of intertextuality as well) that none of the parts are new, and it is repetition rather than radical innovation that is henceforth at stake. The problem lies in the resultant paradox that it is on this renunciation of the new or the novum that the claim to historic originality of postmodernism in general, and postmodern architecture in particular, is founded. What is it, then, that is original (in some new and original sense) in the conception of the "neo" to eschew originality and to embrace repetition in some strong and original fashion? To what degree can we still describe the originalities of spatial construction in the postmodern, when this last has explicitly renounced the great modernist myth of producing a radically new Utopian space capable of transforming the world itself?

As always, however, the dilemmas of the postmodern themselves modify (and are in turn modified by) those of the modern, for which innovation was unambiguous enough as an ideological value, but structurally ambivalent and undecideable in its realization. Judgment of this kind ought to have been facilitated by the forthright identification, in the most programmatic of the moderns (such as Le Corbusier), of formal with radical social change as such, something that presumably offers the usual empirical verifiability, provided you think it is an easy matter to register social regeneration after the fact. The attempt to think through such changes from the perspective of the superstructure seems finally to produce social models or world visions of an essentially religious kind. At any rate, the very concept of space here demonstrates its supremely mediatory function, in the way in which its aesthetic formulation begins at once to entail cognitive consequences on the one hand and sociopolitical consequences on the other.

But this is also why it may be misleading to frame the social consequences of spatial innovation in terms of space itself—the indirection of some third term or interpretant drawn from another realm or medium seems to impose itself. Such was the case in film studies a few years ago when Christian Metz elaborated his film semiotics in a vast rewriting program in which the essentials of filmic structure were reformulated in terms of language and sign systems.[3] The tangible result of such a rewriting program was to produce a dual problem that might never have been articulated or brought into focus had it remained couched in purely cinematographic terms—the problem of the minimal unities and macroforms of what, in the image, might correspond to the sign and its components, not to speak of the word itself; and of what in filmic diegesis might be considered to be a complete utterance, if not a sentence, let alone a larger "textual" paragraph of some sort. But such problems are "produced" within the framework of a larger pseudo-problem that looks ontological (or metaphysical, which amounts to the same thing), and which can take the form of the unanswerable question of whether film is a kind of language (even to assert that it is *like* a language—or like Language—sets off metaphysical resonance). This particular period of film studies seems to have ended, not when the ontological question was identified as a false one, but when the local work of transcoding had reached the limit of its objects, at which point the judgment of the pseudo-problem could be allowed to take its course.

Such a rewriting program may be useful in our present architectural context, provided it is not confused with a semiotics of architecture (which already exists), and provided a second historical and Utopian step is added onto this key one, whose function is not to raise analogous ontological questions (as to whether built space is a kind of language), but rather to awaken the question of the conditions of possibility of this or that spatial form.

As in film, the first questions are those of minimal units: the words of built space, or at least its substantives, would seem to be rooms, categories which are syntactically or syncategorematically related and articulated by the various spatial verbs and adverbs—corridors, doorways, and staircases, for example—modified in turn by adjectives in the form of paint and furnishings, decoration, and ornament (whose puritanical denunciation by Adolf Loos offers some interesting linguistic and literary parallels). Meanwhile, these "sentences"—if that indeed is what a building can be said to "be"—are read by readers whose bodies fill the various shifter-slots and subject-positions; while the larger text into which such units are inserted can be assigned to the text-grammar of the urban as such (or perhaps, in a world system, to even vaster geographies and their syntactic laws).

Once these equivalents have been laid in place, the more interesting questions of historical identity begin to pose themselves—questions not implicit in the linguistic or semiotic apparatus, which begin to obtain when this is itself dialectically challenged. How, for example, are we to think of the fundamental category of the room (as minimal unity)? Are private rooms, public rooms, and rooms for work (white-collar office space, for instance) to be thought of as the same kind of substantive? Can they all be deployed indifferently within the same kind of sentence structure? On one historical reading,[4] however, the modern room comes into being only as a consequence of the invention of the corridor in the seventeenth century; its privacies have little enough to do with those indifferent sleeping spaces that a person used to negotiate by passing through a rat's nest of other rooms and stepping over sleeping bodies. This innovation, thus renarrativized, now generates cognate questions about the origins of the nuclear family and the construction or formation of bourgeois subjectivity fully as much as do queries about related architectural techniques. But it also raises serious doubts about the philosophies of language that in effect produced the formulation in the first place: what is, indeed, the transhistorical status of the word and the sentence? Modern philosophy significantly modified its vision of its own history as well as its conception of its function when it began to appreciate the relationship of its most fundamental (Western) categories to the grammatical structure of ancient Greek (let alone to the latter's approximations in Latin). The repudiation of the category of substance in modern philosophy can be said to be one response to the impact of this experience of historicity, which seemed to discredit the substantive as such. It is not clear that anything similar took place on the macrolevel of the sentence proper, even though the constitutive relationship of linguistics as a discipline to the sentence as its largest conceivable object of study has come to be understood (and is reinforced, rather than dispelled, by the attempt to invent compensatory disciplines like semantics or text-grammar, which dramatically designate the frontiers they would desperately like to transgress or abolish).

Historical speculation is here only exacerbated by the drawing of political and social consequences. The question of the origins of language itself (the ur-formation of the sentence and the word in some galactic magma at the dawn of human time) has been declared illicit by everyone from Kant to Lévi-Strauss, even though it is accompanied by a question about the origins of the social itself (and used to be accompanied by another, related one about the origins of the family). But that of the possible evolution and modification of language is still conceivable and entertains a vital relationship to the Utopian question about the possible modification of society (where that is itself still conceivable). Indeed, the forms taken by just such debates will seem philosophically receivable or on the contrary antiquated and superstitious in strict proportion to your deeper convictions as to whether postmodern society can be changed any longer or not. The Marr debate in the Soviet Union, for example, has been classed with Lysenko as a scientific aberration, largely owing to Marr's hypothesis that the very form and structure of language itself altered according to the mode of production of which it was a superstructure. As Russian had not sensibly evolved since the tsarist period, Stalin put an abrupt end to this speculation with a famous pamphlet ("Marxism and Linguistics"). In our own time, feminism has been virtually alone in attempting to envision the Utopian languages spoken in societies in which gender domination and inequality would have ceased to exist[5]: the result was more than just a glorious moment in recent science fiction, and should continue to set the example for the political value of the Utopian imagination as a form of praxis.

But it is precisely from the perspective of such Utopian praxis that we can return to the problem of the judgment to be made on the innovations of the modern movement in architecture. For just as the expansion of the sentence plays a fundamental role in literary modernism from Mallarmé to Faulkner, so also the metamorphosis of the minimal unit is fundamental in architectural modernism, which may be said to have attempted to transcend the sentence (as such) in its abolition of the street. Le Corbusier's "free plan" may be said in much the same sense to challenge the existence of the traditional room as a syntactic category and to produce an imperative to dwell in some new way, to invent new forms of living and habitation as an ethical and political (and perhaps also as a psychoanalytic) consequence of formal mutation. Everything turns, then, on whether you think the "free plan" is just another room, albeit of a novel type, or whether it transcends that category altogether (just as a language beyond the sentence would transcend our Western conceptuality and our sociality alike). Nor is it only a question of demolishing the older forms, as in the iconoclastic and purifying therapy of dada: this kind of modernism promised the articulation of new spatial categories that might properly merit characterization as Utopian. It is well known that postmodernism is at one with a negative judgment on these aspirations of the high modern, which it claims to have abandoned —but the new name, the sense of a radical break, the enthusiasm that greeted the new kinds of buildings, all testify to the persistence of some notion of novelty or innovation that seems to have survived the modern itself.

Such is at least the problematic framework in which I propose to examine one of the few postmodern buildings which does seem to have some powerful claim on revolutionary spatiality: the house (or single-family dwelling) that the Canadian-American architect Frank Gehry built (or rebuilt) for himself in Santa Monica, California, in 1979. Problems enshroud even this starting point, however: for one thing, it is not clear how Gehry thinks of himself in relationship to postmodern architecture more generally. His style certainly has little enough in common with the ostentatious decorative frivolity and historicist allusion of Michael Graves or Charles Moore or even Venturi himself. Gehry has indeed observed that Venturi "is into storytelling . . . I'm really interested in this hands-on thing, and not in telling stories,"[6] an apt enough characterization of the passion for periodization from which (among other things) the concept of postmodernism comes. Meanwhile, the single-family dwelling may also be less characteristic of the projects of the postmodern: the grandeur of the palace or the villa is clearly increasingly inappropriate to an age which began with the "death of the subject" in the first place. Nor is the nuclear family any specifically postmodern interest or concern. Here too, then, if we win, we may actually have lost; and the more original Gehry's building turns out to be, the less generalizable its features may be for postmodernism in general.

The house is located on the corner of Twenty-second Street and Washington Avenue and is not, properly speaking, a new building but the reconstruction of an older, very conventional frame dwelling.

> *Diamonstein:* One of the works of art that you did manage to create, however, is your very own house. It has been described as suburban anonymity. The original structure was a two-story gambrel-roof clapboard house. You proceeded to build a one-and-one-half-story-high wall of corrugated metal around it, but behind the wall the original structure pokes up from inside the new structure. Can you tell us what your intentions were there?
>
> *Gehry:* It had to do with my wife. She found this nice house —and I love my wife—this cute little house with antiques in it. Very sweet little thing. And we were having a lot of problems finding a house. We bought in Santa Monica at the height of the real estate boom. We paid the highest price possible.
>
> *Diamonstein:* A hundred and sixty thousand dollars, I read.
>
> *Gehry:* A hundred and sixty thousand.
>
> *Diamonstein:* A lot of money.
>
> *Gehry:* A year earlier it was forty. Talk about desperate moves. I

always do that. And we could have lived in that house fine. There was enough room in it and everything.

Diamonstein: A pink house with green shingles?

Gehry: It was all pink asbestos shingle over white clapboard. It had several layers on it. It was already layered, which is a heavy term these days, layering.

Diamonstein: That's part of the appeal to you.

Gehry: Anyway, I decided to get into a dialogue with the old house, which is no different, you know, from what I was saying about the Ron Davis house, where the interiors would join in a dialogue with the exteriors. Here I had it easy, because the old house was already a different aesthetic, and I could play off it. But I wanted to explore the relationship between the two. I got fascinated with the idea that the old house should appear to remain totally intact from the outside, and that you could look through the new house, and see the old house as though it was now packaged in this new skin. The new skin and the windows in the new house would be of a totally different aesthetic than the windows in the old house. So they would constantly be in tension, or whatever, with each other. I wanted each window to have a different aesthetic, which I couldn't accomplish at that time.

Diamonstein: So, the old house was the core, and the new house is the wrapper. Of course, you've used a number of the materials that are familiar in your own vocabulary—metal, plywood, glass, and chain-link fencing—all very inexpensive. On one hand, the house looks unfinished and rough—

Gehry: I'm not sure if it is finished.

Diamonstein: You're not sure?

Gehry: No.

Diamonstein: Is one ever sure?

Gehry: It's confusing. I was wondering the other day what effect this had on my family. I've noticed my wife leaves papers and stuff around on the table so there's a kind of chaos in the organization of how we live in the house. I was beginning to think that it had something to do with her not knowing whether I'm finished or not.[7]

In what follows, I rely heavily on Gavin Macrae-Gibson's *Secret Life of Buildings*,[8] which includes some fine pieces of phenomenological and

Frank Gehry House, Santa Monica, California

formal description. I have visited the house myself and am anxious to avoid the stark methodological aporia of Barthes's *System of Fashion* (which chose to analyze the writing about fashion rather than the physical fashions themselves); but it is certain that even the most seemingly physical or sensory approaches to the architectural "text" are only apparently opposed to expression or interpretation (something we will confront when we return to the peculiar phenomenon of the architectural photograph).

But Macrae-Gibson's book has an even stronger claim on our interest here, owing to the character of its interpretive framework, which remains that of an older high modernism and which can therefore, at crucial conjunctures between description and interpretation, tell us something as revealing about the difference between modernism and postmodernism as Gehry's construction itself.

Macrae-Gibson sorts the Gehry house into three types of space. I will not retain this threefold differentiation, but it gives a useful starting

point: "First, a group of small rooms at the back of the house on both floors consisting of stairs, bedrooms, bathrooms, and closets. Second, the major spaces of the old house, which have become the living room on the ground floor and the master bedroom on the first floor. Lastly, the complex attenuated spaces of the new spatial wrapper, consisting of the entry spaces, kitchen and dining areas, which are five steps below the living room."[9]

Let us work our way back through these three types of space. "The house consists of a corrugated metal shell wrapped around three sides of an existing pretty pink shingled 1920s house in a way that creates new spaces between the shell and the old exterior walls."[10] The old wooden frame remains as a kind of scaffolding memory in places, but the dining area and kitchen have now expanded beyond it and are essentially located in the former driveway and yard (five steps below the level of the former ground floor). These new areas, between the frame and the wrapper, are mostly glassed in and therefore visually open to and indis-

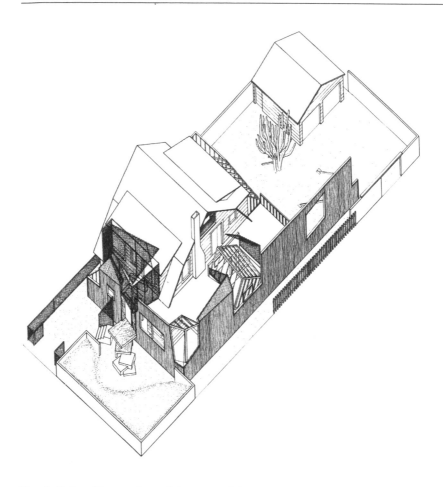

Frank Gehry House, Santa Monica, California

tinguishable from the former "outside" or "outdoors." Whatever aesthetic thrill we get from this formal innovation (it might be a thrill of discomfort or malaise; but, on the other hand, Philip Johnson, who had breakfast there, found it quite *gemütlich*) will clearly have had something to do with an effacement of the categories of inside/outside, or a rearrangement of them.

The stark effect of the corrugated metal frame seems to ruthlessly cut across the older house and brutally stamp the mark and sign of "modern art" on it, yet without wholly dissolving it, as though the peremptory gesture of "art" had been interrupted and abandoned in mid-process.

Besides this dramatic formal intervention (whose use of cheap junk material must also be retained, as we shall see in a moment), the other dramatic feature of the newly wrapped house involves the glassing of the driveway area and, in particular, the new skylighting of the kitchen, which, seen from the outside of the house, appears to protrude into outer space like an enormous glass cube—the "tumbling cube" Gehry has called it—which "marks the junction of the streets with what during the day is a receding void and at night is an advancing solid like a beacon."[11] This characterization by Macrae-Gibson strikes me as interesting, but his interpretation of the cube, which returns to Malevich's mystic quadrilaterals (Gehry once designed a Malevich exhibit, so the reference is not as arbitrary as it might seem), seems to me completely misguided, a willful attempt to reinscribe the old-clothes junk aesthetic of a certain postmodernism within the loftiest metaphysical vocations of an older high modernism. Gehry himself has often insisted on what is obvious to any viewer of his buildings, namely, the cheapness of their materials—"cheapskate architecture" he once called it. Besides the corrugated aluminum of this building, he has an obvious predilection for steel mesh, raw plywood, cinder block, telephone poles, and the like, and even at one time in his career designed (astonishingly ornate) cardboard furniture. Such materials clearly "connote";[12] they annul the projected syntheses of matter and form of the great modern buildings, and they also inscribe what are clearly economic or infrastructural themes in this work, reminding us of the cost of housing and building and, by extension, of the speculation in land values: that constitutive seam between the economic organization of society and the aesthetic production of its (spatial) art, which architecture must live more dramatically than any of the other fine arts (save perhaps film), but whose scars it bears more visibly even than film itself, which must necessarily repress and conceal its economic determinations.

The cube and the slab (of corrugated metal): these ostentatious markers, planted in the older building like some lethal strut transfixing the body of a car crash victim, clearly shatter any illusions of organic form that might be entertained about this construction (and that are among the constitutive ideals of the older modernism). These two spatial phenomena make up the "wrapper"; they violate the older space and are now both parts of the newer construction and at distance from it, like foreign bodies. They also correspond, in my opinion, to the two great constitutive elements of architecture itself which in his postmodern

Frank Gehry House, Santa Monica, California

manifesto, *Learning from Las Vegas*, Robert Venturi disengages from the tradition in order to reformulate the tasks and vocation of the newer aesthetic: namely, the opposition between the façade (or store front) and the shed behind or the barnlike space of the building itself. But Gehry does not remain within this contradiction, playing each term off against the other to produce some interesting but provisional solution. Rather, it seems to me that the corrugated metal front and the tumbling cube *allude* to the two terms of this dilemma, which they attach to something else—the remains of the older house, the persistence of history and the past: a content which can still be seen through the newer elements, literally, as when the simulated window opening of the corrugated wrapper discloses the older windows of the frame house behind them.

But if this is so, then we find ourselves obliged to reorganize Macrae-Gibson's tripartite scheme. His first category—the remnants of traditional suburban space—we retain as such, to be dealt with later. If, however, the wrapper—cube and slab—takes on a life of its own here, as the visible agent of architectural transformation-in-course, then it must be assigned category status in its own right, while Macrae-Gibson's final two types of space—the older "major spaces" along with the new "entry" and kitchen spaces—will be amalgamated as the joint results of the intersection of the first two categories, of the intervention of the "wrapper" into the traditional house.

For our purposes, therefore, the fact that the living room emerges in a space already built in the older house, while the kitchen is in effect an additional room outside of that, does not seem as significant as the sense that both are somehow equally new, in a way that remains to be evaluated. Indeed, both the now sunken living room and the dining areas and kitchen opened up between the loosely draped external wrapper and the "withering away" of the now unnecessary structural frame now seem to me the thing itself, the new postmodern space proper, which our bodies inhabit in malaise or delight, trying to shed the older habits of inside/outside categories and perceptions, still longing for the bourgeois privacy of solid walls (enclosures like the old centered bourgeois ego), yet grateful for the novelty of the incorporation of yucca plants and what Barthes would have called Californianity into our newly reconstructed environment. We must insist, over and over and in a variety of ways, on the troubling ambiguities of this new "hyperspace." This is how Macrae-Gibson does it, evoking

> numerous contradictory perspective lines going to numerous vanishing points above and below a wide variety of horizons. . . . When

nothing is at right angles, nothing seems to vanish to the same point. . . . Gehry's distorted perspective planes and illusionistic use of framing members engender the same feeling in the beholder [as do Ronald Davis's paintings where "the viewer is suspended above the warped perspective grids and tipped towards them"]; the tilting of planes expected to be horizontal or vertical and the converging of studwork members cause one to feel suspended and tipped in various directions oneself.

For Gehry the world vanishes to a multitude of points, and he does not presuppose that any are related to the standing human being. The human eye is still of critical importance in Gehry's world, but the sense of center no longer has its traditional symbolic value.[13]

What this account suggests is nothing quite so much as the alienation of the older phenomenological body (with its right/left, front/back, up/down coordinates) in the outer space of Kubrick's 2001, with the security of the Newtonian earth withdrawn. The feeling is also surely related to that new shapeless space — neither mass nor volume — which characterizes Portman's vast lobbies (according to me)[14] in which stream-ers and hangings remind us like ghostly remanences of older partitioning and structuring boundaries and enclosure categories, while also withdrawing those and offering the illusion of some new and meretricious spatial liberation and play. Gehry's space is, to be sure, far more precise and sculpted than those enormous and crudely melodramatic containers. In a more articulated way it confronts us with the paradoxical impossibilities (not least the impossibilities of representation) which are inherent in this latest evolutionary mutation of late capitalism toward "something else" which is no longer family or neighborhood, city or state, nor even nation, but as abstract and nonsituated as the placelessness of a room in an international chain of motels or the anonymous space of airport terminals that all run together in your mind.

There are, however, other ways of coming at the nature of hyperspace, and Gehry mentioned a different one in the interview I've already quoted when he spoke about the chaos of things inside the house. After all, Venturi's "decorated shed" suggests that contents are relatively indifferent and might as well be strewn all over as stacked neatly in a corner somewhere. This is also how Gehry describes the rebuildable studio he made for Ron Davis: such structures "create a shell. Then the user comes in and puts his junk in the shell in some way. The house I did for Ron Davis was that idea. I built the most beautiful shell I could do, and then let him bring his stuff to it, and convert it to his use."[15] But Gehry's remarks on the messiness of his own house betray a faint malaise which may be worth tracking further (particularly since the continuation of the dialogue introduces a new topic—photography—to which we will be returning shortly):

> *Diamonstein*: There might have been another cue that you have given to the occupants. When that house was photographed with three perfect lilies in one place, and two books in another—you had soap powder for the kitchen sink on the kitchen sink, and some of the cupboard doors open. It was very much a lived-in environment. It seemed evident that this was a deliberate structuring of the photo to reflect an environment in which real people lived real lives.
>
> *Gehry*: Actually, it wasn't structuring the photo.
>
> *Diamonstein*: It was taking a photo of the way you live?
>
> *Gehry*: Yeah. Well, what happens is—I've had a lot of photographers there now. Each one comes in and has a different idea of how the place should look. So they start moving the furniture around. If I get there in time I start putting everything back.[16]

Such discussions imply a displacement of architectural space such that the positioning of its contents—objects and human bodies alike—becomes problematical. It is a feeling that can only be properly evaluated in a historical and comparative context and, in my opinion, on the basis of the following proposition: if the great negative emotions of the modernist moment were anxiety, terror, the being-unto-death, and Kurtz's "horror," what characterizes the newer "intensities" of the postmodern, which have also been characterized in terms of the "bad trip" and of schizophrenic submersion, can just as well be formulated in terms of the messiness of a dispersed existence, existential messiness, the perpetual temporal distraction of post-sixties life. Indeed, one is tempted (without wishing to overload a very minor feature of Gehry's building) to evoke the more general informing context of some larger virtual nightmare, which can be identified as the sixties gone toxic, a whole historical and countercultural "bad trip" in which psychic fragmentation is raised to a qualitatively new power, the structural distraction of the decentered subject now promoted to the very motor and existential logic of late capitalism itself.

At any rate, all these features—the strange new feeling of an absence of inside and outside, the bewilderment and loss of spatial orientation in Portman's hotels, the messiness of an environment in which things and people no longer find their "place"—offer useful symptomatic approaches to the nature of postmodern hyperspace, without giving us any model or explanation of the thing itself.

But such hyperspace—Macrae-Gibson's second and third types of space—is itself the result of the tension between two terms or poles, two distinct kinds of spatial structure and experience, of which we have so far mentioned only one (namely, the cube and the corrugated wall, the external wrapping). We must therefore proceed on to the most archaic parts of the house itself—the older surviving stairs, bedrooms, bathrooms, and closets—to see not merely what it was that had to be even partially transformed but also whether that traditional syntax and grammar is susceptible to Utopian transformation.

In fact, such rooms are preserved as in a museum: untouched, intact, yet now somehow "quoted" and without the slightest modification emptied, as in the transformation of something into an image of itself, of its concrete life, like a Disneyland preserved and perpetuated by Martians for their own delectation and historical research. As you go up the still-old-fashioned stairs of the Gehry house, you reach an old-fashioned door, through which you enter an old-fashioned maid's room (although it might just as well have been the bedroom of a teenager). The door is a time-travel device; when you close it, you are back in the old twentieth-century American suburb—the old concept of the room, which includes my privacy, my treasures, and my kitsch, chintzes, old teddy bears, old LP records. But the time-travel evocation is misleading: on the one hand, we have here praxis and reconstruction, much like Philip K. Dick's Wash-36,[17] a lovingly authentic reconstruction of the Washington of his boyhood in 1936 by a three-hundred-year-old millionaire on a satellite planet (or, if you prefer a quicker reference, like Disneyland or EPCOT); while, on the other hand, it is not exactly a reconstruction of the past at all, since this enclave space is our present and replicates the real dwelling spaces of the other houses on this street or elsewhere in Los Angeles today. Yet it is a present reality that has been transformed into a simulacrum by the process of wrapping, or quotation, and has thereby become not historical but historicist—an allusion to a present out of real history which might just as well be a past removed from real history. The quoted room therefore also has affinities with what in film has come to be called *la mode rétro*, or nostalgia film: the past as fashion plate and glossy image. Suddenly, therefore, this area, retained and preserved from that older house with which Gehry is pursuing a "dialogue," resonates as an aesthetic phenomenon with a whole range of other very different and nonarchitectural phenomena in postmodern art and theory: the transformation into the image or simulacrum, historicism as a substitute for history, quotation, enclaves within the cultural sphere, and so forth. I am even tempted here to reintroduce the whole problem of reference itself, so paradoxical when one has to do with buildings, which, presumably "realer" than the content of literature, painting, or film, are then somehow their own referent. But the theoretical problem of how a building could have a referent (as opposed to a signified or a meaning of some kind) loses its estrangement capacity and shock value when it slips into the weaker issue of what the building might refer to. I mention this because this last is another move in Macrae-Gibson's "modernizing" interpretation of the house, and it results in a brilliant essay on the way in which the house *alludes* to its own position in Santa Monica with a host of marine allusions and imagery. This is a kind of reading we are accustomed to in analyses of works by Le Corbusier or Frank Lloyd Wright, where the operation of such allusions seems perfectly consistent not merely with the modernist aesthetic of such buildings but also with their particular social space and historical situation. If, however, one feels that the city space of the 1980s has for all kinds of multiple and overdetermined reasons lost that particular materiality and placeness or situatedness—that is, we no longer feel Santa Monica in this way as a place whose sites stand in determinate relations to the beach or the freeway and so forth—then such exegesis will come to seem misguided or irrelevant. Not wrong, necessarily, for these structures may be the remnants of an older modernist language subsumed and virtually canceled by the new one, yet persisting feebly and in a pinch decryptable by a bright and stubborn, backward-looking reader and critic.

There are, however, other ways in which the theoretical issue of reference might be framed: most notably, a perspective in which the room itself—characteristic of that mainstream American society and social space into which the Gehry house has been inserted—stands as some last minimal remnant of that older space as it is worked over, canceled, surcharged, volatilized, sublimated, or transformed by some newer system. In that case, the traditional room could be seen as some feeble, ultimate, tenuous reference, or as the last stubborn, truncated core of a referent in the process of wholesale dissolution and liquidation. I believe that nothing like this can be shown for the space of Portman's Bonaventure, unless it be the now marginalized apparatus of the traditional hotel: the wings and stories of claustrophobic and uncomfortable bedrooms hidden away in the towers, a traditional hotel living space whose decorations were so notorious that they have been altered several times since the inauguration of the building and for whose architect they were clearly the least interesting matter on the agenda. In Portman therefore, reference—the traditional room, the traditional language and category—is brutally dissociated from the newer postmodern space of the euphoric central lobby and left to etiolate and dangle slowly in the wind. The force of Gehry's structure would then stem from the active dialectical way in which the tension between the two kinds of space is maintained and exacerbated (if this is a "dialogue," then it has little of the complacency of a Gadamer or of Richard Rorty's "conversations").

I want to add that this conception of reference, which is social and spatial all at once, has real content, and can be developed in very concrete directions. For example, the above described enclave space is in fact a maid's room and thereby becomes invested at once with the content of various kinds of social subalternity, remnants of older hierarchy in the family, and gender and ethnic divisions of labor.

We have essentially rewritten Macrae-Gibson's enumeration of three types of space (traditional rooms, the newer living spaces, and the cube and corrugated wall) into a dynamic model in which two very distinct kinds of space—the bedroom and the abstract architectural forms that open up the older house—intersect to produce new kinds of space (the kitchen and dining area, the living room), space that includes old and new, inside and outside, the framed platforms of the older house and the reconstituted yet strangely amorphous areas between the frame and the wrapper. It is essentially only this last type of space—the result of a dialectical engagement between the two others—which can be characterized as postmodern; that is to say, as some radically new spatiality beyond the traditional and the modern alike which seems to make some historical claim for radical difference and originality. The question of interpretation arises when we try to evaluate this claim and propose hypotheses as to its possible "meaning." Put somewhat differently, such hypotheses necessarily constitute transcoding operations in which we frame equivalents for this architectural and spatial phenomenon in other codes or theoretical languages; or, to use yet another kind of language, they constitute the allegorical projection of the structure of the analysis models. So here, for example, it is evident at the outset that an allegory is being told whereby, from out of what is either a traditional or a realistic moment (but then perhaps, the realism of Hollywood rather than that of Balzac), the lightning bolt of "modernism" seems to generate the postmodern "proper." (Gehry's own private allegorization seems to involve the adaptation or rebuilding of Judaism for a new function, if not simply a survival, in the modern, or even the postmodern, world. Gehry's grandfather "was president of his synagogue, a small, remodeled houselike building, his grandson later recalled, similar, in some ways, to the house in Santa Monica that he himself would remodel in the 1970s. 'My house reminds me of that old building,' Gehry confessed, 'and I frequently think of it when I'm here.'")[18] Even if, as with Kant, such narratives lie exclusively in the eye of the beholder, they require historical explanation and some account of their conditions of possibility, and the reasons why we seem to feel this to be a logical sequence if not a complete story or narrative. But other allegorical constructs are also possible, and an analysis of these will commit us to a long detour back through Macrae-Gibson's interpretive system, which is (as I've said) an essentially modernist one.

I have touched on several interpretive moves in Macrae-Gibson's article without recording the basic formulations in which he frames his sense of the function of this new kind of building. These are as follows: "Perspective illusion and perspective contradiction are used throughout Gehry's house, and many of his other projects, to prevent the formation of an intellectual picture that might destroy the continual immediacy of perceptual shock. . . . Such illusions and contradictions force one to continually question the nature of what one sees, to alter the definition of reality, in the end, from the *memory* of a thing to the *perception* of that thing."[19] Such formulations, with their familiar stress on the vocation of art to restimulate perception, to reconquer a freshness of experience back from the habituated and reified numbness of everyday life in the fallen world, bring us to the very heart of the essential modernism of Macrae-Gibson's aesthetic. The Russian formalists, of course, codified such views most powerfully and durably, but something similar can be found in all the modernist theories, from Pound to surrealism and phenomenology, and across all the arts, from architecture to music and literature (and even film). I believe, for a number of reasons, that this remarkable aesthetic is today meaningless and must be admired as one of the most intense historical achievements of the cultural past (along with the Renaissance or the Greeks or the Tang dynasty). In the wholly built and constructed universe of late capitalism, from which nature has at last been effectively abolished and in which human praxis—in the degraded form of information, manipulation, and reification—has penetrated the older autonomous sphere of culture and even the Unconscious itself, the Utopia of a renewal of perception has no place to go. It is not clear, to put it crudely and succinctly, why, in an environment of sheer advertising simulacra and images, we should even want to sharpen and renew our perception of those things. Can some other function, then, be conceived for culture in our time? The question at least offers a standard by which to evaluate the claims of contemporary postmodernism to some genuine formal and spatial originality: it can at least do so negatively by starkly disclosing the remnants of an unacceptable modernism still at work in the various postmodern manifestos: the concept of irony in Venturi, for example, just as fully as that of defamiliarization seen in the book by Macrae-Gibson. Such older modernist themes are appealed to in extremis when the newer theories require some ultimate conceptual grounding they cannot generate out of their own internal economies (and this not least because the very logic of postmodern theory is inconsistent with and hostile to grounding in the first place, sometimes also stigmatized as essentialism or foundationalism). I will add that I must also refuse Macrae-Gibson's account on a more empirical basis, since, in my experience, the Gehry house does not particularly correspond to the defamiliarizing and perception-renewing description.

Nonetheless I am interested in the description from a somewhat different angle, which is that of its continuing possibility in a postmodernist framework. The account is still plausible, although it should not be any longer, and I think we also need an explanation of why this should be so. Let us look again at the specifics, which suggest that the building has as its primary aesthetic function to subvert (or to block) "the formation of an intellectual picture that might destroy the continual immediacy of perceptual shock." A few sentences later, this "intellectual picture" (which must be resisted, subverted, or blocked) is assimilated to the "*memory* of a thing" (as distinguished from the positive value of the "*perception* of that thing"). We may here detect a slight modification of the older modernist paradigm in the reinforcement and increasing specification of the negative term (that which is to be fragmented, undermined, forestalled). In the older modernisms, that negative term was still relatively general in character and evocative of the nature of social life in a kind of global way; this is the case, for example, with the formalist conception of habituation as a condition of modern life, as well as with the Marxist conception of reification when used in an older systemic way, and even with concepts of the stereotypical, as in Flau-

bert's *bêtise* and *lieux communs*, when these are taken to characterize
the increasingly standardized "consciousness" of the modern or bourgeois person. My sense is that in recent years, although the general
binary scaffolding of the modernist aesthetic remains intact in many
otherwise seemingly more advanced theories, the content of this negative term becomes modified in what then become historically interesting and symptomatic ways: in particular, from a general characterization of social life or consciousness, the negative term now comes to be
reconstituted as a specific sign system. Thus it is no longer fallen social
life generally which is opposed to the brutal freshness of the aesthetic
renewal of perception but, as it were, two types of perception, two kinds
of sign systems, which are now in opposition. It is a development which
can be dramatically documented in the newer film theory and in particular in the so-called representation debate, where despite the essentially modernist cast of the argument and its aesthetic priorities and
solutions, the slogan "representation" now designates something far
more organized and semiotic than older conceptions of habit or even
Flaubert's stereotypes (which are still, despite their novelistic precision, general characteristics of bourgeois consciousness). "Representation" is both some vague bourgeois conception of reality and also a
specific sign system (in the event Hollywood film), and it must now be
defamiliarized not by the intervention of great or authentic art but by
another art, by a radically different practice of signs.

If this is true, then it becomes interesting to detain Macrae-Gibson's
modernist formulations for another moment and to interrogate them a
little more insistently. What would be, for him, this "intellectual picture" which blocks the more authentic perceptual processes of art? I
think that more is at stake here than the simple traditional opposition of
the abstract and the concrete—the difference between intellectualizing
and seeing, between reason or thinking and concrete perception. Still,
it would seem paradoxical to thematize such a concept of the intellectual picture in terms of memory (the opposition between the memory of
a thing and the perception of the thing) in a situation in which both
personal and collective memory have become functions in crisis to
which it is increasingly problematical to appeal. Proust, you will "remember," did it just the other way round and tried to show that it is only
by way of memory that some genuine and more authentic perception of
the thing can be reconstructed. Yet the reference to nostalgia film suggests that Macrae-Gibson's contemporary formulation is not without
some justice if we suppose, as against Proust, that it is memory itself

that has become the degraded repository of images and simulacra, so that the remembered image of the thing now effectively inserts the reified and the stereotypical between the subject and reality or the past itself.

But I believe that we can now identify Macrae-Gibson's "intellectual picture" a little more precisely and concretely: it is, I think, simply the photograph itself and photographic representation, the perception by the machine—a formulation meant to be a little stronger than the more acceptable idea of perception *mediated* by the machine. For bodily perception is already a perception by the physical and organic machine, but we have continued to think of it, over a long tradition, as a matter of consciousness—the mind confronting visible reality or the spiritual body of phenomenology exploring Being itself. But supposing, as Derrida says somewhere, there is no such thing as perception in that sense: supposing that it is already an illusion to imagine ourselves before a building and in the process of grasping its perspectival unities in the form of some glorious image-thing: photography and the various machineries of recording and projecting now suddenly disclose or deconceal the fundamental materiality of that formerly spiritual act of vision. We must therefore displace the architectural question of the unity of a building in much the same way as, in recent film theory, reflections on the filmic apparatus, inserted into a rewriting of the history of painterly perspective and reinforced by Lacanian notions of subject construction and subject position and their relationship to the specular, have displaced older psychological questions of identification and the like in the discussion of the filmic object.

Such displacements are already everywhere at work in contemporary architecture criticism, where a clear tension has long been established between the concrete or already constructed building and that representation of the building to be constructed which is the architect's *project*, the various sketches of the future "work," and this to the point where the work of a certain number of very interesting contemporary or postcontemporary architects consists exclusively of the drawing of imaginary buildings which will never cast a real shadow in the light of day. The project, the drawing, is then one reified substitute for the real building, but a "good" one, that makes infinite Utopian freedom possible. The photograph of the already existing building is another substitute, but let us say a "bad" reification—the illicit substitution of one order of things for another, the transformation of the building into the image of itself, and a spurious image at that. So it is that in our architectural histories and journals, we consume so many photographic images of the classical or modern buildings, coming at length to believe that these are somehow the things themselves. At least since Proust's pictures of Venice we all try to retain our sensitivity to the constitutive visual deceptiveness of the photograph, whose frame and angle always give us something by comparison with which the building itself is always something distinct, something slightly different. All the more so is this true with color photography, where a new set of libidinal forces comes into play so that it is no longer even the building that is now consumed, having itself become a mere pretext for the intensities of the color stock and the gloss of the stiff paper. "The image," said Debord in a famous theoretical move, "is the final form of commodity reification"; but he should have added, "the *material* image," the photographic reproduction. At that point, then, and with those qualifications, we may accept Macrae-Gibson's formulation that the peculiar structure of the Gehry house aims at "preventing the formation of an intellectual picture that might destroy the continual immediacy of perceptual shock." It does this by blocking the choice of photographic point of view, evading the image imperialism of photography, securing a situation in which no photograph of this house will ever be quite right, for it is the photograph alone which offers the possibility of an "intellectual picture" in this sense.

Yet other possible meanings of this curious expression "intellectual picture" suggest themselves if we now lift it completely out of its context: there are, for example, maps that are both pictorial and cognitive, but in a very different way from the visual abstractions of photography. This new tack will lead me on to my final thoughts on the interpretation itself, and to alternative interpretive options from the modernist one which we have already discussed and rejected. In his recent books on cinema, Gilles Deleuze argues that film is a way of thinking, that is, it is also a way of doing philosophy, but in purely filmic terms: its concrete philosophizing has nothing to do with the way in which some film or other might *illustrate* a philosophical concept, and that very precisely because the philosophical concepts of film are filmic concepts, and not ideational or linguistic ones. In a similar move I would like to argue that architectural space is also a way of thinking and philosophizing, of trying to solve philosophical or cognitive problems. To be sure, everyone agrees that architecture is a way of solving architectural problems, just as the novel is a way of solving narrative problems and painting a way of solving visual ones. I want to presuppose that level of the history of each art as a set of problems and solutions and to posit, beyond that, a very different type of perplexity or object of thought (or *pensée sauvage*).

Yet such allegorical transcoding must still begin with space; for if Gehry's house is the meditation on a problem, that problem must initially be a spatial one, or at least be susceptible to formulation and incarnation in properly spatial terms. We have already, in fact, worked up the elements of an account of such a problem: it will somehow involve the incommensurability between the space of the traditional room and tract house and that other space here marked by the corrugated wall and the tumbling cube. To what kind of a problem could this tension and incommensurability correspond? How can we invent a mediation whereby the spatial language in which we describe this purely architectural contradiction can then be rewritten in other nonarchitectural languages and codes?

Macrae-Gibson, as we know, wishes to inscribe the tumbling cube in the tradition of Utopian and mystical modernism, most specifically Malevich, a reading that would oblige us to rewrite the fundamental contradiction in the house as one between traditional American life and modernist Utopianism. Let's look a little more closely:

> What looks like a cube could hardly be more deceptive. The surface that is squashed up against the plane of the exterior wall is rectangular rather than square, and the back face of the cube has been pushed sideways and sheared upwards so that no framing member forms a right angle with any other, except in the front plane. As a result, while the panels of glass in the front plane may be rectangular those on all the other faces are all parallelograms.[20]

What we can retain from this description is the sense of a space existing in two distinct dimensions at once, in one of which it leads a rectangular existence, while in that other simultaneous and unrelated world it is a parallelogram. There can be no question of linking these worlds, or spaces, or fusing them into some organic synthesis; at best, the peculiar shape dramatizes the impossible task of such representation all the while indicating its impossibility (and thereby perhaps at some curious second-degree level representing it all at once anyhow).

So the problem—whatever it turns out to be—will be twofold: it will pose its own internal content as problem or dilemma, and also raise the secondary problem (presumably, however, at one with and "the same as" that one) of even representing itself as a problem in the first place. Let me now dogmatically and allegorically, in an a priori way, say what I think that spatial problem is. We have refused Macrae-Gibson's account of the symbolic way in which the house anchors itself in its space, which is Santa Monica and the relationship to the sea and the city behind it, the ranges of hills, and the other urban prolongations along the coast.[21] Our theoretical refusal was based on the conviction that in that simpler phenomenological or regional sense, place in the United States today no longer exists, or, more precisely, it exists at a much feebler level, surcharged by all kinds of other more powerful but also more abstract spaces. By these last I mean not only Los Angeles itself, as some new hyperurban configuration, but also the increasingly abstract (and communicational) networks of American reality beyond, whose extreme form is the power network of so-called multinational capitalism itself. As individuals, we are in and out of all these overlapping dimensions all the time, something which makes an older kind of existential positioning of ourselves in Being—the human body in the natural landscape, the individual in the older village or organic community, even the citizen in the nation-state—exceedingly problematical. I have found it useful, for an earlier stage of this historical dissolution of place, to refer to a series of once-popular novels which are no longer very much read, in which (essentially for the New Deal period) John O'Hara charts the progressive enlargements of power around but also away from the small town, as these migrate to the higher dialectical levels of the state and finally the federal government. Could one imagine this migration now projected and intensified at a new global level, some new and more acute sense of the problems of contemporary "mapping" and of the positioning in this system of the older individual, might be achieved. The problem is still one of representation, and also of representability: we know that we are caught within these more complex global networks, because we palpably suffer the prolongations of corporate space everywhere in our daily lives. Yet we have no way of thinking about them, of modeling them, however abstractly, in our mind's eye. This cognitive "problem" is then the thing to be thought, the impossible mental puzzle or paradox exemplified by the tumbling cube. And if it is observed that the cube is not the only novel spatial intervention here, and that we have not yet made any interpretive allowance for the wall or fence of corrugated metal, then I will observe that the two features do indeed characterize the problem of thinking about contemporary America. The corrugated aluminum, the chain-linked balcony above, are, one would think, the junk or Third World side of American life today—the production of poverty and misery, people not only out of work but without a place to live, bag people, waste and industrial pollution, squalor, garbage, and obsolescent machinery. All this is surely a very realistic truth, and an inescapable fact, of the most recent years of the superstate. The cognitive and representational problem comes when we try to combine that palpable reality with the equally unquestionable other representation of the United States that inhabits a different and unrelated compartment of our collective mind: namely, the postmodern United States of extraordinary technological and scientific achievement; the most "advanced" country in the world, in all the science fictional senses and connotations of that figure, accompanied by an inconceivable financial system and a combination of abstract wealth and real power in which all of us also believe, without many of us ever really knowing what that might be or look like. These are the two antithetical and incommensurable features, then, of abstract American space, of the superstate or multinational capitalism today, which the cube and the wall mark for us (without offering representational options for them).

The problem, then, which the Gehry house tries to think is the relationship between that abstract knowledge and conviction or belief about the superstate and the existential daily life of people in their traditional rooms and tract houses. There must be a relationship between those two realms or dimensions of reality, or else we are altogether within science fiction without realizing it. But the nature of that relationship eludes the mind. The building then tries to think through this spatial problem in spatial terms. What would be the mark or sign, the index, of a successful resolution for this cognitive but also spatial problem? It could be detected, one would think, in the quality of the new intermediary space itself—the new living space produced by the interaction of the other poles. If that space is meaningful, if you can live in it, if it is somehow comfortable but in a new way, one that opens up historically new and original ways of living—and generates, so to speak, a new Utopian spatial language, a new kind of sentence, a new kind of syntax, radically new words beyond our own grammar—then, one would think, the dilemma, the aporia, has been resolved, if only on the level of space itself. I will not decide that, nor dare to evaluate the outcome. What does seem certain to me is the more modest proposition that Frank Gehry's house is to be considered the attempt to think a material thought.

5

Reading and the Division

of Labor

One can reread Claude Simon—a novel published in 1971[1] remains, after all, "within living memory" —only to find that embarrassing new problems (problems of evaluation) arise on top of the older ones (problems of interpretation), without the latter going away. The new problems spring from the breakdown, or at least the crisis, of the canon, and they include these questions: What is the relationship between fashion and high literature? If the *nouveau roman* is over, can it have been a fad and still have literary or aesthetic value today? Can certain books have become unreadable since feminism? (Does the neutrality of Simon's sexual descriptions—essentially crotch shots without any of Robbe-Grillet's sadoaestheticism, which in any case he makes fun of—not in fact prove the point and turn out to be an essentially masculine part-object voyeurism?) Would even male readers' relationship to such texts change if they discovered that Simon's aesthetic pleasures were not universal but specifically limited to a single special-interest group (even one as large as male literary readers in general)? Do we now feel the Frenchness of this work more strongly and oppressively than in previous decades (when writers like Simon simply represented a non-national vanguard production of Literature as such)? Has the fission we associate with the "new social movements," micropolitics and microgroups, now fastened onto national traditions, such that "French literature" is fully as much a badge of local in-group membership as contemporary poetry, gay literature, or science fiction? Does not, meanwhile, the competition of the media and so-called cultural studies signal a transformation in the role and space of mass culture today which is greater than a mere enlargement and which may increasingly leave no space whatsoever for literary "classics" of this kind? Were the experimental peculiarities of the *nouveau roman* already a harbinger of postmodernism (or a belated, already outmoded rehearsal of a dying modernism)? Does the extinction of the *nouveau roman* have anything to tell us about the survival (or the waning) of the 1960s (including its fashionable—and mostly French!—theories)? Does experimental high literature of this type have any sociological value, and does it tell us anything about its social context and the evolution of late capitalism or its culture? Does its reading have anything to tell us about the transformation of the role and status of intellectuals? Does the seeming gratuitousness of talking about Simon or even reading him confirm Bourdieu's blanket condemnation of the aesthetic as a mere class signal and as conspicuous consumption? Finally, are these "anguished" questions or merely matters of idle academic curiosity?

Some will remember what reading a *nouveau roman* felt like. *Les corps conducteurs* begins with window displays in a downtown street; someone seems to be sick and nauseous, resting on a fire hydrant; conquistadors are struggling through the jungle; an airplane is flying overhead, between North and South America; a man (the same?) is trying vainly by phone to persuade a woman to continue their affair (later on, we see them in bed, presumably during the previous night); a man (the same?) visits a doctor's office (but in Manhattan or in a South American city?); a man (the same?) visits a South American writers' congress in which the social role of art is debated, various works of art (Poussin's *Orion*, a Picasso print) are described or alluded to in the intervals, but we are unable to decide if the "protagonist" has just seen them somewhere. We learn to make an inventory of these plot strings and to coordinate them—something done in two contradictory operations—by learning to tell them apart and by conjecturing their larger interrelationship (the nameless male protagonist must be a single character: he must therefore be on a trip from North to South America, etc.). We will come back to these operations later on. Suffice it for the moment to underscore the historic peculiarity of a reading in which we strain to identify what is happening beneath our eyes (is he sitting down in the street?) while nervously anticipating the next shift without warning to an unrelated plot string, something that can happen in midsentence, although it most often occurs in the gap between them, opening that up to a more profound silence on either side of each utterance than obtains in Flaubert.

Conducting Bodies was, according to most critics, produced within a significant transitional period in Claude Simon's work, at a break between what Celia Britton calls the personal and impersonal novels of his middle and late periods, respectively,[2] between representational and "textual" or "linguistic" works, between a style oriented around memory and expressive evocation and a neutral and combinational practice pre-eminently characteristic of what we call the *nouveau roman*. The fault line is often placed within the preceding novel, *La Bataille de Pharsale*, which begins "personally" and ends "impersonally." Here, in *Les corps conducteurs*, the "personal" qualities of style are almost completely effaced, but something like a protagonist and the remnants of a unified story still persist; while in the next two novels, *Triptyque* and *Leçon de choses*, even that remnant has disappeared. Oddly, the most ambitious work of Simon's late years, the recent *Géorgiques*, reverts mainly to the so-called personal mode.

This peculiar alternation within Simon's oeuvre must serve as our start-ing point, since it does not seem to be a matter of development or evolu-tion but rather of the optional availability of two distinct narrative matri-ces. This suggests Simon's fundamental distance from both aesthetics, with each of which he has an equal but unrelated, dissociated affinity. I will suggest, therefore, that his relationship to *both* is pastiche, a bravura imitation so exact as to include the well-nigh undetectable reproduction of stylistic authenticity itself, of a thoroughgoing commitment of the authorial subject to the phenomenological preconditions of the stylistic practices in question. This is, then, in the largest sense what is postmod-ern about Simon: the evident emptiness of that subject beyond all phe-nomenology, its capacity to embrace another style as though it were another world. The moderns, however, had to invent their own personal worlds first, all by themselves, and at least the first of Simon's stylistic options, the so-called personal one, is clearly of modernist provenance since it very systematically reproduces Faulknerian writing procedures.

Faulkner's style took the situation of memory itself as its formal precondition: the violent action or gesture in the past; a vision that fascinates and obsesses storytellers who cannot but commemorate it in the present and yet who must project it as a complete tableau — "motionless" as well as "furious," "breathless" in the stillness of its agitation, and compelling "stupor" and "amazement" in the viewer. Lan-guage, then, returns over and over again to this gesture out of time, des-perately accumulating its adjectives and qualifiers in an attempt to con-jure, from the outside, what is virtually a seamless gestalt in its own right that can no longer be constructed by the movement of the senten-ces. Thus Faulkner himself exhibits a deeply embedded foreshadowing of the necessary failure of language, which will never coincide with its objects, given in advance. This failure is surely the entry point for

Simon's (or anyone else's) pastiche of Faulkner, since it blocks out a structure in which the "spontaneity" of literary language has already been dissociated into the establishment of a visual, nonverbal content, on the one hand, and a well-nigh interminable rhetorical evocation, on the other. Nothing seems further from the language ethics of the so-called new novel, with its exclusion of rhetoric, and of the subject, and body warmth, until we think of the extraordinary function of the Faulknerian "now," which (generally accompanied by the past tense) shifts gears from the traumatic present of the obsessive memory in the past, across the listeners' situation, to the present of the Faulknerian sentences in our own reading time. Here, suddenly, in a different space from Faulknerian deep time and deep memory (and the rhetoric associated with it), a linguistic and textual mechanism takes form which is structurally comparable to what will be specialized and developed to an advanced degree by the *nouveau roman*.

But the mode of Faulknerian modernism in Simon does not alternate with the practice of another style (personal style in that sense being preeminently a modernist phenomenon), but instead with something rather different, which it may be appropriate to characterize as the codification of the laws of a new "artificial" genre. The genre remains in some sense a "named" phenomenon, although if Robbe-Grillet is its inventor, Jean Ricardou can theoretically be regarded as its Eisenstein; but it is a system of relatively impersonal rules of exclusion, which offers the peculiar appearance (as in genetic engineering) of a completely "man-made" genre itself devised full-blown in imitation of the "natural" ones that have evolved organically over historical time.[3] There is nonetheless here also a distant caricature of Faulknerian structure in the way in which, in Robbe-Grillet as well, content is given in advance and the sentences simply trace and imitate it after the fact. But in Robbe-Grillet that already preformed content is the raw material of cultural stereotypes —situations, characters, mass cultural allusions of all kinds—which the habits of consumption enable us to identify at a glance (like a musical theme of which we have only heard a few notes). Faulkner's raw material was philosophically dignified not merely by its status as memory in a temporality-obsessed age but also by implicit ideologies of perception as such, which so often informed the various modernist aesthetics, beginning (most strategically for Faulkner's own personal development) with Conrad's impressionism ("above all, to make you see!"). The postmodern period, however, eschews temporality for space and has generally grown skeptical about deep phenomenological experience in general, and the very concept of perception itself in particular (see Derrida). Robbe-Grillet's manifestos can in this respect be read today less as an affirmation of the visual over the other senses than as a radical repudiation of phenomenological perception as such. Meanwhile, if it is so, as Celia Britton's excellent book on Simon argues,[4] that Robbe-Grillet's older "disciple" is in fact torn between the incompatible impulses of vision and textuality, then such an irreconcilable tension would go a long way toward explaining his alternation between a Faulknerian evocation of perception and a neo-novelistic practice of textualization (unless it is the other way round, as the Formalists liked to insist, and literary-historical choices predetermine characterological traits of authorial inclinations).

Meanwhile, the widespread impression that the *nouveau roman* had something to do with *things* (and therefore with descriptions)[5] can lead beyond Simon or Robbe-Grillet to some new historical sense of their linguistic situation in general, provided it is neither reformulated in terms of some new aesthetic nor diagnosed in neither personal, psychoanalytic, or "stylistic" terms. What its "description" of things mainly shows is rather the breakdown of description and the failure of language to achieve some of the most obvious things it has been supposed to do. The appearance of an implacable focus on the specific and the particular, for instance—something already present in the more aberrant moderns such as Raymond Roussel, where the effort to describe objects in minute detail is sustained with implacability, at lengths interestingly intolerable for most readers—here at once inverts into its opposite, in a virtually textbook dialectical fashion.

The "package" is not enough all by itself (any more than the "shoebox" is, particularly since this last mutates without warning into the "biscuit tin," reminding us of the persistence of the referent—Venus or the morning star!—in Frege's famous essay on *Sinn* and *Bedeutung*); nor is its position ("under the soldier's left arm," "in a drawer in the doctor's desk") helpful in convincing the reader that we have to do in both cases with *the same* object: "wrapped in brown paper," to be sure, but, on the other hand "the snow, drying, has left darker spots on it, marks with rounded contours, fringed with minuscule festoons; distended, the string has slipped towards one of the corners."[6] Indeed, the very complexity of the attribute ("des cernes plus foncés, traces aux contours arrondis, franges de minuscules festons"), clearly designed to supply the maximum specificity to this object, as if uniqueness were a function of multiplicity, only anticipates the dialectic to come: for these abstract plurals—Robbe-Grillet at his most formalizing—end up evoking any surface at all that has some grain to it; the most concrete turns into the most general under our very eyes; plurality turns out to stand on the side of the universal rather than the particular. But finally—"you cannot get out of language by means of language!"—all the possibilities end up at the same dead end: a single attribute for the box ("brown," "cardboard") would not have done us much more good than some more obviously accidental property (a "rip" or "tear," for example), insofar as all those words also remain general in their very essence. Only the definite article (*the* box, as though there could never be another one) and the present tense try to reanchor these not very satisfactory nouns and adjectives into their proper place in the "text," which is to say this printed novel here, to be read according to generic specifications. Still, one senses the possibility of other kinds of slippage: "little bubbles that cluster in a beige froth against the concave side"[7]: leaving aside the question of the dimensions of observer or observed (but the coffee cup could be as enormous as the galactic one in Godard's *Deux ou trois choses que je sais d'elle!*), only the color warns us not to assimilate this account to that of the wine bottle later on: "little rose bubbles cluster on the liquid's surface, clinging to the sides" (BP 209). This is not to say that color is any more reliable than any other property: "it is now a dull grey" (BP 253). But the "it" of the previous sentence was a pavement, hitherto wet and gleaming with barely perceptible glints of color; in the next it is the skin of the drunken naked soldier, gray from his fall on the dirty floor, but where "little drops of blood begin to seep from scrapes beneath the layer of gray dust covering the whole left side of his body." Examples could be multiplied, but they are useless unless we are able to outwit our apparently irresistible tendency to invent an entity corresponding to our verbal or ideational perception. The sentence sequence leaves the reading mind without an object, which it therefore conveniently supplies itself in the form of an ideal or imaginary literary referent, a kind of subliminal or archetypal image in which a colorless surface oscillates back and forth in time between dull indistinction and the heightened perception of varied points. To this least common denominator both the pavement and the dust-covered skin correspond as so many possible surface manifestations. But this image—whose elaboration might continue with the logically entailed positing of an unconscious subjectivity in which it was formed—does not exist; it is a figment of the interpretive process and a sign of the desperate malfunctioning of the subject position generated by the sentences just read. In effect, the reader seems unable to conclude that language has broken down (some-

thing which would leave her or him without any subject position whatsoever), and therefore—as in a reverse shot in film—constructs some
new imaginary object to justify the persistence of the subject position
already achieved. This imaginary object—which is only one of a whole
range of interpretive temptations we will find Simon's work offering
us—then generates its secondary mirage of subjectivity on the side of
that equally imaginary object, the Author, of whom this particular imaginary object is supposed to be the thought. Thus there is an exchange
and a dialectical multiplication of imaginary entities between subject
and object—or rather between subject position and what we must now
call object position—which confirms Foucault's choice, in *The Order
of Things*, of *Las Meniñas* as a virtual allegory of the construction of the
subject (very much including that "vanishing point" which is the putative "subjectivity" of the writer or artist). We must deduce from this the
necessity of reversing Kant's transcendental deduction: it is not the unity
of the world that demands to be posited on the basis of the unity of the
transcendental subject; rather, the unity or incoherence and fragmentation of the subject—that is, the accessibility of a workable subject position or the absence of one—is itself a correlative of the unity or lack of
unity of the outside world. The subject is certainly no mere "effect" of
the object, but it would not be nearly so erroneous to suggest that the
subject *position* is just such an effect. Meanwhile, it must be understood that what is meant by object here is not some mere perceptual
aggregate of physical things, but a social configuration or ensemble of
social relationships (even physical perception and seemingly rock-bottom
experiences of the body and of matter being mediated by the social).
What one concludes from such an argument is not that the "unified"
subject is unreal or undesirable and inauthentic, but rather that it is
dependent for its construction and existence on a certain kind of society and is menaced, undermined, problematized, or fragmented by other
social arrangements. At any rate, something like this is what I take to be
the allegorical lesson of Simon's novels (or at least his *nouveau roman*
sequence) for questions of subjectivity. Objects are, however, here still
very much a function of language, whose local failure to describe or
even to designate them takes us in a different direction and foregrounds
the unexpected breakdown of a function of language we normally take
for granted—some privileged relationship between words and things
which here gives way to a yawning chasm between the generality of the
words and the sensory particularity of the objects.

In such passages language is being forced to do something we assumed to be virtually its primary function, but which it now—pressed to some absolute limit—proves to be incapable of doing. We need to know what that is before we try to understand why this self-defeating experiment has been conducted in the first place. What seems clear is that nouns are here being asked to function as names, since the proper name is evidently the only term we have for the attempt to match a specific word to a unique object. Yet, virtually simultaneously with the *nouveau roman*, we have learned from Lévi-Strauss that the "proper name" was itself something of a misnomer, since individual proper names were also components of larger linguistic systems that varied according to their generic objects (dogs, race horses, people, cats): so that even this seemingly more concrete linguistic possibility—in which words reach a level of specificity denied to them as mere general nouns—vanishes in advance like a mirage: in *Les corps conducteurs*, however, this false lead and dead end of the promise of proper names gives rise over and over again to a linguistic proliferation in which taxonomic lists fold out aimlessly in all directions: parts of the body, tables of tropical birds, lists of the constellations.[8]

Meanwhile, the other theoretical alternative—one reaches the things themselves not by way of *names* but by way of pointing, or *deixis*—is not so much excluded by the generic impersonality of the *nouveau roman*: Robbe-Grillet's mannerisms of interpolation—"or so it would seem," "perhaps," "as has already been said"—serve a kind of deictic function that is also a technique of modulation or variation. Rather, the failure of *deixis* itself results from the irreducible generality of those words also, along with all the rest, as Hegel demonstrated for "now," "here," "this," and "that" in the opening chapter of the *Phenomenology of Spirit*: a philosophical space which is virtually identical with that of the later *nouveau roman* and in which we find rehearsed the most fundamental doubts as to the capacity of language itself to resolve the fundamental philosophical opposition between the universal and the particular, the general and the specific. It is often suggested that Hegel's conception of the dialectic is somehow prelinguistic (or at least, to use an anachronism, prestructuralist), and in particular that it seems to mobilize logical or conceptual antinomies and contradictions as though these last were somehow prior to language and somehow also more "fundamental" than linguistic properties. This may or may not be so, but the judgment ignores the significance of the *Phenomenology*'s opening section on Consciousness (sense certainty, perception, and force and understanding), whose intent is to settle accounts with language from the outset and to found the necessity of the dialectic on this very failure of language to coordinate the universal and the particular. Meanwhile, whatever ontological status structuralism felt able to confer on language, it is significant that this tradition also finds its starting point (whether in those analyses of Lévi-Strauss referred to above or in the reading mysteries of the *nouveau roman*) in a meditation on just such failures of language.

What Hegel shows is that there can be no unmediated identity between language and our sensory experience of the present, of the here and now of these unique things (also called our "sense certainty"). "If [philosophers] actually wanted to *say* 'this' bit of paper which they mean, if they wanted to *say* it, then this is impossible, because the sensuous This that is meant *cannot be reached* by language, which belongs to consciousness, i.e., to that which is inherently universal."[9] "Universal" is tortuously defined here as an empty concept which can preside over a multiplicity of distinct kinds of content: the "Now" as a "plurality of Nows taken together" constitutes for Hegel "the experience of learning that Now is a *universal*."[10] This may not quite be the "lesson" the *nouveau roman* has in store for us, but the failure of language used by Hegel to teach it is surely part of that more novelistic lesson:

> It is as a universal too that we *utter* what the sensuous [content] is. What we say is: 'This', i.e. the *universal* This; or, 'it is', i.e. *Being in general*. Of course, we do not *envisage* the universal This or Being in general, but we *utter* the universal; in other words, we do not strictly say what in this sense-certainty we *mean* to say. But language, as we see, is the more truthful; in it, we ourselves directly refute what we *mean* to say, and since the universal is the true [content] of sense-certainty and language expresses this true [content] alone, it is just not possible for us ever to say, or express in words, a sensuous being that we *mean*.[11]

In this situation of linguistic failure, the breakdown of the relationship between words and things is for Hegel a happy fall insofar as it redirects philosophical thought toward new forms of the universals themselves. For Simon, however, and the *nouveau roman* generally, it opens up a provisional space in which this breakdown is reexperienced over and over again as a process, a temporary runoff between the habitual onset of linguistic belief and the inevitable degradation of the signified into its material signifier or the sign itself into a mere image.

This provisional and repetitive process is what used to be called reading: what I want to argue here is that in the *nouveau roman*, reading undergoes a remarkable specialization and, very much like older handicraft activity at the onset of the industrial revolution, is dissociated into a variety of distinct processes according to the general law of the division of labor. This internal differentiation, the becoming autonomous of older combined branches of the productive process, then knows a second qualitative leap with Taylorization; that is to say, the planned analytic separation of the various production moments into independent units. That older, but scarcely traditional, activity called reading can now be seen to have been a process of this kind, susceptible to a similar historical development. As such, Niklas Luhmann's more general theory of differentiation (itself the most evolved and specialized theoretical reflection on this process to date) seems very relevant indeed:

> We can conceive of system differentiation as a replication, within a system, of the difference between a system and its environment. Differentiation is thus understood as a reflexive and recursive form of system building. It repeats the same mechanism, using it to amplify its own results. In differentiated systems, as a result, we find two kinds of environment: the external environment common to all subsystems and a separate internal environment for each subsystem. This conception implies that each subsystem reconstructs and, in a sense, *is* the whole system in the special form of a difference between the sub-system and its environment. Differentiation thus reproduces the system in itself, multiplying specialized versions of the original system's identity by splitting it into a number of internal systems and affiliated environments. This is not simply a decomposition into smaller chunks but rather a process of growth by internal disjunction.[12]

Beginning with Ricardou, a great number of fine-grained analyses of local procedures and patterns in Simon have been produced, which mainly end up affirming a kind of "textualist" aesthetic ideology, but which it would perhaps be more interesting today, now that the novelty has passed, to rewrite according to Luhmann's schemes. I myself would suggest that two general processes are at work in Simon's *nouveaux romans* (as opposed to his Faulknerian ones), which largely correspond to Luhmann's distinction between the reproduction of an external environment within the system (or text) and the replication of distinct internal environments for each subsystem. These last correspond to what I have called, above, the degradation of the signified into its material signifier or, if you prefer, the eclipse of the illusion of transparency, the unexpected transformation of a meaning into an object, or, better still, its deconcealment as something already reified, something already opaque in advance, whether that opacity be revealed as the sound and complexion of words or as their printed reproduction and the meaningless spatiality of individual letters. Transparency is, in this respect, something like the organism's or the subsystem's illusion of autonomy; the recall of its materiality then reestablishes what Luhmann calls an internal environment (on the order of the chemical processes at work within the brain, for example). In Simon, on the whole, this material differentiation of former meanings and signifieds takes two general forms. The first may be described as the reading of "reading," a moment in which something in the words ("what a riot of color . . . !") alerts us to the possibility that they may be themselves a quotation, and that we are reading someone else's reading; in the second, the words themselves become mere typography, as with inserted foreign languages or the reproduction of letters printed in other typefaces:

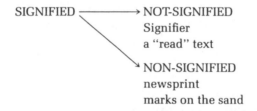

Luhmann's second set of processes, which turn on the external environment itself—or what in literature is generally called the context or even the referent—is exemplified above all in those moments (also characteristic of Robbe-Grillet) in which a narrative in which we have been led to believe (for in literature, what is called the fictive is the equivalent of the referential in other forms of language) suddenly proves to have been a mere image all along, whether that image is simply a painting (which the preceding pseudonarrative has, as it were, animated) or turns out to have been a film, as in the case of the tropical expedition in *Les corps conducteurs*. Here, then, the materialization of the signified by quotation, described above, is replicated diegetically or narratively on the level of the sign as a whole, with new and unexpected results: these passages now lift us from the realm of linguistic problematics and linguistic philosophy into that of image society and the media. (Indeed, the copresence of these two very different microscopic and macroscopic areas of significance and interpretation within the *nouveau roman* goes a long way toward validating our claim for historically novel and intensified forms of differentiation within the latter.) As for the second logically possible permutation on this level of the sign, what can be called the position of the nonsign:

it would seem to consist essentially in the inevitable presence of *noise* as such within any communicational system. In the case of Simon such noise is generally the aleatory or random insertion of irrelevant reference (such as, for example, the traces left behind by the picture book, *Orion aveugle*, which he cannibalized in order to construct *Conducting Bodies* as a novel), but it is, as it were, emblematized or allegorized in this work as an enigmatic pile of rubble in movement across the frames of the individual sentences ("something grayish, shapeless, and awesomely heavy that seems to be inching along inexorably, an avalanche in slow motion on the move for billions of years, patient and insidious, wearing away the floor, the walls" [*CC* 88/72]). Whether this is to be seen as a pathological ocular condition, a disintegration of the film itself within the projector, or a science-fictional being of some sort is not even "undecidable," since this episode evidently has the paradoxical, and indeed contradictory and impossible, function of meaning the meaningless and intending to convey an absence of intention.

But these local effects could also be grasped as mere changes in the raw material of the production process rather than as indications of some radical structural change within this last: as peculiar new things to be coped with by reading rather than any differentiation within reading as such. Any inspection of our own mental processes when we begin to read a *nouveau roman* discloses the presence of new operations as well as that fission and reproduction by multiplication attributed by Luhmann to his differentiating subsystems. The activity of *identification*, for example, as it is inevitably called into play by the opening pages of a novel, here subdivides into two new and as yet unnamed mental operations. In a fashion reminiscent of the possibilities of Barthes's proairetic code, we are given unnamed components of an unidentified segment of an action or a gesture, which must, like magnified fragments of a lost photograph, be put back together in some recognizable form: that is to say, the object of the representation (a man sitting on a fire hydrant in pain, perhaps) must now be *named* or *renamed*. In the traditional novel we do not have to perform this part of the work; the novelist does it for us, clearly labeling the components and the essentials of the story to come; our job, in reading the traditional novel, is to reassemble those components within some larger action not yet "named" (the narrative itself). But this we must *also* go on doing in the *nouveau roman*, for besides deciding what the object is (man on fire hydrant), we must still decide "who" he is, that is to say where he fits into the larger plot. Yet this process has itself internally differentiated: in *Conducting Bodies* it has split into the two very distinct operations of (1) deciding whether the pause on the fire hydrant comes before or after the visit to the doctor's office (or the stop in the bar), and (2) looking for evidence that might establish the identity between the man on the hydrant and the visitor to the Latin American writers' conference, let alone the one with the unhappy love affair. The operation of identification, then, is both combined with and differentiated from that of reordering segments in chronological time and that other process of cross-referencing or cross-relating strings of events—something which in turn reintroduces all the other operations all over again (if the man on the hydrant also traveled to Latin America, did he do so before or after his *crise de foie?*).

Meanwhile, in this situation in which mental activities are colonized and miniaturized, specialized, reorganized like some enormous modern automated factory somewhere, other kinds of mental activities fall out and lead a somewhat different, unorganized or marginal, existence within the reading process. Indeed, not the least pleasure of reading Simon, a wondrous effect that strikes me as having no equivalent elsewhere in literature, is what we may call the first moments in which we feel the train in motion. We are occupied with our various tasks —identifying this or that fragment of a gesture, making some preliminary inventory of the various plot strings as they appear one after the other—when suddenly we also become aware that *something is happening*, that time has begun to move, that the objects, even as imperfectly identified as they are, have begun to change under our very eyes; the book is actually getting on with it, getting written, getting finished. But this extraordinary feeling of aesthetic relief has very little in common with the Aristotelian emotion that accompanies a more traditional mimesis of a completed action.

By the same token, interpretation in its older senses also seems to be a remnant or survival no longer required here, even though it does not seem to me quite right to attribute to Simon what has often elsewhere been taken to constitute one of the fundamental features of the postmodern as such, namely, the absolute exclusion of interpretive possibilities. Here, as in Weber, older kinds of value are rendered obsolete by the rationalization process and the reorganization of work in terms of instrumentality and efficiency, but the older interpretive values live on as residual temptations, which all prove unsatisfying and frustrating. The realist temptation, of course, involves the reassembling of all the raw materials into a single unified action, something which is not frustrated only because of the random presence of other aleatory materials, as we shall see. But there is also something that might be called a modernist interpretive temptation: that of reading the very form of the novel as a stream of perceptions. "What a riot of color when a flock of aras spreads its wings and flies upward in the sunlight! The squawking, chattering flock disappears, leaving behind it a long, dazzling, bright-colored trail across the observer's retina" (CC 174/146). But besides the fact that this interpretive temptation—which is denaturalized in the great vision of the lights of the city at night (CC 83/67) and, later, in the dramatic visual chaos of the city's advertising systems and images (CC 139/116)—has no way of dealing with the content of perceptions as such, it is also profoundly complicitous with that very ideology of perception of which we have spoken above. But the image culture of postmodern is postperceptual, turning on imaginary rather than on material consumption. The analysis of image culture (including its aesthetic products, such as this one of Claude Simon) can thus only be meaningful if it leads us to rethink the "image" itself in some nontraditional and nonphenomenological way.

There remains the structural temptation, until recently the most influential interpretive option, whereby, following Robbe-Grillet and Ricardou, we were encouraged to grasp the text as a game played against Benjamin's automaton and to interpret our reading as a combinational experience in which the event of closure happens when all the permutations are finally exhausted:

> With one of his arms stretched out in front of him, fumbling about in the void, Orion is still advancing in the direction of the rising sun, guided by the voice and the information passed on to him by the little figure perched on his muscular shoulders. There is every indication, however, that he will never reach his goal, since as the sun rises higher and higher in the sky, the stars outlining the giant's

body are gradually growing paler and dimmer, and the fabulous silhouette motionlessly advancing in great strides will thus slowly fade and eventually disappear altogether in the dawn sky. (CC 222/187)

Yet this glorious period, which set all the Geiger counters of interpretation swinging wildly in a frenzy, is utterly unrelated to the other narrative strings (coming to the novel, rather, from Simon's related picture book, *Orion aveugle*). At best a PREPARE TO TERMINATE! on the order of our earlier videotext, it would seem—if read as a climax rather than one textual event among others—to inflect the structuralist reading back on the modernist one and to reinvent the now outmoded aestheticizing self-designations and autoreferentialities of this last.

There is a final possibility, however, no less improbable than the others, to be sure, and this is the reading of the novel as a kind of diary or autobiographical scrapbook in which various real-life experiences (although we can now no longer tell whether Simon himself actually "had" them)—the Latin American trip, the stopover in New York, the affair, the *choses vues* on 42nd Street, and the contemplation of the relevant paintings in the museums (including, perhaps, the great Orion ceiling of Grand Central Station itself)—are all formulated and reassembled in a more satisfying memorial than any photograph album: but one which fulfills the present and triumphantly dispatches it into the past more adequately than the doomed, gallant, vain, peremptory Faulknerian evocation of what has long since vanished. But in that case, the seeming aestheticism of the *nouveau roman* veers dialectically into a form of a very different kind, one capable of fleeing the guilt of the aesthetic generally—Sartre's suggestion that you could not read a *nouveau roman* in a Third World country,[13] along with the Bourdieu-type leisure-class "distinction" of reading it in a First World one—at the same time that it proposes new equipment for registering the raw material of everyday life and a new "libidinal apparatus" for coping with those kaleidoscopic shocks Benjamin, following Baudelaire, associated with the modern industrial landscape. At that point, the reproducibility of the new or artificial, invented *genre* becomes an index of its democratic accessibility; and this was always the reverse side and the progressive implication of the most notorious philistine reproaches to modernist art itself, as, for example to abstract painting, "Anyone could do that!" the answer being, "Of course! but you don't want to, do you? You would have to want to!"

At this point, however, interpretation has turned around in production, and reception has begun to be recycled as use. This particular dialectical reversal—which might also be taken as the very opposite of Luhmann's processes of infinite fission and differentiation, in which all of those new microscopic subsystems are now powerfully reassembled into a unified form of praxis—is perhaps the most interesting the *nouveau roman* has to offer, and the most historically original feature of its innovations (about which it seems less significant that they may themselves already have passed into history as so many false starts or unsuccessful patents). I want to argue, in particular, that it is the linguistic focus of Simon's "new novels" that uniquely—and for one long moment, the one in which we read these texts—renders reception (or consumption) indistinguishable from production. We have to read these sentences word by word, and that is something already fairly unusual (and painfully unfamiliar) in an information society in which a premium is placed on briefing and instant recognition, so that sentences are either skimmed or preprepared for rapid assimilation as so many signs. The discipline of the word by word (Simon's own expression, by the way) is enforced by the practice of cross-cutting, the possibility that the subject may change without warning at any minute. There is, in any case, no point whatsoever to speed-reading books of this kind; they have no supplemental content or information to offer us, nothing to store up and carry away, not even anything to find out (as at the end of a mystery story), unless it is the one simple tragic discovery that there is nothing to find out in the first place.

The economists tell us that automation goes hand in hand with deskilling, so here too that prodigious differential specialization of what used to be called the reading process, and of which we have spoken above, goes hand in hand with new and more rudimentary, plebeian, forms of labor that anyone can do: for under certain conditions—social conditions or, indeed, conditions of socialism!—deskilling also goes hand in hand with democratization (or plebeianization, as I prefer to call it). Is it possible, then, that the reading of so specialized and highly technical an elite literary artifact as *Les corps conducteurs* might offer a figure or *analogon* for nonalienated labor and for the Utopian experience of a radically different, alternate society?

It used to be affirmed that art or the aesthetic in our time offered the closest accessible analogy to, constituted the most adequate symbolic experience of, a nonalienated labor otherwise unimaginable for us. This proposition in its turn derived from the preindustrial speculations of

German idealist philosophy, where the experience of play offered a similar *analogon* to a condition in which the tensions between work and freedom, science and ethical imperatives, might be overcome.

There are, however, good reasons why these propositions about hints, anticipations, or symbolic experiences of nonalienated labor should no longer be persuasive. For one thing, the very experience of art itself today is alienated and made "other" and inaccessible to too many people to serve as a useful vehicle for their imaginative experience. This is so whether it is a question of high art or of mass culture; for in both cases, for very different reasons, the experience of the *production* of such art forms is inaccessible to most people (including critics and intellectuals), who thereby find themselves thrown back on an experience of both kinds of art as sheer reception (whence the attractiveness of those categories for contemporary theory). Specialization, and everything esoteric that accompanies it (special training, collective division of labor, unique technologies, a guild or professionalist mentality, along with the simple indifference that accompanies activities from which we are excluded), characterizes both high art and mass culture: the whole elaborate machinery of contemporary postelectronic music, on the one hand, and the systems of television production, on the other, are not, for example, environments in which most people feel at home, and in any case they inspire very little optimism about that potential control or mastery over processes, oneself, and nature and collective destiny, which nonalienated labor necessarily includes and projects. Thus the older Romantic analogy tends to remain a dead letter because the very artistic production held up as a Utopian model for alternative social living is itself a closed book.

As for play, it may also no longer mean very much as a reminder and an alternative experience in a situation in which leisure is as commodified as work, free time and vacations as organized and planified as the day in the office, the object of whole new industries of mass diversion of various kinds, outfitted with their own distinct high-tech equipment and commodities and saddled with thoroughgoing and themselves fully organized processes of ideological indoctrination. Play once meant children, who were in an older society the stand-in for those more distant representatives of Nature like the savage. But where children are themselves taken in hand and organized, integrated into consumer society, childhood may have lost its capacity to suggest or project ideas like play, which were thought to convey freedom in motion, as a form of active self-invention and self-determination.

Under these circumstances, even more marginal and degraded experiences—such as the *hobby*—are called upon to transmit distant glimpses of what humanly satisfying activities are like, glimpses distorted and amputated by their medium. In the case of the hobby, for example, what is strongly antiofficial—the role of the amateur, doing things after hours, deciding to pass and waste one's time deliberately without guilt, reversion to more archaic handicraft skills—also systematically excludes the collective as such, offering a perspective in which, unlike aesthetic pleasure, we want to keep these satisfactions to ourselves and are not eager to share and confirm them by way of other people's experience (the social dimension, as Gadamer has rightly stressed, of Kant's universalism of aesthetic value). On the other hand, the old-clothes informality of the hobby usefully rebukes and excludes the sacrality developed by some forms of art in the late nineteenth century as a way of distancing the aesthetic from innerworldly commercial activity: the solitary eccentricities of the hobby now displace that priestly unction and make it unnecessary, as in the productions by Roussel or *le facteur Cheval* so admired by the surrealists. In our own (postmodern) period, however, in which the socialization and institutionalization of individual life have intensified beyond any equivalents in an earlier twentieth-century capitalism, we will not be surprised by the paradoxical discovery that the hobby has itself been organized and institutionalized in groups like Oulipo. Indeed, the extraordinary novel by its adherent Georges Perec called *La Vie: mode d'emploi* (*Life: A user's manual*) is surely not only the most striking literary monument produced by an experimental writer after the end of the *nouveau roman* but also a useful exhibit for juxtaposition with Simon's symbolic treatment of work and activity.

In *La vie: mode d'emploi*, indeed, nonalienated labor in the form of the hobby is explicitly thematized in the grotesque obsession that constitutes the novel's central strand: the passion of the millionaire Bartlebooth to distract himself from the empty meaninglessness of existence by a rigorously computed lifelong program: to visit five hundred ports all over the world, one every two weeks for twenty years, in each painting a watercolor which is then applied to wood, segmented into a jigsaw puzzle, and consigned to a box, which will then be reopened during the twenty years that follow the period of travels, each jigsaw puzzle reassembled, the wood glued back together, the paper somehow magically reconnected, the watercolor removed, and the blank sheet returned to its original folder. If it is objected that this peculiar hobby is only one of many pursued within the covers of this novel, then we must grasp global totalization here at work in another way, in the very apartment building itself (owned by this same millionaire) which houses this ensemble of stories, destinies, and hobbies, and returns itself in the form of a miniaturized model on the very last page (miniaturization being, in general, one of the most powerful indices and signals for the presence of production as a process). It is as though the text and its dead models look back on all the agitation of human history from the standpoint of a geological epoch in which human life had become extinct on the planet; this is to say that a prodigious price has had to be paid for the figuration, in our time, of nonalienated labor as such.

But Simon's work does not thematize production and activity in this fashion (until the very last book in the *nouveau roman* series). At best, an approximation is reached in the process of translation (Latin in *La Bataille de Pharsale*, Spanish in *Les Corps conducteurs*), in which producing a sentence is endowed with a kind of opacity and, as it were, the resistance of matter. Simon's novels give us the experience of such production without its identification as such and without its official abstract name: and it must remain an open question whether, in literature, the thematization of such a process—its transformation into a symbol and a meaning, a representation—does not, by way of some mysterious Heisenberg principle of literary language as such, end up transforming it into something else. But the theme does appear in the last *nouveau roman, Leçon de choses* (1975), where it is inserted into the printed text as a kind of looseleaf flier:

> Sensitive to the critiques made of writers who neglect the "great issues," the author has attempted to raise some of those here, such as lodging, manual labor, food, time, space, nature, leisure, education, language, information, adultery, and the destruction and reproduction of human and animal species. A vast program which thousands of works in thousands of libraries have apparently not yet exhausted. Without claiming to offer answers, the present modest work has no other ambition than to contribute as best it can and within the limits of the genre to the general effort.[14]

It does not seem quite right to understand this as irony—except in the sense of a new kind of blank irony, a juxtaposition from which the older ironic conclusions are, for whatever reason, no longer drawn—any more than it seems right to characterize the insertion of the writer's conference as a satiric matter or an attack on Sartrean political values and committed literature. But it is just as surely a very peculiar, if not a historically original, way of handling an ideological dispute: to draw it inside the text in such a way that it also becomes part of the flat surface on which the other materials are spread out and displayed. Perhaps, indeed, this is how ideology ends, on some postmodern replay of the fifties end-of-ideology theses—not by evaporating in the general wallowing around in free elections and consumers' goods but rather by being inscribed on the Möbius strip of the media in such a way that what used to be virulent, subversive, or at least offensive ideas have now been transformed into so many material signifiers at which you gaze for a moment and then pass on.

What the episode does do, of course, is to invert the Sartrean comment quoted above: you may not be able to read the *nouveau roman* in a Third World country (itself a rather doubtful matter since Sarduy and other "new wave" postcolonial writers), but you cannot read the Third World *out* of this particular *nouveau roman*, whose contents are so systematically drawn from the internal Third World of Manhattan along with the external one of Latin America as to envelop all that and hold it within itself. Simon's relationship to such raw materials can in any case be said to be more realistic, on any acceptation of the word, than Robbe-Grillet's, whose pop comic-book narratives—postmodern in sharp contrast to Simon's modernist and painterly relationship to the visual—are in many ways more aestheticizing. The stereotype is what is already preconsumed, aesthetically prepared for consumption, whereas the palpable struggle to get sense data into sentences leaves a residue in its failure, lets you sense the presence of the referent outside the closed door.

That is, however, a door that is likely to remain closed for some time. For better or for worse, art does not seem in our society to offer any direct access to reality, any possibility of unmediated representation or of what used to be called realism. For us today, it is generally the case that what looks like realism turns out at best to offer unmediated access only to what we think about reality, to our images and ideological stereotypes about it (as in Doctorow). That is, of course, also part of the Real, and very much so indeed! But it is also characteristic of our period that we are very disinclined to think so, and that nothing chills us more, or is more calculated to break contact, than the discovery that this or that view of things is in reality "merely" someone else's projection. It needs to be labeled as such and stamped as "Jamesian" point of view: only in the population explosion of the postmodern there have come to be too many of these private worldviews, personal styles, or points of view for anyone to take them seriously, as was done in the modern period.

Art therefore yields social information primarily as symptom. Its specialized machinery (itself obviously symptomatic of social specialization more generally) is capable of registering and recording data with a precision unavailable in other modes of modern experience—in thought, for instance, or in daily life—but that data, reassembled, does not model reality in the form of things or substances, or social or institutional ontology. Rather, it tells of contradictions as such, which constitute the deepest form of social reality in our prehistory and must stand in for the "referent" for a long time to come.

Thus the very contradiction mentioned above in passing—our peculiar postmodern feeling about our own multiple subjectivities and points of view—that we are sick and tired of the subjective as such in its older classical forms (which include deep time and memory) and that we want to live on the surface for a while—this contradiction is fundamental in the development of modern and postmodern narrative, where its configurations allow us to take the temperature of the current situation. *Conducting Bodies* is in this sense a scandal: radicalizing the already scandalous but still tendential developments of *La Bataille de Pharsale*, this "novel" now confronts us with an impossible choice, an intolerable alternative: either we read the whole thing as one elaborate point of view, reconstructing an imaginary protagonist to whom we somehow, as ingeniously as possible, attribute everything (the trip to Manhattan, including the picture galleries, was a *memory* of a previous trip, etc.), or else we follow Simon's own lead and see these pages as a verbal equivalent of Rauschenberg's great collage installations.[15] The first alternative turns the novel back into Nathalie Sarraute or worse; the second retranslates it into the already published *Orion aveugle* and the contingent whimsies of the picture book. But what one should deduce from this contradiction is not some new aesthetic, in which the text is assigned to a new function to eschew each of these strategies of containment and to foreground contradiction as such: the inscription of the symptom can never be planned in advance, it must come after the fact, by indirection, and be the result of the failure or measurable deflection of a real project that has content.

Such a project might be glimpsed, for example, in the linguistic efforts with which we began, and in particular with the attempt to make language concrete, to make sentences somehow the vehicles for what Hegel called sense certainty. This is, however, a historical project, and not a very ancient one at that, for I suspect that few examples of this new vocation of literary language to register the sensory will be found much before the mid-nineteenth century. Why does this begin to happen in the new industrial "human age," and why are such impossible demands now made on language, whose other functions seemed to have performed well enough and given satisfaction in other modes of production? This question of social and historical interpretation is evidently both exacerbated and modified in the postmodern, as the example of Claude Simon testifies. For the high modern period, its paradoxes seem to have corresponded to what, in art, Adorno called nominalism; that is to say, the tendential repudiation of general or universal forms (including genre itself) and the intensifying will of the aesthetic to identify itself ever more closely with the here and now of this unique situation and this unique expression. I have, of course, followed Adorno here in defending the proposition that the work of art registers the logic of social development, production, and contradiction in ways usefully more precise than are available elsewhere,[16] but there is now a distinction to be made between the symptomaticity of high art in the modernist period (in which it stands in radical opposition to the nascent media or culture industry as such) and that of a residual elite culture in our own postmodern age, in which, owing in part to the democratization of culture generally, these two modes (high and low culture) have begun to fold back into one another. If nominalism in Adorno's period meant Schönberg and Beckett, in the postmodern it means a reduction to the body as such, which is less the triumph of ideologies of desire than it is the secret truth of contemporary pornography, as such just as faithfully registered in Simon (as we have seen) as any of the nobler linguistic or aesthetic symptoms. Yet as Deleuze has taught us, even under postmodernism we must distinguish between the body with organs and the body without. Paradoxically, this last, the inauthentic body which constitutes a visual unity and reinforces our sense or illusion of the unity of the personality—the body without organs—is the object of the pornographic and the glossy contents of so many images or strips of film. The body that has organs, however, and lots of them, to the point at which it disintegrates into a set of imperfectly reconnected "desiring machines," that body is the authentic space of pain as such, pain you cannot see or express, but which—"long after the doctor has removed his hands, the feeling of pressure persists, or rather the sensation that an enormous foreign body is still stuck in him like a wedge" (CC 47/36)—accompanies Simon's sentences as their ghostly referent and as a stand-in for the Real itself.

There is, however, another way of ending this discussion, and it has to do with endings themselves. Everything that is mixed and transitional, unclassifiable, about Simon emerges here when we try to think together the problems of the proairetic (identifying a gesture and its "folds" or temporal components), realism, and closure. What has been realistic about *Les corps conducteurs* is the consistent search for ever larger completed actions or events: whether this smaller one can be attached to a larger one and in what order, and finally whether the whole text imitates a single action of some magnitude. What is satisfying, then, is the downward turn, prepare to terminate!, the airplane finally in the process of landing. This is, of course, a valorization of closure which marks Simon as relatively traditional and acknowledges the existence in human life of complete events or experiences. In that respect, then, it is also significant, if not symptomatic, that the airplane does land, but at an intermediary stop somewhere; the flight was not direct; the passengers have to cool their heels at a small local airport in the middle of nowhere. Nor was the love affair conclusive either way, let alone the writers' conference. *Les Corps conducteurs* is, in that respect, one immense shaggy dog story which leads us firmly toward the completion of an incomplete thing. Only the final string seems decisive, the sick man's collapse in the hotel room, body on the floor, a now sightless eye open to the carpet's warp and woof. To reach the hotel room under these circumstances is certainly to achieve something; to turn the perceiving eye off at the end of the book—elsewhere Simon is fascinated by the blank screen of the movie theater, which hearkens back to Baudelaire's curtain rising on the empty stage of death—is to inscribe the form elegantly and autoreferentially within this content, but it may also be permitted to feel that this death is otherwise as much a meaningless interruption as any of the other termini randomly chosen.

6

Utopianism After the End

of Utopia

A certain spatial turn has often seemed to offer one of the more productive ways of distinguishing postmodernism from modernism proper, whose experience of temporality —existential time, along with deep memory—it is henceforth conventional to see as a dominant of the high modern. In hindsight, the "spatial form" of the great modernisms (a description we owe to Joseph Frank) proves to have more in common with the mnemonic unifying emblems of Frances Yates's memory palaces than with the discontinuous spatial experience and confusions of the postmodern, while the single-day urban synchronicity of *Ulysses* today reads more like a record of intermittent associative memories that find their temporal fulfillment in the dream theater of the climactic Nighttown section.

The distinction is between two forms of interrelationship between time and space rather than between these two inseparable categories themselves: even though the postmodern vision of the ideal or heroic schizophrenic (as in Deleuze) marks the impossible effort to imagine something like a pure experience of a spatial present beyond past history and future destiny or project. Yet the ideal schizophrenic's experience is still one of time, albeit of the eternal Nietzschean present. What one means by evoking its spatialization is rather the will to use and to subject time to the service of space, if that is now the right word for it.

And indeed the words and terms have their own complicity with the two epistemes, respectively: if *experience* and *expression* still seem largely apt in the cultural sphere of the modern, they are altogether out of place and anachronistic in a postmodern age, where, if temporality still has its place, it would seem better to speak of the *writing* of it than of any lived experience.

The writing of time, its enregisterment: such is the lesson, for example, of J. G. Ballard's haunting "Voices of Time,"[1] whose apocalyptic vision of the imminent end of the cosmos itself, running down like an unwound clock, and of the human race terminating in sleep (the first narcoma victims constituting "the vanguard of a vast somnabulist army massing for its last march" [85]), may at first resemble fin de siècle Wagnerian modernism or some grandiose and musical sociobiology. But what Ballard works on linguistically are, in fact, the multiple signatures of Time itself, which his own writing reads: as in the specimens and exhibits of his hero's temporal zoo or terminal laboratory. Not merely the deformed chimpanzee but also the mutations of the sea anemone (no longer sensitive to white light, but now to colors), the fruit fly, the enormous spider with blind eyes ("or rather, their optical sensitivity has shifted down the band; the retinas will only register gamma radiation. Your wristwatch has luminous hands. When you moved it across the window he started thinking" [91]), the frogs with antiradiation armor plating, the sunflower now living the *longue durée* of geological epochs ("it literally *sees* time. The older the surrounding environment, the more sluggish its metabolism" [93]), and finally, above all DNA itself, that ultimate script, which is literally deteriorating: "The ribonucleic acid templates which unravel the protein chains in all living organisms are wearing out, the dies enscribing the protoplasmic signatures have become blunted. After all, they've been running now for over a thousand million years. It's time to retool" (97).

It is not merely on the inner clock of the organism that time can be read: the galaxies themselves literally speak it, as when "mysterious emissaries from Orion" meet the *Apollo 7* astronauts on the moon and warn them "that the exploration of deep space was pointless, that they were too late, as the life of the universe is now virtually over!" (103). Meanwhile, numerical signals from Canes Venitici

$$96,688,365,498,695$$
$$96,688,365,498,694$$

beam a countdown to Earth. "The big spirals there are breaking up, and they're saying goodbye . . . it's been estimated that by the time this series reaches zero the universe will have just ended" (109–10). "Thoughtful of them to let us know what the real time is," retorts another character.

The universal fascination of contemporary (or poststructural or postmodern) theory with DNA—the exemplum of the concept of "code" for Jean Baudrillard, for example, who is himself an enthusiastic reader of Ballard—lies not only in its status as a kind of writing (which displaces

biology from the physics model to that of information theory) but also
in its active and productive power as template and as computer program:
a writing that reads you, rather than the other way round. DNA as "the
perforated sheet music of a player piano" (91): Ballard's story is also
very specifically a story about "future" art or postmodern aesthetics
—indeed, the opposition between two new kinds of spatial art, the mandala of the sixties built by the hero in the last stages of his own narcoma, at the center of which he will expire, and the "atrocity exhibit" of
the other, Byronic figure, which foreshadows Ballard's own later work
in its conception of the newer art as a version of that emergent form of
the creative exhibitions of the postmodern museums today, in this case
a collection of the high-tech reproductive traces—from X-rays to printouts—of the most atrocious traumas of the postcontemporary world,
from Hiroshima through Vietnam and the Congo to the multiple car
crashes with which Ballard himself was momentarily obsessed (most
notably in the novel Crash). Yet in the framework of a period concept of
postmodernism, one wants to estrange these multiple figures of writing
or inscription and reposition them within some enlarged conception of
the spatial itself.

The initial approach to this particular "great transformation"—the
displacement of time, the spatialization of the temporal—often registers its novelties by way of a sense of loss. Indeed, it seems just possible
that the pathos of entropy in Ballard may be just that: the *affect* released
by the minute, and not unenthusiastic, exploration of this whole new
world of spatiality, and the sharp pang of the death of the modern that
accompanies it. At any rate, from this nostalgic and regressive perspective—that of the older modern and its temporalities—what is mourned
is the memory of deep memory; what is enacted is a nostalgia for nostalgia, for the grand older extinct questions of origin and telos, of deep
time and the Freudian Unconscious (dispatched by Foucault at one blow
in the *History of Sexuality*), for the dialectic also, as well as all the
monumental forms left high and dry by the ebb tide of the modern
moment, forms whose Absolutes are no longer audible to us, illegible
hieroglyphs of the demiurgic within the technocratic world.

We need a detour through the modern, then, in order to grasp what is
historically original in the postmodern and its spatialisms. Indeed, such
a history lesson is the best cure for nostalgic pathos, minimally teaching us, by way of Necessity, that the way back to the modern is sealed for
good. Presupposed in what follows, of course, is a correlation between
the transition from the modern to the postmodern, and that economic

or systemic transformation of an older monopoly capitalism (the so-called moment of imperialism) into its new multinational and high-tech mutation. Increasingly spatial features of a new type can be derived from such economic accounts, but any concrete account of the new spatial aesthetic and its existential life world demands some intermediary steps, or what the dialectic used to call mediations.

Thus, "conceptual art," too, surely stands under the sign of spatialization, in the sense in which, one is tempted to say, every problematization or dissolution of inherited form leaves us high and dry in space itself. Conceptual art may be described as a Kantian procedure whereby, on the occasion of what first seems to be an encounter with a work of art of some kind, the categories of the mind itself—normally not conscious, and inaccessible to any direct representation or to any thematizable self-consciousness or reflexibility—are flexed, their structuring presence now felt laterally by the viewer like musculature or nerves of which we normally remain insensible, in the form of those peculiar mental experiences Lyotard terms paralogisms—in other words, perceptual paradoxes that we cannot think or unravel by way of conscious abstractions and which bring us up short against the visual occasions. Bruce Nauman's installations, say, or even Sherrie Levine's representations of representations, are infernal machines for generating such unresolvable yet concretely visual and perceptual antinomies that eject the viewing mind once again into the bewildering stages of the paralogical process itself. "Conceptual" here designates the ultimate *subject* of the process (in the experimental sense)—namely, the perceptual categories of the mind itself, provided we also understand that these can never become visible as objects in their own right, and that at every stage of the viewing process all we have are material occasions for it, in the form of what used to be thought of as "works of art." This is the sense in which the conceptual operation spatializes, since it teaches us over and over again that the spatial field is the only element in which we move and the only "certainty" of an experience (but *not* in the sense that these spatial pretexts—called conceptual works—are themselves full forms of materialized meaning in their own right, as the classical work of art claimed to be). The relationship between the vocation of such conceptual art and some of the classic texts of deconstruction (which can be described in much the same way) seems clear but raises the further question of the relationship of this newer *reading* to spatialization itself. Is, for example, the reading closure of a philosophical or theoretical "essay" not in some way analogous to the formal boundaries of the traditional work of art, such that the deconstructive problematization of reading itself also tends to open the frame and leave us elsewhere? That the widespread textualization of the outside world in contemporary thought (the body as a text, the state as a text, consumption as a text) should itself be seen as a fundamental form of postmodern spatialization seems evident and has been presupposed in what follows.

As for conceptual art and its evolution, however, it is worth adding that its later political variant—in the work of Hans Haacke, for example—redirects the deconstruction of perceptual categories specifically onto the framing institutions themselves. Here the paralogisms of the "work" include the museum, by drawing its space back into the material pretext and making a mental circuit through the artistic infrastructure unavoidable. Indeed, in Haacke it is not merely with museum space that we come to rest, but rather the museum itself, as an institution, opens up into its network of trustees, their affiliations with multinational corporations, and finally the global system of late capitalism proper, such that what used to be the limited and Kantian project of a restricted conceptual art expands into the very ambition of cognitive mapping itself (with all its specific representational contradictions). In Haacke, at any rate, the spatializing tendencies inherent from the beginning in conceptual art become overt and inescapable in the uneasy gestalt alternation between a "work of art" that abolishes itself to disclose the museum structure which contains it and one that expands its authority to include not merely that institutional structure but the institutional totality in which it is itself subsumed.

To mention Haacke at this point is, of course, to raise one of the fundamental problems posed by postmodernism generally (and not least by the very spatializing tendencies under discussion here): namely, the possible political content of postmodernist art. That such political content will necessarily be structurally and dialectically very different from what was formally possible in an older modernism (let alone in realism itself) is already implicit in virtually all of the alternative descriptions of the postmodern; but it may be dramatized by a convenient shorthand problem in political aesthetics posed in an earlier chapter: the question why Andy Warhol's Coca-Cola bottles and Campbell's soup cans—so obviously representations of commodity or consumer fetishism—do not seem to function as critical or political statements. As for systematic accounts of the postmodern, however (including my own), when they succeed, they fail. And the more powerfully one has been able to underscore and isolate the antipolitical features of the newer cultural dominant—its loss of historicity, for example—the more one paints oneself into a corner and makes any repolitization of such culture a priori inconceivable. Yet the totalizing account of the postmodern always included a space for various forms of oppositional culture: those of marginal groups, those of radically distinct residual or emergent cultural languages, their existence being already predicated by the necessarily uneven development of late capitalism, whose First World produces a Third World within itself by its own inner dynamic. In this sense postmodernism is "merely" a cultural dominant. To describe it in terms of cultural *hegemony* is not to suggest some massive and uniform cultural homogeneity of the social field but very precisely to imply its coexistence with other resistant and heterogeneous forces which it has a vocation to subdue and incorporate. The case of Haacke poses, however, a radically different problem, for his is a kind of cultural production which is clearly postmodern and equally clearly political and oppositional—something that does not compute within the paradigm and does not seem to have been theoretically foreseen by it.

The scope of the present essay, however, is more restricted than this; if it must specify the ultimate political coordinates of the problem of the evaluation of postmodernism as we have just done, our topic here is the narrower one of the *Utopian* impulses to be detected in various forms of the postmodern today. One wants to insist very strongly on the necessity of the reinvention of the Utopian vision in any contemporary politics: this lesson, which Marcuse first taught us, is part of the legacy of the sixties which must never be abandoned in any reevaluation of that period and of our relationship to it. On the other hand, it also must be acknowledged that Utopian visions are not yet themselves a politics.

Utopia, however, poses its own specific problems for any theory of the postmodern and any periodization of it. For according to one conventional view, postmodernism is also at one with the definitive "end of ideologies," a development announced (along with "postindustrial society") by the conservative ideologues of the fifties (Daniel Bell, Lipset, etc.), "disproven" dramatically by the sixties, only to "come true" in the seventies and eighties. "Ideology" in this sense meant Marxism, and its "end" went hand in hand with the end of Utopia," already secured by the great postwar anti-Stalinist dystopias, such as 1984. But "Utopia" in that period was also a code word that simply meant "socialism" or any revolutionary attempt to create a radically different society, which the ex-radicals of that time identified almost exclusively with Stalin and Soviet communism. This generalized "end of ideology and of Utopia," celebrated by the conservatives in the fifties, was also the burden of Marcuse's *One-Dimensional Man*, which deplored it from a radical perspective. Meanwhile, in our own period virtually all the significant manifestos of postmodernism celebrate a similar development—from Venturi's "irony" to Achille Bonito-Oliva's "deideologization," which now comes to mean the eclipse of "belief" and of the twofold Absolutes of high modernism proper and the "political" (which is to say, of Marxism).

If one inserts the sixties into this historical narrative, everything changes; "Marcuse" virtually becomes the name for a whole explosive renewal of Utopian thinking and imagination, and for a rebirth of the older narrative form. Ursula K. LeGuin's *The Dispossessed* (1974) was the richest literary reinvention of the genre, while Ernest Callenbach's *Ecotopia* (1975) provided a summa of all the disparate sixties Utopia impulses and also revived the (itself properly Utopian) ambition to write a book around which a whole political movement might crystallize, as was the case with Edward Bellamy's *Looking Backward* and the mass movement around his Nationalist party in the analogous earlier stage of North American political Utopianism. The Utopian impulses of the sixties did not, however, coalesce in that way, but rather produced a vital range of micropolitical movements (neighborhood, race, ethnic, gender, and ecological) whose common denominator is the resurgent problematic of Nature in a variety of (often anticapitalist) forms. It is certain that these social and political developments can also be reread within our first paradigm as constituting the repudiation of a traditional left party politics and thereby, in their own way, as another "end of ideology." Nor is it clear to what degree these multiple Utopian impulses have been prolonged into the late seventies and eighties (Margaret Atwood's *Handmaid's Tale* [1985] has, for example, been assessed as the first feminist *dystopia* and thereby the end of the very rich feminist work in the Utopian genre as such). On the other hand, it also seems to be plausible to return to the phenomenon of spatialization already mentioned here, and to see in all these varied Utopian visions as they have emerged from the sixties the development of a whole range of properly spatial Utopias in which the transformation of social relations and political institutions is projected onto the vision of place and landscape, including the human body. Spatialization, then, whatever it may take away in the capacity to think time and History, also opens a door onto a whole new domain for libidinal investment of the Utopian and even the protopolitical type. It is, at any rate, this door ajar

Robert Gober, "Untitled Installation"

that we seek, if not to pry open, then at least to peer through in what follows.

Robert Gober's installation seems an excellent place with which to begin this inquiry since it offers us, at the very least, an empty doorframe. It also forces us to ask—but helps us answer—the obvious question as to the relevance of concepts of spatialization when we are dealing with what are already very obviously spatial arts. But postmodern spatialization here plays itself out in the relationship and the rivalry among the various spatial media—in the claims and formal powers of video over against film, for example, or of photography over against painting as a medium. Indeed, we may speak of spatialization here as the process whereby the traditional fine arts are *mediatized*: that is, they now come to consciousness of themselves as various media within a mediatic system in which their own internal production also constitutes a symbolic message and the taking of a position on the status of the medium in question. Gober's installation—which includes what might once have been called painting, sculpture, writing, and even architecture—thus draws its effects from a place not above the media but within their system of relationships: something it seems better to characterize as a kind of reflexivity rather than the more conventional motion of "mixed media," which normally implies the emergence of a kind of superproduct or transcendental object—the *Gesamtkunstwerk*—from this synthesis or combination. But this installation is very clearly not an art object in that sense.

There is, first of all, no "representation" to look at. The door, the painting, the mound, the text, none of them are in themselves the object of our undivided attention; but one might have said as much for the elements of a Haacke installation as well or, beyond it, of the quintessentially postmodern dispositions of Nam June Paik, where only the most misguided museum visitor would look for the "art" in the content of the video images themselves, for instance. Yet between Haacke, (or even Paik's nonpolitical "conceptual" art), and this particular space—which also in some sense evokes a "concept"—there would seem to be a profound methodological difference, virtually an inversion in the operations in question. Haacke's work is situation-specific, as has been said. It foregrounds the museum as such and in its institutionality: something that, utterly absent from Gober, can be said to reveal the bad or nonpolitical Utopianism of Gober's installation, if not to confirm one's worst fears as to the inherent idealism of the project.

Haacke deconstructs: the fashionable word seems quite unavoidable in thinking of him (and recovers some of its original, strong, political, subversive meaning in his context). His art has a European culture-political corrosiveness; Gober's is as American as the Shakers or Charles Ives, its absent community, its "invisible public" constituted out of readers of Emerson rather than of Adorno. I'm tempted to suggest that this

Nam June Paik, "T.V. Clock"

form of conceptual art—for such it is—differs from its opposite number in that it constructs, not an already existing concept of the type that
Haacke and others take to pieces, but rather the idea of a concept that
does not yet exist.

But as we have already seen in our discussion of architecture, the
Utopian value of a merely cultural modification is an ambiguous judgment, whose signs and symptoms can be read either way—fully as much
as signs of systematic replication as of impending change. So it is that
modernist space offers itself as the *novum*, as the breakthrough onto
new forms of life itself, the radically emergent, that "air from other planets" (Stefan George) that Schönberg, and after him Marcuse, liked to
evoke, the first telltale sign of the dawning of a new age. Now, in the
hindsight of failures of modern architecture, modernist space proves to
have merely reproduced the logic of the system itself at a greater level
of intensification, running on ahead and transferring its spirit of rationalization and functionalism, of therapeutic positivism and standardization, onto built space not yet even dreamed of. The alternatives would
be decideable only by way of the related historical question of whether
modernism in fact completed its mission and its project, or was interrupted and remained fundamentally incomplete and unfilled.

Still, the postmodern now suggests an additional possibility, some-

Nam June Paik, "T.V. Garden"

thing like a third reading, in which the conception of a Utopian anticipation is foregrounded in a theoretical, non-figurative way. It is within
the perspective of this possibility, which seems to renounce the protopolitical vocation of Le Corbusier to transform our built space at once
and against all economic and social obstacles, that Gober's project can
best be grasped. It can be seen, borrowing an expression from Althusser,

not so much as the production of some form of Utopian space but rather as the production of the *concept* of such space. And even this must be understood not in the sense in which contemporary architects have with increasing frequency designed unbuildable "projects" (in the strict architectural sense of plans, drawings, and models) and published grotesque and parodic projections of buildings and urban complexes, unimaginable in any light of day, that resemble the visual records of Piranesi's fantasies more than his views of Rome or Le Corbusier's notebooks. Gober is not an architect, even in that greatly expanded sense of the word, although his own "sculptures" derive very specifically from the inner space of buildings and from those intermundia between furniture and the residential shell which, sometimes thought of as mere plumbing, are the visible apparatus of kitchen and bathroom equipment.

This installation does not seek, like the "projects" mentioned above, to spring the representation of some new kind of dwelling onto the Utopian screen of the mind's eye; and it is as a terminological way of differentiating this operation from such representations, fully as much as an intervention in current notions of conceptual art, that its characterization —the production of a concept of space—systematically functions: it is meant to stress, over against the deconstructive operation, the production of a new kind of mental entity, but at the same time to exclude the assimilation of that entity to any kind of positive representation, and in particular to any sketch for an "affirmative" architecture. The operation is therefore a peculiar one indeed, which merits closer description.

What we are offered is a door with its frame (Gober), a mound (Meg Webster), a traditional American landscape painting (Albert Bierstadt), and what may be called a "postmodernist text" (Richard Prince). The combination of these objects as a unified exhibit within museum space certainly awakens representational anticipations and impulses, and in particular emits an imperative to unify them perceptually, to invent the aesthetic totalization from within which these disparate objects and items can be grasped—if not as parts of a whole, then at least as elements of some complete thing. This is an imperative, as we have suggested, which is systematically thwarted by the "work" itself (if one can still continue to use that word), but not, as has also been suggested, primarily in order to foreground and rebuke our own (Kantian) longing for the form of the "whole" or the "complete thing," or the "work," or "representation" itself, as is the case with analogous frustration in so-called conceptual art.

For one thing, the heterogeneity of Gober's items or elements is not merely the abstract differentiation of uncombinable raw materials or types of content—as is the case with postmodernist "texts" generally —but it is also "doubled" and "strengthened," as it were, by a more genuinely concrete and even social heterogeneity, which is that of collective work itself. The multiple histories of forms that distance each of these items from each other—the "mound" with its aesthetic precursors, the ironic "text" with its own rather different ones, not to mention the Hudson River school and its own specific ancient history—all of these distinct artistic materials, which emit their own discordant formal and material voices, also here summon up the ghostly, but social, presence of real human collaborators, who raise again the issues of the subject and of agency, even the false problems of collective subject and individual intention, along with the nonsolution of "signatures." This second level of the work then amplifies and orchestrates the heterogeneity of the first purely formal problem of aesthetic reception and unification, turning it into a social one without in any way effacing the formal dilemma—how to see all these things together and invent a perceptual relationship between them—which now remains alongside it like a second, no less unbearable, scandal. Meanwhile, the door off its hinges continues to urge us to put all this back together, all the while inscribing itself as disjoined, as we gradually get it through our heads that producing a concept is uncomfortably different from merely having one, or even thinking one through.

Socially, however, this collective presence of the work also begins to acquire a certain historical precision and to differentiate itself, no less uncomfortably, from older, already existing but perhaps no longer functional, categories of the *Mitsein*. For one thing, the family—as the Ur-old notion of some fundamental collective living—is utterly absent from this idea of a room, which does not even feel the need to subvert or deconstruct familial values any longer. This, then, is the final and most decisive feature that separates Gober's Utopian room from any genuinely architectural project (even of the "Utopian" type), since these last must necessarily come to grips with the problem of the family and of the persistence of family structure, even where they seek to collectivize it, as most notably in communal kitchens and dining areas (a preoccupation which is present in Utopian discourse from More all the way to Bellamy's seemingly middle-class apartments in *Looking Backward*—which ostentatiously lack kitchens— and beyond to our own time). The absence of any problematic of the family here can be read as a gender statement, but it also surely displaces the matter of the collective from the domestic to the realm of collective work per se, here identified as artistic collaboration.

But at this point a second historical specification intervenes: for whatever this collaboration may be, it is surely also no longer the vanguard project of the older modernist avant-gardes, whose disappearance or impossibility has, of course, often been taken as the constitutive feature of all the postmodernisms. This installation does not, in other words, project either a stylistic politics of a more generalizable type nor any particular cultural one, as surrealism, or any of the architectural avant-gardes, once preeminently did—either propagating the protopolitical virus through the power of some new period style or invoking a universal program for radical culture-political change by way of this or that individual work or text, building, or painting. Here also, then, as in the other postmodernisms, we are beyond the avant-gardes; yet with this difference that collective work is here still affirmed as something other than mere period likeness or the anecdotal meeting of the minds between individual painters or architects. The ultimate meaning of this affirmation of the collaborative, which eschews the organization of a movement or a school, ignores the vocation of style, and omits the trappings of the manifesto or program, is not the least enigma with which the Gober installation confronts us; but it is an enigma which is at the very least at one with all the new and more properly political questions that the "new social movements" or contemporary "micropolitics" have placed on the agenda.

Returning now to the more formal "reading" of the thing itself, it may first be observed that it involves another matter which any future historians of our own cultural and theoretical moment are bound to consider significant and symptomatic: namely, the return and the revival, if not the reinvention in some unexpected form, of *allegory* as such, including the complex theoretical problems of allegorical interpretation. For the displacement of modernism by postmodernism can also be measured and detected in the crisis of the older aesthetic absolute of the Symbol, as its formal and linguistic values secured their hegemony in the long period from romanticism to New Criticism and the canonization of "modernist" works in the university system in the late 1950s. If the symbolic is (overhastily) assimilated to various organic conceptions of the work of art and of culture itself, then the return of the repressed of its various opposites, and of a whole range of overt or covert theories of the allegorical, can be characterized by a generalized sensitivity, in our own time, to breaks and discontinuities, to the heterogeneous (not merely in works of art), to Difference rather than Identity, to gaps and holes rather than seamless webs and triumphant narrative progressions, to social differentiation rather than to Society as such and its "totality," in which older doctrines of the monumental work and the "concrete universal" bathed and reflected themselves. The allegorical, then —whether those of DeMan or Benjamin, of the revalorization of medieval or of non-European texts, of Althusserian or Lévi-Straussian structuralisms, of Kleinian psychologies or Lacanian psychoanalysis—can be minimally formulated as the question posed to thinking by the awareness of incommensurable distances within its object of thought, and as the various new interpretive answers devised to encompass phenomena about which we are at least minimally agreed that no single thought or theory encompasses any of them. Allegorical interpretation is then first and foremost an interpretive operation which begins by acknowledging the impossibility of interpretation in the older sense, and by including that impossibility in its own provisional or even aleatory movements.

For the newer allegory is horizontal rather than vertical: if it must still attach its one-on-one conceptual labels to its objects after the fashion of *The Pilgrim's Progress*, it does so in the conviction that those objects (along with their labels) are now profoundly relational, indeed are themselves constructed by their relations to each other. When we add to this the inevitable mobility of such relations, we begin to glimpse the process of allegorical interpretation as a kind of scanning that, moving back and forth across the text, readjusts its terms in constant modification of a type quite different from our stereotypes of some static medieval or biblical decoding, and which one would be tempted (were it not also an old-fashioned word!) to characterize as dialectical.

(It is perhaps worth observing, in passing, that the allegorical method evoked here is very much what is demanded and mobilized by the periodizing schema of the modernism/postmodernism break as such. Here again, then, as so often, postmodernism theory is itself an example of what it claims to anatomize: the newer allegorical structures are postmodern and cannot be articulated without the allegory of postmodernism itself.)

Such is, at any rate, the way in which the reading of the Gober installation imposes itself: as a constant movement from one item to another in which each term, as it confronts one of the other three, finds its value and its meaning subtly or not so subtly modified. This movement can be crudely described if it is understood that any direction and any starting point are possible and that what is here offered is only one of the varied trajectories and combinations logically possible (and perhaps one

Robert Gober, "Untitled Installation"

of the more obvious ones). Thus it is only apparently "logical" or "natural" to begin with the frame itself—house, dwelling—which as a built space and a habitation, a product of society and of culture, to stands in most immediate opposition to the mound, itself now marking the place of Nature in a host of seventeenth-century pastoral or Shakespearean senses. On this first reading, both the social (the doorframe) and the natural (the mound) are taken as realities, as ontological dimensions of the world.

What that pairing off of meanings does next is to suggest that the "world" itself—as a combination of the social or cultural and the natural—can be opposed to that rather different matter which is its own *representation*, the aesthetic realm, in which both nature and culture (both the natural and the social) can be objects of representation. Indeed, both are present in dialectical relationship to each other in the Hudson River school painting, insofar as a particular kind of landscape—better still, the ideology of a particular kind of landscape—at one and the same time emits a host of precise ideological messages about the "society" and the social and historical realities, which, absent from it, are no less intensely the implied object of its construction. The traditional landscape painting, then, in this move, retroactively transforms the first two seemingly ontological realities of the social and the natural into ideology and into representation.

But who ever raises the question of representation in our own time at once opens up a new force field in which it is clear that the older painting is itself a historical document and a dead moment in the history of the evolution of North American culture. With this modification of our focus on the landscape painting, we are already in the process of establishing some more scandalous and historicist link with the final item in the collection; namely, the virulent object from the present, the Richard Prince text, whose very enigmatic and "conceptual" structure at once announces the presence of the postmodern and transforms all three previous terms into nostalgia and Americana and unexpectedly projects them into a now distant past, about which not the least embarrassing question is whether, in full postmodernist late capitalism with its perpetual present and its multiple historical amnesias, it has itself any more genuine existence than that of a stereotype or a cultural fantasy.

At this point, however, the signifying trajectory does not come to a halt but rather begins in earnest. For we can now move from the postmodernist text to the equally postmodernist mound and ask ourselves whether—far from marking the place of Nature—it does not rather constitute something like the grave of Nature, as the latter has systematically been eclipsed from the object world and the social relations of a society whose tendential domination over its Other (the nonhuman or the formerly natural) is more complete than at any other moment in human history. From that perspective, as the mourning for a lost object which can scarcely even be remembered as such, the path back through the other objects shows them radically modified and transformed as well. The doorframe—the metonym of human habitation and the social —now turns out to have been not merely cultural, and a representation, but a nostalgic representation of a more natural form of dwelling. It now "opens the door" to a host of economic and historical anxieties about real estate speculation and the disappearance of the construction of older single-family housing which are the other face of the "postmodern" in our own time, and which then draw the landscape painting after themselves into a whole new social reality in which, from a document of cultural history, it becomes an antique and a commodity, a bit of yuppie furnishing, and in that sense no less "contemporary" than its postmodern opposite number. As for this last, however, on our new trajectory, it begins to foreground itself more insistently as language and as communication (rather than as artistic production in any older sense) and brings into this new construction the omnipresence of the media as such, as that has seemed for many to constitute one of the fundamental features of contemporary society.

At this point, however, the victory of the postmodern—its triumph over these older seemingly nostalgic items that accompany it—is by no means secure. For if the framed text is the heightened spice, the jarring note, Barthes's *punctum* in the sense of the most active element, which sets all the rest in bewildering movement, it is also the most fragile of the associated objects, and not merely because in the content of its humor it bears a kind of nostalgia and an older ethnicity within itself. Now, however, in one of those reversals characteristic of any "dominant" —such as the current, largely "structuralist" episteme in which Language as such is grasped as the bottom line, the fundamental reality, the "ultimately determining instance"—this written text comes before us with an insubstantiality that only tends to reconfirm and strengthen the robust visual presence of its neighbors.

What then begins to happen here is that, from mere nostalgic reflexes, these articles slowly take on the positive and active value of conscious resistance, as choices and symbolic acts that now repudiate the dominant poster-and-decorative culture and thereby assert themselves as something emergent rather than something residual. What was the delectation with a fantasy past now turns out to look more like the construction of a Utopian future.

What has been speculatively outlined here is, however, not merely an "in-terminable" trajectory from one provisional "interpretation" to another competing one. It can take many other forms, and to break off our account at this point is not to imply that that "Utopian future" has in any way been secured, even as an image or a representation. The "items" continue to pair off against each other in unstable constellations, and the quality of the "thought" waxes and wanes, brightens and grows more somber again in ceaseless variation.

The installation also emits a different kind of message, which, as has already been intimated, concerns the system of the fine arts as such, or, in more contemporary language, the relations of the various media to each other. Like synesthesia in the literary real (Baudelaire), the ideal of the *Gesamtkunstwerk* respected the "system" of the various fine arts and paid it tribute in the notion of some vaster overarching *synthesis* in which they might all somehow "combine" (the theoretical and philosophical parallel to yesterday's notion of the *interdisciplinary* is striking), generally under the "fraternal leadership" of one of them—in the case of Wagner, of music. The present installation is, as has been suggested, no longer that, not least because the very "system" on which the older synthesis was based has itself become problematical, along with the claim of any one of the individual fine arts to its own intrinsic autonomy or semiautonomy. The media here associated do not, in other words, draw on the inner coherence of a genuinely sculptural language (in Gober himself or in Webster), nor on that of a still internally coherent tradition of painting as such (traditional landscape, postmodern "painting"), nor even on any primacy of the architectural as a set of forms. If this is in some sense "mixed media" (the contemporary equivalent of the *Gesamtkunstwerk* but with all the differences already enumerated), the "mix" comes first and redefines the media involved by implication a posteriori.

Nonetheless, it would seem clear that a secondary message about painting, which it would be exaggerated to describe as the latter's dethronement, is here present and will inevitably be read off the post-contemporary situation itself, and the debates about the status of some properly "postmodern" painting which have become as central to its practice as those around architecture were yesterday. For the differentiation of painting into "landscape" and "text" more brutally problematizes the claims of this particular fine art than anything in the sculptural or architectural components. Meanwhile, that the question of the Utopian impulse is at issue here will be evident not merely from the status of painting generally in an older modernism but, in particular, from John Berger's evaluation of cubism, which we have already alluded to:

> During the first decade of this century a transformed world became theoretically possible and the necessary forces of change could already be recognized as existing. Cubism was the art which reflected the possibility of this transformed world and the confidence it inspired. Thus, in a certain sense, it was the most modern art—as it was also the most philosophically complex—*which has yet existed*."[2]

Berger explicitly glosses these tenses as meaning not merely that the Utopian vocation of painting embodied in cubism was closed off by the war and the failure of global revolution that followed it, but also that this failed cubism of the past is also our future insofar as it expresses a Utopian impulse that we have not yet been able to reinvent. Yet the other avant-gardes all have their specific Utopian moments as well: in dada, an explosive negativity which is not merely critical but embodies the very dynamic of history itself as "the unceasing overthrow of the objective forms that shape the life of man."[3] The Utopian vocation of surrealism lies in its attempt to endow the object world of a damaged and broken industrial society with the mystery and the depth, the "magical" qualities (to speak like either Weber or the Latin Americans), of an Unconscious that seems to speak and vibrate through those things.

It is therefore against these multiple Utopian vocations of modernist painting that the implications of Gober's stance (itself positioned, as we have said, in some new kind of Utopian space) must be read. Yet the new turn of the screw of the contemporary situation results in the transformation of any assessment of postmodern painting into a set of statements about its various media others, and most specifically about photography, whose extraordinary reinvention today (in theory as well as in practice) is a fundamental fact and symptom of the postmodern period —something the photographic segment of the present exhibit triumphantly demonstrates at the same time that it secures its consonance with the installation segment by revealing an unsuspected Utopian vocation of its own. One's sense is indeed that the various photographic movements that were contemporaneous with the modern movement in painting still tended to borrow their aesthetic and apologetic justifications from that medium, at best seeing their task as a "redemption of physical reality" (Kracauer's characterization of filmic realism) by way a revelation of the visible world which was also, in various modes and styles, the latter's unmasking. The vocation of contemporary photography may now be somewhat different from that, as we will try to show. The demonstration demands a detour through the equally transformed apologetics of postmodern painting, in which, however, the dialectics of construction and deconstruction which we have found helpful in evaluating Gober's installation will unexpectedly reappear in new context.

What is initially certain, at any rate, is that the spokespeople for postmodern painting, whatever the particular tendency they promote within that pluralism which is its most enthusiastically celebrated feature, agree on the renunciation, by contemporary neofigurative painting, of painting's older (modernist) Utopian vocations: it is no longer to do anything beyond itself (including the transaesthetic thrust of the great modernisms). With the loss of such ideological missions, and the liberation from the history of its forms as a kind of telos, painting is now free to follow "a nomadic attitude which advocates the reversibility of all the languages of the past" (IT 6)[4] a conception which wishes "to deprive language of meaning," tending "to consider the language of painting entirely interchangeable, removing it from fixation and mania and delivering it to a practice which sees value in inconstancy. . . . The contiguity of different styles produces a chain of images, all of which work on the basis of shifting and progression which is fluid rather than planned . . . " (IT 18–20). "In this way meaning is bewildered, attenuated, made relative, and related to other semantic substances which float behind the recovery of this innumerable systems of marks. There results a sort of mildness of the work, which no longer speaks peremptorily, nor bases its appeal on ideological fixity, but dissolves in multidirectional digression" (IT 24). These very interesting and pertinent characterizations unequally raise two related issues about the newer painting. The first is what is sometimes called its historicism; namely, its secession from a genuine history or dialectic of its styles and of the content of its forms, something which "frees" it to recover "painting styles . . . as a sort of objct trouvé, detached from their semantic references as from every metaphorical association. They are consumed in the execution of the work, which becomes the crucible in which their exemplarity is purified. For this reason, it is possible to renew references that are otherwise irreconcilable, and to interweave different cultural temperatures," grafting "unheard-of hybrids and different dislocations of language with respect to their historical situation" (IT 56–58). "A neomanneristic sensibility takes over, a sensibility that runs through the history of art without rhetoric and pathetic identification, displaying instead flexible laterality capable of translating the historic depth of the recovered languages into a disenchanted and uninhibited *superficiality*" (IT 66–68). The other feature of the postmodern condition implied but not addressed in such remarks is, of course, our old friend "the death of the subject," the end of individuality, the eclipse of subjectivity in a new anonymity that is not puritanical extinction or repression but probably not often either that schizophrenic flux and nomadic release it has often been celebrated as.

Surrealism without the Unconscious: such is the way in which one is also tempted to characterize the newer painting, in which the most uncontrolled kinds of figuration emerge with a depthlessness that is not even hallucinatory, like the free association of an impersonal collective subject, without the charge and investment either of a personal Unconscious or of a group one: Chagall's folk iconography without Judaism or the peasants, Klee's stick drawings without his peculiar personal project, schizophrenic art without schizophrenia, "surrealism" without its manifesto or its avant-garde. Does this mean that what we used to call the Unconscious was itself a mere historical illusion produced by certain kinds of theories in a certain situation-specific configuration of the social field (including certain kinds of urban objects and certain kinds of urban people)? The point, however, is to search out radical historical difference, and not to take sides or hand out historical certificates of value.

It strikes one then, in that spirit, that neofigurative painting today is very much that extraordinary space through which all the images and icons of the culture spill and float, haphazard, like a logjam of the visual, bearing off with them everything from the past under the name of "tradition" that arrived in the present in time to be reified visually, broken into pieces, and swept away with the rest. This is the sense in which I associated such painting with the term *deconstructive*, for it constitutes an immense analytic dissection of everything and a lancing of the visual abscess. Whether the operation has therapeutic value—in the sense in which Susan Sontag once evoked a kind of "ecology" of images, an anticonsumerist hunger or water cure for image society[5]—is far from clear. It is in any case difficult to see the function of a concept like "the cure" in the absence of either an individual or a collective subject. Yet a powerful movement of interference—clouds of electrical short circuits, the sizzling of specular or even scopophilic burnt flesh—disengages itself from such painting at its best, as in the work of David Salle. His archetypal category (for it is not a form, exactly) seems to be the empty organization of the dyptich or double panel (sometimes rewritten in the form of superpositions, overdrawing and overdoodling), where, however, the content that traditionally accompanied such a gesture ("look now upon this picture and on this")—authentification and deauthentification, unmasking, the puncturing of one sign system in the name of another, or of "reality" itself—remains absent; while at the same time the end of ideology, in particular the end of Freud and the end of psychoanalysis, ensures the incapacity of any hermeneutic or interpretive system to domesticate these juxtapositions and turn them into usable meanings. When they work, therefore, it is difficult to distinguish between the shock that certifies them as "working" and that "mildness" of which Bonito-Oliva spoke, which results from the abstention of the art object to address and hector you for ideological purposes, but also from its dissolution into "multidimensional digression."

David Salle, "Wild Locusts Ride"

In this respect, then, it seems useful and instructive to juxtapose this practice of fragmentation within the picture—dyptich framing, sequential collage, scissored images, which it may be best to term *screen segmentation*—as it is practiced in what I'm tempted to call the base-and-superstructure features of David Salle and also in various ways in the photographers exhibited here: Wasow's rephotographed and recombined images, Simpson's "iris"es and illustrative captions, Larry Johnson's mottoes, Cypis's multipaneled anatomy exhibits, Welling's literal *analyses*; even Wall's transparencies may be looked at in this way, if the actual photograph is separated from the luminous or even stereoscopic performance to which it is subjected (like a dimension underneath, rather than, as in Salle, the overprint or the side by side). The parts and segments of these "works" or "texts" do not demystify one another, I am tempted to say (although Simpson's art comes the closest, and the "feminist" components of Cypis's—that is to say, the pieces of women's bodies—ensure a certain obligatory effort at radical reading). But the matter may best be approached by way of perception: we're told, for example, that photographic perception very much depends on *identifi-*

cation as such, on some prior effort to recognize the thing at least generically, after which we can explore what is unexpected about this particular view or exposure of it. A certain prior knowledge, a nomenclature or a general terminology: perhaps these also played a crucial role in the first moments of the inspection of the great tradition of representational painting down to the modern period; but they now seem to have migrated into contemporary *photography*, where you have to recognize and identify the stylistic pieces, whose individual identification then leads to absolute separation from the other elements; whence the coexistence and conflict of these "semiotic substances."

My sense is that the segmentation of contemporary photography does not necessarily operate in the "deconstructive" fashion of the painters, but it may show signs of newer structures for which we as yet lack the right historical and formal categories.

Some difference in temperature between the sixties and the eighties, for example, can be taken by reflecting on what J. G. Ballard might have called (in *The Atrocity Exhibition*) the spinal landscapes of Oliver Wasow's photographs. (See #146 reproduced in chapter I.) What is absent from Wasow, indeed, is the background level of sixties violence and pain, in which Vietnam and the Congo retrieve Hiroshima in the form of multivehicle car crashes on the lunar landscape of decaying high rises and collapsing superhighways. Yet the layering of the vision has odd similarities with those evoked by Ballard in the following "paragraph," entitled "The Persistence of Memory":

> An empty beach with its fused sand. Here clock time is no longer valid. Even the embryo, symbol of secret growth and possibility, is drained and limp. These images are the residues of a remembered moment of time. For Talbot the most disturbing elements are the rectilinear sections of the beach and sea. The displacement of these two images through time, and their marriage with his own continuum, has warped them into rigid and unyielding structures of his own consciousness. Later, walking along the flyover, he realized that the rectilinear forms of his conscious reality were warped elements from some placid and harmonious future.[6]

The title phrase here surely must be read against that (apparently pseudoscientific) doctrine of the "persistence of vision" that has played so great and emblematic a role in film theory, where the illusion of continuity is generated by the overlap of static afterimages on the retina. Ballard now projects this overlap into our experience of the world itself and its multiple realities, whose discontinuities reappear at the moment of individual and collective crisis and breakdown—separating into the layered bands of beach and sea. The apparatus of distress and trauma, the enabling instrumentation of social and historical disaster, seem absent from Wasow's X-rays (unless they are for his later generation so deeply interiorized that Ballard's affect is no longer detectable). Yet Ballard here—uniquely in his work, I believe—also invokes the Utopian "epoch of rest" (William Morris), that "placid and harmonious future" whose unimaginable messages and signals somehow penetrate our ravaged postatomic ecosystem and make their absent presence felt by the empty form of striated volumes, levels, superimposed bands of absent substances as distinct as primary colors, or the primal elements of the pre-Socratics, or some regressive dream of the ultimate simplicities of the state of nature. In the climactic moment of "The Voices of Time," also, the spatial components of the universe spoke to the protagonist, but they spoke in the distinct languages and emissions of various rates of entropy:

> Powers suddenly felt the massive weight of the escarpment rising up into the dark sky like a cliff of luminous chalk. . . . Not only could he see the escarpment, but he was aware of its enormous age. . . . The ragged crests . . . all carried a distinct image of themselves across to him, a thousand voices that together told of the total time elapsed in the life of the escarpment. . . . Turning his eyes away from the hill face he felt a second wave of time sweep across the first. The image was broader but of shorter perspectives, radiating from the wide disk of the salt lake. . . . Closing his eyes, Powers lay back and steered the car along the interval between the two time fronts, feeling the images deepen and strengthen within his mind.[7]

To these are added at length the voices from galactic space, all of which finally converge on the ultimate target, Powers's body at the center of his mandala. Yet the reassuring extinction fantasies of early Ballard, which no longer seem possible in the world cataclysms of the sixties, paradoxically exchange formulations of entropy and the geological past for the fragile acknowledgment of a future and a Utopia out of reach, all the more powerful for the toxic atmosphere it has to penetrate. With Wasow we are now in the eighties, and the dark, hallucinatory colors of his Utopian spinal bands have something of that tranquil and unearthly conflagration of sunsets over Santa Monica whose optical effects are due, we are told, to the extreme density of chemical pollution in the atmosphere.

My sense is that it is precisely by way of such internal differentiation —bands within the image which resonate with each other—that the Utopian vocation of the newer photography is secured. The traditional pleasures of photography include, besides the stiff glossiness of the object as well as its incorporation of the machine as such, a referentiality which painting has traditionally sought to abolish. As in the dialectic of the name,[8] which separates itself from its object and now stands across from it, the photograph always dramatized its independence as a repro-duction from the object from which it was "indistinguishable." What we have observed in contemporary painting, however, is that to the degree that modern society becomes "acculturated" and that social reality takes on a more specifically cultural form—stereotypes, collective images, and the like—postmodern painting recovers a kind of reference and reinvents the "referent" in the form of just such collective cultural fantasies.

Photography, then, in its contemporary and even postmodern version, would seem to have evolved in the opposite direction, renouncing refer-ence as such in order to elaborate an autonomous vision which has no external equivalent. Internal differentiation now stands as the mark and the moment of a decisive displacement in which the older relationship of image to referent is superceded by an inner or an interiorized one (where, as a consequence, none of the "bands" in Wasow's images has any referential priority over the other). To speak more psychologically, the attention of the viewer is now engaged by a differential opposition within the image itself, so that he or she has little energy left over for intentness to that older "likeness" or "matching" operation which com-pares the image to some putative thing outside. Paradoxically, however, it is precisely attention to that "outside"—but an outside that now enters consciousness itself in the form of the external realities of collective fantasies and the materials of the Culture Industry—that determines the novel character of postmodern painting such as Salle's.

Whether this newer Utopian photography will know the fate of an older experimental type of art-photography (abstractions, blowups of now unrecognizable milk drops, trick mechanics of all kinds)—whose aesthetic Barthes is not alone in loathing—remains to be seen. What speaks against such assimilation is, among other things, the very modification in our conception of what art and culture are: for among the now intolerable messages emitted by the older art photography was the claim to be "art" (rather than photographic journalism), a claim these newer pictures do not seem to have to defend or enounce. That such Utopianism is an ideology—including an aesthetic ideology—seems clear enough; but at a time when we have minimally agreed that *everything* is ideology, or better still, that there is nothing outside of ideology, that does not seem a very damaging admission either. Yet in our time, where the claims of the officially political seem extraordinarily enfeebled and where the taking of older kinds of political positions seems to inspire widespread embarrassment, it should also be noted that one finds everywhere today—not least among artists and writers—something like an unacknowledged "party of Utopia": an underground party whose numbers are difficult to determine, whose program remains unannounced and perhaps even unformulated, whose existence is unknown to the citizenry at large and to the authorities, but whose members seem to recognize one another by means of secret Masonic signals. One even has the feeling that some of the present exhibitors may be among its adherents.

7

Immanence and Nominalism

in Postmodern Theoretical Discourse

Part I. Immanence and the New Historicism

Few recent works of American criticism display the interpretive brilliance and intellectual energy of Walter Benn Michaels's *The Gold Standard and the Logic of Naturalism*.[1] Besides addressing a period whose formal tendencies—naturalism in particular—have always presented peculiar problems for literary history, and confronting unique writers —Norris above all—who seem to have proven unusually resistant to classification and evaluation, this book also is said to exemplify in its own special way that new thing called the "New Historicism," which has been the object of so much fascination to current polemicists. It also seems called on to "illustrate" a provocative and controversial theoretical text by Michaels himself (with Stephen Knapp), "Against Theory,"[2] presumably by demonstrating what you can still go on to do when "theory" is abandoned. Besides all this, alertness to the problematic of photography provides some stimulating interventions into what is currently perhaps the most exciting artistic medium (in postmodernism); while attention to the questions of romance and realism (as well as of the modern itself), conjoined with the central problem of naturalism raised above, reinscribe genre and periodization on the agenda in a welcome and productive fashion. Finally, the book deploys strong (and to some, offensive) political attitudes, whose relationship to the literary critical attitudes is on the face of it unclear. Any one of these topics by itself would merit closer attention; taken together they suggest that Michaels's collection (but I will argue that it is more than that) offers a signal occasion for taking the temperature of contemporary (or post-contemporary) criticism and theory.

"Theory," in the Michaels-Knapp program essay, proved to be a reassuringly restricted category, which oddly ignored the bulk of all those now voluminous continental materials that this word has seemed to conjure up for many of us over the last twenty years. The frame of reference of the essay will surely strike un-American and European-oriented "theorists" as peculiarly Anglo-American and as a return to just those English department concerns (what is the validity of this reading of the canonical poem or passage in question?) from which the rest of us were in flight, and in place of which "theory" (in its structural or poststructural, or in its German or dialectical sense) promised the relief of new problems and new interests. Gadamer appears here, to be sure, but as the rival of Hirsch; Derrida is here not merely because of his American connections but, above all, on the strength of his polemic with Searle: it is as though naturalization now depended on having sound Anglo-American enemies. But I will argue later that the great continental themes and issues also resurface in *The Gold Standard*; and that the logic of Michaels's argument drives him into rediscovering and reinventing them. This is indeed, in my opinion, the most extraordinary and admirable feature of this book that it exhibits a philosophical discovery process at work before our eyes, and that Michaels has given himself over so completely to the logic of his content and the inner dynamic of his objects that the great problems appear, as it were, under their own momentum, not summoned in from the outside on the strength of this or that current theoretical trend or slogan. Perhaps this may serve as the deeper moment of truth of the otherwise provocative program of "Against Theory": that with the proper combination of alertness and receptivity, problems may be expected to pose themselves in ways that allow us to make a detour around the reifications of current theoretical discourse.

That is not, however, what that essay "meant" by "theory," something that can now be recapitulated with all the concision of its authors, namely, "the tendency to generate theoretical problems by splitting apart terms that are in fact inseparable" (AT 12). This tendency is then identified and localized in two kinds of privileged error: the separation of "authorial intention and the meaning of texts" (AT 12), and a larger, or more "epistemological" pathology, in which "knowledge" is separated from "beliefs," generating the notion that we can somehow "stand outside our beliefs" (AT 27), such that "theory" now becomes "the name for all the ways people have tried to stand outside practice in order to govern practice from without" (AT 30). Both issues will return again, and it is tempting to suggest that a different code or terminology would separate them out into issues of the subject, on the one hand, and of ideology, on the other, before somehow putting them back together. That is a discussion which would be prematurely broken off by the facile objection that the Michaels-Knapp argument ignores the most interesting problem about its targets: why "splitting apart terms that are in fact inseparable" is so persistent a mistake or an error, to use their terms, and why so many people keep on making it, or make it in the first place. Mistakes and errors are presumably personal affairs, the result of stupidity or fuzzy thinking: this one now takes on the proportions of a historical mystery, to which the appropriate first response is Michaels's own characteristic reaction, throughout *The Gold Standard*, that such thoughts are "odd" or "weird." And this is finally why few readers can have taken seriously the rather alarming reassurance (borrowed from Stanley Fish) that to stop doing theory will have no (practical) consequences whatsoever: it is not that such readers have any clear counter-image of the consequences in question, but rather that we feel very strongly that we are being told to *stop* doing something, that new taboos whose motivation we cannot quite grasp are being erected with passionate energy and conviction. There is thus something "weird" about the new taboo on "theory" itself.

One of the tantalizing and enigmatic silences of this proposal has to do with the status philosophy will have after the end of "theory"; that "end" itself can usefully be recast in philosophical terms as a rehearsal of the old tension between "immanence" and "transcendence." In the realm of literary criticism, the New Critics also worried eloquently and productively about this problem, opting for that well-known primacy of textual immanence we now sometimes in hindsight dismiss with the shorthand term *formalism*. Their words for immanence and transcendence were "intrinsic" and "extrinsic"; the forms of theoretical transcendence they sought to repel were extrinsic historical and biographical information, but also political opinions, sociological generalizations, and "Freudian" concerns: the "old" historicism plus Marx and Freud. To put it this way is to realize that during its triumphant ascent—from the Marxist thirties to the academic canonization of the fifties—the New Criticism encountered very few "theories" on its path. The intellectual atmosphere was still relatively unpolluted by the theoretical proliferation that set in with a vengeance in subsequent years; even the philosophy departments had yet to feel the first fresh stirrings of the gale-force winds unleashed by existentialism. Only an old-fashioned communism and an old-fashioned psychoanalysis stood out upon the agrarian landscape like immense and ugly foreign bodies, history itself (equally old-fashioned in those days) being very effectively consigned to the dusty ash can of "scholarship." Immanence in those days meant writing poetry and also reading it, something then a good deal more exciting than any theory.

To put it this way is to realize that criticism and theory confront an utterly different situation in the United States today. When the proliferation of what I may call "named" theories is so intense, both in their rhythm and their number, as to saturate the cultural and intellectual atmosphere incomparably, and to render the New Critical separatism of the "intrinsic" meaningless, such separatism, however conceived, then simply becomes another named theory. And as for the two earlier theories mentioned, the plurality of Marxisms today, like the plurality of schools of psychoanalysis, seems to render them less threatening as well, or at least less obviously "extrinsic." What Paul DeMan called the "resistance to theory" (meaning, of course, merely his own "theory") can therefore be expected to take complicated, second-degree forms, which are only apparently comparable to the older resistances. Even the slogan of the "return to history" (if that is really the way the New Historicism is to be characterized) is misleading insofar as "history" is itself today not the opposite of "theory" but rather very precisely itself a lively plurality of various historical and historiographic "theories" (*Annales* school, metahistory, psychohistory, Thompsonian history, etc., etc.). But "pluralism" is itself a rather "extrinsic" way of describing the current intellectual situation.

Virtually the first problem we face in circumscribing the New Historicism and telling the story of its emergence has to do with the name itself, which presupposes its existence as a "school" or "movement" (or a "theory" or "method"), whereas actually, as I will try to show in a moment, it is a shared writing practice rather than any ideological content or conviction that seem to mark its various participants. Perhaps this accounts for their own mixed feelings about a label, which, however it originated among them, now comes to them from the outside as a kind of accusation. Few recent intellectual movements (if we may still loosely use that word) have generated quite as much passion and antagonism as this one (with the exception of deconstruction itself), and from the Right fully as much as from the Left. Indeed, if there is any merit in characterizing the postmodern moment constitutively as one in which the traditional avant-gardes and collective movements have become impossible, then it seems possible that forms of *ressentiment* are at work in the denunciation of something that seems to be a collective movement of that older type (or is accused as passing itself off as such a movement, or as its simulacrum). This odd situation at the very least again raises the issue of what a genuine avant-garde movement was, at the moment in which its structural impossibility is affirmed.

It also accounts for some of the malaise of those considered to be New Historicists; who feel, not without some justice, that their books have been turned into examples of some vague general idea or -ism, with which they are then reproached. Indeed, in what follows, we will be guilty of just this, and we will occasionally read *The Gold Standard* as just such an illustration, for good or ill, of New Historicist method. But this dilemma is unavoidable, as Sartre showed long ago: a crucial component of my *particular* situation as a unique individual is always the *general* category to which I am also condemned by other people and which I must therefore come to terms with (Sartre said, *assume*) in any way I like—shame, pride, avoidance behavior—but which I cannot expect to have removed just because I'm somebody special. As with other targets of "discrimination," so with New Historicists: a New Historicist, as Sartre might have said, is one whom other people consider a New Historicist. In our other terminology, this means, in effect, that individual immanence is here in tension with a certain transcendence, in the form of seemingly external, collective labels and identities. The theoretical form of "denial," however, consists in arguing that the transcendent dimension does not exist in the first place because it is not empirically given and has no real ontological or conceptual status: no one has ever seen such collectives or experienced them immediately, while the -isms that correspond to them seem to involve the shabbiest stereotypes or the vaguest generalizing thinking. It follows, to take only the most dramatic examples of such denial of the transcendent, that social classes do not exist, or that, in literary history, concepts like "modernism" are crude substitutes for that very different and qualitatively discriminate experience of reading an individual text (about which there is no longer even any point in identifying it as somehow "modernist"). Contemporary thought and culture are in this sense profoundly *nominalist* (to expand a diagnosis Adorno made about the tendencies of modern art), postmodernism more thoroughly so than anything that preceded it. But the contradiction between immanence and transcendence remains as before, however the zeitgeist decides to handle it, and it is, if anything, intensified by the extraordinary systematizing and unifying forces of late capitalism which are so omnipresent as to be invisible, so that their transcendent operation does not seem to pose the intellectual problem of transcendence itself so tangibly and dramatically as it did in earlier stages when capital was less complete and more intermittent.

It is therefore as inappropriate as it is unavoidable to read *The Gold Standard* as a characteristic specimen of New Historicism, an operation which now requires us to develop or to abstract some useful stereotype of this "movement." This can only be done, I think, by storytelling (we had this, and now we have *this*); and it is a story I propose to tell by way of the changes wrought by the introduction of the concept of a "text." Those changes do not at first take place in the literary area, but they return to it later from an "outside" modified by the notion of textuality, which now seems to reorganize the objects of other disciplines and to make it possible to deal with them in new ways which suspend the troublesome notion of "objectivity." So it is that political power becomes a "text" that you can read; daily life becomes a text to be activated and deciphered by walking or shopping; consumers' goods are unveiled as a textual system, along with any number of other conceivable "systems" (the star system, the genre system of Hollywood film, etc.); war becomes a readable text, along with the city and the urban; and finally the body itself proves to be a palimpsest whose stabs of pain and symptoms, along with its deeper impulses and its sensory apparatus, can be *read* fully as much as any other text. That this reconstruction of basic objects of study was welcome and liberated us from a whole range of constricting false problems no one can doubt, that it brought with it new false problems in its own right no one could fail to anticipate. Of interest to us here are the formal dilemmas this conception of textuality begins to pose for expository writing (or *Darstellung*, to use the classical term which includes, but means something a little more fundamental than, mere "representation").

Those dilemmas do not surface within any particular homogeneous discipline, where, for example, power is read as a text without the interference of materials of a different kind. But where several types of materials or objects are juxtaposed, a representational problem arises which can only be solved by a "theory" (which sometimes looks like a "method"). Thus, within the broad range of Lévi-Strauss's interests, a number of heterogeneous objects of study raise their discordant claims: the kinship system above all, but also "social structure" in the narrower sense of dualistic or ternary organizations, and finally culture itself, whether in the form of the visual "style" of a given tribal society or in their oral stories. Family, class, daily life, the visual, and narrative: each of these "texts" presents specific problems, which, however, combine into problems of a qualitatively heightened type when we try to read them side by side and incorporate them into a single, relatively unified discourse. Lévi-Strauss, anticipating postmodern social thought, evades the establishment of some fictive totalizing entity such as Society itself, under which more local and heterogeneous entities of the type already enumerated used to be organically and hierarchically ordered. But he can do so only by inventing a different kind of fictive (or transcendent) entity, in terms of which the various independent "texts" of kinship, village organization, and visual form can be read as somehow being "the same": this is the method of the *homology*. As distinct as they are from each other, these various local and concrete "texts" can nonetheless be read as homologous with each other insofar as we disengage an abstract *structure* which seems to be at work in all of them, according to their own specific internal dynamics. In principle, the "theory" of structure, which justifies the practice of homology as a method, then allows one to avoid the establishment of ontological priorities. The structure of kinship is then, at least in principle, no more fundamental or causally prior than the spatial organization of the village (even though, in fact, slippage seems inevitable here, and Lévi-Strauss frequently seems to imply just such priorities and "deeper" levels). But in order to secure that indifference or nonhierarchy of the various subsystems, an external category is required, that of "structure" itself. My own sense is that the influence of "structuralism" (and the extraordinary richness of new analyses that it opened up) is rather to be attributed to the possibility of making homologies than to the operative pretext—the concept of structure—which was its philosophical presupposition and its working fiction (or ideology). At the same time, it must be said that the notion of the homology rapidly proved to be an embarrassment and turned out to be as crude and vulgar an idea as "base and superstructure" ever was, the excuse for the vaguest kind of general formulations and the most unenlightening assertions of "identity" between entities of utterly distinct magnitude and properties. Indeed, with some modifications (whose implications will be discussed later on), Michaels's own critique of "theory" might be invoked for the indictment of this particular one: from a concrete entity or "text" (kinship phenomena, say, or the emplacement of a village), a kind of "intention"—the underlying *structure*—has been abstracted or separated out, such that the concrete text comes to look like the expression or realization of that independently formulated intention.

The solution, however, will evidently not lie in the regression to the styles of the older, pretextual disciplines; in other words, in going back to separate, specialized discussions of all those heterogeneous materials or "texts." The discursive progress marked by the "structuralist moment," or by the "theory" of structure that authorized the practice of homology, was the enlargement of the object and the possibility of establishing a whole range of new relationships between materials of divers kinds. This is not to be abandoned now, whatever one's position on the "theoretical" component turns out to be. The ambiguity of the Michaels-Knapp manifesto, in other words, lay in the possibility of reading it as a call to return to a pre-theoretical procedure; whereas it also, in the practice of New Historicism, proves to open up a whole post-theoretical set of operations that retain the discursive conquest of a range of heterogeneous materials while quietly abandoning the theoretical component that once justified that enlargement, omitting the transcendental interpretations that had once seemed to be the very aim and purpose of homologies in the first place.

We will therefore describe the New Historicism as a return to immanence and to a prolongation of the procedures of "homology" which eschews homology's theory and abandons the concept of "structure." This is also an aesthetic (or a writing convention, or mode of Darstellung) for which a formal rule emerges governing something like a ban or taboo on theoretical discussion and on the taking of interpretive distance from the material, the drawing up of a provisional balance sheet, the summary of the "points" that have been made. Elegance here consists in constructing bridge passages between the various concrete analyses, transitions or modulations inventive enough to preclude the posing of theoretical or interpretive questions. Immanence, the suppression of distance, must be maintained during these crucial transitional moments in such a way as to keep the mind involved in detail and immediacy. Whence, in the most successful of such artifacts, that sense of breathlessness, of admiration for the brilliance of the performance, but yet bewilderment, at the conclusion of the essay, from which one seems to emerge with empty hands—without ideas and interpretations to carry away with us.

From this perspective the inaugural volume of the New Historicism, Stephen Greenblatt's *Renaissance Self-Fashioning*, in hindsight looks like one of those classical and paradigmatic scientific discoveries achieved by triumphant accident in the process of attempting to solve a false problem (Kepler's or Galileo's Platonism). As the title indicates, the starting point, or the framework, seems to have been a rather old-fashioned conception of the "self" and of "identity"—very specifically high-modernist ideologies and values these—which the working through ends up thoroughly dismantling and discrediting, although this outcome is never theorized and its implications are never drawn in theoretical fashion. There is here a remarkable combination of interpretive sophistication, of intense intellection and theoretical energy, with an exclusion of self-consciousness or reflexivity of the classical type, which will then characterize all the most successful productions of the New Historicism. It was, of course, Greenblatt's peculiar material whose inner logic itself determined the deconstruction of the ideological framework: selves capable of modifying their shapes so effectively that they ultimately call the very idea of the self into question. But the overt thematics of the volume seem to have been its least influential feature, which lies rather in the way the theme overtly pursued opens an axis between theology and imperialism, an axis on which documentary material ranging from the institution of confession or the editions of Tyndale's English Bible to accounts of grisly atrocities in Ireland or in the Bahamas is inscribed. A thematic association initially identified as the "self" and grasped with all the analytic sophistication of psychoanalysis is not dismissed but refashioned and, as it were, transcoded: "in all my texts and documents, there were, so far as I could see, no moments of pure, unfettered subjectivity; indeed, the human subject itself began to seem remarkably unfree, the ideological product of the relations of power in a particular society."[3] But this new, retroactive version of the thematic leitmotif, which now finally seems to *name* the homology or structure as Power itself, strikes me as being itself something of a "motivation of the device," an entity invoked after the fact to rationalize the practice of a collage or montage of multiple materials. "Power" is here not an interpretive concept, not a "transcendental" theoretical object on which the text works and which it seeks to produce, but rather a reassurance that secures its immanence and allows the reader's attention to dwell and persist in the detail without guilt or discomfort.

This is, at least, what happens when *Renaissance Self-Fashioning* is read as a paradigm of the procedures of the New Historicism; that is, as the demonstration of a "method" (or a discourse) that can be redeployed elsewhere (in the Victorian period or, as in the present instance, in the moment of American naturalism). For it must be added that the book is structurally ambiguous. When read as a contribution to Renaissance scholarship, what emerges is something quite different from what I have described above, namely, a historical proposition and the tentative sketch of a historical narrative in which an appearance of subjectivity or inwardness seems to emerge at the moment of Tyndale and More (but an appearance only, which oscillates between the security of two institutions), becomes secularized in Wyatt, and then, in the Elizabethan period, is swept into the fictionality and the dramatic pageantry of a new kind of nonsubject, with Marlowe and Shakespeare. Here too the category of the subject is invoked only to be "deconstructed"; but the rudiments of a transcendental historical interpretation remain, which can be used and debated in a very different way. Their eventual abandonment in New Historicism is here foreshadowed by the relative truncation of the historical segment, which makes it difficult to determine whether a larger tendency is identified or only a local point-to-point transformation.

Another way of thinking about the immanence of the New Historicism needs to be acknowledged and dismissed, and that is that it simply reflects the malaise of the historian with theoretical generalizations (generally of a sociological or protosociological type, since it is most often the constitutive tension between history and sociology that is in question in this situation). The procedures of the *Annales* historians, or Ginzburg, or even one of the impulses of Thompson's attack on Althusser, display a highly theoretical reluctance to "theorize" which bears some family likeness to the New Historicism. As for the other related disciplinary tendency, "narrative" anthropology, its leading figures (Geertz, Turner, etc.) are explicitly evoked by Greenblatt in his first book, although he did not at that time know the codification of this tendency by George Marcus and James Clifford, which surely is much more closely related to the New Historicism itself and something like a productive reaction to its emergence. As far as the historians go, however, the resemblance might better be discussed in terms of overdetermination: which is to say that the ideological kinship of the New Historicism with them adds a certain supplementary resonance to its reception and evaluation, its prestige as a new movement, but does not go very far toward explaining the meaning and function of this new historical phenomenon in its own, literary-critical and theoretical, context.

We will therefore formulate the discourse of the New Historicism as a "montage of historical attractions," to adapt Eisenstein's famous phrase, in which extreme theoretical energy is captured and deployed, but repressed by a valorization of immanence and nominalism that can either look like a return to the "thing itself" or a "resistance to theory." Such elaborate montages work more vividly in short form and can be viewed to stunning effect in two such different essays as Greenblatt's own "Invisible Bullets" and Catherine Gallagher's "The Bio-economics of *Our Mutual Friend*." In Greenblatt's essay police surveillance, the Virginia colony, and the counterfeiting of gold coins are juxtaposed with Renaissance grammars and language teaching and Shakespeare's mimicry of dialects. In Gallagher's study Malthus, themes of death, the nineteenth-century hygienic movement, and emergent conceptions of life or the vital are constellated, under the sign of Value, with the representation of the disposal of garbage and sewage in Dickens's novel. It will, however, be clear from what has already been said that I regard the ostensible subjects of these essays—the Other and value—as pretexts for the montage in question rather than as "concepts" in their own right.

Even a figurative use, in passing, of Eisenstein's language, however, reminds us that analogies to New Historicist forms exist well beyond the bounds of related disciplines like history and anthropology, while the staging of these discursive pieces in terms of their aesthetic, or their form or *Darstellung*, already suggests more general historical parallels of which I will only mention two. How new forms of montage in film are to be related to a pedagogy that stimulates thinking and prods the spectator out of some merely immanent contemplation of visual images is not merely the classical problem of an Eisenstein or a Brecht but also the more immediate and contemporary space in which Godard's films desperately and far more problematically wrestle with that heritage; that Godard had "ideas" no less theoretical than Brecht or Eisenstein, ideas about consumer society and Maoist politics which it was the task of the film somehow to convey, seems undeniable. But in Godard the status of those "ideas" seems to have become as undecidable as those of the New Historicism (power, the Other, value), something which at least suggests that we have to do here not with mere personal choices or inclinations on the part of the individual authors in question but with some more general historical situation and dilemma for which conceptual positions as such (what we have been calling discursive "transcendence") are delegitimized and discredited by the more general movement toward immanence or what Adorno called nominalism. It is no longer certain, for instance, that the heavily charged and monitory juxtapositions in a Godard film—an advertising image, a printed slogan, newsreels, an interview with a philosopher, and the *gestus* of this or that fictive character—will be put back together by the spectator in the form of a message, let alone the right message. As for Adorno, and despite the fact that *Negative Dialectics* can in many ways be read as his attempt to deal productively with this same historical dilemma of immanence and transcendence (which for him cannot be solved as such), he confronted the dilemma more starkly in the (for him) inadmissible practice of Benjamin in the latter's Arcades project: the letters between the two on that occasion draw the line beyond which Adorno was unwilling to go when faced with Benjamin's reluctance to tell the reader of his historical "constellations" or montages what they meant and how to interpret them. In the Anglo-American tradition, this anxiety of immanence finds its genealogy in Pound's notion of the ideogram and in the pedagogical dilemmas of *The Cantos*. We have every interest in resituating the phenomenon of the New Historicism in this wider historical and formal context, in which its own local solutions (or evasions) find a more exemplary historical resonance.

The Gold Standard and the Logic of Naturalism is, of course, yet another such montage, working on the twin levels of the individual chapters and of the book as a whole. This extended demonstration of New Historicist form (or "method") has the additional interest for us of being staged without the scaffolding of traditional or conventional "themes," such as the "self" in Greenblatt's pioneering work (even though the occasional gesture toward a thematics of "writing," as in the introduction, seems designed misleadingly to reassure the reader that we are embarked on a more familiar enterprise).

Three distinct rhythms seem to course unevenly through this book, attention to any one of which backgrounds the others and produces a rather different reading. These are (1) the practice of the homologies as such, or, in other words, that "montage of historical attractions" in which we saw the most distinctive formal principle of New Historicist discourse; (2) the polemics ostensibly waged against liberal or radical interpretations but which also in fact recapitulate the "position" outlined in "Against Theory"; and (3) a protohistorical narrative in which something is affirmed about the specificity of this particular period, including its waning and its imminent transformation into something else —this narrative is most clearly grasped in economic terms (the ideology of the gold standard, the debates on contracts, the coming into being of the trusts), but can also be reconstructed in terms of literary movements or genres (realism, romance, naturalism), and even in terms of representation as such in the remarkable pages on trompe-l'oeil painting and photography (where the discussions of écriture probably also belong). Not the least interest of *The Gold Standard* lies in this unplanned polyphony, which is therefore to be distinguished from some putative New Historicist norm by the presence of other features or levels (in particular, the second or polemic one).

The homologies, however, still capture the primary attention of any first reading, owing to the dazzling heterogeneity of their raw materials, which include medicine, gambling, land tenure, masochism, slavery, photography, contracts, hysteria, and, not least, money itself. The legitimation of money and its related projections (trust law, the futures market, the rhetoric of gold) as a respectable topic of literary-critical discussion may be thought of as something of a Michaels trademark (just as the emphasis on travel narrative and imperialism was a Greenblatt trademark). What is remarkable is that the sounding of the economic motif has today shed all of its (once inevitable) Marxist connotations. Not very long ago, the very act of including the economic background, however briefly, alongside the customary "intellectual context" (science, religion, "worldviews") within a literary or critical essay had political meaning and consequences, whatever the content of the historical interpretation in question. It is true that "money" is no longer exactly coterminous with "the economic" in this sense: Jean-Joseph Goux's *Numismatiques* was still a "contribution" to Marxist thinking; Marc Shell's pathbreaking books on money and coinage were already a good deal more neutral than that; while, in Michaels, "money" is merely another "text," albeit a kind of final frontier and an arid zone into which humanists without his stamina are still generally reluctant to venture. Paradoxically, the political stakes here are not invested in the issue of the development of North American capitalism (the monopolies), but rather, as we shall see, in the much more contemporary issues of the market and consumption. (Imperialism, in Greenblatt, still remains a much more intensely political issue, but in a situation today in which a kind of alternate radicalism, of a Foucauldian and Third World, more exclusively antiimperialist, type, has opened up alongside the Marxist one.)

Money in *The Gold Standard* enters the picture as supporting evidence rather than as the thing itself. Here is an early statement of the mechanisms that allow us to shift from one level to another (the starting point is the peculiar doodling and "production" of marks by the heroine of Charlotte Perkins Gilman's *The Yellow Wallpaper*):

> From this perspective, the hysterical woman embodies not only the *economic* primacy of work but also the connection between the economic primacy of work and the *philosophical* problem of personal identity. The economic question — How do I produce myself?

—and the therapeutic question—How do I stay myself?—find their parallel in the *epistemological* question, How do I know myself?— or more specifically, as James puts it, How do I know today that "I am the same self that I was yesterday"? What does "consciousness" "mean when it calls the present self the *same* with one of the past selves which it has in mind?" (GS 7, italics mine)

This articulation is misleadingly neat and final; in reality, it merely triggers the homological or analogizing process, which will quickly spread to a variety of other areas. Nor is it clear that the "structure" here identified and named—the "self"—has anything in common with the concept from which Greenblatt set out: this Humean self is already philosophically discredited and annulled from the outset; we see the bottom through it in advance; whatever sham stability it devises will have to come from outside, from other instances and resources, that are eventually identified as a "level" not mentioned in this passage, namely, forms of *property*. Another way of saying this is that it is not at all clear that Michaels is here guided by an abstract problematic of the self. One could argue just as plausibly that the language of self here simply designates another crucial piece of textual evidence of raw material, namely, the books of William James, whose *Principles of Psychology* are as basic to *The Gold Standard* as anything by Dreiser, Norris, Hawthorne, Wharton, and the rest. In that case, notions of "self" fall from solutions or explanatory frameworks to the status of textual problems, exhibits among many others, whose conceptual language no longer has any privilege.

In fact, James himself provides the mediation that allows us to shift gears away from the psychological (or even the psychoanalytic) to the categories of property rights. By way of a remarkable passage in which James compares the persistence of personal identity among our various memories of the past to the branding of cattle with our own distinctive "mark," we reach a more satisfactory formulation, in which the language of production has been replaced by the language of juridical right:

Our mistake, James thinks, has been to imagine the [present] thought as *establishing* ownership over past thoughts; instead, we should think of it as *already* owning them. The owner has "inherited his 'title.'" His own "birth" is always coincident with "the death of another owner"; indeed, the very existence of an owner must coincide with the coming into existence of the owned. "Each Thought is thus born an owner, and dies owned, transmitting whatever it realized as its Self to its own later proprietor." (GS 9)

With this reformulation, which substitutes the analogy of property rights for that of production, the royal road to the associative work of the later chapters is thrown open: now at once we can pass on to the question of romance and photography in Hawthorne. "Romance" will then offer the stability of "uncontested title and inalienable right" (GS 95) and security against the market fluctuations of real estate value, while against all expectation, the practice of photography (the profession of Holgrave in *The House of Seven Gables*) will turn out to be "an artistic enterprise hostile to imitation" (GS 96). If mimesis is associated with realism (and thereby with the threatening dynamic of the market), this strangeness and "hyperreality" of the first photographs, or Daguerrotypes, will be registered as something else, as a hermeneutic activity that "actually brings out the secret character with a truth that no painter would ever venture upon" (Hawthorne, p. 91, quoted in GS 99).

This particular homology with aberrant or marginal forms of "art" (romance rather than realism, photography rather than the great tradition of then emergent modern painting) will be picked up again when, with Norris and with the trompe l'oeil of Peto and Harnett, we confront that other aberrant phenomenon which is "naturalism"; such minor media do not here annul the grand linear narrative of the telos of artistic or literary history, but they stand, as it were, on its margins, much as in Deleuze's treatment of the instinctual naturalism and fetishism of Stroheim and Buñuel in his film typology. The impossible solution of *The House of the Seven Gables*—permanent title beyond the market, "immunity to appropriation"—now leads more immediately to the possibility of imagining different kinds of conceptual relationships between property and the self (the *political* question raised by this reading of Hawthorne—namely, whether this romance-vision is then not to be seen as a critique or Utopian transcendence of the market—will be dealt with later). But extreme conceptual possibilities are given in attempts to theorize slavery and in Sacher-Masoch's "weird" contractual arrangements for his "masochistic" practices. We must pass over Michaels's excellent discussion of these matters, except to observe that the issue of slavery anchors the book in the mainstream of American history, while the apparently aberrant foray into Eastern European materials in reality sets up the fundamental test case of *The Gold Standard* as a whole; namely, the combination, in Norris and above all in *McTeague*, of the twin phenomena of miserliness and masochism (in the person of Trina). Gold now finally makes its triumphant appearance in the "reality" of the naturalist text (as opposed to the phantasms and imaginary resolutions of juridical "theories" of slavery, on the one hand, or the "canon law" of masochism, on the other). The long excursus through land and property, however, has endowed this new combination of value and the self with the supplementary "level" of the juridical and of contract theory, which will shortly, as we shall see, free itself from these constraints and become autonomous.

Michaels's ingenious reading of *McTeague* has the merit of "producing the problem" of this novel by way of a "solution" that will not necessarily convince all his readers (any more than the reading of Charlotte Perkins Gilman): "The contradiction, then, is that Trina belongs to McTeague, but her money doesn't. . . . The simultaneous desires to own and to be owned constitute the emotional paradox Norris sets himself to elaborate in *McTeague*" (GS 123). If you don't like this way of doing it, you nonetheless henceforth find yourself confronted with the disassociation of the "themes" of money and instinctual violence as the problem to be solved by any future reading. This particular solution allows Michaels to make the connection between miserliness in this text and the passion of the spendthrift elsewhere (*Vandover and the Brute*); both, via Simmel, turn out to be "tragic" attempts to escape the market system as such and to abolish money:

> It is as if, from the spendthrift's point of view, the miser's refusal to spend money represents a failed attempt to withdraw from the money economy, failed because in a money economy, the power of money to buy can never be denied. It will always at least buy itself. Going the miser one better, the spendthrift tries to buy his way out of the money economy. If the miser is always exchanging his money for itself, the spendthrift tries to exchange his for nothing and so, by staging the disappearance of money's purchasing power, to stage the disappearance of money itself. (GS 144)

The reappearance here of the notion of the "market" alerts us to a polemic, that is to say, a political function of this passage, to which we will return at the proper time. The analysis also allows Michaels to cut away (perhaps prematurely) all those traditional readings of naturalism (including those of the naturalists themselves) in terms of instinct, atavism, archaic libido, and obsession (the great inhuman rages that seize on characters of Zola or Norris and shake them by the neck like forces of Nature); what looks like the unconscious or instinct is here (via William James again) decoded as intentional (if vain and contradictory) behavior.

The reading then finally allows Michaels to set in place the central demonstration promised by his title; namely, the analysis of the "gold standard" itself, or rather the passionate and even obsessive belief in the *natural* value of gold, as the ultimate form in which the longing to escape the market is fantasized. Stepping back from the immediacy of the welter of period documents through which he leads us, it will not be difficult to grasp a family likeness between Michaels's local diagnoses and a range of now characteristic poststructural denunciations of the ideologies of nature and the "authentic." Barthes's earlier Brechtian unmaskings of the strategies of "naturality" and naturalizing myths (in *Mythologies*) should not be too hastily taken as the source for this particular crusade (both Derrida and DeMan on Rousseau are more immediately relevant), which finds its most substantial full-dress rehearsal in Dean MacCannell's *The Tourist* and its full-dress ideological program in Baudrillard, in particular the Baudrillard of the critique of concepts of "need" and "use value." Meanwhile, the aesthetic consequences of the debate over nature, gold, and authenticity are also central and find their expression in the (equally postcontemporary and canonical) critiques of *representation* as such, which resurface here in the few brilliant pages on trompe l'oeil where Michaels uses and undermines Greenberg's conception of the modern all at once: "The painting that can represent nothing and still remain a painting is 'money itself,' and the modernist (or, perhaps, literalist) aesthetic of freedom from representation is a goldbug aesthetic" (GS 165). This is an ungrateful way of treating one's allies, but it underscores the problematic position of modernism at the present time. The ideology of the modern achieved its hegemony by repudiating and repressing the naturalist moment with which it radically broke; thus even a literary revindication of this peculiar moment, which does not seem to fit into the triumphant modernist narrative (or into a realistic optic either), will involve serious mixed feelings about the classical positions of high modernism (even where those derive from painting rather than from poetry). As a consequence, the very revival of naturalism itself today, in full postmodernism, can be seen as something like a return of the repressed, whose relationship to postmodern readings of the modern (such as Michael Fried's) must remain ambivalent at best. Trompe l'oeil—so old-fashioned yet so simulated and hyperreal (see Baudrillard himself on just such artifacts) —now offers an Archimedean point outside the modern, from which the (modernist) critique of representation can be staged in nonmodernist fashion.

Finally, however, there is a certain shift in emphasis between Michaels's positions and those of the older critics of authenticity, a shift I hesitate to characterize in terms of the differences between the seventies and the eighties. Nonetheless, the moral and political urgency of the older positions Michaels still shares seems lacking here; the polemic has evidently been restructured, its new stridency now combined with celebratory accents that find some echo and analogy in Lyotard rather than in Baudrillard.

Before examining this more polemic layer of Michaels's book, however, it may be worth pausing to measure the distance we have come from that thematics of the self with which we began: it will unexpectedly reemerge, after a remarkable sea change, but for the moment the "self" seems to have been mainly useful in opening up terrains such as slavery, contracts, representation, and money, which have the merit of allowing us to leave psychology behind. Still, there remains an open question that is at one with the very procedures of homology itself: namely, whether any of these levels has some ultimate priority or privileged explanatory value. Or, to put it the other way around, can one invent a way of doing homologies without begin sucked back into the ideology of "structure" itself and finding oneself establishing priorities and hierarchies against one's own will? Michaels is aware of the problem, which he rehearses intermittently and fitfully but without forming or formulating any very satisfying conclusion: "Thus, the social involvement of these texts depends not on their direct representation of the money controversies but on their indirect representation of the conditions that the money controversies themselves articulated" (GS 175).

The definitive answer will come, of course, with the conception of a "logic of naturalism" that informs the other half of his title. For the moment there remains the nagging feeling that all this *does* come down to the "self" after all, and that the desperate or passional fantasies of productionism, romance, slavery, masochism, the gold standard, and hoarding or spending are all somehow attempts to square the circle and come to terms with the antinomy of the self as private property. This is nowhere affirmed as such, yet the theoretical or interpretive void in the endless chain of homologies somehow draws the reading mind toward what we may call the existential (if not the psychoanalytic) solution: the ontological priority of explanations in terms of the self over all the other levels. This is, in general, the fate of philosophies without "content" (in the Hegelian sense of the word), and in particular of philosophies that seek to exclude content as such: a kind of Lacanian "foreclusion" in which content is reintroduced back from the outside in the form of some compensatory and generally psychoanalytic bottom line (as in *Tel Quel* and some places in Derrida), the materials of the "self" proving more serviceable in the completion of a formalist system than the materials of history or the social.

What is being described is the formal tendency of a system or a method to complete itself and to endow itself, against its own will and vocation, with a foundation that grounds it. This general observation about the tendency of "foundations" to return via some extreme form of the return of the repressed within the most antifoundational outlooks must be distinguished from judgments on the specific foundational level in question; in this case that identification of the self and private property which fitfully offers an alternate reading—an interpretive temptation, waxing and waning throughout Michaels's text—of a book about which we can affirm with some confidence that it is not the correct reading and by no means corresponds to the author's intention. That alternate reading according to which the self is constituted like private property, or even on the model of private property resonates across some very different zones of modern thought, above all in those areas where the ego or personal identity has been the most strongly experienced as an unstable construction. In Adorno, for instance, "coupled with the subject's historic enthronement as a mind was the delusion of its inalienability,"[4] where Michaels's juridical implications are also formally linked to the death anxiety (very much present in *The Gold Standard*, as we shall see). Meanwhile, in Lacan, particularly in the notion of the ego or personality as a defense mechanism, indeed as a kind of fortress, that he borrows from Reich's *Character Analysis*, the figure of landed property takes on well-nigh feudal and territorial proportions. If, in spite of that, we do not feel the intellectual kinship very strongly, this surely has at least something to do with the absence in Michaels of the inevitable next step, the speculation as to what it would be like to live without that juridical protection, and as to the forms the subject itself must once have had, or might invent in the future, in the absence of this powerful but historical legal category of property. More than that, however, the difference in spirit between Michaels's formulation and these other philosophical ones—even that of William James himself—lies in our uncertainty as to whether the former is still really an "idea" at all, our perplexity as to the status of this thought or theory, which, shorn of some more general philosophical power, has been functionally limited and pressed into merely local service in the establishment of connections or bridge passages between concrete historical descriptions.

Even the "theories" here have therefore been therapeutically restricted, preprepared, and transformed back into more historical "textual" materials (the "self as private property" being no longer an idea but a written formulation by William James), very much in the spirit of "Against Theory." Now it is time to see the polemic forms this spirit takes in *The Gold Standard*, or, in other words, to move to the second impulse of this work, which (most often in the footnotes) draws active and protopolitical consequences from the more neutral work of the establishment of homologies in the main body of the text. These no longer seem to turn on matters of intention in the reading of this or that lyric crux (but we will reestablish the connection shortly); rather, particularly in the case of readings of *Sister Carrie*, they have to do with the evaluation of commodification and consumption, in a writer conventionally thought to be a realist and a social critic, who was associated with left-wing causes and movements all his life. The narrower argument turns on the character of Ames and on the question of whether the artistic ambitions he inspires in Carrie are to be read as a radical break with her earlier and more "materialistic" impulses. Michaels argues that they are not, and I think he is right, but the argument is instructively formulated: "The ideal that Ames represents to Carrie is thus an ideal of dissatisfaction, of perpetual desire" (GS 42). We never do get out of commodity lust in Dreiser; there is no "alternate vision"; no counterimpulse can be sensed; no experience remains uncontaminated by it; nothing negates this omnipresent element, which Michaels equally rightly identifies as "the market." Or at least nothing social, for in his most electrifying pages Michaels identifies what is, for Dreiser, the true Other of the market and of commodity consumption, namely, death itself: "In *Sister Carrie*, satisfaction itself is never desirable; it is instead the sign of incipient failure, decay, and finally death" (GS 42). (Something similar was at work in the Hawthorne reading, where the solution—inalienability of title, romance, immunity to the market—is equally one of *aphanisis*: "Alice Pyncheon fancies herself immune to possession . . . simply because she feels no desire" [GS 108].) If "realism" has any kind of meaning, then, it means that the Hurstwood parts of *Sister Carrie*, the representation of the deathly Other of the market and desire, a "literature only of exhausted desire and economic failure" (GS 46). The "realisms"—like that of poor old Howells—that evoke some pastoral withdrawal from the market into some other (imaginary) inner-worldly space are all weak and sentimental fantasies, though *The House of the Seven Gables* is signally excepted from this judgment because it explicitly marks itself as a nonrealism and confronts the contradiction head-on in its very form.

Now the polemic is given another, supplementary turn: for it follows, according to Michaels, that since Dreiser's is a work of absolute *immanence* to the market, Dreiser criticism can only dishonestly exhibit these texts as the market's *critique*. Suddenly, therefore, we are confronted with the unexpected reemergence of one of the central problematics of all radical or Marxist literary or cultural criticism: namely, how the negative is to be conceived in practice and, in particular, how one can impute critical value to works that are ideologically or representationally complicitous with the "system." What is at first blush politically shocking in Michaels, then, is not the evaluation of Dreiser himself (despite the writer's conscious ideological positions). It is what was shocking in a classic version of this debate which turned on a writer fully as ambiguous as Dreiser, namely, Balzac, in whose works commodity lust is also very much an issue, along with Tory fantasies of landed squireship and overt monarchist positions (of a very different complexion from Dreiser's). One is, I think, permitted to disagree with Marx and Engels and to judge Balzac to be far more deeply corrupt and irrecuperable than they thought (although in that case their position—that Balzac was able to register contradictory social forces more acutely than merely "liberal" writers—is the more complicated and interesting one). What is probably more shocking about such discussions in *The Gold Standard* is the very presence of this problematic itself, which has never interested formalist or aestheticist criticism and which we thought belonged to us: that the "other side" should now draw up its battle lines on our own terrain—and offer to fight it out on matters of literary and cultural "subversion" or negative, critical value—is now even more alarming that the appropriation of those economic materials and topics mentioned earlier and hitherto associated with the Left. Doubts about the viability of critical and mostly dialectical models of the negative function of culture have, of course, come to be widespread in the poststructural period: but they have mostly been expressed by writers who remained political and "hommes de gauche," and whose "methods," like deconstruction, promised to be more subversive and more "revolutionary" than the traditional ones. But Michaels no longer raises, I think, any more than the New Historicism in general, any claim of "revolutionary" or subversive value for his own work.

"Subversion" indeed can serve as shorthand for a position or a principle that Michaels is concerned to deny in a variety of forms: we have already seen how various ideologies of nature, the natural, and authenticity (which range from debates about gold to political and economic positions on the "natural wealth" embodied by oil or wheat) are systematically targeted. Now it is clear that their deeper vice lies in their attempt to secure some Utopian space outside the dynamics of the market, which can (for Michaels) be characterized as necessarily and constitutively "impure," as an infinite "supplementarity" which can never know fulfillment (or "satisfaction") and which draws all other kinds of space within itself. Another name for the illusory dream of an alternate non-market space is, of course, "production" itself, something provocatively exercised in the introduction, which stages Charlotte Perkins Gilman's attempt to conquer autonomy through self-production as a fantasy deconstructed by her own text (so that texts can apparently still undermine or "subvert" themselves, but in an immanence very reminiscent of Derridean deconstruction). But Michaels is clear that his conceptual enemies extend well beyond the Marxists and the feminists: Continental ideologies of "desire" also get their share of attention, in a critique of Leo Bersani that would hold, mutatis mutandis, for Kristeva and Deleuze as well (Lyotard's *Economie libidinale* is slipperier). It is not hard to show that the force of desire alleged to undermine the rigidities of late capitalism is, in fact, very precisely what keeps the consumer system going in the first place: "the 'disruptive' element in desire that Bersani finds attractive is for Dreiser not subversive of the capitalist economy but constitutive of its power" (*GS* 48). This telling reversal can perhaps be read as the epitaph of one of the principal political positions of the 1960s, for which capitalism, by awakening needs and desires it was unable to fulfill, would somehow subvert itself; and it is certainly as part of a general systemic reaction against the 1960s that Michaels is in this respect to be read.

What must now be emphasized, however, is the consonance of these polemics with the seemingly more limited positions of "Against Theory," where, it will be recalled, a two-level offensive was waged on the "ontology" as well as the "epistemology" of so-called theory. On the ontological level, the vice of such thinking lay in a critical practice which somehow tried to isolate the author's "intention" from the text itself. What is wrong with this is then clarified by the more philosophical discussion of the "epistemological" level in which the error is succinctly described as one of trying "to stand outside our beliefs in a neutral encounter with the objects of interpretation" (*GS* 27). The concept (or pseudoconcept) of "subversion" now suggests an illusion of this same type with respect to the "system" as a whole: the illusion, that Dreiser's work, which is immanent to the market system and its dynamics and deeply complicitous with it, could somehow also "stand outside" that, achieve a "transcendence" with respect to it (normally even characterized as critical *distance*), and function as a criticism of it, if not indeed some outright political repudiation of it. But this obviously goes very far indeed: it was always implicit in the theoreticians of the "total system," such as Foucault, that if the system was as tendentially totalizing as he said it was, then all local revolts, let alone "revolutionary" impulses, remained inside that and were in reality a function of its immanent dynamic. Nonetheless Foucault himself still seemed able to act out and endorse a kind of local guerrilla warfare against the system. But of Foucault one might also say that since he did not believe in "desire," he was not equipped to measure the "seductions" of the market as such. It remained for Baudrillard to give the most dramatic and "paranoiac-critical" expression of this dilemma, in his demonstrations of the ways in which conscious ideologies of revolt, revolution, and even negative critique are—far from merely being "co-opted" by the system—an integral and functional part of the system's own internal strategies.

In the United States, what has survived of all this in the eighties is evidently the critique of consumption or consumer society itself: these are Michaels's principal adversaries (which also explains why Dreiser becomes the crucial exhibit or battlefield), and it is worth quoting his crucial footnote on the matter at some length:

> I cite [Richard Wightman] Fox and [T. Jackson] Lears here and Alan Trachtenberg and Ann Douglas below not because they seem to me particularly egregious instances of the genteel or Progressive tradition in American cultural history but—just the opposite—because they are exemplary in their attempts to imagine alternative views of American culture. Which makes it all the more striking that they do not finally dissent from the genteel/Progressive view of important works of art as in some sense transcending or opposing the market. My further point here is that American literary criticism (even more than American cultural history) has customarily understood itself and the objects of its admiration as being opposed to consumer culture—and, with a few exceptions, continues to do so. No doubt the newly politicized proponents of "oppositional" criticism would reject this assimilation of their work to the genteel tradition. But transforming the moral handwringing of the fifties and

sixties first into the epistemological handwringing of the seventies
and now into the political handwringing of the eighties does not
seem to be much of an advance. (GS 14, n. 16)

Leaving Michaels himself out of it for the moment, this passage seems
to be useful and therapeutic because of the uncomfortable way in which
it raises a very American problem that is still very much with us: namely,
the relationship between "liberalism" and "radicalism." Michaels is in
effect impolitely suggesting that critics today who imagine themselves
to be radicals are really nothing more than liberals, in all the weak and
"handwringing" senses of that word. Michaels thus offers us an opportunity for "criticism/self-criticism" of a significant and even urgent type
at a moment when the self-definitions of the Left are at best confused, if
not aimless. His incisive formulations will be helpful in this process;
here is another one:

> What exactly did it mean to think of Dreiser as approving (or disap-
> proving) consumer culture? Although transcending your origins in
> order to evaluate them has been the opening move in cultural criti-
> cism at least since Jeremiah, it is surely a mistake to take this move
> at face value: not so much because you can't really transcend your
> culture but because, if you could, you wouldn't have any terms of
> evaluation left—except, perhaps, theological ones. It thus seems
> wrong to think of the culture you live in as the object of your
> affections: you don't like it or dislike it, you exist in it, and the
> things you like and dislike exist in it too. Even Bartleby-like refus-
> als of the world remain inextricably linked to it—what could count
> as a more powerful exercize of the right to freedom of contract than
> Bartleby's successful refusal to enter into any contracts? (GS 18–19)

This takes us all the way with the dilemma of getting out of the total
system (which Michaels reinvents here): however it is conceived—
whether the market and capitalism, or the American character and
exceptional experience (American culture)—the power with which the
system is theorized outsmarts the local act of judging or resisting it from
within, revealing that to have been yet another feature of the system
itself, whether ruse or incest taboo, programmed into it in advance.
Although the form of the dilemma replicates the more abstract model of
"Against Theory," Michaels's specific topic here is "cultural criticism,"
an activity even more forcefully specified by the traditional German
word (*Kulturkritik*), on which Adorno has forceful things to say in the

great program essay that opens *Prisms*, an essay that includes Michaels's strictures within a much larger framework and raises issues significantly absent here: the status of intellectuals, the nature of culture itself as well as of its concept, and even the antinomy from which the dialectic itself emerges and in which it finds its reason for being—namely, how to do something which is impossible, yet indispensable, and in any case inevitable. Even Michaels's own peremptory solution—to *stop* doing it— does not engage the matter this far, although it surely includes the awareness that people will continue on with theory or cultural *criticism* as though nothing had ever happened.

A final rehearsal of the matter:

> do texts refer to social reality? if they do, do they merely reflect it, or do they imagine utopian alternatives to it? Like the question of whether Dreiser liked or disliked capitalism, these questions [Michaels wrongly limits them to questions of *realistic* representation] seem to me to posit a space outside the culture in order then to interrogate the relations between that space (here defined as literary) and the culture. But the spaces I have tried to explore are all very much within the culture, and so the project of interrogation makes no sense. (GS 27)

In effect, Michaels here replays the great debate about the ethical (and vaguely Kantian) nature of Second International socialism: among others, but with greater precision, Lukács diagnosed it as a moral imperative that summons us to create something which does not exist and can therefore virtually by definition never be realized. The projection of "socialism" as a radical ethical alternate to the existing order virtually ensures the impossibility of its coming into being: and this, not despite its plausibility and power as an ethical critique of capitalism, but virtually in proportion to it. On an empirical level (but Lukács's is also a telling critique of the very category of the ethical in Kant's thought), it is clear that the more corrupt and evil the existing order is, the less likelihood for anything better to emerge from it. Lukács rightly suggests that Marx's own (dialectical) account of the emergence of socialism from capitalism is very different from this one. The force of Marxism as such, as Marx himself projected it, was to have combined an argument about the desirability of socialism (and the intolerability of capitalism) with a demonstration of the ways in which socialism was *already* coming into being *within* capitalism, in which capitalism by some features of its logic was already creating the structures of socialism, and in which socialism is not staged as an ideal or a Utopia but a tendential and emergent set of already existing structures. This is the essential realism of Marx's view, which the word *inevitability* somehow misrepresents in other ways and in which the strong or full form of what Marx meant by "contradiction" can be observed and examined. It is always worth adding that Marx was not wrong about this diagnosis, particularly if we take the long temporal perspective of the *Grundrisse* in place of the foreshortened apocalyptic prophecies of *Capital* itself. To take only one feature of Lukács's analysis, processes of collectivization can today be observed to have replaced market individualism on a range of levels, all the way down to the microexperiences of daily life, something reflected in the "molecular politics" of the so-called new social movements. This model of the presence of the future within the present is then clearly quite different from the attempt to "step outside" actually existing reality into some other space: the workers of the commune, as Marx put it in perhaps his most incisive formulation, "have no ideals to realize but to set free the elements of the new society with which old collapsing bourgeois society itself is pregnant."[5]

The point is that systems, even total systems, change; but the question about the tendencies and the laws of motion of that change is also accompanied by the relatively distinct question of the role of human agency in the process (which may, of course, by a Hegelian "ruse of history" end up doing something very different from what it "intended"). Marx's notion of change is not in that sense a completely immanent one: even if they have no "ideal," the communards have a program, and their consciousness of it reflects the limits imposed on them by the very situation the program is designed to change: "mankind always raises only those problems which it is already in a position to solve."

This is then the spirit in which we need to return to the more immediate matter of the "market" and the Utopian critique of consumption and consumerism. It seems to me very important to persuade ourselves, as Michaels tirelessly insists here, that we are *inside* the culture of the market and that the inner dynamic of the culture of consumption is an infernal machine from which one does not escape by the taking of thought (or moralizing positions), an infinite propagation and replication of "desire" that feeds on itself and has no outside and no fulfillment. It is a process whose dangerous power can be more tangibly observed in the socialist countries today, which are attempting to solve the basic problem of the production and distribution of urgently needed and desirable consumers' goods without any great awareness of the autonomous dynamic of that "culture of consumption" thereby unleashed and in which we ourselves are plunged to the point of being unable to imagine anything else. This first moment, then, of a sense of the constriction of the total system, of its inescapability even for the imagination, is what can help us once again draw a firmer line between "radicalism" and "liberalism." For the liberal view is generally characterized by the belief that the "system" is not really total in that sense, that we can ameliorate it, reorganize it, and regulate it in such a way that it becomes tolerable and we thereby have the "best of both worlds." Susan Sontag's wonderful book on photography is exemplary in this respect (her conception of "image lust" is a cognate of Michaels's vision of the market and consumption, but also a significant variant and alternate way of talking about that): her conclusion about contemporary image culture is the classically liberal recommendation of a kind of "diet cure" for images,[6] what she calls a "conservationist remedy": "If there can be a better way for the real world to include the one of images, it will require an ecology not only of real things but of images as well."[7] But this solution—nothing in excess!—is in reality determined by the phantasm of an alternate "radical" one, namely, Plato, or the puritanical suppression of images altogether (her concrete example of this is Maoist China). I suspect that this kind of deep-seated fear—what I have elsewhere called the "anxiety of Utopia"—is also at work in defenses of the market which fantasize the utter removal of consumption, images, and desire at the very moment when the socialist countries themselves are edging closer to all those things.

I would therefore draw the opposite conclusion from Michaels: critiques of consumption and commodification can only be truly radical when they specifically include reflection, not merely on the problem of the market itself but, above all, on the nature of socialism as an alternative system. Unless the possibility of such an alternate system is grappled with and theorized explicitly, then I would agree that the critique of commodification tends fatally to turn back into a merely moral discussion, into mere Kulturkritik in the bad sense and a matter of "handwringing." The conquest of discursive hegemony in the 1980s by what it seems more accurate to call Thatcherism rather than Reaganism combined the naturalization of a set of economic dogmas (budgets must be balanced, production must be "efficient") with the seemingly now universally accepted conviction that "socialism does not work," a conviction largely achieved by discursive struggles (as Stuart Hall has tirelessly shown us), reinforced by the disintegration of any clear conception of what socialism ought to be and how it ought to function, particularly in the socialist countries themselves. One would think, however, that rather than dropping the whole business in embarrassed silence, this would very precisely be the moment to discuss it publicly. I say all this because the problem of the market is itself central to the problem of theorizing or conceptualizing socialism: there has emerged in recent years the beginnings of a rigorous debate on the Left around the market, largely but not exclusively written by Marxist economists in the West. Virtually the most important achievement of Michaels's own book has then been to place this topic back inescapably on the agenda, and on the agenda of cultural criticism itself, which must now shake itself out of its immanence and include the heterogeneous materials of economic and market debate alongside its textual analyses.[8] These political issues —the market and socialism—are, as he shows us only too well, the ultimate consequences, the ultimate stake, in this kind of literary or cultural analysis; it would be ironic for us to leave the field to him.

All of which seems to imply that we can step outside our system or our culture after all. But this powerful objection, which Michaels tellingly formulates for us over and over again, seems to me to involve a misunderstanding of the uses and function of Utopian thought and even Utopian critique. (I will leave out of the discussion the occasional usage by some of us whereby the code word is simply a euphemism for socialism itself.) To posit such discourse and its interest is not at all to affirm its possibility, or, in Michaels's language, its capacity in any fully realized sense to step outside our own system. That would be a still relatively representational view of the matter, leading us to inspect More or Skinner—to make an inventory of their positivities and then to add up and compare their visionary achievements. What they achieved, however, was something rather different from achieved positivity; they demonstrated, for their own time and culture, the *impossibility* of imagining Utopia. It is thus the limits, the systemic restrictions and repressions, or empty places, in the Utopian blueprint that are the most interesting, for these alone testify to the ways a culture or a system marks the most visionary mind and contains its movement toward transcendence. But such limits, which can also be discussed in terms of ideological restriction, are concrete and articulated in the great Utopian visions: they do not become visible except in the desperate attempt to imagine something else; so that a relaxed consent to immanence—a consciousness in advance of the necessary failure of the project that leads us to renounce it—can yield no experimental information as to the shape of the system and its boundaries, the specific social and historical fashion in which an outside is unattainable and we are turned back in on ourselves.

This is also, in a more restricted way, the relationship we need to develop to the radical impulses of earlier literature and culture. That Dreiser or Gilman failed to think their way out of the systems that surrounded them as some ultimate horizon of thought is scarcely surprising; but these are specific and concrete failures that yield some insight into the way in which a radical movement toward something else is also part and parcel of the system it seeks to evade or outsmart, so that at some outer limit these very gestures of revolt are also those programmed into the system. Nor is such a process merely a matter of thinking new thoughts, but rather that quite different and more tangible thing, the production of *representations*; indeed, the priority of literary and cultural analysis over philosophical and ideological investigation in this respect lies very precisely in the concrete fullness of detail afforded by every representation as to its own failure. It is the failure of imagination that is important, and not its achievement, since in any case all representations fail and it is always impossible to imagine. This is also to say that in terms of political positions and ideologies, all the radical positions of the past are flawed, precisely because they failed. The productive use of earlier radicalisms such as populism, Gilman's feminism, or even these anticommodity impulses and attitudes that Lears and others have begun to explore lies not in their triumphant reassemblage as a radical precursor tradition but in their tragic failure to constitute such a tradition in the first place. History progresses by failure rather than by success, as Benjamin never tired of insisting; and it would be better to think of Lenin or Brecht (to pick a few illustrious names at random) as failures—that is, as actors and agents constrained by their own ideological limits and those of their moment of history—than as triumphant examples and models in some hagiographic or celebratory sense. Dreiser's corruption is very much to the point here; what Michaels does not take into account in his denunciations of radical misreadings of Dreiser is why readers made them in the first place, and continue to do so—why something in the text should so imperiously tempt us to assume that this elaborate anatomy of commodity lust might spring from some inner distance from it rather than from the sheerest complacency. But this is the very ambiguity of naming a phenomenon and designating or foregrounding it: once isolated in the mind's eye, it becomes an object for judgment irrespective of authorial intention; and misreaders of Michaels himself will then be forgiven for sometimes assuming that he himself judges commodity lust in Dreiser in a positive way despite his frequent assertions that it cannot, in fact, be judged at all in that sense, positively or negatively, and that we cannot take positions like that on what exists.

Indeed, the "moment of truth" of Michaels's antiliberalism (one cannot, I think, call it conservatism in any positive or substantial ideological sense) can perhaps better be grasped by analogy with what I will call the ontological commitments of the various stages of the modern (or better still, the bourgeois) novel. What Lukács called the great realists, that is, the principal realistic novelists of the nineteenth century, can be characterized in terms of a kind of aesthetic vested interest in Being itself (which is to say, in the apprehension of society as a form of stable Being), which, despite its convulsions and the inner rhythms of its lawful transformations, can somehow eventually be grasped as such and registered. However progressive some of them may have been, they therefore could, by virtue of their calling and their aesthetic, have no stake in a vision of the social world that allows for abrupt modifications and, as it were, dialectical transformations in the very laws of that order and its local form of "human nature." The deeper formal kinship between such novelists and the historians themselves suggests that this second profession equally determines a kind of ontological commitment to the massive density of social being and experience. Michaels's own interests as a historical critic (of a new type) seem to me essentially to converge with these, for the theorists he considers radical threaten the stability of the object of study (sometimes here known simply as "the market") and, by seeming to suggest that it can be replaced by something else, tend to trivialize and undermine the research project.

All this seems to me to change with what is called modernism, where the experience of real social change in industrialism now inspires serious doubts as to the stability of being and equally serious premonitions of the constructed or demiurgic nature of the social; while, that process having been completed in the postmodern, the artists of this final period can scarcely be bothered with Being itself at all in their conviction as to the weightlessness and textualization of multiple social realities. This more postmodern position would seem, however, rather to characterize the left wing of the New Historicism, so to speak, while that of high modernism should probably be reserved for a different kind of historiography altogether, such as that of Hayden White.

A consideration of Michaels's own conception of the market will now lead us on into the third strand of his book and raise the question of that historical paradigm that sometimes seems implicitly to subtend it and at others to take center stage and become its official topic and central issue. What must first be noted is that "the market" is in Michaels what is today often contemptuously described as a totalizing concept. In this he parts company with the mainstream of the New Historicism, which, in both its Renaissance and Victorian variants, does not seem to pose or presuppose any absent yet all-informing totality or system of this kind. It seems superfluous to point out what Michaels systematically exploits in a variety of ways: namely, that this particular way of "naming the system" displaces the emphasis—and the types of explanations called for—from production or distribution to exchange and consumption. Michaels's polemic against the rhetoric of production is not explicitly directed against Marxism (which does not figure here as a topic); indeed, its principal occasion is rather the feminism of Charlotte Perkins Gilman. Still, to avoid misunderstandings, it is worth affirming that Marx's analysis of capital is not (pace Baudrillard) a "productionist" one, and that the great 1857 draft introduction to the *Grundrisse* affirms the dialectical indissolubility of the three dimensions of production, distribution, and consumption. If in spite of that Marx has always been (rightly) understood as seeing production as the key to understanding the other processes, that is because the mainstream of economic thought before and since (and including Michaels) persists in absolutizing consumption and the market. The affirmation of the "primacy of production," (whatever that might mean exactly), offers the most effective and powerful way of defamiliarizing and demystifying ideologies of the market itself and consumption-oriented models of capitalism. As a vision of capitalism, then, the affirmation of the primacy of the market is sheer ideology.

It is also, however, something else in Michaels, and this now needs to be addressed. We have already noted the tendency of a homologizing method to pose, implicitly or explicitly, some kind of "structure" that would justify the analogizing juxtaposition of the various raw materials or documents and provide the form or terms by which they can somehow be affirmed to be "the same." But in Lévi-Strauss, despite his agile methodological footwork, this common "structure" remains a transcendent mechanism which never completely folds back into any one of its surface manifestations, no matter how privileged, and therefore never utterly vanishes into the immanence of ethnographic description. As we have seen, however, the whole thrust and originality of the New Historicism lay in its discomfort with such transcendent entities and its effort to do without them altogether while preserving the discursive gains of the homological method. Michaels clearly shares this working position, but just as clearly distances himself from New Historicist practice in his effort to stage this absent common "structure" as an asphyxiating total system—the market—and thereby to endow his readings with a rather different kind of effect, that of some all-embracing closure, some all-encompassing fatality. But how can this procedure be theorized? The "market" is surely not any longer to be grasped as some old-fashioned worldview or zeitgeist; its effects in Michaels have some family likeness with the Foucauldian episteme, but that, as its very designation suggests, continues to be couched and described in terms of knowledge and to yield accounts, first, of some specific order and pattern of thinking, and, later on, of an order of discursive rules that preselect certain kinds of verbal possibilities and exclude others. That also does not exactly seem to be what is happening here. The Foucault of the prisons book—with its "biotechnologies of the body" and its tendential grid of power and control—produced effects more consonant with Michaels's baleful deployment of the market here, but, unlike Greenblatt, Michaels does not seem to be much interested in power. His own word for the matter is the best one after all: he calls all this the "logic" of naturalism, and by extension seems also to imply some deeper logic or dynamic of the market, in terms of which that specific aesthetic logic (and also those of the other exhibits, of non-naturalists like Gilman or Hawthorne) can be grasped.[9] This observation is not, in a book with the title of this one, a criticism; in my opinion, it is diagnostically more productive to have a totalizing concept than to try to make one's way without one. The Frankfurt School did not proceed otherwise, with its often somewhat fuzzy conception of "late capitalism" (or, alternately, the more Weberian "administered society").

My point lies elsewhere: namely, that such an organizing concept or system would seem to raise real problems for the schema of "Against Theory," with its individualist emphasis on authorial "intention" (even though we're not supposed to use that word any longer) and with its more general restriction to categories of the individual subject. In an Anglo-American empiricist world of individual subjects and decision makers, what can possibly be the status of this transsubjective "logic" of the market? For those formed in "Continental" theory such questions were always the most mysterious and perplexing absences in the earlier essay: surely the Freudian unconscious, to take one "theoretical" reference point, does not always "say what it means" and "mean what it says." What became of Freud, or Marxian conceptions of ideology, let alone the Foucauldian episteme mentioned above, or Baudrillard's "code," or Hegel's "ruse of reason," then seemed a very urgent problem indeed, one omitted from the antitheorists' list of exceptions ("narratology, stylistics and prosody") and conspicuous by signal lack of mention altogether. Yet these transindividual entities are the very locus of *interpretation* today, in its strongest sense (for good or ill). Far more than the debates over authorial intention, such continental concepts have provided the most frequent alibis for critical hypotheses about meanings not intended by their authors (nor does the Gadamer-Hirsch exchange really do justice to the complexity of such issues).

At this point, however, *The Gold Standard* seeks to answer this question and implicitly to enlarge the framework of "Against Theory" and its problematic. For one thing, Freud here at last makes his fateful appearance: he pops up unexpectedly among the photographers in the last chapter, reminding one a little of *Ragtime* (not bad history either!); therewith the most astonishing, and astonishingly pertinent, of the homologies comes into view: photography and psychoanalysis as events roughly contemporaneous with each other and as phenomena sharing a common structure, or at least turning on a similar structural problem. We have already seen Michaels arguing, on the occasion of Hawthorne, that photography was not "photographic realism" or representation; that it was somehow *less* representational than painting or "realism." That argument, still relatively ostentatious in its ingenuity, cited Hawthorne as authority for the sense that somehow photography was more hermeneutic and penetrated behind the surface of things in a distinctive and mysterious way. Meanwhile, one had the sense that photography—whose peculiar and untheorizable processes have unexpectedly become central to postmodernism, promoted, as it were, to the very top of the latter's new hierarchy of the fine arts, virtually for the first time in its short life span—shares with naturalism at least the ec-centricity of an unclassifiable cultural convulsion, familiar surfaces subtended by a whole archaic world of libido, which, however, vanishes when you try to fix it head-on with the naked eye. Now the place of the unconscious comes centrally into view: it is what *exceeds* intention, what is not mastered by the intentional act or the intentional expression; in short, it is chance, accident, the unforeseeable. (Michaels does not mention the fact that in this same period, with statistics and probability theory, mathematics is also in the process of mastering and outthinking chance: as witness Mallarmé and *Un coup de dés*.) For however the photographer chooses his angle and viewpoint, a host of unforeseen, unplannable detail will be registered on the final plate (something later on celebrated in film theory, in Bazin's glorification of the deep shot in Welles and Renoir as the very space of being itself, where the "world-ness of world" opens up and deconceals itself beyond all the petty "intentions" of the mere individual human subject). But chance will also be the stumbling block for the art photographers of the period — Stieglitz above all — who, seeking to promote photography as an art *like* painting and with a dignity equal to painting's (whereas its ultimate achievement of this status in the postmodern involved a *demotion* of painting and "art" as such), found themselves running up against the fact that as artists they could not lay claim to everything within their artifact because significant zones of it had nothing to do with them and escaped their direction or control: how to argue that the final product was in any aesthetic or demiurgic sense really *theirs*? This is the moment when Freud enters the picture; it turns out that the "unconscious" (slips of the tongue, dreams, neurotic symptoms, *chance* in the largest sense of the word) is not some *other* of consciousness — the other scene or stage, as Freud liked to call it — but rather very precisely an *enlargement* of consciousness, a widening of the very concept of intention so as to catch these aberrant phenomena also in its net and to make them "willed" and deliberate, to confer on them also the meaningfulness of the conscious act. "The discovery of the unconscious thus problematizes agency only to extend it, finding actions where only accidents had been" (GS 222). It is enough; with this turn of the screw Michaels outsmarts the "Continental" objections to "Against Theory" at the same time that he triggers the operation of a new homological series that comes to include machinery (via Peirce, GS 230) and gambling (Wharton's *House of Mirth*). He also thereby turns Freud back into a local, historical text, and just another of his exhibits, no less privileged than the other documents but no more so either: psychoanalysis will now definitively be set back in place as the "compulsion not to let chance count as chance" (GS 236).

This is, however, not quite the end of the story; that the adventures of agency, of consciousness and intention, are not really concluded here becomes clearer when we recall the matter of the market, whose status as something like agency on an utterly impersonal scale is scarcely addressed in the skirmish with Freud. In fact, the political unconscious of Michaels's book has not stopped thinking about the problem in another, more consequent way; and it has something rather different to tell us: not a theory, exactly, not a "solution," but an evolution and a restructuration of the problematic itself that is even more significant an

acknowledgment of the deeper issues than the settling of accounts
between intention and psychoanalysis. The "market," after all, first sent
us back to individual subjects—Dreiser, Gilman, Hawthorne, Norris, et
al. and their characters—who, caught in its logic of consumption, acted
out and demonstrated the impossibility of getting out of that into something else. Getting out of that simply meant dying (when not the romance
fantasy of immortal property rights, as in Hawthorne). But what if this
particular search could be prolonged in an unexpected and more consequent way? What if, in the failure to theorize the "system," the impossibility of thinking some nonindividual, meaningful, collective yet impersonal agency (what Marxism calls the "mode of production"), another
possibility opened up to grasp a different kind of agency—still somehow a "subject," like the individual consciousness, yet now immortal,
impersonal in another way, collective beyond the dreams of populism,
and embodied, institutionalized in so rigorous a fashion as to give it
social and historical objectivity beyond all fantasy?

The third strand of Michaels's book then consists in watching the
emergence of this other kind of "character" so different from the anthropomorphic ones—the first signs, straws in the wind, redoubled reference,
insistence growing more than significant, and finally the thing itself,
full-dress and full-blown, in its ultimate triumph. To keep the frame of
reference, it is a little like those amazing final pages in Norris's *Octopus*
when we finally penetrate the outer offices and come face to face with
God himself, behind the chairman's desk (in modernism, this will turn
back into an encounter with the Author, as in Unamuno's *Mist*). The
futures market already gave us some sense of what would happen to time
itself and to individual uncertainty when you got the proper handle on it.
Now, however, through the welter of merely empirical fact (the Rockefel-
lers and their "handwringing" enemy Ida M. Tarbell), we break through
to the new thing and its category: the trust, the monopoly, the "soulful"
corporation, with its new corporate law. This new "subject of history"
now abolishes the individual characters of laissez-faire, with their false
problems; it supersedes the opposition between production and consumption; it finally does something to the very category of the machine
itself (which figured rather differently in the photography chapter):

In fact, following Seltzer's lead, we can say that the "discourse of
force" not only undoes the opposition between body and machine
but, perhaps more surprisingly, undoes the opposition between the
body/machine and the soul, between something that is *all* body

and something that is no body at all. Thus Davis can think of the corporation as simultaneously "intangible" (no body) and a "machine"
(all body), not because he is inconsistent but because these two
conditions are more like one another than either is like the alternative, a soul in a body. (GS 201)

"Much the same," he concludes, "can be said about *The Octopus*."
Indeed, it must be, for the corporation is not first and foremost a matter
of power or of thinking and philosophizing (although it is also the occasion for Royce's concept of the "community of interpretation" GS 188),
nor even of the invention of new juridical categories or the application
of traditional ones in some new way; it is first and foremost a matter of
representation. This is the *modernist* moment: not merely the emergence of reflexivity about the process of fiction-making (the weakest of
all accounts of modernism) but rather the dawning sense of that necessary failure that is now to be forestalled, or better still, to be transformed
into a new kind of success and triumph, by reckoning the very impossibility of the representation back into the thing itself: "Hence the corporation comes to seem the embodiment of figurality that makes personhood possible, rather than appearing as a figurative extension of
personhood" (GS 205). Suprapersonal agencies are unthinkable for the
individual mind: that is, at least, what they tell us when we use words
like *class* or *class consciousness*, and woefully anthropomorphic categories like Lukács's much-derided *subject of history*. And yet they exist
and we name them: one thing might be believing in the existence of the
new entity; and another, grasping it as a figure for what we can't really
think or represent in the first place. At any rate, Michaels here yanks
the last bit of rug out from under the individual subject or "character,"
which turns out not to be what we project onto the suprapersonal entity
to make it look like a person but rather to be itself an effect and a figure,
a projection back from the collective, a second-order illusion generated
by the priorities of history itself.

Being immortal, the corporation also stills those fears of death and
dying aroused as we have seen, by individual consumption. But this is
now a relatively insignificant feature of the process whereby *The Gold
Standard* rises to the occasion and produces a concept of the collective
itself and of collective agency. In some philosophical or theoretical sense,
of course, the problem has not been solved but compounded, for we
now find ourselves in the presence of two such concepts—in other
words, of the contradiction between the corporation and our old friend

the market, which has persisted in life throughout this other, seemingly momentous, change. On one level of history, something has happened: the corporate and the trust have consigned individualism (and its forms and categories) to the ash can of history. On the other level, nothing has changed and the market continues as before, as far as the eye can reach. If the market means capitalism as a system, however, and the trust only one moment, or restructuration, of that system, then the contradiction is no longer very damaging except on the level of the text and of detail, where we continue to shuttle between one code and the other. But is the market finally an instance of the same order as the newly immortal soulful transindividual character of the great trust? Is the market also somehow a "person" or an effect of the figurality of personhood? What is the relationship between such a "logic" and the actors—consumers, writers, and trusts alike—caught up in its ineluctable machinery? What current developments in neopragmatist theory suggest is that the "market" bears the same relationship to individual subjects, with their desires and their commodity lust, as the charged term *belief* to the conscious, "theoretical" attempts (sometimes designated as "knowledge") to step outside that, to theorize or even to change it. *Belief* is here the missing totalization, the other term you can never get out of, some ultimate and definitive form of ideology fixed for all time (or what Sartre called the "originary choice of being"): "the only relevant truth about belief is that you can't go outside it, and, far from being unlivable, this is a truth you can't help but live. It has no practical consequences not because it can never be *united* with practice but because it can never be *separated* from practice" (AT 29). But have we not gotten a little out of "belief" just by calling it "the market" and giving it that figuration? And in that case, which comes first? Is it the condemnation of human beings to "belief" in this absolute sense which generates the infernal dynamic of the market? Or is it the market which somehow "produces" today this odd concept of "belief"? Is not the very separation of belief from knowledge presupposed here itself an example of the production of a theory by way of the artificial creation of two abstract entities out of an inseparable reality?

Part 2. Deconstruction as Nominalism

One's occasional feeling that, for poststructuralism, all enemies are on the left, and that the principal target always turns out to be this or that form of *historical* thinking, could conceivably lead to something other than impatience and exasperation if we drew a rather different kind of consequence. For it does not follow, for that tireless and implacable search-and-destroy mission of poststructuralism that finds traces and contaminations of the diachronic with more precision than any previous theoretical or philosophical technology, that it is *synchronic* thought that is thereby privileged. Synchronic thought is not particularly vindicated by the deficiencies of the diachronic; indeed, it remains peculiarly contradictory and incoherent (the demonstration of this is often referred to as the "critique of structuralism"), with this difference: unlike the diachronic, the conceptual antinomies of the synchronic are at once obvious and unavoidable; synchronic "thought" is a contradiction in terms, it cannot even pass itself off as thinking, and with it the last traditional vocation of classical philosophy vanishes.

What results then is the paradox that the diachronic becomes coterminous with "thinking" itself and is established as the privileged terrain of philosophy by the very force of the onslaughts upon it. If "poststructuralism," or, as I prefer, "theoretical discourse," is at one with the demonstration of the necessary incoherence and impossibility of all thinking, then by virtue of the very persistence of its critiques of the diachronic, and by way of the targeting mechanism itself, which consistently finds temporal and historical conceptualities positioned at the center of its objective, the attempt to think "history" — in however confused or internally contradictory a fashion — at length becomes identified with the very vocation of thought itself. These crude images (*Vorstellungen*) of time and change, and the cumbersome machinery of the dialectic, are palpable failures of representation, much like the naïve wingspans of the first birdmen when compared with the Wright brothers' airplane. Only in this connection we have no airplane to compare them with. Nonetheless, one can perfectly well imagine the first sophisticated hominid philosophers, already skeptics of an advanced sort, complaining among themselves about the awkwardness of the rocks their fellows use to beat and break and pound. These clumsy objects, they feel, do not even reach approximation with their concept, the "instrument" or "tool"; they are of a piece with the level and quality of social life of the hominid population itself, who, archeologists now tell us, bumped into each other a lot, were frequently confused, had short attention spans, and generally milled around aimlessly without identifiable purpose or goals. Would our hominid philosophers need some more advanced concept to make such a critique (the notion, for example, of a specialized handle and a head whose function was sharply differentiated from that—the gleaming first Platonic idea of a hammer)? Or might they not equally well have concluded that the achievement of genuine instrumentality (and differentiation) was impossible for humankind, and that even the machinery latent in the most advanced human thought—as far as the mind can reach—is doomed to a kind of comical incoherence and a representational inadequacy with its concept, space rockets fully as much as hammers, computers fully as much as blackened fire sticks? For *intention* is somehow always deeply comical: we do not need the banana skin and the interruption of an intended action for the human act, from this perspective, always to strike us as ontologically inadequate (Homeric laughter). For that, it is enough for the intention itself to be separated out from the act and to hover alongside it as a now no longer quite internal standard of judgment: at that point the very project of a human being to walk—even without slipping—is a matter of some hilarity. The implication, however, is that we should at least dispel all the ideological illusions of technological progress; and that something has been gained when we restore to all human action and thought this ineradicable dimension of clumsiness—its home-made characteristics, its unspecialized core of popular mechanics and uncoordinated infantile experimentation. The objects may be as complicated as you like, as complex as the history of philosophy itself, but when one comes to the great acts of thought and conceptualization—those of Kant or Hegel, Galileo or Einstein—what must be recaptured is the crude and preemptory simplicity—when not simple-mindedness—with which they finally decide to shatter one rock upon another.

Rousseau, another of those "great" hominids, decided to invent the concept of "history"; in his case, we can all the more easily leave aside the complex story of his precursors and his conditions of possibility, since he himself, *faux naïf*, liked to think of the matter as starting from scratch, cobbling together "an ingenious piece of home-made furniture" (as T. S. Eliot wonderfully puts it about Blake's philosophy, except that he thought "tradition" was something other than that; and in general the problem with the idea of bricolage lies in its presupposition that there is another, more efficient way of doing things). It is the interest of Rousseau, as one of the great cruxes and white elephants of Western philosophy, to offer the spectacle of this crude new thought—history— on the moment of its invention out of nothingness.

It is important to add at once, however, that the "greatness" of Rousseau's most advanced critic and analyst, Paul DeMan, is of the same order as this. The grandiose architectonics of the Rousseau half of *Alle-*

gories of Reading—the immense building up of the fundamental blocks of metaphor, self, allegory, allegory of reading, promises, and excuses—a *Darstellung* of which he (like the Marx who had just finished the first volume of *Capital*) had reason to be proud, is no less an "ingenious piece of home-made furniture" than the peculiar compositions it took as its object of study. The very crudeness of its emergent philosophical generalizations is now to be grasped as a matter of honor and a title of glory: to begin from zero in the realm of thinking is not an achievement given to everyone. DeMan kept faith with Rousseau precisely in this aboriginal construction of the text itself; and it seems to me more productive to insist on the relationship between the difficulty of his own book and the stark simplicity of its newly forged thoughts than to evoke a hypersophisticated "thought of the other" so complex and subtle as to stand forever out of reach, and thereby to stimulate those feelings of textual envy which Harpham has identified in DeMan's critics. To put it in another, more aesthetic, way, restoring the clumsiness of some initial thought process means returning to the act of thinking as praxis and stripping away the reifications that sediment around that act when it has become an object. Gertrude Stein liked to say that "every masterpiece came into the world with a measure of ugliness in it. . . . It's our business as critics to stand in front of it to recover its ugliness."[10]

DeMan's "status" as a critic and thinker is so absolutely bound up with that of Rousseau that the uncertainties about the latter's historical specificity (as there are multiple, but not infinite, possibilities of reckoning this, I prefer to avoid the word *indecidability*) project uncertainties about DeMan's own project.

For one thing, few contemporaries have lived the crisis in history, the crisis in historiography, the crisis in the narrative language of the diachronic, so intensely as DeMan: the possibility of returning afresh to this extreme experience—however he himself decided to handle it theoretically—is then one of the sources of the value and significance of his reflection on it for us. "I began to read Rousseau seriously," he tells us, "in preparation for a historical reflection on Romanticism and found myself unable to progress beyond local difficulties of interpretation. In trying to cope with this, I had to shift from historical definition to the problematics of reading. This shift, which is typical of my generation, is of more interest in its results than in its causes."[11] This final sentence shrewdly attempts to cut his own "solutions" off from the historical perspective which he found himself unable to adopt for his own objects of study; if respected, therefore, this cautionary note is self-fulfilling and validates the subsequent positions themselves. One understands, obviously, what he meant by both features of the passage just quoted: the vacuousness of the narratives of manuals of literary history, which are constitutively unable to confront the texts themselves except as examples; and the crude causalities of the history of ideas, which sometimes reach their formulation in psychoanalysis (something for which he had a lifelong aversion), or else (less frequently) their generalization in the form of vulgar sociology. It would be a mistake, however, to limit the originality of DeMan's experience of this problem to some mere shift from diachrony to synchrony (the form it might take, for example, in some *future* manual of the history of ideas of our own period).

But the repudiation of the periodizing categories of the manuals is a complicated and dialectical one, since they are also *retained* in DeMan's work, in which notions of the radical difference between the Enlightenment and romanticism remain in force, along with a certain more hesitant distinction between romanticism and modernism. Romanticism is, among other things, the moment of Schiller and of the vulgarization of eighteenth-century thought (or its transformation into an ideology, to use a different language). Romanticism thus becomes a dangerous moment, a moment of *seductiveness* (to use DeMan's central ethical category); but what seduces us here is a thought system or an ideological synthesis (the dialectic would also be included, when we call it *that* and mobilize it at that level of generality), whereas the modern marks the triumph of a more properly verbal and sensory seductiveness (a point to which we will return). It was therefore crucial for DeMan to secure the historical specificity of the eighteenth century, as is clear in his otherwise seemingly unmotivated warning in the preface to *The Rhetoric of Romanticism*: "Except for some passing allusions, *Allegories of Reading* is in no way a book about romanticism or its heritage,"[12] a correction that implied the tendency of at least some readers to assimilate the descriptions in that book (and Rousseau's texts) to his readings of the texts of other periods. "The trouble with Marxism," he once observed in private conversation, "is that it has no way of understanding the eighteenth century." Unfamiliar with the literature, he could not have been aware how shrewd an insight this was into the "transition" debates, as well as those about "bourgeois revolution" and the relationship of state power to capitalism.

In the manuals the eighteenth century is customarily identified as the moment of the birth of History — of historicity and the sense of history as well as the possibilities (if not yet the practice) of modern historiography. How this characterization is to be related to its other pseudonym, the Age of Reason, lies in the peculiar coordination between the exercise of reason and the emergence of those new historical realities (the discovery of older radically different modes of production in the Americas and Tahiti, the conflict of modes of production in prerevolutionary Europe) with which it had never previously had to deal. Now, for one long moment, Reason will "set all the facts aside"[13] (to reproduce one of Rousseau's most scandalous gestures) and try to work history up by sheer abstract deduction or reduction. In other words, to think its way back to the origins of this or that (virtually the central category in this philosophical debate on "history") by removing what is inessential from the materials of contemporary life. Kant's word for this procedure, which he follows in his own philosophical reasoning, was rather freely rendered by an early translator as "to annihilate in thought"[14] After the richer empirical historiography that developed in the nineteenth century, the procedure will cease to characterize the exercise of philosophical Reason in any central way, and fall to the status of the "thought experiment," or, in phenomenology, Merleau-Ponty's notion of the "phantom member" (feeling in a limb that has already been amputated as a dramatization of the impossibility of grasping something we can never be without, such as Language, or Being itself, or the body). The epistemological privilege of the eighteenth century, then, its value for us as a unique conceptual laboratory, lies in the paradoxical situation that (particularly with Rousseau) it not merely produced the concept of "origins" but also, virtually simultaneously, its most devastating critique. This seems in part to have been what made Rousseau an ideal object of study for DeMan.

Rousseau can also be read as opening that conceptual space later on secured by the dialectic itself; but DeMan's chapter on that fundamental dialectical text which is the *Discourse on the Origin and Foundations of Inequality* (hereinafter called simply the *Second Discourse*) does not give (nor does it try to give) an adequate picture of the larger narrative form of this essay, in part because his central illustration, the giant as metaphor, is drawn from a secondary fragment (draft or sequel to this one, no one quite knows which) called the "Essay on the Origins of Language."

Rousseau's thoughts on language in the *Second Discourse* are certainly interesting enough, but as much for their function and narrative position as for their content. They can serve as a fundamental demonstration of that "reduction in thought" just referred to, and of the way in which Rousseau necessarily "sets all the facts aside" to arrive at what is at least a negative concept of the "state of nature": peeling away successive layers of everything artificial and "unnecessary," social, luxurious, and thereby immoral, from human reality in order to see what remains when those inessentials are stripped away. At that point, Rousseau will then reverse the process in order to reconstruct the history by which these degraded supplements came into being and human society as we know it today emerged. His is therefore virtually the first example of that "progressive-regressive method" Sartre attributed to Henri Lefebvre, but which the latter credited to Marx himself (in the 1857 preface to the *Grundrisse*).[15]

In Rousseau, however, this reversal is not unproblematical, something made obvious by his remarks on language, itself very precisely one of those "nonessential" social additions and auxiliaries which Reason's reduction by thought feels able to remove from essential human life. The problem is that Rousseau has talked himself so powerfully into the proof that language could never have come into being in the first place that he must break off in embarrassment, since it obviously did. The "Essay" then returns to this conundrum, which it worries in a variety of ways, none of them conclusive.

His narrative, however, evidently requires a new kind of causal concept —a detonator—in order to reverse itself and to explain the beginnings of History as such, in the sense of the dynamism of Lévi-Strauss's "hot societies" or the origins of state power in the Marxian sense. It is clearly incorrect to attribute to Rousseau any univocal (and thus quasireligious) vision of this Fall, or any single form of causality or determination. The *Second Discourse* indeed posits or hypothesizes a variety of local starting points, which at various moments include sexuality (which stimulates fights among men by way of love and jealousy, and thus not merely institutes inequality but also generates the need for language [*RSD* 134, 147]) and, more famously, private property itself ("the first person, who having fenced off a plot of ground, took it into his head to say, *this is mine.*" . . . [*RSD* 141]). What is, however, dialectical, or at least proto-dialectical, in Rousseau[16] is the double valence of "perfectibility" itself, which defines everything distinctive about human beings as such and also determines the well-nigh inevitable fatality of their fall into degradation, corruption, and civilization (*RSD* 114–15).

What justifies DeMan's "linguistic" reading is that this process is in Rousseau everywhere described in terms of differentiation: the class experience of the eighteenth century was, above all, one of the intolerability of caste distinctions, rank, the overweening pride of the great, and obsessions with "degree" and face, all of which are powerfully concentrated in the eponymous word *inequality* in a feudal and social more than an economic sense. Such differentiation is also, however, explicitly characterized by Rousseau in protolinguistic terms and as the deeper meaning of the origin of language itself, as we shall see shortly.

A final narrative shift deserves mention here, because it forms the climax of the *Second Discourse* and amounts to something like a potentiation or dialectical intensification of the first "inequalities"; namely, the origin of the state itself and state power, about which Rousseau wishes to show that its sham contract is an enormous swindle and hoax (thereby initially motivating his own version of a genuine "social contract," which we will examine below).

Of DeMan's more personal affinities with Rousseau, we learn virtually nothing and can only speculate (that a Belgian would be interested in the marginality of Switzerland with respect to the great Parisian fact seems, for example, obvious enough). But there are a few lapses; I think of the moment in his *Mythologies* when Barthes, having evoked their demystificatory function, admits that he has here and there indulged some more ontological and Bachelardian description for relief. So also DeMan surrenders to the seductive temptation of a very different kind of criticism (mostly explicitly repudiated by him) when he observes, about *La Nouvelle Heloïse*:

> Passions are then conceived as pathological needs, which is also why they are affectively valorized in terms of pleasure and pain. The allegory inevitably shifts to a eudaemonic vocabulary. In its more domestic versions, this vocabulary generates the mixture of erotic sweetness and deceit, of "doux modèle" with "âcres baisers" that hangs over much of Rousseau's fictions. He himself compared *Julie* to the "soave licor" (Tasso) that covers up the bitterness of the actual statement, and this slightly nauseating flavor catches the quintessential aroma of Rousseau's necessarily "bad" taste. One can always console oneself from this cloyness with the hygienically brisk *Social Contract.* (AR 209)

Still, it can be agreed that this particular bodily or phenomenological dimension of Rousseau's texts is repulsive enough to secure it against all "seduction." The epistemological dimension is more revealing: "for a mind as distrustful as Rousseau's, little inclined to have faith in any voice, including his own, it seems unlikely that such a chain of displacements could be mastered without further complications" (AR 225). Here paranoia and self-loathing, which might have tempted another critic on to existential psychoanalysis of this or that variety, become a "happy fall" and a "fortunate accident" which define the epistemological privilege of Rousseau's thinking and writing. This now uniquely allows us to observe the forging of a historical conceptuality ex nihilo and its simultaneous dismantling out of suspicion and distrust—a construction followed immediately in the same text by a deconstruction. Although some more general rhetoric of "deconstruction" (as an ideology) goes on to suggest that all "great" texts thus deconstruct themselves, or that literary language as such always does so, these assertions cannot be generalized on the basis of the analysis of Rousseau; while in the meantime, further "explanations" of Rousseau's privileged epistemological possibilities in this respect—his "paranoia" or his social and historical situation—have already been strategically blocked in DeMan ("of more interest in its results than in its causes").

The crucial topic for DeMan's analysis will then be the way in which Rousseau's mind constructed the so-called state of nature: not just the past in general, or any historical past, but the *necessary* historical past —what remains, what must have been there, when we remove the artifice and the decadent frivolity and luxury of "civilization" as that has already been identified and denounced in the *First Discourse*. This is the point at which it is crucial to distinguish DeMan's perspective on the *Second Discourse* ("On the Inequality of Humankind") from Derrida's (in *Of Grammatology*). Indeed, it seems to me a useful working hypothesis, at least for the moment and in a situation in which their names are so often evoked together and subsumed under the rubric of "deconstruction," to assume from the outset that these two bodies of "signed" theory have nothing whatsoever to do with each other. This therapeutic working hypothesis will indeed be more deeply justified by the picture of DeMan's metaphysics I want to develop here, which will look very different from the positions generally associated with Derrida.

In this particular instance, however—the matter of the "state of nature" —certain initial differences in emphasis can be clearly marked. DeMan will characterize the state of nature as a "fiction" (AR 136), just as he will consider Rousseau's political philosophy (including the constitutions devised by the *philosphe*) as a set of "promises," and his narrative of his own past as a set of "excuses." These terms already oddly disqualify what lies beyond the present as a set of subjective projections; or rather, since we have already had occasion to mark DeMan's hostility to the "subjective" as such (and will do so again), as a set of conventions of a relatively flimsy social sort. To think, for example, of the Constitution of the United States as a "promise," however defamiliarizing that description may be, is somehow to adopt a perspective on it from which the force of institutions (and of Althusser's Ideological State Apparatuses) seems oddly invisible. Existential guilt will also become a kind of "motivation of the device" in the Russian formalist sense, an after-effect of sentence structure (AR 299). As for "fiction," it seems an oddly antiquated and "aesthetic" category in the current atmosphere of simulacra and image-society theory; of the prolongation of contemporary trends in psychoanalysis also, where "fantasy" and the imaginary often seem to have more powerful effectivity than reality or reason; and of historiographic theory as well, where the various empirical pasts of history sometimes do not seem much more compelling ideologically than Rousseau's particular "fiction." If narrative theory today has accomplished anything substantial, it is to have powerfully displaced the old category of the "fictive" (along with that, equally important to DeMan, beneath all suitable transformations, of "literary language"). For the moment, however, it is enough to signal the operative presence in DeMan's texts of older categories like "fiction" or "irony," which the Derridean text does not seem particularly to respect or acknowledge. Derrida's interest (to summarize it overhastily) bears not on the fictionality of the "experience" of the past that Rousseau's account seems to presuppose but on the internal contradictions of his formulation. To work our way back mentally to a situation that must have once existed (language must have once upon a time emerged for hominids; there must have been a time when surpluses did not exist, when social and tribal institutions themselves slowly came into being) requires us to postulate, either in language or in writing, a condition from which both of those "properties" are absent, something whose many incoherences and contradictions can at least be dramatized by this one: namely, the difficulty for a being who "possesses" speech/writing to imagine what their absence could possibly entail. This particular focus then strikes at all imagination of radical change or difference and poses the question of how a being informed by one system in the present could possibly have any appreciation of a condition radically different, since by definition the thesis of difference and change means just that, that the past is inaccessible and unimaginable. But the force of Derrida's argument requires the political and intellectual precondition that we do go on "believing" in the difference of the past, despite the incoherence of this

conceptuality; DeMan's fictionality no longer seems to stage that agonizing double bind. The state of nature falls to an optional standing; or
rather its historical content is displaced by a rather different kind of
philosophical interest, which it would be misleading to characterize as
epistemological and in which the problem of origins is also somehow
transformed: this is the whole question of the birth of *abstraction* and
indeed philosophical conceptuality as such, emphasis on which will
now yield a very different reading of Rousseau's text and indeed of the
rest of his work.

The analysis is staged under the sign of metaphor, a word and concept that should always be approached cautiously in DeMan's writing,
since its traditionally celebratory function in literary and aesthetic writing (metaphor as the hallmark of genius or as the very essence of poetic
language) is here always ruthlessly excluded. Indeed, paradoxically, metaphor "is essentially anti-poetic" (*AR* 47); even more paradoxically, far
from being the very heartland of the figural and the space in which
language is liberated from the literal and the referential (in general, the
viewpoint of romantic and modernist aesthetics, at least when these
become ideologies of the aesthetic and are loosely transmitted as general ideas), metaphor is for DeMan something like the source and origin, the deeper cause, of the literal and referential illusions themselves:
"Metaphor overlooks the fictional, textual element in the nature of the
entity it connotes. It assumes a world in which intra- and extra-textual
events, literal and figural forms of language, can be distinguished, a
world in which the literal and the figural are properties that can be
isolated and, consequently, exchanged and substituted for each other"
(*AR* 152). "This is an error," he adds, "although it can be said that no
language would be possible without this error." It is thus clear that whatever the status of the tropes in DeMan, we must not suppose that metaphor is here dethroned in order to promote some other figure (meton-
ymy, for example, or catachresis) to the central position in some putative
poetic structure. We will return to the question of rhetoric in a moment,
and in particular to the peculiar problem it presents here of depending
on a distinction between the literal and the figurative which it is simultaneously concerned to undermine. Suffice it for the moment to use this
passage as an illustration of what is most taxing and perplexing in
DeMan's argumentation, and perhaps also most "dialectical": namely,
just this shift from structure to event, from the positing of a structural
relationship within a textual moment to the attention to its subsequent
effects, which then disaggregate the initial structure. This is the sense

in which metaphor is and is not an "error": it generates illusions; yet insofar as it is inescapable and part of the very fabric of language itself, "error" does not seem a particularly suitable word for it, since we have no space available that might allow us to get outside language and to make such judgments. (Such was, however, Rousseau's procedure and his epistemological illusion; and there is a sense in which, as we shall see, DeMan's extraordinary effort replicates Rousseau's on a more theoretically sophisticated level, and may thus also be said to constitute a late form of eighteenth-century rationalism.)

The *Second Discourse* will then be staged—using Rousseau's own categories—as a tension between names and metaphors or, if you prefer, as an exemplary slippage from names to metaphors. The "name" is here, following Rousseau, taken relatively unproblematically as a use of language which isolates the *particular* in its strong sense of the absolutely unique and individual, the "heterogeneous," to use contemporary terminology, what cannot be subsumed under the general or the universal: an intersection between human language and the radical "difference" of things among each other and from us. To put it this way is to begin to awaken some sense of the peculiarity, and indeed the very perversity and impossibility, inherent in the act of nomination itself: "tree" already no longer seems to be a "name" for the particular "great-rooted blossomer" I gaze at out this window; while, if some people find themselves able to name their favorite car, we do not normally name our favorite armchair or our favorite comb or toothbrush. As for those other names, the "proper" ones, Lévi-Strauss in particular has richly taught us the ways in which names are part of classification systems, something which at once subverts the pretension of the individual name to uniqueness (in other linguistics this particularizing function is taken over by the virtually wordless operation of the *deictic*—the "this" or "that," the pointing at the otherwise ineffable specificity of the unique object in the here and now). But DeMan's arguments are not particularly vitiated by these considerations, which only draw the second, metaphorical operation back one stage in time and confirm the vanity of language itself in general, whose ineradicably generalizing and conceptualizing, universalizing, "properties" slip across the surface of a world of unique and ungeneralizable things. Thinking about it this way then inevitably stages an ontological (or metaphysical) picture of the world and language (to which we will return later).

But language *emerges*; we do name and talk about things, whether in error or not; and the rationalizing procedures of the eighteenth century

led Rousseau to try to "understand" (or "explain") this situation by genet-
ically or historically deducing a stage in which it was not yet present:
"The repeated contacts between man and various entities, and between
the entities themselves, must necessarily engender in the mind of man
the perception of relationships" (Rousseau, quoted in *AR* 155). Such
relationships—first, comparisons ("large, small, strong, weak"), and then
number itself—mark the birth of true conceptualization and abstraction; or, if you prefer, of an abstraction that grasps itself as such (unlike
nomination, which still purports to respect the particular, and *not* to
compare). Sheer conceptual relationship would then seem to wash back
over the particular and convert it into a series of equivalences or identities: you cannot, in other words, evoke the quantitative differences
between two entities (this tree is *larger* than that one) without having
somehow posed their equivalence (or their resemblance), at least in that
respect. The reign of the name therefore ends at that point, and that of
the word, the concept, the abstraction, the universal, begins. DeMan
will, of course, now crucially identify this transformation as the operation of metaphor. The concept implies some preliminary decision about
the resemblance of a specific group of entities among themselves (we
call them henceforth men, trees, armchairs, or whatever). Yet on that
level of the preliminary decision, the entities have nothing in common
with each other; they are all distinct existents, and therefore, at that
virtually prelinguistic moment, to "compare" two distinct "blossomers"
is as outrageous a linguistic act as to describe "my love" as a "red, red
rose." This identification of the emergence of abstraction as a metaphorical operation is, of course, a good deal more than a gloss on this specific
passage in Rousseau: it is also a strategic act which enables DeMan's
unique "rhetorical" system to come into being, as we shall see. A pause
at this point in the process of "theoretical construction" allows us to see
a little more clearly what the otherwise seemingly unique and unclassifiable work of DeMan has in common with certain other bodies of contemporary thought.

Adorno is the most proximate of those whose vision of the tyranny of
the concept—so-called identity theory, the violence imposed on the
heterogeneous by the abstract identities of Reason (Rousseau's resem-
blances, DeMan's metaphors)—has a cognate diagnostic function (something again detectable in the frequent temptations to compare his
"negative dialectics" with some form of Derridean "deconstruction").
Bracketing the difference between a philosophy that describes these
phenomena on the level of the concept and a theory that searches them

out in the pattern of linguistic events themselves involves adjourning the (perhaps metaphysical) question of the ontological priority of language over consciousness; but it requires us to observe in passing the greater internal narrativity of DeMan's account, as opposed to something like an external narrativity in the "dialectic of enlightenment." In DeMan, as we shall see, the structural fact of metaphorization has eventlike consequences for the text and its content, consequences that will eventually be sorted out and typologized in the various kinds of allegories. In Adorno the tyranny of the concept, the abstract, "identity," can be outsmarted in various ways, of which the proposal for a "negative dialectics" is something like a codification and a whole strategic program. In Adorno also, however, as with metaphor for DeMan, the concept remains binding and is an ineradicable component of thought (such that "error" is here also both an appropriate and an inadequate characterization). But Adorno—like Rousseau in this respect, and very unlike DeMan—feels able to reconstruct an external historical narrative which can account for the emergence of abstraction (resemblance in Rousseau, reason or the enlightenment "mastery" over nature in Adorno and Horkheimer). This narrative turns centrally in both versions around fear and the hominids' vulnerability to a massively threatening nature, to which only thinking offers a durable instrument of protection and control. DeMan, who can be thought to have had a historical experience of fear and vulnerability greater than most North Americans, excludes explanations of this kind, which he would doubtless have characterized as "less interesting."

The deeper affinities with DeMan's problematic here lie in Marx himself, and in particular in the latter's account of the four stages of value (an account which can, of course, also be read as an emergence narrative, although it need not be). DeMan did not live to explore and articulate the encounter with Marxism that he promised us in his last years. *Allegories of Reading*, however, already includes a substantial hint, which displaces the encounter with Marxism from the anthropological (needs, human nature, etc.) to what he calls "linguistic conceptualization":

> But an economic foundation of political theory in Rousseau is not
> rooted in a theory of needs, appetites, and interests that could lead
> to ethical principles of right and wrong; it is the correlative of lin-
> guistic conceptualization and is therefore neither materialistic, nor
> idealistic, nor merely dialectical since language is deprived of rep-

resentational as well as of transcendental authority. The complex relationship between Rousseau's and Marx's economic determinism could and should only be approached from this point of view. (AR 158)

Like Derrida, DeMan's theoretical encounters with Marxism seem to have been primarily mediated by Althusser, whose work on Rousseau DeMan admired (he seems to have felt [AR 224] that it was an *interesting* misreading and more useful than the banal misreadings of psychoanalytic, biographical, thematic, and disciplinary approaches). It must be confessed that Rousseau has generally been an embarrassment for Marxism (as for almost everybody else); the absorption of eighteenth-century mechanical materialism into the Marxian tradition has not been accompanied by any greater benevolence for Rousseau's "idealism," "sentimentalism," etc. But to reread *The Social Contract* is to find the Convention rising up vividly before our eyes; while debates about the Jacobin strand (so prophetically articulated by Rousseau here) in the subsequent history of left or Marxian political formations generally have not adequately addressed the continuing relevance of *The Social Contract* for problems of the party and the state, of the "dictatorship of the proletariat" and the need to project a vision of some more advanced socialist democracy beyond the forms of bourgeois parliamentary representation. DeMan's shrewd and valuable suggestion, however, warns us to postpone these comparative generalities of political philosophy and to engage, first, the more difficult activity of sorting through the linguistic tissue of these ideas or "values." Indeed, we will see in a moment that *The Social Contract* itself not only cries out for such reading but is virtually incomprehensible without it.

The more immediate problematic, however, in which Marxism and DeManian deconstruction overlap, can be identified, from the Marxist perspective, as the "theory of value." This juxtaposition is made less perplexing by the reminder that in Marx, "the whole mystery of the form of value lies hidden"[17] in the even more mysterious phenomenon of equivalence, on which exchange value and the very possibility of exchanging one object for another, different, one, are somehow founded. (In order to avoid terminological confusion, the reader needs to remember that "use value" at once drops out of the picture on the opening page of *Capital*: it marks our existential relationship to unique things, something to which I will return in a moment, but is not in that sense subject to the law of value or equivalence. In contemporary terminology, then, we might say that "use value" is the realm of difference and differentiation as such, whereas "exchange value" will, as we shall see, come to be described as the realm of identities. But what this terminological usage means in Marx is that henceforth value as such and "exchange value" are synonymous.)

The discussion of the four stages of value in *Capital*[18] should also be distinguished from the "construction" of the so-called labor theory of value, which, following Adam Smith, identifies the value of a produced commodity in the amount of labor time it contains. Whether this theory entails or amounts to an anthropology (in the sense in which Althusser or DeMan himself might denounce that) is a very interesting question; but the matter of production is the other face, or the other dimension, of the phenomenon of the "value form" that concerns us here; it grounds the market and exchange and culminates in the emergence of that peculiar thing called money.

Viewed linguistically or "rhetorically," Marx's analysis drives the exploration of "metaphoric identification" a good deal further—into fresh thickets and complexities—than does that of Rousseau (or DeMan, for whom metaphor is here only the starting point and enabling act of his reading). Marx seeks to defamiliarize—to "estrange," if you prefer —the seemingly natural set whereby we weigh distinct kinds of objects against each other and even occasionally exchange them as though they were somehow the same. The mystery then consists in trying to fathom what a pound of salt could possibly have in common with three hammers, and in what way it makes sense to affirm of them that they are, somehow, "the same." Marx sharpens the problem by specifying two objects which are in principle more closely related to each other, namely, "twenty yards of linen" and "one coat," presumably the coat into which that linen has been made. This choice is obviously designed to lay in place the rather different problem of the production of *new* value, which will be his central concern later on in *Capital*.

We are here clearly again in the realm of metaphor, which is surely what we have to call this kind of identification of two distinct objects with one another if the identification is not thinkable, if it remains a mystery, or if it cannot be justified by conceptual reason. My sense is that for Marx also, the positing of equivalence remains in that sense nonthinkable, even though it can also be explained (the labor theory of value) in structural and historical ways different from and surely superior to the rather mythic "explanations," in terms of sheer fear and weakness, of Rousseau or Adorno. There is thus a sense in which the Marxian analysis of equivalence is fully compatible with DeMan's rhetorical account: seeing this primal metaphorical violence, by which two commodities are decreed to be "the same," in terms of the linguistic function of the trope itself is surely a welcome enrichment of Marx's schema. But Marx in turn surely adds something else to the linguistic account in his "explanation," in his narrative of the process of the emergence of value (and what position that "something else" might occupy in the DeManian scheme could only be determined by comparing Marx's "narrative" to DeMan's "story" of the "birth of allegory out of primal metaphor," which we have not yet outlined here).

There is, however, also a way in which the staging of the "mystery" in Marx and the nature of the objects involved greatly expands and modifies Rousseau's starting point, which turned on two relatively simple situations: the "identity" of objects and the apprehension of the other human being as being somehow "the same" as myself (pity, sympathy). Indeed, DeMan's very interesting discussion of the second of these zones of the metaphorical act (the Other, the giant, "man") has the disadvantage of neglecting the first one, or indeed of somehow conflating our relations to objects with our relations to other people. But in Marx it is no longer a question of understanding how one tree might be juxtaposed with another very different one in order that the "name" and the "concept" tree thereby somehow emerge; it is rather a question of understanding how altogether distinct objects (the salt, the hammers, the linen, the coat) could be somehow considered equivalences. The most exciting Marxian epistemological work then follows Marx's anti-Cartesian and dialectical methodological lesson; namely, that we do not build up complex ideas out of simple ones, but rather, the other way around, that it is the intuition of the complex form that gives us the key to grasping the simpler one. From the law of value, or the mystery of the equivalence of radically different things, we can then return in a new way to the simpler problem of universals and particulars; or if you prefer, abstraction itself and conceptual thought (DeMan's "linguistic conceptualization") must first be positioned in the larger field of the operation of the law of value before its more specialized philosophical and linguistic effects can be understood. Or finally, to be even more "vulgar" (that is to say, more ontological) about it, philosophical and linguistic abstraction is itself an effect and a by-product of exchange.

In Marx's description of the way in which, of the two terms of the equivalence, one comes to serve as the *expression* of the other ("the linen expresses its value in the coat; the coat serves as the material in which that value is expressed: [MC 139]), we can see a richer dialectical anticipation of the doctrine of metaphor as tenor and vehicle. Meanwhile, the very irreversibility of the equation by which the two objects are affirmed as being "the same" in value then introduces a "temporal" process into this structure, in a way compatible with DeMan's accounts of the generation of "narrative" out of metaphor and the subsequent "allegorical" forms which result from that structural tendency. But the word *temporal* should not be taken to imply the participation here of "real" lived or existential time, nor of historical time either. As I have suggested, it is possible to read Marx's account of the four forms of value in a genealogical, narrative, "continuist," or historical way: the first equivalences are formed at the intersection between two autonomous systems or self-sufficient social formations: salt has no "exchange value" within our tribe, but as we have no metals, and as the neighbors seem interested in salt and willing to exchange metallic objects for it, an "accidental" form of equivalence comes into being. When this mode of comparing different objects and positing their equivalences is drawn within an autarchic social formation, a new kind of movement results whereby a host of now provisional equivalences seizes on a great range of objects in turn: "metaphoric" moments spring up fitfully in punctual exchanges and then disappear again, only to reemerge at distant points on the social network. This is then the "total or expanded form of value," a kind of infinite and infinitely provisional chain of equivalence that courses through the object world of a social formation, and in which the objects ceaselessly change places in the two poles of the value equation (which, as we have said, is not reversible). People ceaselessly exchange, without any stability in the process: "the relative expression of value of the commodity is incomplete, because the series of its representations never comes to an end. The chain, of which each equation of value is a link, is liable at any moment to be lengthened by a newly created commodity, which will provide the material for a fresh expression of value" (MC 156). This moment can, of course, also be described from a different perspective, one in which emphasis is laid on the provisionality of the moments and on the ceaseless dissolution of value that follows them: the very "law" of value, not yet institutionalized and solidified in a medium, at all points is then totally consumed and vanishes into smoke with each transaction. Such a description corresponds to what Baudrillard calls symbolic exchange (the Utopian moment of his own view of history, whose name has been significantly modified from Mauss; Malinowski's kula system has sometimes been taken to be a formalized projection of this moment, although it could just as easily be considered its reification and transformation into something else; while the relationship of Baudrillard's reading to Bataille's anthropological celebration of excess, destruction, and the potlatch should also be apparent).

This infinite, in-terminable chain of exchanges proving intolerable, the "general form of value" emerges to seal the uniformity of the process by producing, as it were, its concept of itself ("value" as a general idea or universal property), which it then embodies in a single object designed to serve as the "standard" for all the rest. But this is a very peculiar and contradictory operation: "the new form we have just obtained expresses the values of the world of commodities through one single kind of commodity set apart from the world" (*MC* 158). The object thus elected has an impossible role to fulfill because it is both a thing in the world, with a potential value just like all the other things, and something removed from the object world that is called upon, from the outside, to mediate the latter's new value system. It is not terribly astonishing to find cows thus selected (Evans-Pritchard's classic description of the Nuer); at least they can accompany you on their own legs and momentum; but the horrendous cumbersomeness of the process is also apparent. Gayatri Spivak has proposed that we rethink the formation of the literary canon in terms of this dialectic of the stages of value—a suggestive notion indeed.[19] But I would have been tempted myself to correlate this peculiar third stage, in which an inner-worldly object comes to do double duty as the nascent universal equivalent, with the symbol and the symbolic moment of thought: culturally in the various modernist efforts to endow this or that sensory representation of a worldview with a kind of universal force (those new universal "myths" Mr. Eliot thought he saw emergent in Joyce); but philosophically in the universalizing turn of *pensée sauvage* on the point of reaching conceptual abstraction, as in the pre-Socratics where a single inner-worldly element ("all is water; all is fire") is posited as the ground of being.

What follows, then, will not only be abstraction; it will be allegory, and a desperate effort to reach the "concept" which necessarily fails and thereupon marks itself as failure in order to succeed despite itself. This is, of course, in Marx, the money form, and the famous pages on commodity fetishism which ensue are Marx's dramatic rehearsal of just this success and failure of the peculiar consequences that result from it. For our purposes here, it will be useful to transcode "commodity fetishism" into a vast process of abstraction that seethes through the social order. If we recall Guy Debord's remarkable formulation of the image as the "final form of commodity reification" (in *The Society of the Specta-cle*), the relevance of the theory to contemporary society, to the media, to postmodernism itself, is at once secured. Meanwhile, if there is any plausibility in my suggestion that DeMan's exploration of the conse-quences of the inaugural metaphorical moment has deeper affinities with Marx's staging of the emergence of value, then this affinity also opens up a possible relationship between the former's notions of textu-ality and those more postmodern concerns with the peculiar dynamics of media signification that at first seem so distant from him.

At any rate, this retelling of the "stages" of the notion of value should also make it possible to affirm that Marx's *Darstellung* is not exactly a narrative either: for the first stages, as it were, fall outside narrative and are only reconstructed genealogically. In this, "value" has a dynamic comparable to that attributed to language itself by Lévi-Strauss: as this last is for him a system, it cannot come into being piecemeal. Either it exists all at once or it does not exist at all, which is to say only that it is abusive (but inevitable) to transfer terms that are meaningful only for a linguistic system to the random bits and pieces, the grunts and gestures, which in hindsight seem to prepare it.

It is a pity that DeMan does not insist more strongly on the replica-tion of this drama of the universal and the particular in the *Second Discourse* on the larger "political" arena of *The Social Contract* (he seems to have feared that the word *metaphoric* used so distinctively by him in these contexts, would there degenerate into some weaker "organic" stereotype calculated to reinforce the standard misreadings of this text). But the situation is altogether comparable, as his interest-ing characterization of "the metaphorical structure of the number sys-tem" (*AR* 256) (the One of the state, the Many of the people) suggests in passing. At this later stage in his own *Darstellung*, however, DeMan has moved on to what we may call the "indeterminacy" of legal language, that is to say, its capacity to function meaningfully in altogether unfore-seeable new contexts, something characterized, on the one hand, as a "promise," and on the other, as the tension between two functions of language, the constative and the performative ("grammatical logic can function only if its referential consequences are disregarded" [*AR* 269]).

But surely there is no more dramatic instance of the artificial emer-gence of metaphoric abstraction and of the conceptual universal from the realm of particularity and heterogeneity than the appearance—or rather, for Rousseau, the deconcealment, for it was always the primal act that secured the existence of "society" in the first place—of the general will itself. DeMan rightly insists that the structural consequences of this primal or unification on the social level are quite different textually from what we find in the *Second Discourse*. But the dilemma is, if anything, more acute here, since in Rousseau it becomes very difficult to redescend from the universality of law on the level of the general will to the contingent decisions whereby that law is somehow adjusted to specific conflicts or, as he would put it, referential circumstances. Yet this is another locus in which the intersection with Marxism might have proved fruitful: the complaints about the underdeveloped nature of the political dimension in Marxism must surely lead eventually to some new attentiveness to the relationship between "economic" abstraction (value) and that other abstract or universal instance which is the state or the general will.

In staging this lengthy confluence between the concerns of *Allegories of Reading* and the Marxist problematic, something must finally be said about these codes themselves as terminological instruments which permit or exclude certain kinds of work. The advantage of the Marxian code of "value"—as opposed to DeManian "rhetoric" or Adorno's notion of "identity" or the "concept"—is that it displaces or transforms the philosophical problem of "error" which has embarrassed us throughout this exposition. It is too facile, but not wrong, to suggest that conceptions of error, as they inform the positions both of DeMan and Adorno, logically presuppose some prior fantasy about "truth"—the adequation of language or of the concept to their respective objects—which, as in unrequited love, is perpetuated in its henceforth disabused and skeptical conclusions. Nothing of this sort can arise in the terminological field governed by the word *value*. The terminology of error always suggests, in spite of itself, that we could somehow get rid of it by one last effort of the mind. In fact, much of the tortuousness of DeManian as well as Adornian prose results from the need to short-circuit this unwanted implication and to insist over and over again on the "objectivity" of such errors or illusions, which are part and parcel of language or thinking and cannot be in that sense rectified, or at least not now and not here. In this DeMan seems at his furthest not merely from Adorno but also from Derrida himself, where hints abound that some radical transformation of the social system and of history itself may open the possibility of thinking new kinds of thoughts and concepts: something quite inconceivable in DeMan's view of language. The notion of value, however, usefully ceases to imply and entail any of these issues of error or truth: its instances may be judged in other ways (thus, both Lukács and

Gramsci saw the central purpose of revolution as the very abolition of the law of value), but its abstractions are objective, historical, and institutional, and thus they redirect our critiques of abstraction in new directions.

Another way of saying all this is to grasp the ways in which DeMan's own conceptual apparatus—sometimes called "rhetoric"—also has a mediatory function. Our discussion of his peculiar use of the term *metaphor* to designate conceptualization in general suggests that what is at work here is a little more complicated than some simple (or appropriately elaborate) rewriting of textual materials in terms of tropology: something that might better characterize the work of Hayden White or Lotman or the *mu* group (from which DeMan always sought strategically to distance himself). Rather, the larger mediatory use of the notion of metaphor then allows tropology to become attached terminologically to a range of other objects and materials (political, philosophical, literary, psychological, autobiographical) where a certain account of the tropes and their movement then becomes autonomous. Metaphor is thus the crucial locus of what we have called transcoding in DeMan: it is not at first a narrowly tropological concept but rather the place in which the dynamics of the tropes is pronounced to be "the same" as a whole range of phenomena identified by other codes or theoretical discourses in utterly unrelated and unrelatable ways (abstraction is the language we have used here). Metaphor, in DeMan, is therefore itself a metaphorical act and a violent yoking together of distinct and heterogeneous objects.

Meanwhile, something similar can be said about the other kinds of linguistic or rhetorical instruments that are pressed into occasional service throughout *Allegories of Reading*. In particular, it has frequently been observed that the omnibus term *rhetoric* (or the alternate term *reading* itself) does not quite cover over the incompatibility between the terminology of the tropes and the very different terminology of J. L. Austin that distinguishes between performative and constative speech acts of various kinds. But Austin's remarkable fortunes in later theory are surely at least in part due to the structural limits of linguistics itself, which must constitute itself by excluding whatever lies outside the sentence (action, "reality," and so forth); Austin suddenly invents a way of talking about that excluded nonlinguistic reality in "linguistic" terms, as a kind of new "other" within language-philosophy which by seeming to secure a place for action *inside* the new linguistic terminology now justifies the extension of that terminology to "everything." We have seen DeMan rehearse the Austinian opposition in terms of "grammar" and "rhetoric": something which acknowledges the tension but incorporates it back into language without "resolving" it (I do not, however, want to be understood as suggesting that it *can* be resolved). Here too, then, we find a kind of strategic transcoding, but of a somewhat different type: the incorporation of the structural other or excluded of a given system by endowing it with a name drawn from the terminological field of the system itself.

What, finally, of the ontological argument so often used to buttress the primacy of one code over against another (which comes first, language or production?)? That language is unique and sui generis can be admitted, even though it is hard to see how essentially linguistic beings such as ourselves could even have the possibility of attaining that limited insight; that DeMan went further than most people in his tireless and self-punishing effort to grasp the mechanics of language at the very moment of its operation is also evident. But the primacy of a linguistic code or hermeneutics is not thereby secured, if for no other reason than the Nietzschean one that the primacy of no code can ever be secured. "If all language is about language" (*AR* 153), that is to say, if "all language is language about denomination, that is, a conceptual, figural, metaphorical metalanguage" (*AR* 152–53), it by no means follows that a theoretical code organized around the theme or topic of language has some ultimate, ontological primacy. All language may in that sense be "about language," but talking about language is finally no different from talking about anything else. Or, as Stanley Fish might put it, no practical consequences flow from these "discoveries" about the deeper dysfunctionality of all uses of words. But not all the contradictions in DeMan's work (not even the most interesting ones) spring from his attempt to transform analysis into method and to generalize a working ideology (and even a metaphysic) from his extraordinary readings of individual texts and individual sentences.

For example, these essentially philosophical questions about the primacy of language are to be sharply distinguished from methodological ones, in which a certain approach to the language of a variety of different kinds of texts is defended. Unlike what has been shown for the New Historicism, distinct also from certain occasional moments in Derrida (particularly those that flirt with psychoanalytic motifs), homologies play no part in DeMan because they imply analogies between objects, content, or raw materials within discourse; whereas in DeMan we witness, as it were, the very emergence of discourse itself, so that such content cannot even yet be said to be present for inspection (and when it does come into view, after the fashion of the Russian formalists' "motivation of the device," our peculiar perspective will require us to grasp it rather as the pretext of the discourse in question and its projection: "guilt" is the mirage produced by confessional discourse). Nor would it be altogether correct to say that the various ways in which discourse emerges are homologous to one another, although the temptation to read DeMan's varieties of allegories as so many variations on a structure is great. Rather, as with multilinear evolution in the Marxist tradition, we are encouraged to see the peculiar and multiple ways in which language wrestles with its unresolvable problem of denomination as provisional knots and strands, so many distinct and specific local text formations that cannot be theorized and ordered into a law (although he sometimes also does just that).

The function of the theory—and what gives it the appearance of a method that can be transported from one kind of verbal object to another—seems to be rather to lie in its effort to discredit the autonomy of the academic disciplines, and thereby the classification of texts they perpetuate, into political philosophies, historical and social speculation, novels and plays, philosophy, and autobiographical writing, each of which is claimed by a separate tradition. Here, then, finally, is the other deeper reason why Rousseau becomes the privileged object of study: like few other writers, he not only practiced a variety of genres and discursive forms (but then, in that case, the "eighteenth century" itself is privileged insofar as all of those are still held together under the category of "belles lettres" and produced by every intellectual indifferently), but, as a kind of autodidacte, he seems to have felt he reinvented all of them ex nihilo, so that his extraordinary home-made productions seem to give us access to the very origins of genre itself. The imperialism whereby political and philosophical texts are here reattached to literary study (or rather to the very special kind of rhetorical reading DeMan had in mind)—as well as the courtesy with which he shows his contempt for the shoddiness with which other disciplines have overhastily turned verbal structures into vague, general ideas (AR 226)—will look a little different if we remember that he felt the same about most "literary" analyses as well. These are therapeutic lessons whose usefulness will vary according to the state of the discipline in question; the most timely and striking one is destined less for a field than for a tendency, namely, the psychological and the psychoanalytic. The *Pygmalion* chapter firmly dismantles notions of the "self" (AR 236), while the *Julie* chapter effectively does away with the "author." The demolition here has been so complete that paradoxically, by the time we get to the *Confessions*, very little of that particular program remains to be carried out, so that DeMan indulges in his own version of a psychoanalytic reading (in the—to be sure only possible or optional—reading of Rousseau's deeper desire for exposure [AR 285]). Here what is more basically at stake is the transformation of the existential—feeling, emotion, instinct, drives—into an "effect" of the text: as this aim is also shared by Lacan (and Althusser in another way), peculiar resonances and interferences are given off by this final chapter, until the unexpected introduction of the *machine* (AR 294) produces a well-nigh Deleuzian optical illusion (but the machine is not that of Deleuze but of eighteenth-century mechanical materialism, as we shall see shortly). The distance from the opening discussion of the *Second Discourse* to this final one seems very great indeed, and suggests two opposing interpretations: on the one hand, to posit a lapse of time in the composition of these chapters and the gradual emergence of a whole set of new interests, and, on the other, to see here something like a dialectical progression in which the content determines radical modifications in the form and method themselves. But it would be somewhat more consistent to adopt DeMan's own way of using narrative, as again in the *Pygmalion* chapter, where the thesis about the existence or nonexistence of a stable self (and a stable other) is tested against a story about which the principal problem the reader (or spectator) has is whether anything really happens in it or not (that is, whether change takes place). DeMan concludes that it does not and that what looks like progression is little more than iteration or repetition: we will also assume that this is the case with his own Rousseau sequence.

This is not quite the same as saying that the same thing happens in every chapter, for what each one tells, in a different way and with a different outcome, is the birth of allegory out of the primal metaphorical dilemma. It would be a mistake to assume that a single coherent theory of allegory is to be disengaged from the book (even though the latter is subtended by a single coherent theory of metaphor): DeMan is at least postcontemporary in his belief that a transcendent theory is undesired and undesirable; it is not an aim in itself but rather a conceptual distance that allows the reader apprehension of a language it has already transformed (so theory is here very much that effort to "stand outside" the text, and even to stand outside language itself, that Knapp and Michaels deplored; but it is that only for a moment).

This proposition can be demonstrated by the fact that when we get to the consequences of metaphor, those consequences are not specified as allegory but rather more generally designated as narrative: "if the self is not, in principle, a privileged category, the sequel to any theory of metaphor will be a theory of narrative centered on the question of referential meaning" (*AR* 188). The metaphoric act constitutively involves the forgetting or repression of itself: concepts generated by metaphor at once conceal their origins and stage themselves as true or referential; they emit a claim to being literal language. The metaphoric and the literal are thus at one, at least insofar as they are the twin inevitable moments of the same process. That process, then, generates a variety of illusions, of which the eudaimonic (pleasure and pain) deserves mention (we shall return to it), as well as the notion of the practical or the useful ("the proor regression from love to economic dependence is a constant characteristic of all moral or social systems based on the authority of noncontested metaphorical systems" [*AR* 239]).

But as for the next stage of the process—narrative itself—anyone with the slightest media familiarity with "deconstruction" will have guessed that it will somehow involve an "undoing" of this first illusory moment. The complications arise when we approach the concrete varieties of that, and also when we seek to come to terms with DeMan's evident temptation—which he also resists—to forge some new typology and lay out a "semiotic" theory of the kind he has tirelessly denounced in the earlier chapters of *Allegories of Reading*.

If such a "theory" exists (if it is not, in other words, simply a question of a useful and portable opposition), then it consists in positing two distinct moments of the deconstructive narrative, the second succeeding the first and incorporating it at some higher dialectical level of complexity. First, the initial metaphor is undone—undermined as soon as it has been posited by some deep suspicion of this particular linguistic act. Yet in a second moment, that very suspicion washes back over the first and becomes generalized: what was at first only an acute doubt as to the viability of this particular resemblance and this particular concept —a doubt about speaking and thinking—now becomes a deeper skepticism about language in general, about the linguistic process, or about what DeMan calls *reading*, a term which usefully excludes general ideas about Language itself:

> The paradigm for all texts consists of a figure (or a system of figures) and its deconstruction. But since this model cannot be closed off by a final reading, it engenders, in its turn, a supplementary figural

superposition which narrates the unreadability of the prior narration. As distinguished from primary deconstructive narratives centered on figures and ultimately always on metaphor, we can call such narratives to the second (or the third) degree *allegories*. Allegorical narratives tell the story of the failure to read whereas tropological narratives, such as the *Second Discourse*, tell the story of the failure to denominate. The difference is only a difference of degree and the allegory does not erase the figure. Allegories are always allegories of metaphor and, as such, they are always allegories of the impossibility of reading—a sentence in which the genitive "of" has itself to be "read" as a metaphor. (*AR* 205)

The terminology is sometimes uncertain: are the allegories referred to here the same as what later on, in connection with the *Confessions*, "can be called an allegory of figure" (*AR* 300)? What happens when the allegorical process is contained or repressed? Such questions have the merit of forcing us to the obvious conclusion that since the initial problem cannot be solved (there is no "solution" to the metaphorical dilemma), it admits of no single outcome either, but yields a variety of attempted solutions whose mode of failure, although logical after the fact, cannot be predicted or theorized in advance. Here again the theory of allegory, since it cannot be completed, sends us back to the individual texts themselves, whose in-terminable "reading" merely reconfirms the initial description while focusing attention on the unique structural failure of each specific text. Whence the productive confusion, for example, about the nature of the *Social Contract:*

Is Rousseau himself the "lawgiver" of the Social Contract and his treatise the Deuteronomy of the modern State? If this were the case, then The Social Contract would become a monological referential statement. It could not be called an allegory . . . instead, by praising the suspicion that the Sermon on the Mount may be the Machiavellian invention of a master politician, [Rousseau] clearly undermines the authority of his own legislative discourse. Would we then have to conclude that the Social Contract is a deconstructive narrative like the Second Discourse? But this is not the case either, because the Social Contract is clearly productive and generative as well as deconstructive in a manner that the Second Discourse is not. To the extent that it never ceases to advocate the necessity for political legislation and to elaborate the principles on which such a legislation could be based, it resorts to the principles of authority that it undermines. We know this structure to be characteristic of what we have called allegories of unreadability. Such an allegory is metafigural: it is an allegory of a figure (for example, metaphor) which relapses into the figure it deconstructs. The Social Contract falls under this heading to the extent that it is indeed structured like an aporia: it persists in performing what it has shown to be impossible to do. As such we can call it an allegory. But is it the allegory of a figure? The question can be answered by asking what it is the Social Contract performs, what it keeps doing despite the fact that it has established that it could not be done. (AR 275)

As the title of the chapter ("Promises") indicates, that new impossible thing *The Social Contract* continues to do is to *promise*: so that the seeming heterogeneity of DeMan's final chapters here can now be rejustified in terms of the wider variety of impossible "solutions" to the textual dilemma. The disparity between the terminology of speech acts (promises, excuses) and that of allegories and figures can now be seen as one last ambitious effort to open up a wider mediatory code which will finally encompass personal life and History itself ("textual allegories on this level of rhetorical complexity generate history" [AR 277], a concluding sentence which seems to mark a provisional end to DeMan's own quest for historicity as that has been characterized above).

DeMan's multiple accounts of allegory therefore seem to fall under the general heading of what I have elsewhere called "dialectical narratives"; that is to say, narratives which by reflexive mechanisms restlessly shift themselves to higher levels of complexity, transforming all their terms and starting points in the process, which they cancel but continue to include (as he himself points out). The crucial problem for such narratives, particularly in the contemporary intellectual situation, where phenomenological notions of consciousness and the "self" have been sharply problematized, lies clearly in the moment of "reflexivity" itself and the way in which this moment (about which I begged the question above by neutrally designating it as a mechanism) is staged: it will be persuasive today only if the seemingly inevitable temptation to turn it back into this or that form of "self-consciousness" is excluded. Whether or not the impact of psychoanalysis and linguistics, on the one hand, or the end of individualism, on the other, are satisfactory explanations, it is certain that the notion of "self-consciousness" is today in crisis and no longer seems to do the work it was thought able to perform in the past; it no longer strikes people as an adequate foundation for what it used to ground or complete. Whether the dialectic is itself inextricably bound up with this now traditional valorization of self-consciousness (something often meant by loose repudiations of Hegel, which ignore passages where something very different seems to be going on) must remain an open question; nor is the loss of the concept of self-consciousness (or indeed that of consciousness either) necessarily fatal to the very conception of agency itself. In the case of DeMan's work, however, I feel that it is fatally menaced at every point by a resurgence of some notion of self-consciousness that its language vigilantly attempts to ward off. Surely the deconstructive narrative always risks slipping back into that simpler story in which the initial figure, having brought illusion into being, then somehow achieves some more heightened awareness of its own activity; while the allegory of reading, or of unreadability, comes before us in his work with a heightened charge of renewed consciousness of its own processes, consciousness ever more intensely becoming conscious of itself, "to the second (or third) degree," in a never-ending progression. All this falls out rather differently in Derrida, where the emphasis on in-terminability and on what Gayatri Spivak has called "the impossibility of a full undoing"[20] meet the problem of self-consciousness head-on by acknowledging it as a necessarily thwarted aim and drive. In DeMan, however, it persists as something like a ghostly "return of the repressed," a misreading so powerful that even its denial reawakens it; and this is not the only peculiar survival of an older conceptuality in the "uneven development" of DeMan's intensely postcontemporary system.

What I will call DeMan's metaphysics is, from one perspective, just such a survival—the most dramatic but perhaps not the most significant —even though in another sense, if we replace the word *metaphysics* with *ideology*, it will be less astonishing to assert that a contemporary secular thinker who frequently characterized his own positions as "materialist" also "had" an ideology. But, of course, one does not exactly "have" an ideology; rather, every "system" of thought (no matter how scientific) is susceptible to *representation* (DeMan would have called it "thematization," in one of his shrewdest terminological moves) such that it can be apprehended as an ideological "vision of the world": it is, for example, well known that even the most thoroughgoing existentialisms or nihilisms—which affirm the meaninglessness of life or the world and the senselessness of questions about "meaning"—also end up projecting their own meaningful vision of the world as something lacking meaning.

In DeMan, however, this susceptibility to ideological representation is the correlative of his own rigorous picture of the functioning, or the systematic dysfunctionality, of language as such: in spite of itself and against its own will, the attention to and focus on the linguistic apparatus ends up conjuring an impossible picture of what falls outside language and what language cannot assimilate, absorb, or process. That realm, inaccessible by definition (that is to say, inaccessible to language, which remains the element beyond which we cannot think), is nowhere present in DeMan's texts, although it is present in Rousseau, particularly in the most "religious" and "philosophical" of his writings, the *Profession de foi du vicaire savoyard*, which will therefore become virtually the crucial test case for DeMan's reading. But it is the dialectical correlative of what is there present and, as it were (to use another language), its *non-dit*, its *impensé*. The affirmation of this absent metaphysics is therefore implicit in our earlier remarks about the way in which the practical claim to get a handle on how language works generally continues to replicate, in a different way, the more rationalist eighteenth-century procedure of deducing a stage in which language did not yet exist and working back from that. There is no way that even the most suspicious and alert theoretician can take sufficient precautions to exclude such slippage into ideology and metaphysics. DeMan had to know this very well, as his frequent warnings about the inevitability of the referential illusion (and its silliness: "silliness being deeply associated with reference" [AR 209]) testify; on the other hand, as we shall see later, his strategic definition of "text" does attempt to conjure ideological *writing* as such, on my view not altogether successfully.

From this perspective DeMan was an eighteenth-century mechanical materialist, and much that strikes the postcontemporary reader as peculiar and idiosyncratic about his work will be clarified by juxtaposition with the cultural politics of the great Enlightenment philosophes: their horror of religion, their campaign against superstition and error (or "metaphysics"). In that sense, deconstruction itself, as closely or distantly related to Marxian ideological analysis as Islam to Christianity, can be seen to be an essentially eighteenth-century philosophical strategy. What ensues from this, as a mechanical-materialist "vision" of the world, is a representation so delirious that—contradiction in terms—it can only reach linguistic figuration by way of revelation, as in d'Alembert's famous dream: "Le monde commence et finit sans cesse; il est à chaque instant à son commencement et à sa fin; il n'en a jamais eu d'autre et n'en aura jamais d'autre. Dans cet immense océan de matière, pas une molécule qui ressemble à une molécule, pas une molécule qui se ressemble à elle-même un instant."[21] But even Diderot cheated, as DeMan points out, for he rescued his vision of absolute heterogeneity by positing the totality of matter as a kind of vast organic being. Rousseau was more consequent: "Yet this visible universe consists of matter, scattered and dead matter, which as a *whole* has none of the cohesion, organization or the common feeling of the *parts* of a living body, for it is certain that we, who are *parts*, have no feeling of ourselves in the *whole*" (*Profession*, quoted in *AR* 230). This is evidently inconsistent with the notion of a pious and theistic Rousseau traditionally associated with the *Profession* and other writings: removal of that inconsistency, however, is the tour de force of DeMan's chapter on this text. This is done by shifting the place of what has been taken as theistic belief, and in particular the idea of God, from the realm of ontological propositions to the "faculty" of judgment itself (*AR* 228). "God" and the accompanying conceptuality is therefore not to be read as a resolution of the intolerable vision of matter evoked above, and not as some later intervention in it, which substitutes for its scandal some more reassuring worldview (that the manuals of intellectual history designate as "theism"); rather, the idea named "God" and the other matters associated with "inner assent" are transferred, by way of a kind of bracketing, to the function of the mind, or better still, to that of language itself and its capacity to make what is epistemologically termed "an act of judgment." To displace and redistribute the problem in this fashion (DeMan plausibly asserts that it is Rousseau who does this himself and not his deconstructive reader) is to recognize our old friend, the metaphoric act, the linguistic affirmation of resemblance and identity. Now these "religious beliefs" are no longer exactly Rousseau's; they are linguistic and conceptual forms floating through his mind with all the disembodied objectivity of the generic and universal "concepts" of language itself; the *Profession* now no longer argues for them but merely seeks to examine something like their operative conditions of possibility (something which converts this work from a neo-Cartesian text into a pre-Kantian one [*AR* 229]).

But in that case the "religious" conceptuality is left suspended above the prelinguistic realm of meaningless matter as effectively as the metaphoric concept floats above the individual particulars or entities it is supposed to subsume, or the general will above the unique passions and violent particularities who inhabit its domain as individual subjects. Rousseau's "theism" is undecidable (*AR* 245) in exactly the same way, for, far from making a bridge from the realm of the particular to the realm of universals and language, Rousseau's whole operation has consisted precisely in problematizing that relationship and casting its very possibility into question at the same time that universals, concepts, language, and even "theism" continue to be "used."

I am inclined to think that this materialistic or "pessimistic" vision (what some people seem to like to call "nihilism") can in fact be transferred to DeMan himself by way of the intermediation of the other great alter ego, Kant (with whom DeMan's affinities, besides the mutual link to Rousseau, are, I think, founded on precisely the same dual vision). A passage like the following only superficially conveys the horror of Kant's "worldview":

> Everywhere around us we observe a chain of causes and effects, of means and ends, of death and birth; and, as nothing has entered of itself into the condition in which we find it, we are constantly referred to some other thing, which itself suggests the same inquiry regarding its cause, and thus the universe must sink into the abyss of nothingness, unless we admit that, besides this infinite chain of contingencies, there exists something else that is primal and self-subsistent—something which as the cause of this phenomenal world, secures its continuance and preservation.[22]

Yet this passage still characterizes the world of phenomena, the empirical world of our own experience. It is rather the world of the noumena, and the things-in-themselves, that in Kant is the true home of the uncanny and corresponds more closely to the atomistic or materialist visions present in earlier philosophy with certain fundamental new twists. The thing-in-itself is, for example, not representable in Diderot's fashion because it is not representable at all, by definition: it is a kind of empty concept that cannot correspond to any form of experience. Nonetheless, it sometimes seems to me that we have some advantage over tradition, not so much because we have new terminologies and new conceptualities (as Lacan and Althusser thought about their rewriting of Freud and Marx) but rather because we have new technologies. Film in particular may allow us to square this particular circle in a new way and to represent a little better what was fundamentally defined as escaping representation altogether. If indeed the philosophical meaning of film, in Stanley Cavell's great insight[23] is to show us what the world might look like in our own absence—"la nature sans les hommes," as Sartre used to say—then perhaps today the noumenon can come before us with a properly filmic *Unheimlichkeit*, as some grisly set of eerily lit volumes projecting a kind of internal visibility out of themselves like an infrared light: the element of horror films and trick photography, of the flight across the dimensions of Kubrick's *2001* if not the loathsomeness of the field of vision of some occult Other. This might, with all appropriately shabby disreputableness, be a contemporary way of matching the dizziness with which the classical materialists imagined themselves to gaze into the very pores of matter as that meaninglessly subtended the realm of appearance of the ordinary human world. For Kant's noumenal realm has nothing to do with that deeper level of Hegelian essence, that truer dimension beneath phenomenal appearance into which Marx invites us on leaving the marketplace ("let us therefore, in company with the owner of money and the owner of labor-power, leave this noisy sphere, where everything takes place on the surface and in full view of everyone, and follow them into the hidden abode of production, on whose threshold there hangs the notice 'No admittance except on business'" [MC 279–80]). Kant's things-in-themselves, along with the material universe of Rousseau's Vicar and also, perhaps, of DeMan himself, cannot be visited in that fashion, since they correspond to what lies beyond anthropomorphism, beyond human categories and human senses —what is here before us *without* us, unseen and untouched, independent of the phenomenological centering of the human body and above all beyond the categories of the human mind (or, in DeMan, the operations of language and the tropes). As for "freedom" as a noumenon, it marks the same "lack of perspective" taken on the self, on human consciousness and identity, as some monstrous thing we cannot imagine seeing from the outside—that nameless alien being we domesticate by means of the more banal anthropomorphic concepts of reasons, choices, motives, leaps of faith, irresistible compulsions, and the like. To see Kant as positing an insuperably dualistic world in which human appearance coexists and is impossibly superimposed with an unthinkable and nonhuman world of things-in-themselves (including our own "selves") is to understand a little better why Kant should offer so useful a set of coordinates for DeMan, whose linguistic "categories" replace Kant's cognitive ones and effectively rule out the Kantian ethical compromise at the same time that they close the door, with a certain glacial skepticism, on the "theistic" solution of Rousseau, which scarcely turns out to be theism any more in any traditional "religious" sense.

Thus, unlike Rousseau, DeMan did not even seek to make such a bridge between the universal and the particular (although he acknowledged the inevitability of assuming it to exist, that is, of continuing to use language). Is his practice then to be described, as people have loosely done (particularly in the last few years), as a "nihilism"? DeMan consistently described himself as a materialist, but that is surely not the same thing. Nihilism evokes a kind of global ideology or "pessimistic" worldview of the type to which he was in general allergic. The more precise designation of his "philosophical" position lies elsewhere and opens up an even more archaic and unseasonable problematic behind the already seemingly antiquated one of eighteenth-century materialism. What DeMan clearly was was not a nihilist but a *nominalist*, and the scandalized reception that greeted his views on language when they finally became clear to his readers is comparable to nothing quite so much as the agitation of Thomist clerks confronted unexpectedly with the nominalist enormity. Exploring these philosophical affinities, clearly a task that cannot be undertaken here,[24] might yield yet another DeMan, one whose ideology was at the very least no longer that of eighteenth-century materialism. What is more interesting for us in the present context is the way his nominalism can now be reinscribed into the very logic of contemporary thought and culture, from which he otherwise stood aloof, unique and unclassifiable. Adorno has for one already explored the ways in which modern art centrally faces a logic of nominalism as its situation and its dilemma; he borrowed the word from Croce, who used it largely to discredit the kinds of genre thinking at work in the art appreciation of his own day, generalities and generic classifications he felt to be inconsistent with the experience of the individual work of art. In Adorno, nominalism enters the very production of the modern work as a destiny; and his formal diagnosis is also implicit in his work on the history of modern philosophical concepts, which are now fatally driven back from the universalizing possibilities of traditional philosophy (about which he is not particularly nostalgic).

What is now wanted is some larger social and cultural diagnosis of the nominalist imperative in contemporary times: the tendency toward immanence, the flight from transcendence characterized in our opening section, in this light becomes a private or negative phenomenon, whose positive side is only disclosed by the hypothesis of "nominalism" as a social and existential force in its own right (postmodern politics and the postmodern inflection of the older concept of "democracy" can also be interpreted in this way, as a growing feeling that the reality of social particulars and individuals is somehow inconsistent with older ways of thinking of society and the social, including the ideology of "individualism" itself). Within such a context DeMan's work takes on a somewhat different and less exceptional resonance, as the place in which a certain experience of nominalism, in the specialized realm of linguistic production itself, was, as it were, lived to the absolute and theorized with a forbidding and rigorous purity.

But our discussion of Rousseau's theism remains incomplete, for we have not yet mentioned the way in which the "theistic" conceptuality —which clearly enough failed to "take on" the realm of matter itself —nonetheless won a certain autonomy in its own right by way of libidinal cathexion. (DeMan's very different language describes this moment as a "turn towards eudaemonic valorization" [AR 243], the transformation of the locus of judgment into a kind of "spectacle" [AR 242] henceforth susceptible to a language of pleasure and pain, and beyond that into that general erotic and sentimental attitudinizing we associate with the eighteenth century.[25] But what is to be done with this resurgence of the matter of pleasure opens up the issues and problems of the aesthetic as such—in DeMan's work rather than in that of Rousseau.

It is certain that DeMan's form of deconstruction can be seen as a last-minute rescue operation and a salvaging of the aesthetic—even a defense and valorization of literary study and a privileging of specifically literary language—at the moment in which it seemed about to disappear without a trace. This he first secured through a strategic redefinition of the concept of a *text*, which is now restricted to apply only to those writings that "deconstruct themselves," to speak loosely. "The paradigm of all texts consists of a figure (or a system of figures) and its deconstruction" (AR 205); this formulation, which we have already encountered in our effort to grasp the initial metaphoric moment of language, can now also be seen to have the very different function of aesthetic valorization. Expelled from it are the vulgarizers and the ideologists—Herder and Schiller, for example—who imagine that Rousseau is merely a philosopher, whose "ideas" one can borrow and adapt, develop and add to; they are blissfully unendowed with the deeper "suspicion" that informs the two basic types of writing—allegories of figure and allegories of reading—encompassed in the larger designation "text." This is surely an assertion of value (if not of a kind of canonicity); one might, however, object that it is not exactly an assertion of *aesthetic* value. Texts can be so categorized and classified because they are linguistically reflexive, deconstruct themselves, and are somehow self-conscious about their own operations. Perhaps such judgments might better be consigned, as DeMan so often seems to do, to rhetoric rather than to aesthetics? But there is a final turn of the screw here,

for text also in DeMan becomes the very definition of "literary language" as such, at which point something suspiciously resembling
aesthetic evaluation and literary study itself becomes triumphantly
reestablished.

But it would be wrong to conclude from this that DeMan's operation
turns out to be reassuringly traditionalist after all; for there is yet another
piece of this puzzle, namely, the unexpected intervention of what Geoffrey Galt Harpham has called the "ascetic imperative."[26] We have indeed
frequently had occasion to observe DeMan's use of a vocabulary of "temptation" and "seduction"; particularly, but not exclusively, in connection
with interpretive options: it is now time to say that these are no mere
habits of style but correspond to a more fundamental feature of DeMan's
philosophical view of language as well as of his aesthetic. This is also
the point at which his work can be seen crucially to intersect with the
current debate over modernism and postmodernism, terms of which he
would not particularly have approved, especially in the periodizing fashion in which I plan to use them. If we drew up the battle lines between
those committed to positing some deep continuity between Romanticism and modernism and those intent on stressing a radical break
between them, DeMan would surely have belonged in the first camp,
even though the radical difference of the individual text (or rather the
individual auteur, for DeMan remains committed to auteur theory even
in the problematization of authorship as such) intervenes to discredit
the larger concepts.

It is, however, as though Romantic poetry remained somehow closer
to the sources of Rousseau's suspicion of language (DeMan's affinitive
elections among the theorists tend, as is well known, after Nietzsche,
toward Friedrich Schlegel): the capacity of the language of the moderns
is therefore richer in lies and delusions, in seductions, so that it seems
fitting that DeMan's most extraordinary full-dress deconstruction of
poetic language as such should take Rilke as its occasion. For the
moment, then, the deconstruction of the seductiveness of poetic language is at one with the deconstruction of "modernism" itself.

"Since it is commonly admitted that value-seductions are tolerated
(and even admired) in so-called literary texts in a manner that would
not pass muster in 'philosophical' writings, the value of these values is
itself linked to the possibility of distinguishing philosophical from literary texts" (AR 119). Rilke's "seductions" (AR 20) are articulated in a
four-step account, in which each step finds resonances elsewhere in
DeMan's writing. The first, the awakening of complicity in the reader, is

often thought to be paradigmatic of the modern in general ("hypocrite lecteur! mon semblable, mon frère!"); in a second moment a fullness of objects and a fascination with their surfaces is identified, which takes a specific thematic form in Rilke but is also in one way or another paradigmatic of a significant intensification of the sensory in the modern generally. The third step now converts these gains into what we may call an ideological implementation: they are now "to affirm and promise, as few other [works] do, a form of existential salvation": "Hiersein ist herrlich!" It will not be surprising to find that this operation awakens DeMan's vigilance most immediately: indeed, by the end of this monographic study (written as an introduction to a French selection of Rilke, an occasion which perhaps explains its relatively unusual accessibility and also its systematic character as a general survey and totalizing analysis), the great philosophical poems, the *Duino Elegies* and the *Sonnets to Orpheus*, have been displaced, reduced to a more marginal and humbled position in the Rilke canon, where they have been dethroned by the sparser and more fragmentary, well-nigh minimalist fragments, that seem to foreshadow Celan and in their very refusal of plenitude to embody something like a "deconstructive" aesthetic (nor is this minimalism a structural accident: "this 'liberating theory of the Signifier' also implies a complete drying up of thematic possibilities" [AR 48]).

Yet the other features of Rilke's seductive strategy are finally just as suspicious as this one; not least the final, or fourth, moment, in which the preceding three steps are crystallized into poetic language as such; this is the emergence of a single sensory channel: euphony, which makes "language sing like a violin" (AR 38), a well-nigh "phonocentric Eargod on which Rilke, from the start, has wagered the outcome of his entire poetic success" (AR 55): "Possibilities of representation and of expression are eliminated in an askesis which tolerates no other referent than the formal attributes of the vehicle. Since sound is the only property of language that is truly immanent to it and that bears no relation to anything that would be situated outside language itself, it will remain as the only available resource" (AR 32). It is odd to find this extraordinary musicality, familiar to every addicted reader of Rilke, described as an *askesis*. The word is designed to mediate between this formal peculiarity and Rilke's religious thematics, which are in effect here both justified and acted out by the renunciation of all the other senses that Rilke is sometimes pleased to think of as sainthood. Meanwhile the characterization also cuts deeply across the historical phenomenon of the reification and separation of the senses in modern times, and the subsequent autonomization of each, which thereby, as also, in modern painting gains an extraordinary new intensity. The new bodily sensorium has mostly been celebrated by readers (and writers) who have gained some historical sense of its novelty: phenomenology, and the more contemporary ideologies of desire, take their point of departure in this fragmentation that has happened to the body in modern times. DeMan's peculiar perspective is therefore defamiliarizing in a way that can only be welcomed: coldly suspending the tempting richness of the new sense (euphony), he insists on its price and on everything that must be renounced in order for the sounds of language to become autonomous.

But this must also surely be described as an askesis on his part as well; and nowhere is *Allegories of Reading* more ferocious than in its mocking rehearsal of Nietzsche's own apologia for the supreme power of music itself:

> Who would dare admit, after such a passage, to not being one of the happy few among the "authentic musicians"? The page could only have been written with conviction if Nietzsche's personal identification would make him into the King Mark of a triangular relationship. It has all the trappings of a statement made in bad faith: parallel rhetorical questions, an abundance of clichés, obvious catering to its audience. The "deadly" power of music is a myth that cannot withstand the ridicule of literal description, yet Nietzsche is compelled, by the rhetorical mode of his text, to present it in the absurdity of its facticity. (AR 97–98)[27]

I want to stress the degree to which, above and beyond this or that local identification and unmasking of a specific linguistic seduction (all of which in one way or another reenact the referential illusions—including desire—generated by the initial metaphoric act), DeMan's work is unique among that of modern critics and theorists in its ascetic repudiation of pleasure, desire, and the intoxication of the sensory.

Yet even more crucial matters lie behind these fashionably contemporary ones, in particular the great traditional preoccupation of philosophical aesthetics from Plato to German idealism; namely, the question of the status of *Schein*, or aesthetic appearance (reduced, in postcontemporary debates, to the somewhat more limited issue called *representation*). How one stands on the guilt of art and the status of the cultural intellectual (not to speak of the aesthete as such) depends very much, as Adorno never tired of showing us, on one's attitude toward aesthetic appearance, which can be repudiated for political reasons as a social

luxury or privilege, or alternately celebrated or rationalized in any number of different ideological ways (which have themselves been modified
since the emergence of mass media culture). DeMan uniquely combined
both these positions in an idiosyncratic synthesis, assigning to *Schein*
and sensory appearance the negative status of aesthetic ideology and
falsehood or bad faith while retaining art itself (or at least literature) as
the privileged realm in which language deconstructs itself and in which,
therefore, some very late version of "truth" might still be available. Aesthetic experience is thus again valorized, but *without* those tempting
aesthetic pleasures that always used to seem its very essence, as though
art were a pill one had to swallow in spite of its sugarcoating; or more
traditionally, a relatively Wagnerian vale of necessary magical illusion
and phantasmagoria.

Juxtaposed with someone like Roland Barthes, DeMan's puritanism
takes on virtually Platonic proportions (save for the latter's social plans
for art itself), alongside which a Barthes then comes to seem the very
epitome of irresponsible self-indulgence and the surrender to delusion.
I'm afraid I am personally unable to take seriously the ethical sugges-
tions which accompany DeMan's text (that is, no doubt, my problem);
but *Allegories of Reading* does seem prophetic of the 1980s, less for
some putative "new morality" than for the judgment of bankruptcy it
pronounces on the elaborate celebration of liberation, the body, desire,
and the senses which was one of the principal "gains" and battlefields
of the 1960s.

Yet, as we have already seen, this remarkable and devastating diagnosis of the modern and of its sensory rhetoric (we cannot recapitulate the
detailed deconstruction of Rilke's figures that follows) is followed almost
immediately by the reinstatement of the primacy of literary and poetic
language. This is plausible enough, since if what is wanted is the undoing of the sensory illusions of language, then these must have been awak-
ened to their fullest extent for the definitive strong case against them to
be made.

We must therefore read DeMan's aesthetic against a larger historical
context in which it offers the spectacle of an incompletely liquidated
modernism: the positions and the arguments are "postmodern," then,
even if the conclusions are not. Why such ultimate consequences are
then not drawn becomes our final question, which cannot be fully
answered. In a very general way, however, as has been asserted in previous chapters, a fully autonomous and self-justifying postmodernism
seems finally impossible as an ideology. If one likes to use a language of

antifoundationalism (but this is only one of the codes or themes in which the drama is acted out), this amounts to the assertion that the anti-foundational position is always susceptible to slippage into a new kind of foundational role in its own right. Yet the survival of properly modernist values in DeMan—above all, the supreme privilege and value of the aesthetic and of poetic language—is too peremptory and full-throated, particularly alongside its extraordinarily detailed indictment of virtually all the formal features of the modernist aesthetic, to be explained only in this way.

I suppose that what is being observed here is the feeling one sometimes has, with a certain distance and a certain shift in perspective, that historically and culturally DeMan was a very old-fashioned figure indeed, whose values were more characteristic of a pre-World War II European intelligentsia (something generally calculated to remain invisible to contemporary North Americans). What needs to be explained, then, is not so much the imperfect liquidation of the modern heritage in DeMan but the very project of liquidating it in the first place.

I have not until the present wanted to pronounce myself on the now notorious "revelations," the discovery of DeMan's work as a cultural journalist in the first years of the German occupation of Belgium. I'm afraid that much of the debate aroused by these materials has struck me as what Walter Benn Michaels likes to call "handwringing." For one thing, it does not seem to me that North American intellectuals have generally had the kind of experience of history that would qualify them to judge the actions and choices of people under military occupation (unless indeed the situation of the Vietnam War is taken to offer some rough analogy). For another, the exclusive emphasis on anti-Semitism ignores and politically neutralizes its other constitutive feature in the Nazi period: namely, anticommunism. That the very possibility of the Judeo-cide was absolutely at one with and inseparable from the anticommunist and radical right-wing mission of National Socialism is the burden of Arno J. Mayer's conclusive new history, *Why Did the Heavens Not Darken?* But put this way, it seems at once clear that DeMan was neither an anticommunist nor a right-winger: had he taken such positions in his student days (at a time when the student movements of Europe were overwhelmingly conservative or reactionary), they would have been public knowledge, inasmuch as he was the nephew of one of the most famous figures of European socialism. (Meanwhile, a certain background political ideology in these texts, utterly devoid of any personal originality or distinctiveness, simply rehearses the general period corporatism common across the board from Nazism and Italian fascism, through the New Deal and Henrik DeMan's post-Marxian social democracy, all the way to Stalinism.)[28]

What Paul DeMan clearly was, however, as the articles testify, can be seen to be a fairly unremarkable specimen of the then conventional high-modernist aesthete, and the apolitical aesthete at that. This is clearly a very different matter from Heidegger (although it seems unquestionable that the twin Heidegger and DeMan "scandals" have been carefully orchestrated to delegitimate Derridean deconstruction). Heidegger may have been "politically naïve," as they like to say, but he was certainly political, and believed for a time that the Hitlerian seizure of power was a genuine national revolution that would result in a moral and social reconstruction of the nation.[29] As rector of Freiburg University, and in the best reactionary and McCarthyite spirit, he worked at purging the place of its doubtful elements (although one should remember that genuinely radical or leftist "elements" were very scarce in the German university system of the 1920s, compared to the Hollywood of the 1940s or the Federal Republic of the 1970s). His ultimate disappointment with Hitler was shared by a number of people on the revolutionary (anticapitalist) left within National Socialism, who failed for some time to understand Hitler's pragmatic position as a moderate or centrist or his crucial relationship to big business. I know I will be misunderstood if I add that I have some sneaking admiration for Heidegger's attempt at political commitment, and find the attempt itself morally and aesthetically preferable to apolitical liberalism (provided its ideals remain unrealized).

Nothing of this has any relevance to Paul DeMan, for whom the thing dramatically called "collaboration" was simply a job,[30] in a Europe henceforth and for the foreseeable future united and German, and who as long as I knew him personally was simply a good liberal (and a nonanticommunist one at that). Can one nonetheless follow one of the classic scenarios of *Ideologiekritik* and argue that the evolution of a whole complex later line of thought was in some way determined by an initial trauma that it seeks to undo? This therapeutic language can, of course, be replaced by a more tactical one, as in Bourdieu's magisterial discussion of the way in which Heidegger's famous *Kehre* (the turn of his existentialism toward matters of being) constitutes a calculated rhetorical disengagement from the earlier political affirmation of the Nazi "revolution";[31] but (in that, unlike Blanchot) DeMan had no such sympathies to begin with. One can also, however, plausibly discuss such deconversions in terms of trauma itself, as the experience of violence and radical fear: thus, in *Conversation in the Cathedral* (so oddly prophetic of his own later apostasy from the Left), Vargas Llosa shows how the very experience of being *burned* by history (in this case being beaten up after a student demonstration, but in more serious cases torture itself) installs a crippling structure of self-censorship and a well-nigh Pavlovian avoidance of future political commitment (a kind of peculiar inversion of the canonical Fanonian liberatory act of violence).

It seems ludicrous to suggest that all the complex procedures of DeManian deconstruction came into being in some way to atone for or to undo a "Nazi past" that never existed in the first place. They certainly effectively undid his uncritically modernist aesthetic values (while finally, as we have seen, "saving the text" in another way). As for the notorious "anti-Semitic" article,[32] I believe that is has been consistently misread: it strikes me as the ingenious effort at resistance of a young man altogether too smart for his own good. For the message of this "intervention" is the following: "you garden-variety anti-Semites and intellectuals (we will leave the lofty 'religious' anti-Semitism of the Third Reich out of it) in fact do your own cause a disservice. You have not understood that if 'Jewish literature' is as dangerous and virulent as you claim it is, it follows that Aryan literature does not amount to much, and in particular lacks the stamina to resist a Jewish culture which is supposed to be, under other canonical 'anti-Semitic' accounts, valueless. You would therefore under these circumstances be better advised to stop talking about the Jews altogether and to cultivate your own garden."

It is ironic, although absolutely characteristic of irony as such, that this irony should be so disastrously misunderstood and misread (DeMan seems to have at once understood that the piece was most easily readable as the expression of anti-Semitism rather than the latter's undermining). Perhaps the rigors of deconstructive reading—so passionately pursued and taught in later years—are calculated to "undo" this disaster in the sense of forming readers capable at least of resisting this kind of elementary interpretive blunder. But most of his disciples seem to have made it anyway on first confronting this "text"; and in any case a certain further "irony" is afforded by the fact that DeMan's pedagogy, so remarkable in other respects, should have left his students singularly ill-prepared to confront this type of political and historical issue, which it bracketed from the outset.

The ultimate irony, however, lies in the survival of Irony itself—the

supreme theoretical concept and value of traditional modernism and
the very locus of the notion of self-consciousness and the reflexive[33]—in
the otherwise complete debacle of the repertoire of modernism in
DeMan's mature work. Indeed, it rises again serenely as the latter's climax, on the final page of *Allegories of Reading*.

8

Postmodernism and

the Market

Linguistics has a useful scheme that is unfortunately lacking in ideological analysis: it can mark a given word as either "word" or "idea" by alternating slash marks or brackets. Thus the word *market*, with its various dialect pronunciations and its etymological origins in the Latin for trade and merchandise, is printed as /market/; on the other hand, the concept, as it has been theorized by philosophers and ideologues down through the ages, from Aristotle to Milton Friedman, would be printed <<market>>. One thinks for a moment that this would solve so many of our problems in dealing with a subject of this kind, which is at one and the same time an ideology and a set of practical institutional problems, until one remembers the great flanking and pincer movements of the opening section of the *Grundrisse*, where Marx undoes the hopes and longings for simplification of the Proudhonists, who thought they would get rid of all the problems of money by abolishing money, without seeing that it is the very contradiction of the exchange system that is objectified and expressed in money proper and would continue to objectify and express itself in any of its simpler substitutes, like work-time coupons. These last, Marx observes dryly, would under ongoing capitalism simply turn back into money itself, and all the previous contradictions would return in force.

So also with the attempt to separate ideology and reality: the ideology of the market is unfortunately not some supplementary ideational or representational luxury or embellishment that can be removed from the economic problem and then sent over to some cultural or superstructural morgue, to be dissected by specialists over there. It is somehow generated by the thing itself, as its objectively necessary afterimage; somehow both dimensions must be registered together, in their identity as well as in their difference. They are, to use a contemporary but already outmoded language, semiautonomous; which means, if it is to mean anything, that they are not really autonomous or independent from each other, but they are not really at one with each other, either. The Marxian concept of *ideology* was always meant to respect and to rehearse and flex the paradox of the mere semiautonomy of the ideological concept, for example, the ideologies of the market, with respect to the thing itself—or in this case the problems of market and planning in late capitalism as well as in the socialist countries today. But the classical Marxian concept (including the very word *ideology*, itself something like the ideology of the thing, as opposed to its reality) often broke down in precisely this respect, becoming purely autonomous and then drifting off as sheer "epiphenomenon" into the world of the superstructures, while reality remained below, the real-life responsibility of professional economists.

There are, of course, many professional models of ideology in Marx himself. The following one from the *Grundrisse* and turning on the delusions of the Proudhonists has been less often remarked and studied but is very rich and suggestive indeed. Marx is here discussing a very central feature of our current topic, namely, the relationship of the ideas and values of freedom and equality to the exchange system; and he argues, just like Milton Friedman, that these concepts and values are real and objective, organically generated by the market system itself, and dialectically are indissolubly linked to it. He goes on to add—I was going to say now *unlike* Milton Friedman, but a pause for reflection allows me to remember that even these unpleasant consequences are also acknowledged, and sometimes even celebrated, by the neoliberals —that in practice this freedom and equality turn out to be unfreedom and inequality. Meanwhile, however, it is a question of the attitude of the Proudhonists to this reversal, and of their miscomprehension of the ideological dimension of the exchange system and how that functions —both true and false, both objective and delusional, what we used to try to render with the Hegelian expression "objective appearance":

> Exchange value, or, more precisely, the money system, is indeed the system of freedom and equality, and what disturbs [the Proudhonists] in the more recent development of the system are disturbances immanent to the system, i.e., the very realization of *equality and freedom*, which turn out to be inequality and unfreedom. It is an aspiration as pious as it is stupid to wish that exchange value would not develop into capital, or that labor which produces exchange

value would not develop into wage labor. What distinguishes these gentlemen [in other words, the Proudhonists, or as we might say today, the social democrats] from the bourgeois apologists is, on the one hand, their awareness of the contradictions inherent in the system, and, on the other, their utopianism, manifest in their failure to grasp the inevitable difference between the real and the ideal shape of bourgeois society, and the consequent desire to undertake the superfluous task of changing the ideal expression itself back into reality, whereas it is in fact merely the photographic image [*Lichtbild*] of this reality.[1]

So it is very much a cultural question (in the contemporary sense of the word), turning on the problem of representation itself: the Proudhonists are realists, we might say, of the correspondence model variety. They think (along with the Habermassians today, perhaps) that the revolutionary ideals of the bourgeois system—freedom and equality—are properties of real societies, and they note that, while still present in the Utopian ideal image or portrait of bourgeois market society, these same features are absent and woefully lacking when we turn to the reality which sat as the model for that ideal portrait. It will then be enough to change and improve the model and make freedom and equality finally appear, for real, in flesh and blood, in the market system.

But Marx is, so to speak, a modernist; and this particular theorization of ideology—drawing, only twenty years after the invention of photography, on very contemporary photographic figures (where previously Marx and Engels had favored the pictorial tradition, with its various camera obscuras—suggests that the ideological dimension is intrinsically embedded within the reality, which secretes it as a necessary feature of its own structure. That dimension is thus profoundly *imaginary* in a real and positive sense; that is to say, it exists and is real insofar as it is an image, marked and destined to remain as such, its very unreality and unrealizability being what is real about it. I think of episodes in Sartre's plays which might serve as useful textbook allegories of this peculiar process: for example, the passionate desire of Electra to murder her mother, which, however, turns out not to have been intended for realization. Electra, after the fact, discovers that she did not really want her mother dead (<<dead>>, i.e., dead in reality); what she wanted was to go on longing in rage and resentment to have her /dead/. And so it is, as we shall see with those two rather contradictory features of the market system, freedom and equality: everybody wants to want them; but they cannot be realized. The only thing that can happen to them is for the system that generates them to disappear, thereby abolishing the "ideals" along with the reality itself.

But to restore to "ideology" this complex way of dealing with its roots in its own social reality would mean reinventing the dialectic, something every generation fails in its own way to do. Ours has, indeed, not even tried; and the last attempt, the Althusserian moment, long since passed under the horizon along with the hurricanes of yesteryear. Meanwhile, I have the impression that only so-called discourse theory has tried to fill the void left when the concept of ideology was yanked along with the rest of classical Marxism into the abyss. One may readily endorse Stuart Hall's program based, as I understand it, on the notion that the fundamental level on which political struggle is waged is that of the struggle over the legitimacy of concepts and ideologies; that political legitimation comes from that; and that, for example, Thatcherism and its cultural counterrevolution were founded fully as much on the delegitimation of welfare-state or social-democratic (we used to call it liberal) ideology as on the inherent structural problems of the welfare state itself.

This allows me to express my thesis in its strongest form, which is that the rhetoric of the market has been a fundamental and central component of this ideological struggle, this struggle for the legitimation or delegitimation of left discourse. The surrender to the various forms of market ideology—on the *left*, I mean, not to mention everybody else —has been imperceptible but alarmingly universal. Everyone is now willing to mumble, as though it were an inconsequential concession in passing to public opinion and current received wisdom (or shared communicational presuppositions) that no society can function efficiently without the market and that planning is obviously impossible. This is the second shoe of the destiny of that older piece of discourse, "nationalization," which it follows some twenty years later, just as, in general, full postmodernism (particularly in the political field) has turned out to be the sequel, continuation, and fulfillment of the old fifties "end of ideology" episode. At any rate, we were then willing to murmur agreement to the increasingly widespread proposition that socialism had nothing to do with nationalization; the consequence is that today we find ourselves having to agree to the proposition that socialism really has nothing to do with socialism itself any longer. "The market is in human nature" is the proposition that cannot be allowed to stand unchallenged; in my opinion, it is the most crucial terrain of ideological struggle in our time. If you let it pass because it seems an inconsequential admission or, worse yet, because you've really come to believe in it yourself, in your "heart of hearts," then socialism and Marxism alike will have effectively become delegitimated, at least for a time. Sweezy reminds us that capitalism failed to catch on in a number of places before it finally arrived in England; and that if the actually existing socialisms go down the drain, there will be other, better, ones later on. I believe this also, but we don't have to make it a self-fulfilling prophecy. In the same spirit I want to add to the formulations and tactics of Stuart Hall's "discourse analysis" the same kind of historical qualifier: the fundamental level on which political struggle is waged is that of the legitimacy of concepts like *planning* or *the market*—at least *right now* and in our current situation. At future times, politics will take more activist forms from that, just as it has done in the past.

It must finally be added, on this methodological point, that the conceptual framework of discourse analysis—although allowing us conveniently, in a postmodern age, to practice ideological analysis without calling it that—is no more satisfactory than the reveries of the Proudhonists: autonomizing the dimension of the /concept/ and calling it "discourse" suggests that this dimension is potentially unrelated to reality and can be left to float off on its own, to found its own subdiscipline and develop its own specialists. I still prefer to call /market/ what it is, namely, an ideologeme, and to premise about it what one must premise about all ideologies: that, unfortunately, we have to talk about the realities fully as much as the concepts. Is market discourse merely a rhetoric? It is and isn't (to rehearse the great formal logic of the identity of identity and nonidentity); and to get it right, you have to talk about real markets just as much as about metaphysics, psychology, advertising, culture, representations, and libidinal apparatuses.

But this means somehow skirting the vast continent of political philosophy as such, itself a kind of ideological "market" in its own right, in which, as in some gigantic combinational system, all possible variants and combinations of political "values," options, and "solutions" are available, on condition you think you are free to choose among them. In this great emporium, for example, we may combine the ratio of freedom to equality according to our individual temperament, as when state intervention is opposed because of its damage to this or that fantasy of individual or personal freedom; or equality is deplored because its values lead to demands for the correction of market mechanisms and the intervention of other kinds of "values" and priorities. The theory of ideology excludes this optionality of political theories, not merely because "values" as such have deeper class and unconscious sources than those of the conscious mind but also because theory is itself a kind of form determined by social content, and it reflects social reality in more complicated ways than a solution "reflects" its problem. What can be observed at work here is the fundamental dialectical law of the determination of a form by its content—something not active in theories or disciplines in which there is no differentiation between a level of "appearance" and a level of "essence," and in which phenomena like ethics or sheer political *opinion* as such are modifiable by conscious decision or rational persuasion. Indeed, an extraordinary remark of Mallarmé—"il n'existe d'ouvert à la recherche mentale que deux voies, en tout, où bifurque notre besoin, à savoir, l'esthétique d'une part et aussi l'économie politique"[2]—suggests that the deeper affinities between a Marxian conception of political economy in general and the realm of the aesthetic (as, for instance, in Adorno's or Benjamin's work) are to be located precisely here, in the perception shared by both disciplines of this immense dual movement of a plane of form and a plane of substance (to use an alternative language from the linguist Hjemslev).

This would seem to confirm the traditional complaint about Marxism that it lacks any autonomous political reflection as such, something which, however, tends to strike one as a strength rather than a weakness. Marxism is indeed not a political philosophy of the weltanschauung variety, and in no way "on all fours" with conservation, liberalism, radicalism, populism, or whatever. There is certainly a Marxist practice of politics, but political thinking in Marxism, when it is not practical in that way, has exclusively to do with the economic organization of society and how people cooperate to organize production. This means that "socialism" is not exactly a political idea, or, if you like, that it presupposes the end of a certain political thinking. It also means that we do have our homologues among the bourgeois thinkers, but they are not the fascists (who have very little in the way of thought in that sense, and have in any case become historically extinct), but rather the neoliberals and the market people: for them also, political philosophy is worthless (at least once you get rid of the arguments of the Marxist, collectivist enemy), and "politics" now means simply the care and feeding of the economic apparatus (in this case the market rather than the collectively owned and organized means of production). Indeed, I will argue the proposition that we have much in common with the neoliberals, in fact virtually everything—save the essentials!

But the obvious must first be said, namely, that the slogan of the market not only covers a great variety of different referents or concerns but it is also virtually always a misnomer. For one thing, no free market exists today in the realm of oligopolies and multinationals: indeed, Galbraith suggested long ago that oligopolies were our imperfect substitute for planning and planification of the socialist type.

Meanwhile, on its general use, market as a concept rarely has anything to do with choice or freedom, since those are all determined for us in advance, whether we are talking about new model cars, toys, or television programs: we select among those, no doubt, but we can scarcely be said to have a say in actually choosing any of them. Thus the homology with freedom is at best a homology with parliamentary democracy of our representative type.

Then too, the market in the socialist countries would seem to have more to do with production than consumption, since it is above all a question of supplying spare parts, components, and raw materials to other production units that is foregrounded as the most urgent problem (and to which the Western-type market is then fantasized as a solution). But presumably the slogan of the market and all its accompanying rhetoric was devised to secure a decisive shift and displacement from the conceptuality of production to that of distribution and consumption: something it rarely seems in fact to do.

It also seems, incidentally, to screen out the rather crucial matter of property, with which conservatives have had notorious intellectual difficulty: here, the exclusion of "the justification of original property titles"[3] will be viewed as a synchronic framing that excludes the dimension of history and systemic historical change.

Finally, it should be noted that in the view of many neoliberals, not only do we not yet have a free market, but what we have in its place (and what is sometimes otherwise defended as a "free market" against the Soviet Union)[4]—namely, a mutual compromise and buying off of pressure groups, special interests, and the like—is in itself, according to the New Right, a structure absolutely inimical to the real free market and its establishment. This kind of analysis (sometimes called public choice theory) is the right-wing equivalent of the left analysis of the media and consumerism (in other words, the obligatory theory of *resistance*, the account of what in the public area and the public sphere generally *prevents* people from adopting a better system and impedes their very understanding and reception of such a system).

The reasons for the success of market ideology can therefore not be sought in the market itself (even when you have sorted out exactly which of these many phenomena is being designated by the word). But it is best to begin with the strongest and most comprehensive metaphysical version, which associates the market with human nature. This view comes in many, often imperceptible, forms, but it has been conveniently formalized into a whole method by Gary Becker in his admirably totalizing approach: "I am saying that the economic approach provides a valuable unified framework for understanding *all* human behavior."[5] Thus, for example, marriage is susceptible to a kind of market analysis: "My analysis implies that likes or unlikes mate when that maximizes total household commodity output over all marriages, regardless of whether the trait is financial (like wage rates and property income), or genetical (like height and intelligence), or psychological (like aggressiveness and passiveness)."[6] But here the clarifying footnote is crucial and marks a beginning toward grasping what is really at stake in Becker's interesting proposal: "Let me emphasize again that commodity output is not the same as national product as usually measured, but includes children, companionship, health, and a variety of other commodities." What immediately leaps to the eye, therefore, is the paradox—of the greatest symptomatic significance for the Marxian theoretical tourist —that this most scandalous of all market models is in reality a production model! In it consumption is explicitly described as the production of a commodity or a specific utility; in other words, a use value which can be anything from sexual gratification to a convenient place to take it out on your children if the outside world proves inclement. Here is Becker's core description:

> The household production function framework emphasizes the parallel services performed by firms and households as organizational units. Similar to the typical firm analyzed in standard production theory, the household invests in capital assets (savings), capital equipment (durable goods), and capital embodied in its "labor force" (human capital of family members). As an organizational entity, the household, like the firm, engages in production using this labor and capital. Each is viewed as maximizing its objective function subject to resource and technological constraints. The production model not only emphasizes that the household is the appropriate basic unit of analysis in consumption theory, it also brings out the interdependence of several household decisions: decisions about family labor supply and time and goods expenditures in a single

> time-period analysis, and decisions about marriage, family size, labor force attachment, and expenditures on goods and human capital investments in a life cycle analysis.
>
> The recognition of the importance of time as a scarce resource in the household has played an integral role in the development of empirical applications of the household production function approach.[7]

I have to admit that I think one can accept this, and that it provides a perfectly realistic and sensible view not only of *this* human world but of *all* of them, going back to the earliest hominids. Let me underscore a few crucial features of the Becker model: the first is the stress on time itself as a resource (another fundamental essay is entitled "A Theory of the Allocation of Time"). This is, of course, very much Marx's own view of temporality, as that supremely disengages itself from the *Grundrisse*, where finally all value is a matter of time. I also want to suggest the consistency and kinship between this peculiar proposal and much of contemporary theory or philosophy, which has involved a prodigious expansion in what we consider to be rational or meaningful behavior. My sense is that, particularly after the diffusion of psychoanalysis but also with the gradual evaporation of "otherness" on a shrinking globe and in a media-suffused society, very little remains that can be considered "irrational" in the older sense of "incomprehensible": the vilest forms of human decision-making and behavior—torture by sadists and overt or covert foreign intervention by government leaders—are now for all of us comprehensible (in terms of a Diltheyan *Verstehen*, say), whatever we think of them. Whether such an enormously expanded concept of Reason then has any further normative value (as Habermas still thinks) in a situation in which its opposite, the irrational, has shrunk to virtual nonexistence, is another, and an interesting, question. But Becker's calculations (and the word does not at all in him imply homo economicus, but rather very much unreflective, everyday, "preconscious" behavior of all kinds) belong in that mainstream; indeed, the system makes me think more than anything else of Sartrean freedom insofar as it implies a responsibility for everything we do—Sartrean choice (which, of course, in the same way takes place on a non-self-conscious everyday behavioral level) means the individual or collective production at every moment of Becker's "commodities" (which need not be hedonistic in any narrow sense, altruism being, for example, just such a commodity or pleasure). The representational consequences of a view like this will now lead us belatedly to pronounce the word *postmodernism* for the first time. Only Sartre's novels indeed (and they are samples; enormous, unfinished fragments) give any sense of what a representation of life that interpreted and narrated every human act and gesture, desire and decision in terms of Becker's maximization model would look like. Such representation would reveal a world peculiarly without transcendence and without perspective (death is here, for example, just another matter of utility maximization), and indeed without plot in any traditional sense, since all choices would be equidistant and on the same level. The analogy with Sartre, however, suggests that this kind of reading — which ought to be very much a demystifying eyeball-to-eyeball encounter with daily life, with no distance and no embellishments — might not be altogether postmodern in the more fantastic senses of that aesthetic. Becker seems to have missed the wilder forms of consumption available in the postmodern, which is elsewhere capable of staging a virtual delirium of the consumption of the very idea of consumption: in the postmodern, indeed, it is the very idea of the market that is consumed with the most prodigious gratification; as it were, a bonus or surplus of the commodification process. Becker's sober calculations fall far short of that, not necessarily because postmodernism is inconsistent or incompatible with political conservatism but rather primarily because his is finally a production and not a consumption model at all, as has been suggested above. Shades of the great introduction to the *Grundrisse*, in which production turns into consumption and distribution and then ceaselessly returns to its basic productive form (in the enlarged systemic category of production Marx wishes to substitute for the thematic or analytic one)! Indeed, it seems possible to complain that the current celebrants of the market — the theoretical conservatives — fail to show much enjoyment or *jouissance* (as we will see below, their market mainly serves as a policeman meant to keep Stalin from the gates, where in addition one suspects that Stalin in turn is merely a code word for Roosevelt).

As description, then, Becker's model seems to me impeccable and very faithful indeed to the facts of life as we know it; when it becomes prescriptive, of course, we face the most insidious forms of reaction (my two favorite practical consequences are, first, that oppressed minorities only make it worse for themselves by fighting back; and, second, that "household production," in his special sense [see above], is seriously lowered in productivity when the wife has a job). But it is easy to see how this should be so. The Becker model is postmodern in its structure as a transcoding; two separate explanatory systems are combined here by way of the assertion of a fundamental identity (about which it is always protested that it is *not metaphorical*, the surest sign of an intent to metaphorize): human behavior (preeminently the family or the *oikos*), on the one hand, the firm or enterprise, on the other. Much force and clarity is then generated by the rewriting of phenomena like spare time and personality traits in terms of potential raw materials. It does not follow, however, that the figural bracket can then be removed, as a veil is triumphantly snatched from a statue, allowing one then to reason about domestic matters in terms of money or the economic as such. But that is very precisely how Becker goes about "deducing" his practical-political conclusions. Here too, then, he fails of absolute postmodernity, where the transcoding process has as a consequence the suspension of everything that used to be "literal." Becker wants to marshal the equipment of metaphor and figural identification, only to return in a final moment to the literal level (which has in the meantime in late capitalism evaporated out from under him).

Why do I find none of this particularly scandalous, and what could possibly be its "proper use"? As with Sartre, in Becker choice takes place within an already pregiven environment, which Sartre theorizes as such (he calls it the "situation") but which Becker neglects. In both we have a welcome reduction of the old-fashioned subject (or individual, or ego), who is now little more than a point of consciousness directed onto the stockpile of materials available in the outside world, and making decisions on that information which are "rational" in the new enlarged sense of what any other human being could understand (in Dilthey's sense, or in Rousseau's, what every other human being could "sympathize" with). That means that we are freed from all kinds of more properly "irrational" myths about subjectivity and can turn our attention to that situation itself, that available inventory of resources, which is the outside world itself and which must now indeed be called History. The Sartrean concept of the situation is a new way of thinking history as such; Becker avoids any comparable move, for good reasons. I have implied that even under socialism (as in earlier modes of production) people can very well be imagined operating under the Becker model. What will be different is then the *situation* itself: the nature of the "household," the stock of raw materials; indeed, the very form and shape of the "commodities" therein to be produced. Becker's market thus by no means ends up as just another celebration of the market system but rather as an involuntary redirection of our attention toward history itself and the variety of alternative situations it offers.

We must suspect, therefore, that essentialist defenses of the market in reality involve other themes and issues altogether: the pleasures of consumption are little more than the ideological fantasy consequences available for ideological consumers who buy into the market theory, of which they are not themselves a part. Indeed, one of the great crises in the new conservative cultural revolution—and by the same token one of its great internal contradictions—was displayed by these same ideologues when some nervousness began to appear over the success with which consumer America had overcome the Protestant ethic and was able to throw its savings (and future income) to the winds in exercising its new nature as the full-time professional shopper. But obviously you can't have it both ways; there is no such thing as a booming, functioning market whose customer personnel is staffed by Calvinists and hard-working traditionalists knowing the value of the dollar.

The passion for the market was indeed always political, as Albert O. Hirschman's great book *The Passions and the Interests* taught us. The market, finally, for "market ideology," has less to do with consumption than it has to do with government intervention, and indeed with the evils of freedom and human nature itself. A representative description of the famous market "mechanism" is provided by Barry:

> By a natural process Smith meant what would occur, or which pattern of events would emerge, from individual interaction in the absence of some specific human intervention, either of a political kind or from violence.
>
> The behaviour of a market is an obvious example of such natural phenomena. The self-regulating properties of the market system are not the product of a designing mind but are a spontaneous outcome of the price mechanism. Now from certain uniformities in human nature, including, of course, the natural desire to "better ourselves," it can be deduced what will happen when government disturbs this self-regulating process. Thus Smith shows how apprenticeship laws, restraints on international trade, the privileges of corporations, and so on, disrupt, but cannot entirely suppress, natural economic tendencies. The spontaneous order of the market is brought about by the *interdependency* of its constituent parts and any intervention with this order is simply self-defeating: "No regulation of commerce can increase the quantity of industry in any part of society beyond what its capital can maintain. It can only

divert a part of it into a direction which it otherwise would not have gone." By the phrase "natural liberty" Smith meant that system in which every man, provided that he does not violate the (negative) laws of justice, is left perfectly free to pursue his own interest in his own way and bring both his industry and capital into competition with those of any other man.[8]

The force, then, of the concept of the market lies in its "totalizing" structure, as they say nowadays; that is, in its capacity to afford a model of a social totality. It offers another way of displacing the Marxian model: distinct from the now familiar Weberian and post-Weberian shift from economics to politics, from production to power and domination. But the displacement from production to circulation is no less a profound and ideological one, and it has the advantage of replacing the rather antediluvian fantasy representations that accompanied the "domination" model from 1984 and Oriental Despotism all the way to Foucault —narratives rather comical for the new postmodern age—with representations of a wholly different order. (I will argue in a moment that these are not primarily consumptive ones, either.)

What we first need to grasp, however, are the conditions of possibility of this alternate concept of the social totality. Marx suggests (again, in the Grundrisse) that the circulation or market model will historically and epistemologically precede other forms of mapping and offer the first representation by which the social totality is grasped:

> Circulation is the movement in which general alienation appears as general appropriation, and general appropriation as general alienation. Though the whole of this movement may well appear as a social process, and though the individual elements of this movement originate from the conscious will and particular purposes of individuals, nevertheless the totality of the process appears as an objective relationship arising spontaneously; a relationship which results from the interaction of conscious individuals, but which is neither part of their consciousness nor as a whole subsumed under them. Their collisions give rise to an *alien* social power standing above them. Their own interaction [appears] as a process and force independent of them. Because circulation is a totality of the social process, it is also the first form in which not only the social relation appears as something independent of individuals as, say, in a coin or an exchange value, but the whole of the social movement itself.[9]

What is remarkable about the movement of these reflections is that they seem to identify two things which have most often been thought to be very different from each other as concepts: Hobbes's "bellum omnium contra omnes" and Adam Smith's "invisible hand" (here appearing disguised as Hegel's "ruse of reason"). I would argue that Marx's concept of "civil society" is something like what happens when these two concepts (like matter and antimatter) are unexpectedly combined. Here, however, what is significant is that what Hobbes fears is somehow the same as what gives Smith confidence (the deeper nature of Hobbesian terror is in any case peculiarly illuminated by the complacency of Mr. Milton Friedman's definition: "A liberal is fundamentally fearful of concentrated power."[10] The conception of some ferocious violence inherent in human nature and acted out in the English revolution, whence it is theorized ("fearfully") by Hobbes, is not modified and ameliorated by Hirschman's "douceur du commerce";[11] it is rigorously identical (in Marx) with market competition as such. The difference is not political-ideological but historical: Hobbes needs state power to tame and control the violence of human nature and competition; in Adam Smith (and Hegel on some other metaphysical plane) the competitive system, the market, does the taming and controlling all by itself, no longer needing the absolute state. But what is clear throughout the conservative tradition is its motivation by fear and by anxieties in which civil war or urban crime are themselves mere figures for class struggle. The market is thus Leviathan in sheep's clothing: its function is not to encourage and perpetuate freedom (let alone freedom of a political variety) but rather to repress it; and about such visions, indeed, one may revive the slogans of the existential years—the fear of freedom, the flight from freedom. Market ideology assures us that human beings make a mess of it when they try to control their destinies ("socialism is impossible") and that we are fortunate in possessing an interpersonal mechanism —the market—which can substitute for human hubris and planning and replace human decisions altogether. We only need to keep it clean and well oiled, and it now—like the monarch so many centuries ago —will see to us and keep us in line.

Why this consoling replacement for the divinity should be so universally attractive at the present time, however, is a different kind of historical question. The attribution of the newfound embrace of market freedom to the fear of Stalinism and Stalin is touching but just slightly misplaced in time, although certainly the current Gulag Industry has been a crucial component in the "legitimation" of these ideological representations (along with the Holocaust Industry, whose peculiar relations to the rhetoric of the Gulag demand closer cultural and ideological study).

The most intelligent criticism ever offered me on a long analysis of the sixties I once published[12] I owe to Wlad Godzich, who expressed Socratic amazement at the absence, from my global model, of the Second World, and in particular the Soviet Union. Our experience of perestroika has revealed dimensions of Soviet history that powerfully reinforce Godzich's point and make my own lapse all the more deplorable; so I will here make amends by exaggerating in the other direction. My feeling has, in fact, come to be that the failure of the Khrushchev experiment was not disastrous merely for the Soviet Union, but somehow fundamentally crucial for the rest of global history, and not least the future of socialism itself. In the Soviet Union, indeed, we are given to understand that the Khrushchev generation was the last to believe in the possibility of a renewal of Marxism, let alone socialism; or rather, the other way around, that it was their failure which now determines the utter indifference to Marxism and socialism of several generations of younger intellectuals. But I think this failure was also determinant of the most basic developments in other countries as well, and while one does not want the Russian comrades to bear all the responsibility for global history, there does seem to me to be some similarity between what the Soviet revolution meant for the rest of the world positively and the negative effects of this last, missed, opportunity to restore that revolution and to transform the party in the process. Both the anarchism of the sixties in the West and the Cultural Revolution in China are to be attributed to that failure, whose prolongation, long after the end of both, explains the universal triumph of what Sloterdijk calls "cynical reason" in the omnipresent consumerism of the postmodern today. It is therefore no wonder that such profound disillusionment with political praxis should result in the popularity of the rhetoric of market abnegation and the surrender of human freedom to a now lavish invisible hand.

None of these things, however, which still involve thinking and reasoning, go very far toward explaining the most astonishing feature of this discursive development; namely, how the dreariness of business and private property, the dustiness of entrepreneurship, and the well-nigh Dickensian flavor of title and appropriation, coupon-clipping, mergers, investment banking, and other such transactions (after the close of the heroic, or robber-baron, stage of business) should in our time have proved to be so *sexy*. In my opinion, the excitement of the once tiresome old fifties representation of the free market derives from its illicit metaphorical association with a very different kind of representation; namely, the media itself in its largest contemporary and global sense (including an infrastructure of all the latest media gadgets and high technology). The operation is the postmodern one alluded to above, in which two systems of codes are identified in such a way as to allow the libidinal energies of the one to suffuse the other, without, however (as in older moments of our cultural and intellectual history), producing a synthesis, a new combination, a new combined language, or whatever.

Horkheimer and Adorno observed long ago, in the age of radio, the peculiarity of the structure of a commercial "culture industry" in which the products were free.[13] The analogy between media and market is in fact cemented by this mechanism: it is not because the media is *like* a market that the two things are comparable; rather it is because the "market" is as un*like* its "concept" (or Platonic idea) as the media is unlike its own concept that the two things are comparable. The media offers free programs in whose content and assortment the consumer has no choice whatsoever but whose selection is then rebaptized "free choice."

In the gradual disappearance of the physical marketplace, of course, and the tendential identification of the commodity with its image (or brand name or logo), another, more intimate, symbiosis between the market and the media is effectuated, in which boundaries are washed over (in ways profoundly characteristic of the postmodern) and an indifferentiation of levels gradually takes the place of an older separation between thing and concept (or indeed, economics and culture, base and superstructure). For one thing, the products sold on the market become the very content of the media image, so that, as it were, the same referent seems to maintain in both domains. This is very different from a more primitive situation in which to a series of informational signals (news reports, feuilletons, articles) a rider is appended touting an unrelated commercial product. Today the products are, as it were, diffused throughout the space and time of the entertainment (or even news) segments, as part of that content, so that in a few well-publicized cases (most notably the series *Dynasty*)[14] it is sometimes not clear when the narrative segment has ended and the commercial has begun (since the same actors appear in the commercial segment as well).

This interpenetration by way of the content is then augmented in a somewhat different way by the nature of the products themselves: one's sense, particularly when dealing with foreigners who have been enflamed by American consumerism, is that the products form a kind of hierarchy whose climax lies very precisely in the technology of reproduction itself, which now, of course, fans out well beyond the classical television set and has come in general to epitomize the new informational or computer technology of the third stage of capitalism. We must therefore also posit another type of consumption: consumption of the very process of consumption itself, above and beyond its content and the immediate commercial products. It is necessary to speak of a kind of technological bonus of pleasure afforded by the new machinery and, as it were, symbolically reenacted and ritually devoured at each session of official media consumption itself. It is indeed no accident that the conservative rhetoric that often used to accompany the market rhetoric in question here (but that in my opinion represented a somewhat different strategy of delegitimation) had to do with the end of social classes—a conclusion always demonstrated and "proved" by the presence of TV in the workers' housing. Much of the euphoria of postmodernism derives from this celebration of the very process of high-tech informatization (the prevalence of current theories of communication, language, or signs being an ideological spinoff of this more general "worldview"). This is, then, as Marx might have put it, a second moment in which (like "capital in general" as opposed to the "many capitals") the media "in general" as a unified process is somehow foregrounded and experienced (as opposed to the content of individual media projections); and it would seem to be this "totalization" that allows a bridge to be made to fantasy images of "the market in general" or "the market as a unified process."

The third feature of the complex set of analogies between media and market that underlies the force of the latter's current rhetoric may then be located in the form itself. This is the place at which we need to return to the theory of the image, recalling Guy Debord's remarkable theoretical derivation (the image as the final form of commodity reification).[15] At this point the process is reversed, and it is not the commercial products of the market which in advertising become images but rather the very entertainment and narrative processes of commercial television, which are, in their turn, reified and turned into so many commodities: from the serial narrative itself, with its well-nigh formulaic and rigid temporal segments and breaks, to what the camera shots do to space, story, characters, and fashion, and very much including a new process of the production of stars and celebrities that seems distinct from the older and more familiar historical experience of these matters and that now converges with the hitherto "secular" phenomena of the former public sphere itself (real people and events in your nightly news broadcast, the transformation of names into something like news logos, etc.). Many analyses have shown how the news broadcasts are structured exactly like narrative serials; meanwhile, some of us in that other precinct of an official, or "high," culture, have tried to show the waning and obsolescence of categories like "fiction" (in the sense of something opposed to either the "literal" or the "factual"). But here I think a profound modification of the public sphere needs to be theorized: the emergence of a new realm of image reality that is both fictional (narrative) and factual (even the characters in the serials are grasped as real "named" stars with external histories to read about), and which now—like the former classical "sphere of culture"—becomes semiautonomous and floats above reality, with this fundamental historical difference that in the classical period reality persisted independently of that sentimental and romantic "cultural sphere," whereas today it seems to have lost that separate mode of existence. Today, culture impacts back on reality in ways that make any independent and, as it were, non- or extracultural form of it problematical (in a kind of Heisenberg principle of mass culture which intervenes between your eye and the thing itself), so that finally the theorists unite their voices in the new doxa that the "referent" no longer exists.

At any rate, in this third moment the contents of the media itself have now become commodities, which are then flung out on some wider version of the market with which they become affiliated until the two things are indistinguishable. Here, then, the media, as which the market was itself fantasized, now returns into the market and by becoming a part of it seals and certifies the formerly metaphorical or analogical identification as a "literal" reality.

What must finally be added to these abstract discussions of the market is a pragmatic qualifier, a secret functionality such as sometimes sheds a whole new light—striking at a lurid mid-level height—on the ostensible discourse itself. This is what Barry, at the conclusion of his useful book, blurts out either in desperation or exasperation; namely, that the philosophical test of the various neoliberal theories can only be applied in a single fundamental situation, which we may call (not without irony) "the transition from socialism to capitalism."[16] Market theories, in other words, remain Utopian insofar as they are not applicable to this fundamental process of systemic "deregulation." Barry himself has already illustrated the significance of the judgment in an earlier chapter when, discussing the rational choice people, he points out that the ideal market situation is for them as Utopian and unrealizable under present-day conditions as, for the Left, socialist revolution or transformation in the advanced capitalist countries today. One wants to add that the referent here is twofold: not merely the processes in the various Eastern countries which have been understood as an attempt to reestablish the market in one way or another, but also those efforts in the West, particularly under Reagan and Thatcher, to do away with the "regulations" of the welfare state and return to some purer form of market conditions. We need to take into account the possibility that both of these efforts may fail for structural reasons; but we also need to point out tirelessly the interesting development that the "market" turns out finally to be as Utopian as socialism has recently been held to be. Under these circumstances, nothing is served by substituting one inert institutional structure (bureaucratic planning) for another inert institutional structure (namely, the market itself). What is wanted is a great collective project in which an active majority of the population participates, as something belonging to it and constructed by its own energies. The setting of social priorities—also known in the socialist literature as planning—would have to be a part of such a collective project. It should be clear, however, that virtually by definition the market cannot be a project at all.

9

Nostalgia for the Present

There is a novel by Philip K. Dick, which, published in 1959, evokes the fifties: President Eisenhower's stroke; Main Street, U.S.A.; Marilyn Monroe; a world of neighbors and PTAs; small retail chain stores (the produce trucked in from the outside); favorite television programs; mild flirtations with the housewife next door; game shows and contests; sputniks distantly revolving overhead, mere blinking lights in the firmament, hard to distinguish from airliners or flying saucers. If you were interested in constructing a time capsule or an "only yesterday" compendium or documentary-nostalgia video film of the 1950s, this might serve as a beginning: to which you could add short haircuts, early rock and roll, longer skirts, and so on. The list is not a list of facts or historical realities (although its items are not invented and are in some sense "authentic"), but rather a list of stereotypes, of ideas of facts and historical realities. It suggests several fundamental questions.

First of all, did the "period" see itself this way? Did the literature of the period deal with this kind of small-town American life as its central preoccupation; and if not, why not? What other kinds of preoccupations seemed more important? To be sure, in retrospect, the fifties have been summed up culturally as so many forms of protest against the fifties "themselves"; against the Eisenhower era and its complacency, against the sealed self-content of the American small (white, middle-class) town, against the conformist and the family-centered ethnocentrism of a prosperous United States learning to consume in the first big boom after the shortages and privations of the war, whose immediacy has by now largely lost its edge. The first Beat poets; and occasional "antihero" with "existentionalist" overtones; a few daring Hollywood impulses; nascent rock and roll itself; the compensatory importation of

European books, movements, and art films; a lonely and premature political rebel or theorist like C. Wright Mills: such, in retrospect, seems to be the balance sheet of fifties culture. All the rest is Peyton Place, best-sellers, and TV series. And it is indeed just those series—living-room comedies, single-family homes menaced by Twilight Zone, on the one hand, and gangsters and escaped convicts from the outside world, on the other—that give us the content of our positive image of the fifties in the first place. If there is "realism" in the 1950s, in other words, it is presumably to be found there, in mass cultural representation, the only kind of art willing (and able) to deal with the stifling Eisenhower realities of the happy family in the small town, of normalcy and nondeviant everyday life. High art apparently cannot deal with this kind of subject matter except by way of the oppositional: the satire of Lewis, the pathos and solitude of Hopper or Sherwood Anderson. Of naturalism, long after the fact, the Germans used to say that it "stank of cabbage"; that is, it exuded the misery and boredom of its subject matter, poverty itself. Here too the content seems somehow to contaminate the form, only the misery here is the misery of happiness, or at least contentment (which is in reality complacency), of Marcuse's "false" happiness, the gratifications of the new car, the TV dinner and your favorite program on the sofa—which are now themselves secretly a misery, an unhappiness that doesn't know its name, that has no way of telling itself apart from genuine satisfaction and fulfillment since it has presumably never encountered this last.

When the notion of the oppositional is contested, however, in the mid eighties, we will know a fifties revival in which much of this "degraded mass culture" returns for possible reevaluation. In the fifties, however, it is high culture that is still authorized to pass judgment on reality, to say what real life is and what is, on the other hand, mere appearance; and it is by leaving out, by ignoring, by passing over in silence and with the repugnance one may feel for the dreary stereotypes of television series, that high art palpably issues its judgments. Faulkner and Hemingway, the southerners and the New Yorkers, pass this small-town U.S. raw material by in a detour considerably greater than the proverbial ten-foot pole; indeed, of the great writers of the period, only Dick himself comes to mind as the virtual poet laureate of this material: of squabbling couples and marital dramas, of petit bourgeois shopkeepers, neighborhoods, and afternoons in front of television, and all the rest. But, of course, he does something to it, and it was already California anyway.

This small-town content was not, in the postwar period, really "provincial" any longer (as in Lewis or John O'Hara, let alone Dreiser): you might want to leave, you might still long for the big city, but something had happened—perhaps something as simple as television and the other media—to remove the pain and sting of absence from the center, from the metropolis. On the other hand, today, none of it exists any longer, even though we still have small towns (whose downtowns are now in decay—but so are the big cities). What has happened is that the autonomy of the small town (in the provincial period a source of claustrophobia and anxiety; in the fifties the ground for a certain comfort and even a certain reassurance) has vanished. What was once a separate point on the map has become an imperceptible thickening in a continuum of identical products and standardized spaces from coast to coast. One has the feeling, however, that the autonomy of the small town, its complacent independence, also functioned as an allegorical expression for the situation of Eisenhower America in the outside world as a whole —contented with itself, secure in the sense of its radical difference from other populations and cultures, insulated from their vicissitudes and from the flaws in human nature so palpably acted out in their violent and alien histories.

This is clearly, however, to shift from the realities of the 1950s to the representation of that rather different thing, the "fifties," a shift which obligates us in addition to underscore the cultural sources of all the attributes with which we have endowed the period, many of which seem very precisely to derive from its own television programs; in other words, its own representation of itself. However, although one does not confuse a person with what he or she thinks of himself/herself, such self-images are surely very relevant indeed and constitute an essential part of the more objective description or definition. Nonetheless, it seems possible that the deeper realities of the period—read, for example, against the very different scale of, say, diachronic and secular economic rhythms, or of synchronic and systemic global interrelationships, have little to do with either our cultural stereotypes of years thus labeled and defined in terms of generational decades. The concept of "classicism," for example, has a precise and functional meaning in German cultural and literary history which disappears when we move to a European perspective in which those few key years vanish without a trace into some vaster opposition between Enlightenment and Romanticism. But this is a speculation which presupposes the possibility that at an outer limit, the sense people have of themselves and their own moment of history may ultimately have *nothing* whatsoever to do with its reality:

that the existential may be absolutely distinct, as some ultimate "false consciousness," from the structural and social significance of a collective phenomenon, surely a possibility rendered more plausible by the fact of global imperialism, in terms of which the meaning of a given nation-state—for everyone else on the globe—may be wildly at odds from their own inner experiences and their own interior daily life. Eisenhower wore a well-known smile for us but an equally well-known scowl for foreigners beyond our borders, as the state portraits in any U.S. consulate during those years dramatically attested.

There is, however, an even more radical possibility; namely, that period concepts finally correspond to no realities whatsoever, and that whether they are formulated in terms of generational logic, or by the names of reigning monarchs, or according to some other category or typological and classificatory system, the collective reality of the multitudinous lives encompassed by such terms is nonthinkable (or nontotalizable, to use a current expression) and can never be described, characterized, labeled, or conceptualized. This is, I suppose, what one could call the Nietzschean position, for which there are no such things as "periods," nor have there ever been. In that case, of course, there is no such thing as "history" either, which was probably the basic philosophical point such arguments sought to make in the first place.

This is the moment, however, to return to Dick's novel and record the twist that turns it into science fiction: for it transpires, from an increasing accumulation of tiny but aberrant details, that the environment of the novel, in which we watch the characters act and move, is not really the fifties after all (I do not know that Dick ever uses this particular word). It is a Potemkin village of a historical kind: a reproduction of the 1950s—including induced and introjected memories and character structures in its human population—constructed (for reasons that need not detain us here) in 1997, in the midst of an interstellar atomic civil war. I will only note that a twofold determination plays across the main character, who must thus be read according to a negative and a positive hermeneutic simultaneously. The village has been constructed in order to trick him, against his will, into performing an essential wartime task for the government. In that sense, he is the victim of this manipulation, which awakens all our fantasies of mind control and unconscious exploitation, of anti-Cartesian predestination and determinism. On this reading, then, Dick's novel is a nightmare and the expression of deep, unconscious, collective fears about our social life and its tendencies.

Yet Dick also takes pains to make clear that the 1950s village is also

very specifically the result of infantile regression on the part of the protagonist, who has also, in a sense, unconsciously chosen his own delusion and has fled the anxieties of the civil war for the domestic and
reassuring comforts of his own childhood during the period in question. From this perspective, then, the novel is a collective wish-
fulfillment, and the expression of a deep, unconscious yearning for a
simpler and more human social system and a small-town Utopia very
much in the North American frontier tradition.

We should also note that the very structure of the novel articulates the
position of Eisenhower America in the world itself and is thereby to be
read as a kind of distorted form of cognitive mapping, an unconscious
and figurative projection of some more "realistic" account of our situation, as it has been described earlier: the hometown reality of the United
States surrounded by the implacable menace of world communism (and,
in this period to a much lesser degree, of Third World poverty). This is
also, of course, the period of the classic science fiction films, with their
more overtly ideological representations of external threats and impending alien invasions (also generally set in small towns). Dick's novel can
be read in that way—the grimmer "reality" disclosed behind the benign
and deceptive appearance—or it can be taken as a certain approach to
self-consciousness about the representations themselves.

What is more significant from the present perspective, however, is the
paradigmatic value of Dick's novel for questions of history and historicity in general. One of the ways of thinking about the subgenre to which
this novel belongs—that "category" called science fiction, which can
be either expanded and dignified by the addition of all the classical
satiric and Utopian literature from Lucian on or restricted and degraded to the pulp-and-adventure tradition—is as a historically new
and original form which offers analogies with the emergence of the
historical novel in the early nineteenth century. Lukács has interpreted
this last as a formal innovation (by Sir Walter Scott) which provided
figuration for the new and equally emergent sense of history of the
triumphant middle classes (or bourgeoisie), as that class sought to
project its own vision of its past and its future and to articulate its
social and collective project in a temporal narrative distinct in form
from those of earlier "subjects of history" such as the feudal nobility.
In that form, the historical novel—and its related emanations, such
as the costume film—has fallen into disrepute and infrequency, not
merely because, in the postmodern age, we no longer tell ourselves
our history in that fashion, but also because we no longer experience

it that way, and, indeed, perhaps no longer experience it at all.

One would want, in short, to stress the conditions of possibility of such a form—and of its emergence and eclipse—less in the existential experience of history of people at this or that historical moment than rather in the very structure of their socioeconomic system, in its relative opacity or transparency, and the access its mechanisms provide to some greater cognitive as well as existential contact with the thing itself. This is the context in which it seems interesting to explore the hypothesis that science fiction as a genre entertains a dialectical and structural relationship with the historical novel—a relationship of kinship and inversion all at once, of opposition and homology (just as comedy and tragedy have often been supposed to do, or lyric and epic, or satire and Utopia, as Robert C. Elliott analyzed them). But time itself plays a crucial role in this generic opposition, which is also something of an evolutionary compensation. For if the historical novel "corresponded" to the emergence of historicity, of a sense of history in its strong modern post-eighteenth-century sense, science fiction equally corresponds to the waning or the blockage of that historicity, and, particularly in our own time (in the postmodern era), to its crisis and paralysis, its enfeeblement and repression. Only by means of a violent formal and narrative dislocation could a narrative apparatus come into being capable of restoring life and feeling to this only intermittently functioning organ that is our capacity to organize and live time historically. Nor should it be thought overhastily that the two forms are symmetrical on the grounds that the historical novel stages the past and science fiction the future.

Historicity is, in fact, neither a representation of the past nor a representation of the future (although its various forms use such representations): it can first and foremost be defined as a perception of the present as history; that is, as a relationship to the present which somehow defamiliarizes it and allows us that distance from immediacy which is at length characterized as a historical perspective. It is appropriate, in other words, also to insist on the historicality of the operation itself, which is our way of conceiving of historicity in this particular society and mode of production; appropriate also to observe that what is at stake is essentially a process of reification whereby we draw back from our immersion in the here and now (not yet identified as a "present") and grasp it as a kind of thing—not merely a "present" but a present that can be dated and called the eighties or the fifties. Our presupposition has been that today this is more difficult to achieve than at the time of Sir Walter Scott, when a contemplation of the past seemed able to renew our sense of our own reading present as the sequel, if not particularly the culmination, of that genetic series.

Time Out of Joint, however, offers a very different machine for producing historicity than Sir Walter Scott's apparatus: what one might in the strong sense call a trope of the future anterior—the estrangement and renewal as history of our own reading present, the fifties, by way of the apprehension of that present as the past of a specific future. The future itself—Dick's 1997—is not, however, centrally significant as a representation or an anticipation; it is the narrative means to a very different end, namely the brutal transformation of a realistic representation of the present, of Eisenhower America and the 1950s small town, into a memory and a reconstruction. Reification is here indeed built into the novel itself and, as it were, defused and recuperated as a form of praxis: the fifties is a thing, but a thing that we can build, just as the science fiction writer builds his own small-scale model. At that point, then, reification ceases to be a baleful and alienating process, a noxious side-effect of our mode of production, if not, indeed, its fundamental dynamic, and is rather transferred to the side of human energies and human possibilities. (The reappropriation has, of course, a good deal to do with the specificity of Dick's own themes and ideology—in particular, the nostalgia about the past and the "petit bourgeois" valorization of small craftsmanship, as well as small business and collecting.)

This novel has necessarily become for us a historical one: for its present —the 1950s—has become our past in a rather different sense than that proposed by the text itself. The latter still "works": we can still feel and appreciate the transformation and reification of its readers' present into a historical period; we can even, by analogy, extrapolate something similar for our own moment in time. Whether such a process today can be realized concretely, in a cultural artifact, is, however, a rather different question. The accumulation of books like *Future Shock*, the incorporation of habits of "futurology" into our everyday life, the modification of our perception of things to include their "tendency" and of our reading of time to approximate a scanning of complex probabilities—this new relationship to our own present both includes elements formerly incorporated in the experience of the "future" and blocks or forestalls any global vision of the latter as a radically transformed and different system. If catastrophic "near-future" visions of, say, overpopulation, famine, and anarchic violence are no longer as effective as they were a few years ago, the weakening of those effects and of the narrative forms that were designed to produce them is not necessarily due only to overfamiliarity and overexposure; or rather, this last is perhaps also to be seen as a modification in our relationship to those imaginary near futures, which no longer strike us with the horror of otherness and radical difference. Here a certain Nietzscheanism operates to defuse anxiety and even fear: the conviction, however gradually learned and acquired, that there is only the present and that it is always "ours," is a kind of wisdom that cuts both ways. For it was always clear that the terror of such near futures —like the analogous terror of an older naturalism—was class based and deeply rooted in class comfort and privilege. The older naturalism let us briefly experience the life and the life world of the various under-classes, only to return with relief to our own living rooms and armchairs: the good resolutions it may also have encouraged were always, then, a form of philanthropy. In the same way, yesterday's terror of the over-crowded conurbations of the immediate future could just as easily be read as a pretext for complacency with our own historical present, in which we do not yet have to live like that. In both cases, at any rate, the fear is that of proletarianization, of slipping down the ladder, of losing a comfort and a set of privileges which we tend increasingly to think of in spatial terms: privacy, empty rooms, silence, walling other people out, protection against crowds and other bodies. Nietzschean wisdom, then, tells us to let go of that kind of fear and reminds us that whatever social and spatial form our future misery may take, it will not be alien because it will by definition be ours. *Dasein ist je mein eigenes*—defamiliariza-tion, the shock of otherness, is a mere aesthetic effect and a lie.

Perhaps, however, what is implied is simply an ultimate historicist breakdown in which we can no longer imagine the future at all, under any form—Utopian or catastrophic. Under those circumstances, where a formerly futurological science fiction (such as so-called cyberpunk today) turns into mere "realism" and an outright representation of the present, the possibility Dick offered us—an experience of our present as past and as history—is slowly excluded. Yet everything in our cul-ture suggests that we have not, for all that, ceased to be preoccupied by history; indeed, at the very moment in which we complain, as here, of the eclipse of historicity, we also universally diagnose contemporary culture as irredeemably historicist, in the bad sense of an omnipresent and indiscriminate appetite for dead styles and fashions; indeed, for all the styles and fashions of a dead past. Meanwhile, a certain caricature of historical thinking—which we may not even call *generational* any longer, so rapid has its momentum become—has also become univer-sal and includes at least the will and intent to return upon our present circumstances in order to think of them—as the nineties, say—and to draw the appropriate marketing and forecasting conclusions. Why is this not historicity with a vengeance? and what is the difference between this now generalized approach to the present and Dick's rather cumbersome and primitive laboratory approach to a "concept" of his own fifties?

In my opinion, it is the structure of the two operations which is instructively different: the one mobilizing a vision of the future in order to determine its return to a now historical present; the other mobilizing, but in some new allegorical way, a vision of the past, or of a certain moment of the past. Several recent films (I will here mention *Something Wild* and *Blue Velvet*) encourage us to see the newer process in terms of an allegorical encounter; yet even this formal possibility will not be properly grasped unless we set in place its preconditions in the development of nostalgia film generally. For it is by way of so-called nostalgia films that some properly allegorical processing of the past becomes possible: it is because the formal apparatus of nostalgia films has trained us to consume the past in the form of glossy images that new and more complex "postnostalgia" statements and forms become possible. I have elsewhere tried to identify the privileged raw material or historical content of this particular operation of reification and of the transformation into the image in the crucial antithesis between the twenties and the thirties, and in the historicist revival of the very stylistic expression of that antithesis in art deco. The symbolic working out of that tension—as it were, between Aristocracy and Worker—evidently involves something like the symbolic reinvention or production of a new Bourgeoisie, a new form of identity. Yet like photorealism, the products themselves are bland in their very visual elegance, while the plot structures of such films suffer from a schematization (or typification) which seems to be inherent in the project. While we may anticipate more of these, therefore, and while the taste for them corresponds to more durable features and needs in our present economicopsychic constitution (image fixation cum historicist cravings), it was perhaps only to be expected that some new and more complicated and interesting formal sequel would rapidly develop.

What was more unexpected—but very "dialectical" indeed, in a virtually textbook way—was the emergence of this new form from a kind of cross, if not synthesis, between the two filmic modes we had until now been imagining as antithetical: namely, the high elegance of nostalgia films, on the one hand, and the grade-B simulations of iconoclastic punk film, on the other. We failed to see that both were significantly mortgaged to music, because the musical signifiers were rather different in the two cases—the sequences of high-class dance music, on the one hand, the contemporary proliferation of rock groups, on the other. Meanwhile, any "dialectical" textbook of the type already referred to might have alerted us to the probability that an ideologeme of "elegance" depends in some measure on an opposite of some kind, an opposite and a negation which seems in our time to have shed its class content (still feebly alive when the "beats" were felt to entertain a twin opposition to bourgeois respectability and high modernist aestheticism), and to have gradually migrated into that new complex of meanings that bears the name *punk*.

The new films, therefore, will first and foremost be allegories of that, of their own coming into being as a synthesis of nostalgia-deco and punk: they will in one way or another tell their own stories as the need and search for this "marriage" (the wonderful thing about aesthetics —unlike politics, alas—being that the "search" automatically becomes the thing itself: to set it up is by definition to realize it). Yet this resolution of an aesthetic contradiction is not gratuitous, because the formal contradiction itself has a socially and historically symbolic significance of its own.

But now the stories of these two films need to be briefly outlined. In *Something Wild* a young "organization man" is abducted by a crazy girl, who initiates him into cutting corners and cheating on credit cards, until her husband, an ex-convict, shows up and, bent on vengeance, pursues the couple. In *Blue Velvet*, on the other hand, a young high-school graduate discovers a severed ear, which puts him on the trail of a torch singer mysteriously victimized by a local drug dealer, from whom he is able to save her.

Such films indeed invite us to return somehow to history: the central scene of *Something Wild*—or at least the one on which the plot structure pivots decisively—is a class reunion, the kind of event which specifically demands historical judgments of its participants: narratives of historical trajectories, as well as evaluations of moments of the past nostalgically reevoked but necessarily rejected or reaffirmed. This is the wedge, or opening, through which a hitherto aimless but lively filmic narrative suddenly falls into the deeper past (or that deeper past into it); for the ten-year reunion in reality takes us back twenty more, to a time when the "villain" unexpectedly emerges, over your shoulder, marked as "familiar" in all his unfamiliarity to the spectator (he is the heroine's husband, Ray, and worse). "Ray" is, of course, in one way yet another reworking of that boring and exhausted paradigm, the gothic, where—on the individualized level—a sheltered woman of some kind is terrorized and victimized by an "evil" male. I think it would be a great mistake to read such literature as a kind of protofeminist denunciation of patriarchy and, in particular, a protopolitical protest against rape. Certainly the gothic mobilizes anxieties about rape, but its structure gives us the clue to a more central feature of its content which I have tried to underscore by means of the word *sheltered*.

Gothics are indeed ultimately a class fantasy (or nightmare) in which the dialectic of privilege and shelter is exercised: your privileges seal you off from other people, but by the same token they constitute a protective wall through which you cannot see, and behind which therefore all kinds of envious forces may be imagined in the process of assembling, plotting, preparing to give assault; it is, if you like, the shower-curtain syndrome (alluding to Hitchcock's *Psycho*). That its classical form turns on the privileged content of the situation of middle-class women—the isolation, but also the domestic idleness, imposed on them by newer forms of middle-class marriage—adds such texts, as symptoms, to the history of women's situations but does not lend them any particular political significance (unless that significance consists merely in a coming to self-consciousness of the disadvantages of privilege in the first place). But the form can also, under certain circumstances, be reorganized around young men, to whom some similarly protective distance is imputed: intellectuals, for example, or "sheltered" young briefcase-carrying bureaucrats, as in *Something Wild* itself. (That this gender substitution risks awakening all kinds of supplementary sexual overtones is here self-consciously dramatized in the extraordinary tableau moment in which the stabbing, seen from behind—and from the woman's visual perspective—looks like a passionate embrace between the two men.) The more formal leap, however, will come when for the individual "victim"—male or female—is substituted the collectivity itself, the U.S. public, which now lives out the anxieties of its economic privileges and its sheltered "exceptionalism" in a pseudo-political version of the gothic—under the threats of stereotypical madmen and "terrorists" (mostly Arabs or Iranians for some reason). These collective fantasies are less to be explained by some increasing "feminization" of the American public self than by its guilt and the dynamics of comfort already referred to. And like the private version of the traditional gothic romance, they depend for their effects on the revitalization of *ethics* as a set of mental categories, and on the reinflation and artificial reinvigoration of that tired and antiquated binary opposition between virtue and vice, which the eighteenth century cleansed of its theological remnants and thoroughly sexualized before passing it on down to us.

The modern gothic, in other words—whether in its rape-victim or its political-paranoid forms—depends absolutely in its central operation on the construction of *evil* (forms of the good are notoriously more difficult to construct, and generally draw their light from the darker concept, as though the sun drew its reflected radiance from the moon). Evil is here, however, the emptiest form of sheer Otherness (into which any type of social content can be poured at will). I have so often been taken to task for my arguments against ethics (in politics as well as in aesthetics) that it seems worth observing in passing that Otherness is a very dangerous category, one we are well off without; but fortunately, in literature and culture, it has also become a very tedious one. Ridley Scott's *Alien* may still get away with it (but then, for science fiction, all of Lem's work—in particular the recent *Fiasco*—can be read as an argument against the use of such a category even there); but surely Ray of *Something Wild* and Frank Booth of *Blue Velvet* don't scare anybody any longer; nor ought we really to require our flesh to creep before reaching a sober and political decision as to the people and forces who are collectively "evil" in our contemporary world.

On the other hand, it is only fair to say that Ray is not staged demonically, as a representation of evil as such, but rather as the representation of someone *playing at being evil*, which is a rather different matter. Nothing about Ray, indeed, is particularly authentic; his malevolence is as false as his smile; but his clothes and hairstyle give a further clue and point us in a different direction from the ethical one. For not only does Ray offer a simulation of evil, he also offers a simulation of the *fifties*, and that seems to me a far more significant matter. I speak of the oppositional fifties, to be sure: the fifties of Elvis rather than the fifties of Ike, but I'm not sure we can really tell the difference any more, as we peer across our historical gap and try to focus the landscape of the past through nostalgia-tinted spectacles.

At this point, however, the gothic trappings of *Something Wild* fall away and it becomes clear that we have to do here with an essentially allegorical narrative in which the 1980s meet the 1950s. What kind of accounts actuality has to settle with this particular historicist ghost (and whether it manages to do so) is for the moment less crucial than how the encounter was arranged in the first place: by the intermediary and the good offices of the 1960s, of course—inadvertent good offices to be sure, since Audrey/Lulu has very little reason to desire the connection, or even to be reminded of her own past, or Ray's (he has just come out of prison).

Everything turns, therefore, or so one would think, on this distinction between the sixties and the fifties: the first desirable (like a fascinating woman), the second fearful and ominous, untrustworthy (like the leader of a motorcycle gang). As the title suggests, it is the nature of "something wild" which is at stake, the inquiry into it focused by Audrey's first glimpse of Charley's nonconformist character (he skips out on his lunch bill). Indeed, the nonpaying of bills seems to function as the principal index for Charley's "hipness" or "squareness"—it being understood that neither of these categories (nor those of conformity/nonconformity used above) corresponds to the logic of this film, which can be seen as an attempt very precisely to construct new categories with which to replace those older, historically dated and period-bound (uncontemporary, unpostmodern) ones. We may describe this particular "test" as involving white-collar crime, as opposed to the "real," or lower-class, crime—grand theft and mayhem—practiced by Ray himself. Only it is a petit-bourgeois white-collar crime (even Charley's illicit use of company credit cards is scarcely commensurable with the genuine criminality his corporation can be expected, virtually by definition, to imply). Nor are such class markers present in the film itself, which can in another sense be seen very precisely as an effort to repress the language and categories of class and class differentiation and to substitute for them other kinds of semic oppositions still to be invented.

Those necessarily emerge in the framework of the Lulu character, within the sixties allegory (which is something like the "black box" of this particular semic transformation). The fifties stands for genuine rebellion, with genuine violence and genuine consequences, but also for the *romantic representations* of such rebellion, in the films of Brando and James Dean. Ray thus functions both as a kind of gothic villain, within this particular narrative, and also, on the allegorical level, as the sheer *idea* of the romantic hero—the tragic protagonist of another kind of film, that can no longer be made. Lulu is not herself an alternate possibility, unlike the heroine of *Desperately Seeking Susan*. The framework here remains exclusively male, as the lamentable ending—her chastening, or taming—testifies, along with the significance of clothing, which we will look at in a moment. Everything depends, therefore, on the new kind of *hero* Lulu somehow allows or enables Charley to become, by virtue of her own semic composition (since she is a good deal more than a mere woman's body or fetish).

What is interesting about that composition is that it first of all gives us the sixties seen, as it were, through the fifties (or the eighties?): alcohol rather than drugs. The schizophrenic, drug-cultural side of the sixties is here systematically excluded along with its politics. What is dangerous, in other words, is not Lulu at her most frenzied but rather Ray; not the sixties and its countercultures and "life-styles" but the fifties and its revolts. Yet the continuity between the fifties and the sixties lay in what was being revolted *against*, in what life-style the "new" life-styles were alternatives *to*. It is, however, difficult to find any content in Lulu's stimulating behavior, which seems organized around sheer caprice; that is to say, around the supreme value of remaining unpredictable and immune to reification and categorization. Shades of André Gide, in *Lafcadio's Adventures*, or of all those Sartrean characters desperately attempting to evade that ultimate objectification by another's Look (it is impossible, and they end up simply being labeled "capricious"). The costume changes lend this otherwise purely formal unpredictability a certain visual content; they translate it into the language of image culture and afford a purely specular pleasure in Lulu's metamorphoses (which are not really psychic).

Yet viewers and protagonist still have to feel that they are on their way somewhere (at least until the appearance of Ray gives the film a different kind of direction): as thrilling and improvised as it seems, therefore, Lulu's abduction of Charley from New York has at least an empty form that will be instructive, for it is the archetypal descent into Middle America, into the "real" United States, either of lynching and bigotry or of true, wholesome family life and American ideals; one doesn't quite know which. Nonetheless, like those Russian populist intellectuals in the nineteenth century setting forth on foot to discover "the people," something like this journey is or was the *scène à faire* for any American allegory worthy of its vocation: what this one reveals, however, is that there is no longer anything to discover at the end of the line. For Lulu/Audrey's family—reduced in this case to a mother—is no longer the bourgeoisie of sinister memory: neither the sexual repression and respectability of the fifties nor the Johnsonian authoritarianism of the sixties. This mother plays the harpsichord, "understands" her daughter, and is fully as much an oddball as everybody else. No Oedipal revolts are possible any longer in this American small town, and with them all the tension goes out of the social and cultural dynamics of the period. Yet if there are no longer any "middle classes" to be found in the heartland, there is something else that may serve as something for a substitute for them, at least in the dynamic of narrative structure itself: for what we find at Lulu's class reunion (besides Ray and her own past) is Charley's business colleague, that is to say, a yuppie bureaucrat, along with his pregnant wife. These are unquestionably the baleful parents we sought, but of some distant and not quite imaginable future, not of the older, traditional American past: they occupy the semic slot of the "squares," but without any social basis or content any longer (they can scarcely be read as embodiments of the Protestant ethic, for example, or of puritanism or white racism or patriarchy). But they at least help us to identify the deeper ideological purpose of this film, which is to differentiate Charley from his fellow yuppies by making him over into a hero or protagonist of a different generic type than Ray. Unpredictability, as we have shown, in a matter of *fashion* (clothing, hairstyle, and general body language): Charley himself must therefore pass through this particular matrix, and his metamorphosis is concretely realized, appropriately enough, when he sheds his suit for a more relaxed and tourist-type disguise (T-shirt, shorts, dark glasses, etc.). At the end of the film, of course, he also sheds his corporate job; but it would probably be asking too much to wonder what he does or can become in its stead, except in the "relationship" itself, where he becomes the master and the senior partner. The semic organization of all this might be laid out as follows (and symmetry preserved by seeing the pregnant and disapproving yuppie wife as the concrete manifestation of the neutral term):

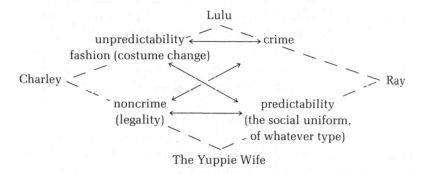

We have not yet mentioned the handcuffs, which can serve as the transition to a similar type of narrative allegory, one whose combinations and atmosphere are very different from this one. *Blue Velvet*, indeed, tries to place sadomasochism squarely on the mass-cultural map with an earnestness altogether lacking in the Demme movie (whose handcuff love scene is as sexy as it is "frivolous"). S&M thus becomes the latest and the last in the long line of those taboo forms of content which, beginning with Nabokov's nymphets in the 1950s, rise one after the other to the surface of public art in that successive and even progressive widening of transgressions which we once called the counterculture, or the sixties. In *Blue Velvet*, however, it is explicitly related to drugs, and therefore to crime—although not exactly organized crime, rather to a collectivity of misfits and oddballs—the transgressive nature of this complex of things being tediously reinforced by repetitive obscenity (on the part of the Dennis Hopper character).

Yet if history is discreetly evoked and invoked in *Something Wild*, it is rather its opposite—Nature—which is given us as the overall frame and inhuman, transhuman perspective in which to contemplate the events of *Blue Velvet*. The father's stroke, which opens the film like an incomprehensible catastrophe—an act of God which is peculiarly an act of scandalous violence within this peaceful American small town—is itself positioned by David Lynch (director of *Eraserhead* and *Dune*) within the more science fictional horizon of the Darwinian violence of all nature. From the shot of the father lying paralyzed, the camera withdraws into the bushes surrounding the house, enlarging its microscopic focus as it does so, until we confront a horrible churning which we take first and generically, in good horror-film format, to be the hidden presence of the maniac, until it proves to be the mandibles of an insatiable insect. The later insistence on robins with worms twisting desperately in their beaks also reinforces this cosmic sense of the dizzying and nauseating violence of all nature—as though within this ferocity without boundaries, this ceaseless bloodshed of the universe as far as the eye can see or thought can reach, a single peaceful oasis had been conquered by the progress of humanity and whatever divine providence guided it; namely—unique in the animal kingdom as well as in the horrors of human history as well—the North American small town. Into this precious and fragile conquest of civilized decorum wrenched from a menacing outside world, then, comes violence—in the form of a severed ear; in the form of an underground drug culture and of a sado-masochism about which it is finally not yet really clear whether it is a pleasure or a duty, a matter of sexual gratification or just another way of expressing yourself.

History therefore enters *Blue Velvet* in the form of ideology, if not of myth: the Garden and the Fall, American exceptionalism, a small town far more lovingly preserved in its details like a simulacrum or Disneyland under glass somewhere than anything the protagonists of Something Wild were able to locate on their travels, complete with high-school leads on the order of the most authentic fifties movies. Even a fifties-style pop psychoanalysis can be invoked around this fairy tale, since besides a mythic and sociobiological perspective of the violence of nature, the film's events are also framed by the crisis in the paternal function—the stroke that suspends paternal power and authority in the opening sequence, the recovery of the father and his return from the hospital in the idyllic final scene. That the other father is a police detective lends a certain plausibility to this kind of interpretation, which is also strengthened by the abduction and torture of the third, absent, father, of whom we only see the ear. Nonetheless the message is not particularly patriarchal-authoritarian, particularly since the young hero manages to assume the paternal function very handily: rather, this particular call for a return to the fifties coats the pill by insistence on the unobtrusive benevolence of all these fathers—and, contrariwise, on the unalloyed nastiness of their opposite number.

For this gothic subverts itself fully as much as Something Wild, but in a rather different way. There, it was the simulated nature of Ray's evil that was underscored for us even while he remained a real threat: revolt, statutory illegality, physical violence, and ex-convicts are all genuine and serious matters. What Blue Velvet gives us to understand about the sixties, in contrast, is that despite the grotesque and horrendous tableaux of maimed bodies, this kind of evil is more distasteful than it is fearful, more disgusting than threatening: here evil has finally become an image, and the simulated replay of the fifties has generalized itself into a whole simulacrum in its own right. Now the boy without fear of the fairy tale can set out to undo this world of baleful enchantment, free its princess (while marrying another), and kill the magician. The lesson implied by all this—which is rather different from the lesson it transmits—is that it is better to fight drugs by portraying them as vicious and silly, than by awakening the full tonal range of ethical judgments and indignations and thereby endowing them with the otherwise glamorous prestige of genuine Evil, of the Transgressive in its most august religious majesty. Indeed, this particular parable of the end of the sixties is also, on another metacritical level, a parable of the end of theories of transgression as well, which so fascinated that whole period and its intellectuals. The S&M materials, then—even though contemporary with a whole new postmodern punk scene—are finally called on to undo themselves and to abolish the very logic on which their attraction/ repulsion was based in the first place.

Thus these films can be read as dual symptoms: they show a collective unconscious in the process of trying to identify its own present at the same time that they illuminate the failure of this attempt, which seems to reduce itself to the recombination of various stereotypes of the past. Perhaps, indeed, what follows upon a strongly generational self-consciousness, such as what the "people of the sixties" felt, is often a peculiar aimlessness. What if the crucial identifying feature of the next "decade" is, for example, a lack of just such strong self-consciousness, which is to say a constitutive lack of identity in the first place? This is what many of us felt about the seventies, whose specificity seemed most of the time to consist in having no specificity, particularly after the uniqueness of the preceding period. Things began to pick up again in the eighties, and in a variety of ways. But the identity process is not a cyclical one, and this is essentially the dilemma. Of the eighties, as against the seventies, one could say that there were new political straws in the wind, that things were moving again, that some impossible "return of the sixties" seemed to be in the air and in the ground. But the eighties, politically and otherwise, have not really resembled the sixties, especially, particularly if one tried to define them as a return or a reversion. Even that enabling costume-party self-deception of which Marx spoke—the wearing of the costumes of the great moments of the past—is no longer on the cards in an ahistorical period of history. The generational *combinatoire* thus seems to have broken down at the moment it confronted serious historicity, and the rather different self-concept of "postmodernism" has taken its place.

Dick used science fiction to see his present as (past) history; the classical nostalgia film, while evading its present altogether, registered its historicist deficiency by losing itself in mesmerized fascination in lavish images of specific generational pasts. The two 1986 movies, while scarcely pioneering a wholly new form (or mode of historicity), nonetheless seem, in their allegorical complexity, to mark the end of that and the now open space for something else.

10

Secondary Elaborations

I. Prolegomena to Future Confrontations Between the Modern and the Postmodern

Marxism and postmodernism: people often seem to find this combination peculiar or paradoxical, and somehow intensely unstable, so that some are led to conclude that, in my own case, having "become" a postmodernist I must have ceased to be a Marxist in any meaningful (or in other words, stereotypical) sense. For the two terms (in full postmodernism) carry with them a whole freight of pop nostalgia images, "Marxism" perhaps distilling itself into yellowing period photographs of Lenin and the Soviet revolution, and "postmodernism" quickly yielding a vista of the gaudiest new hotels. The overhasty unconscious then rapidly assembles the image of a small, painstakingly reproduced nostalgia restaurant—decorated with old photographs, with Soviet waiters sluggishly serving bad Russian food—hidden away within some gleaming new pink-and-blue architectural extravaganza.

If I may indulge in a personal note, it has happened to me before to have been oddly and comically identified with an object of study: a book I published years ago on structuralism elicited letters, some of which addressed me as a "foremost" spokesperson for structuralism, while the others appealed to me as an "eminent" critic and opponent of that movement. I was really neither of those things, but I have to conclude that I must have been "neither" in some relatively complicated and unusual way that it seemed hard for people to grasp. As far as postmodernism is concerned, and despite the trouble I took in my principal essay on the subject to explain how it was not possible intellectually or politically simply to celebrate postmodernism or to "disavow" it (whatever that might mean), avant-garde art critics quickly identified me as a vulgar Marxist hatchet man, while some of the more simple-hearted comrades concluded that, following the example of so many illustrious predecessors, I had finally gone off the deep end and become a "post-Marxist" (which is to say, in one language, a renegade and a turncoat, and in another, someone who would rather switch than fight).

Many of these reactions seemed to confuse taste (or opinion), analysis, and evaluation, three things I would have thought we had some interest in keeping separate. "Taste," in the loosest media sense of personal preferences, would seem to correspond to what used to be nobly and philosophically designated as "aesthetic judgment" (the change in codes and the barometrical fall in lexical dignity is at least one index of the displacement of traditional aesthetics and the transformation of the cultural sphere in modern times). "Analysis" I take to be that peculiar and rigorous conjuncture of formal and historical analysis that constitutes the specific task of literary and cultural study; to describe this further as the investigation of the historical conditions of possibility of specific forms may perhaps convey the way in which these twin perspectives (often thought to be irreconcilable or incommensurable in the past) can be said to constitute their object and thereby to be inseparable. Analysis in this sense can be seen to be a very different set of operations from a cultural journalism oriented around taste and opinion; what it would now be important to secure is the difference between such journalism—with its indispensable reviewing functions—and what I will call "evaluation," which no longer turns on whether a work is "good" (after the fashion of an older aesthetic judgment), but rather tries to keep alive (or to reinvent) assessments of a sociopolitical kind that interrogate the quality of social life itself by way of the text or individual work of art, or hazard an assessment of the political effects of cultural currents or movements with less utilitarianism and a greater sympathy for the dynamics of everyday life than the imprimaturs and indexes of earlier traditions.

As far as taste is concerned (and as readers of the preceding chapters will have become aware), culturally I write as a relatively enthusiastic consumer of postmodernism, at least of some parts of it: I like the architecture and a lot of the newer visual work, in particular the newer photography. The music is not bad to listen to, or the poetry to read; the novel is the weakest of the newer cultural areas and is considerably excelled by its narrative counterparts in film and video (at least the high literary novel is; subgeneric narratives, however, are very good, indeed, and in the Third World of course all this falls out very differently). Food and fashion have also greatly improved, as has the life world generally. My sense is that this is essentially a visual culture, wired for sound —but one where the linguistic element (for which some stronger term than "standardization" needs to be invented, and which is in addition marbled by the worst kind of junk-language, such as "life-style" or "sexual preference") is slack and flabby, and not to be made interesting without ingenuity, daring, and keen motivation.

These are tastes, giving rise to opinions; they have little to do with the analysis of the function of such a culture and how it got to be that way. In any case, even the opinions are probably not satisfactory in this form either, since the second thing people want to know, for the obvious contextual reason, is how this compares to an older modernist canon. The architecture is generally a great improvement; the novels are much worse. Photography and video are incomparable (the latter for a very obvious reason indeed); also we're fortunate today in having interesting new painting to look at and poetry to read.

Music, however (after Schopenhauer, Nietzsche, and Thomas Mann), ought to lead us into something more interesting and complicated than mere opinion. For one thing, it remains a fundamental class marker, the index of that cultural capital Pierre Bourdieu calls social "distinction": whence the passions that highbrow and lowbrow, or elite and mass, musical tastes (and the theories that correspond to them, Adorno, on the one hand, Simon Frith, on the other) still arouse. Meanwhile, music also includes history in a more thoroughgoing and irrevocable fashion, since, as background and mood stimulus, it mediates our historical past along with our private or existential one and can scarcely be woven out of the memory any longer.

The most crucial relationship of music to the postmodern, however, surely passes through space itself (on my analysis, one of the distinguishing or even constitutive traits of the new "culture" or cultural dominant). MTV above all can be taken as a spatialization of music, or, if you prefer, as the telltale revelation that it had already, in our time, become profoundly spatialized in the first place. Technologies of the musical, to be sure, whether of production, reproduction, reception, or consumption, already worked to fashion a new sonorous space around the individual or the collective listener: in music, too, "representationality"—in the sense of drawing up your *fauteuil* and gazing across at the spectacle unfolded before you—has known its crisis and its specific historical disintegration. You no longer offer a musical object for contemplation and gustation; you wire up the context and make space musical around the consumer. In that situation, *narrative* offers multiple and proteiform mediations between the sounds in time and the body in place, coordinating a narrativized visual fragment—an image shard marked as narrative, which does not have to come from any story you ever heard of—with an event on the sound track. Particularly in the postmodern it is crucial to distinguish between narrativization and any specific narrative segment as such: failure to do so results in confusions between "old-fashioned realistic" stories and novels, and putatively modern or postmodern antinarrative ones. The story is, however, only one of the forms narrative or narrativization can take; and it is worth entertaining the possibility that today the mere intent to produce a story may be enough, as in Lem's imaginary book reviews (Ken Russell, when asked why he had shifted over into MTV, prophesied that in the twenty-first century no fiction film would last longer than fifteen minutes). What MTV does to music, therefore, is not some inversion of that defunct nineteenth-century form called program music but rather the nailing of sounds (using Lacan's carpet tacks, no doubt) onto visible space and spatial segments: here, as in the video form more generally, the older paradigm—that lights up in genealogical hindsight as this one's predecessor (but not the basic influence on it)—is *animation* itself. The cartoon—particularly in its more delirious and surreal varieties—was the first laboratory in which "text" tried out its vocation to mediate between sight and sound (think of Walt's own lowbrow obsession with highbrow music) and ended up spatializing time.

We therefore begin to make some progress on turning our tastes into "postmodernism theory" when we step back and attend to the "system of the fine arts" itself: the ratio between the forms and media (indeed, the very shape that "media" itself has taken on, supplanting form and genre alike), the way in which the generic system itself, as a restructuration and a new configuration (however minimally modified), expresses the postmodern, and through it, all the other things that are happening to us.

But descriptions like these seem not only to involve the obligatory comparison with the modern as such, they also let questions back in by way of the "canon": surely only a very old-fashioned critic or cultural journalist would be interested in proving the obvious, that Yeats is "greater" than Paul Muldoon, or Auden than Bob Perelman—unless the word *great* is simply an expression of enthusiasm, in which case you might well sometimes want to do it the other way round. The rejoinder here is the rather different one that you cannot even realistically "compare" the "greatness" of "great writers" *within* a single paradigm or period. Adorno's notion of an internecine war among the individual works, aesthetic monads that repel each other, is surely the one that better corresponds to most people's aesthetic experience, explaining why it is intolerable to be asked to decide whether Keats is greater than Wordsworth, or to measure the worth of the Pompidou Center on the scale of the Guggenheim, or the preeminence of Dos Passos over Doctorow, let alone the question of Mallarmé and Ashbery.

We do, however, make comparisons of this kind and seem to enjoy the process, however meaningless it may be; one can therefore only conclude that such compulsive matchings and rankings *must mean something else*. Indeed, I've argued in another place[1] that in the political unconscious of an age, such comparisons — whether of individual works or cultural styles more generally — are in reality the figuration and the expressive raw material of a deeper comparison between the modes of production themselves, which confront and judge each other by way of the individual contact between reader and text. The example of the modern/postmodern, however, shows that this also holds good for stages within a single mode of production, in this case for the confrontation between the modernist (or imperialist, or monopoly) stage of capitalism and its postmodern (or multinational) stage.

All the enumeration of sheerly cultural traits comes down to this catachresis, or four-term metaphor: we concoct some proposition about the qualitative superiority of the musical production of the eighteenth-century German principalities only in order to censure or to celebrate the commercial-technological engenderment of music in our own. That manifest comparison is the cover and the vehicle for a latent one in which we try to construct a feeling for daily life in the ancien régime so as, in a next step, to reconstruct a feeling for what is peculiar and specific, original and historic, in the present. Under the guise of specialized history, therefore, we are still doing general or universal history, which is destined to end up in postmodernism theory, as the sequence of Brechtian estrangement operations outlined above makes plain. These are then the terms and conditions under which we can argue about the respective "greatness" of Mahler and Phil Glass, or Eisenstein and MTV, but they extend far beyond the aesthetic or the cultural as such, becoming meaningful or intelligible only when they reach the terrain of the production of material life and the limits and potentialities it (dialectically) imposes on human praxis, including cultural praxis. What is now at stake is relative systemic alienation itself and the dialectical relationship between the limits of the base and the possibilities of the super-structure within any given system or systemic moment: its internal quotient of misery and the determinate potentiality of bodily and spiritual transfiguration it also affords, or conquers.

That is, for modernism, a whole investigation in its own right, about which only a few first notes are here appended. As for the feeling entertained about the "end of the modern" within the postmodern, that is another matter entirely, and a constitutive one (which does not necessarily have much to do with historical modernism, or historical modernity either). A second set of notes therefore configures this topic, which is sometimes confused with the ethical and aesthetic "comparison" between modernism and postmodernism; nor does it afford the socioeconomic comparison proposed in what follows.

II. Notes Toward a Theory of the Modern

The "classics" of the modern can certainly be postmodernized, or transformed into "texts," if not into precursors of "textuality": the two operations are relatively different, insofar as the precursors—Raymond Roussel, Gertrude Stein, Marcel Duchamp—always fit uneasily into some modernist canon anyway. They are the exemplars and the eyewitness exhibits in some cases for the identity between modernism and postmodernism, since, in them, the slightest modification, the merest breath of perversity in shifting the chairs around, makes what ought to be the most classical high modernist aesthetic values into something uncomfortable and remote (but closer to us!). It is as though they constituted some opposition within the opposition, an aesthetic negation of the negation; against the already anti-hegemonic minority art of the modern, they staged their own even more minoritarian and private rebellion, which will of course itself become canonical when the modern freezes over and becomes a drafty set of museums.

As for the mainstream moderns, however, those waiting patiently in line for a room in just such a museum, any number of them seem capable of a thoroughgoing rewriting into the postmodern text (one hesitates to think of the process in the same way as the adaptation of a novel to the screen, particularly since one of the features of postmodern cinema is the increasing scarcity of just such screen adaptations). But that we are rewriting high modernism in new ways today seems to me beyond doubt, at least for certain crucial writers: that besides being a realist, Flaubert also turned into a modernist when Joyce learned him by heart, then unexpectedly turned into something like a postmodernist in the hands of Nathalie Sarraute—that is a familiar story. As for Joyce himself, Colin MacCabe has projected a new Joyce for us today, a feminist and a creole or multiethnic Joyce, which would seem to be very consonant with the times and to offer at least one Joyce we might be willing to celebrate as postmodern. Meanwhile, on my side, I've tried to invoke a Third World and anti-imperialist Joyce more consistent with a contemporary than with a modernist aesthetic.[2] But are all the classics of yesteryear rewritable in this fashion? Is the Proust of Gilles Deleuze a postmodern Proust? Deleuze's Kafka is certainly a postmodern Kafka, a Kafka of ethnicity and microgroups, very much a Third World and dialect minority Kafka in tune with postmodern politics and the "new social movements." But is T. S. Eliot recuperable? What ever happened to Thomas Mann and André Gide? Frank Lentricchia has kept Wallace Stevens alive throughout this momentous climatological transformation, but Paul Valéry has vanished without a trace, and he was central to the modernist movement internationally. What is suspicious about the matter, and about the questions that it raises, is their overwhelming family likeness with familiar discussions of the nature of the classic itself, the "inexhaustible" text, capable of being reinvented and used in new ways by successive generations—something like a great manor house, handed down and redecorated over and over by successive heirs, who can install the latest Parisian fashions or Japanese technology. Meanwhile, the non-survivors are proof that "posterity" really does exist, even in our own postmodern media age; the losers are a crucial component of the argument, who document the necessary pastness of the past by showing that not all its "great books" are still of any interest to us. This approach conveniently masks out those parts of the problem that reidentify it with the older historicist dilemma and prevents us from learning something about our own postmodernity by way of the boredom inspired by the high modern "classics" we can no longer read. But boredom is a very useful instrument with which to explore the past, and to stage a meeting between it and the present.

As for the others who did survive—at the price of a certain renovation or "immaculation,"[3] a certain *Umfunktionierung* (Flaubert has to be read much more slowly, for example, in order to undo the storyline and turn the sentences into the moments of a postmodern "text")—they will evidently have something to tell us about a situation of "modernity" we still share. We need, in fact, to inflect the root adjective into three distinct substantives—beyond "modernism" proper, the less familiar one of "modernity," and then of "modernization"—in order not only to grasp the dimensions of the problem, but to appreciate how differently the various academic disciplines, as well as the various national traditions, have framed it. "Modernism" has come only recently to France, "modernity" only recently to us, "modernization" belongs to the sociologists, Spanish has two separate words for the artistic movements ("modernismo" and "vanguardismo"), etc. A comparative lexicon would be a four- or five-dimensional affair, registering the chronological appearance of these terms in the various language groups, while recording the uneven development observable between them.[4] A comparative sociology of modernism and its cultures—a sociology which like Weber's remained committed to measuring the extraordinary impact of capitalism on hitherto traditional cultures, the social and psychic damage done to now irrevocable older forms of human life and perception—would alone offer an adequate framework for rethinking "modernism" today, provided it worked both sides of the street and dug its tunnel from both directions; one must, in other words, not only deduce modernism from modernization, but also scan the sedimented traces of modernization within the aesthetic work itself.

It should also be obvious that it is the fact of the relationship itself that counts and not its content. The various modernisms have just as often constituted violent reactions against modernization as they have replicated its values and tendencies by their own formal insistence on novelty, innovation, the transformation of older forms, therapeutic iconoclasm and the processing of new (aesthetic) wonder-working technologies. If, for example, modernization has something to do with industrial progress, rationalization, reorganization of production and administration along more efficient lines, electricity, the assembly line, parliamentary democracy, and cheap newspapers—then we will have to conclude that at least one strand of artistic modernism is anti-modern and comes into being in violent or muffled protest against modernization, now grasped as technological progress in the largest sense. These anti-modern modernisms sometimes involve pastoral visions or Luddite gestures but are mostly symbolic, and, especially at the turn of the century, involve what is sometimes referred to as a new wave of anti-positivist, spiritualistic, irrational reactions against triumphant enlightenment progress or reason.

Perry Anderson reminds me, however, that in this respect the deepest and most fundamental feature shared by all the modernisms is not so much their hostility to a technology some (like the Futurists) actually celebrated, but rather their hostility to the market itself. The centrality of this feature is then confirmed by its inversion in the various postmodernisms, which, even more wildly different from each other than the various modernisms, all at least share a resonant affirmation, when not an outright celebration, of the market as such.

That the experience of the machine is in any case a crucial marker here can be deduced, in my view, from the rhythm of the successive waves of aesthetic modernism: a long first wave in the late nineteenth century, organized around organic forms and exemplified in some priv-ileged way in *symbolisme*; a second one acquiring its momentum from the turn of the century on and characterized by the dual markers of an enthusiasm for machine technology and an organization into more paramilitary-type avant-gardes (Futurism can serve as the strong form of this moment). To these should be added the modernism of the iso-lated "genius," organized, unlike the two periodic movements (with their emphasis on the organic transformation of the life-world, and on the avant-garde and its social mission, respectively), around the great Work, the Book of the World—secular scripture, sacred text, ultimate ritual mass (Mallarmé's Livre) for an unimaginable new social order. And we should probably also make some place (but not as late as he does) for what Charles Jencks has come to call "late modernism"—the last sur-vivals of a properly modernist view of art and the world after the great political and economic break of the Depression, where, under Stalinism or the Popular Front, Hitler or the New Deal, some new conception of social realism achieves the status of momentary cultural dominance by way of collective anxiety and world war. Jencks's late moderns are those who persist into postmodernism, and the idea makes sense architectur-ally; a literary frame of reference, however, throws up names like Borges and Nabokov, Beckett, poets like Olson or Zukovsky, and composers like Milton Babbitt, who had the misfortune to span two eras and the luck to find a time capsule of isolation or exile in which to spin out unseason-able forms.

Of the most canonical of these four moments or tendencies, that of the great demiurges and prophets—Frank Lloyd Wright and his cape and porkpie hat, Proust in his cork-lined room, the "force of nature" Picasso, and the "tragic," uniquely doomed Kafka (all as idiosyncratic and eccentric as the best Great Detectives in the classical detective stories) —something more needs to be said to discourage the view that, from the hindsight of postmodern fashion and commerciality, modernism was still a time of giants and legendary powers no longer available to us. But

if the poststructuralist motif of the "death of the subject" means anything socially, it signals the end of the entrepreneurial and inner-directed
individualism, with its "charisma" and its accompanying categorial pan-
oply of quaint romantic values such as that of the "genius" in the first
place. Seen thus, the extinction of the "great moderns" is not necessarily an occasion for pathos. Our social order is richer in information and
more literate, and socially, at least, more "democratic" in the sense of
the universalization of wage labor (I have always felt that Brecht's term
"plebeianization" is politically more suitable and sociologically more
exact in designating this leveling process, which people on the left can
surely only welcome); this new order no longer needs prophets and
seers of the high modernist and charismatic type, whether among its
cultural producers or its politicians. Such figures no longer hold any
charm or magic for the subjects of a corporate, collectivized, post-
individualistic age; in that case, goodbye to them without regrets, as
Brecht might have put it: woe to the country that needs geniuses, prophets, Great Writers, or demiurges!

What one must retain historically is the fact that the phenomenon
did once exist; a postmodern view of the "great" modernist creators
ought not to argue away the social and historical specificity of those
now doubtful "centered subjects," but rather provide new ways of understanding their conditions of possibility.

A beginning is made on that process by grasping the once-famous
names no longer as characters larger than life or great souls of one kind
or another, but rather—non- and anti-anthropomorphically—as *careers*,
that is to say as objective situations in which an ambitious young artist
around the turn of the century could see the objective possibility of
turning himself into the "greatest painter" (or poet or novelist or com-
poser) "of the age." That objective possibility is now given, not in subjective talent as such or some inner richness or inspiration, but rather
in strategies of a well-nigh military character, based on superiority of
technique and terrain, assessment of the counterforces, a shrew maximization of one's own specific and idiosyncratic resources. This approach to "genius," however, which we now associate with the name of
Pierre Bourdieu,[5] should be sharply distinguished from a debunking or
demystifying *ressentiment* like what Tolstoy seems to have felt about
Shakespeare, and, *mutatis mutandis*, about the role of "great men" generally in history. Despite Tolstoy, I think we still do admire the great
generals (along with their counterparts, the great artists),[6] but the admiration has been displaced from their innate subjectivity to their histori-

cal flair, their capacity to assess the "current situation" and to evaluate its potential permutation system on the spot. This is, it seems to me, a properly postmodern revision in biographical historiography, which characteristically substitutes the horizontal for the vertical, space for time, system for depth.

But there is a deeper reason for the disappearance of the Great Writer under postmodernism, and it is simply this, sometimes called "uneven development": in an age of monopolies (and trade unions), of increasing institutionalized collectivization, there is always a lag. Some parts of the economy are still archaic, handicraft enclaves; some are more modern and futuristic than the future itself. Modern art, in this respect, drew its power and its possibilities from being a backwater and an archaic holdover within a modernizing economy: it glorified, celebrated, and dramatized older forms of individual production which the new mode of production was elsewhere on the point of displacing and blotting out. Aesthetic production then offered the Utopian vision of a more human production generally; and in the world of the monopoly stage of capitalism it exercised a fascination by way of the image it offered of a Utopian transformation of human life. Joyce in his rooms in Paris single-handedly produces a whole world, all by himself and beholden to no one; but the human beings in the streets outside those rooms have no comparable sense of power and control, of human productivity; none of the feeling of freedom and autonomy that comes when, like Joyce, you can make or at least share in making your own decisions. As a form of production, then, modernism (including the Great Artists and producers) gives off a message that has little to do with the content of the individual works: it is the aesthetic as sheer autonomy, as the satisfactions of handicraft transfigured.

Modernism must thus be seen as uniquely corresponding to an uneven moment of social development, or to what Ernst Bloch called the "simultaniety of the nonsimultaneous," the "synchronicity of the non-synchronous" (Gleichzeitigkeit des Ungleichzeitigen):[7] the coexistence of realities from radically different moments of history—handicrafts alongside the great cartels, peasant fields with the Krupp factories or the Ford plant in the distance. But a less programmatic demonstration of unevenness is afforded by the work of Kafka, about which Adorno once said that it stood as a definitive rebuke to anyone who wanted to think about art in terms of pleasure. I think he was wrong about this, at least from a postmodern perspective; the refutation can be staged in a much more wide-ranging way from those perverse-seeming descriptions of Kafka as a "mystical humorist" (Thomas Mann) and as a joyous and Chaplinesque writer, although it is certain that when you remember Chaplin during your reading of Kafka, Chaplin doesn't look the same any more either.

More must therefore be said on the subject of the pleasurability and even the joyous nature of Kafka's nightmares. Benjamin once observed that there were at least two current interpretations of Kafka that we needed to get rid of for good: one was the psychoanalytic (Kafka's Oedipus complex—he certainly had one, but his are hardly psychological works as such); the other was the theological (the idea of salvation is certainly there in Kafka, but there is nothing otherworldly about it, or about salvation in general). Perhaps we might today also add the existential interpretation: the human condition, anxiety, and the like also offer only too familiar themes and considerations which, as you might have imagined, can certainly not be judged to be very postmodern). And we must also briefly evoke about what used to be thought of as the "Marxist" interpretation: *The Trial* as the representation of the ramshackle bureaucracy of an Austro-Hungarian Empire on the eve of collapse. There is much truth to this interpretation also, except for the suggestion that the Austro-Hungarian Empire was in any way a nightmare. On the contrary, besides being the last of the old archaic empires, it was also the first multinational and multiethnic state: comfortably inefficient when compared with Prussia, humane and tolerant when juxtaposed with the czars; finally not a bad arrangement at all, and an intriguing model in our own postnational period, still riven by nationalisms. The K.-and-K. structure plays a part in Kafka, but not exactly in the way in which the "bureaucracy-as-nightmare" interpretation (the Empire as a foretaste of Auschwitz) wants to suggest.

Returning to the idea of the simultaneity of the nonsimultaneous, of the coexistence of distinct moments of history, what you first notice in reading *The Trial* is the presence of a modern, well-nigh corporate, workweek and business routine; Joseph K. is a young banker (a "junior executive" or "confidential clerk") who lives for his work, a bachelor who spends his empty evenings in a tavern and whose Sundays are miserable, when they are not made even more miserable by invitations from business colleagues to intolerable professional social outings. Into this boredom of organized modernity something rather different suddenly comes—and it is precisely that archaic, older legal bureaucracy associated with the Empire's political structure. So we have here a very striking coexistence: a modern, or at least modernizing, economy, and an old-fashioned political structure, something that Orson Welles's great film of *The Trial* captured vividly by way of space itself: Joseph K. lives in the worse kind of faceless anonymous modern housing but visits a court housed in shabby baroque splendor (when not in ancient tenement-like rooms), the interspace being occupied by the empty rubble and vacant lots of urban development to come (he will eventually die in one of those bombed-out spaces). The pleasures of Kafka, the pleasures of the nightmare in Kafka, then come from the way in which the archaic livens up routine and boredom, and an old-fashioned juridical and bureaucratic paranoia enters the empty workweek of the corporate age and makes something at least happen! The morale would now seem to be that the worst is better than nothing at all, and that nightmares are a welcome relief from the work week. There is in Kafka a hunger for the sheer event as such in a situation in which it seems as rare as a miracle; in his language, an avidness to register, in a virtually musical economic notation, the slightest tremors in the life world that might betray the faintest presence of something "taking place." This appropriation of the negative by a positive, indeed Utopian, force that wraps itself in its wolf's clothing, is scarcely psychologically unfamiliar; it is for example well-known, to cite a more postcontemporary malady, how the deeper satisfaction afforded by paranoia and its various delusions of persecution and espionage lies in the reassuring certainty that everyone is always looking at you all the time!

It is then, in Kafka as elsewhere, the peculiar overlap of future and past, in this case, the resistance of archaic feudal structures to irresistible modernizing tendencies—of tendential organization and the residual survival of the not yet "modern" in some other sense—that is the condition of possibility for high modernism as such, and for its production of aesthetic forms and messages that may no longer have anything to do with the unevenness from which it alone springs.

What follows paradoxically as a consequence is that in that case the postmodern must be characterized as a situation in which the survival, the residue, the holdover, the archaic, has finally been swept away without a trace. In the postmodern, then, the past itself has disappeared (along with the well-known "sense of the past" or historicity and collective memory). Where its buildings still remain, renovation and restoration allow them to be transferred to the present in their entirety as those other, very different and postmodern things called *simulacra*. Everything is now organized and planned; nature has been triumphantly blotted out, along with peasants, petit-bourgeois commerce, handicraft,

feudal aristocracies and imperial bureaucracies. Ours is a more homo-
geneously modernized condition; we no longer are encumbered with
the embarrassment of non-simultaneities and non-synchronicities. Everything has reached the same hour on the great clock of development or
rationalization (at least from the perspective of the "West"). This is the
sense in which we can affirm, either that modernism is characterized by
a situation of incomplete *modernization*, or that postmodernism is *more*
modern than modernism itself.

Perhaps it can also be added that what is also thereby lost from the
postmodern is *modernity* as such, in the sense in which that word can
be taken to mean something specific and distinct from either modernism and modernization. Indeed, our old friends base and superstructure seem fatally to reimpose themselves: if modernization is something
that happens to the base, and modernism the form the superstructure
takes in reaction to that ambivalent development, then perhaps modernity characterizes the attempt to make something coherent out of their
relationship. Modernity would then in that case describe the way "modern" people feel about themselves; the word would seem to have something to do not with the products (either cultural or industrial) but with
the producers and the consumers, and how they feel either producing
the products or living among them. This modern feeling now seems to
consist in the conviction that we ourselves are somehow new, that a
new age is beginning, that everything is possible and nothing can ever
be the same again; nor do we want anything to be the same again, we
want to "make it new," get rid of all those old objects, values, mentali-
ties, and ways of doing things, and to be somehow transfigured. "Il faut
être absolument moderne," cried Rimbaud; we have to be somehow absolutely, radically modern; which is to say (presumably) that we have to
make ourselves modern, too; it's something we do, not merely something that happens to us. Is this the way we feel today, in full postmodernism? We certainly don't feel ourselves living among dusty, traditional,
boring, ancient things and ideas. Apollinaire's great poetic outburst
against the ancient buildings of 1910 Europe, and against the very space
of Europe itself: "A la fin tu es las de ce monde ancien!" (you're suddenly sick and tired of this antiquated world!) probably does not express
the contemporary (the postcontemporary) feeling about the supermar-
ket or the credit card. The word *new* doesn't seem to have the same
resonance for us any longer; the word itself is no longer new or pristine.
What does that suggest about the postmodern experience of time
or change or history?

It implies first of all that we are using "time" or historical "lived experience" and historicity as a mediation between the socioeconomic structure and our cultural and ideological evaluation of it, as well as a provisionally privileged theme by which to stage our systemic comparison between the modern and the postmodern moments of capital. Later on, we will want to develop the matter further in two directions: first, around that sense of unique historical difference from other societies that a certain experience of the New (in the modern) seems to encourage and perpetuate; and second, in analyzing the role of new technologies (and their consumption) in a postmodernity evidently disinterested in thematizing and valorizing the New as such any longer.

For the moment, we conclude that the keen sense of the New in the modern period was only possible because of the mixed, uneven, transitional nature of that period, in which the old coexisted with what was then coming into being. Apollinaire's Paris included both grimy medieval monuments and cramped Renaissance tenements, *and* motorcars and airplanes, telephones, electricity, and the latest fashions in clothing and culture. You know and experience these last as new and modern only because the old and traditional are also present. One way of telling the story of the transition from the modern to the postmodern lies then in showing how at length modernization triumphs and wipes the old completely out: nature is abolished along with the traditional countryside and traditional agriculture; even the surviving historical monuments, now all cleaned up, become glittering simulacra of the past, and not its survival. Now everything is new; but by the same token, the very category of the new then loses its meaning and becomes itself something of a modernist survival.

Whoever says "new," however, or deplores the loss of its concept in a postmodern age, also fatally raises the spectre of Revolution itself, in the sense in which its concept once embodied the ultimate vision of the Novum become absolute and extending itself into the smallest crannies and details of a lifeworld transformed. The inveterate recourse to a vocabulary of political revolution, and the aesthetic avant-garde's often narcissistic affectation of the trappings of their political opposite numbers, suggest a politicality in the very form of the modernisms that casts some doubt on the reassurances of their academic ideologies, who taught us again and again that the moderns were not political, or even socially very conscious. Indeed, their work was said to represent a new "inward turn" and the opening up of some new reflexive deep subjectivity: the "carnival of interiorized fetishism," Lukács once called it. And certainly modernist texts in their range and variety do seem to offer the appearance of so many Geiger counters picking up all kinds of new subjective impulses and signals and registering those in new ways and according to new "inscription devices."

One can also argue against this impression with empirical and biographical evidence about the writers' sympathies. For one thing, Joyce and Kafka were socialists; even Proust was a Dreyfusard (although also a snob); Mayakovsky and the surrealists were communists; Thomas Mann was at some points at least a progressive and an antifascist; only the Anglo-Americans (along with Yeats) were true reactionaries of the blackest stamp.

But something more fundamental can be argued from the spirit of the works themselves, and in particular from a renewed scrutiny of the same high-modernist celebration of the self that the anti-political critics adduced to support a notion of the modernists' subjectivism (in this, they joined hands with the Stalinist tradition). I want, however, to propose the alternative proposition that modernism's introspective probing of the deeper impulses of consciousness, and even of the unconscious itself, was always accompanied by a Utopian sense of the impending transformation or transfiguration of the "self" in question. "You have to change your life!" Rilke's archaic Greek torso tells him paradigmatically; and D. H. Lawrence is filled with intimations of this momentous new sea change from which new people are sure to emerge. What we now have to grasp is that those feelings, expressed in connection with the self, could only come into being in correlation with a similar feeling about society and the object world itself. It is because that object world, in the throes of industrialization and modernization, seems to tremble at the brink of an equally momentous and even Utopian transformation that the "self" can also be felt to be on the point of change. For this is not merely the moment of Taylorization and the new factories; it also marks the emergence of most of Europe into a parliamentary system in which new and vast working-class parties play their part for the first time, and feel themselves, particularly in Germany, on the point of achieving hegemony. Perry Anderson has argued persuasively that modernism in the arts (although he rejects the category of modernism as such for other reasons) is intimately related to the winds of change blowing from the great new radical social movements.[8] High modernism does not express those values as such; rather it emerges in a space opened by them, and its formal values of the New and of innovation, along with its Utopian sense of the transfiguration of the self and the world, are, in ways that remain to be explored, very much to be seen as echoes and resonances of the hopes and optimism of that great period dominated by the Second International. As for the works themselves, John Berger's exemplary essays on cubism[9] offer a more detailed analysis of the way in which this seemingly very formalist new painting is infused by a Utopian spirit that will be crushed by the grisly uses of industrialization on the battlefields of World War I. This new Utopianism is only in part a glorification of new machinery, as in futurism; it expresses itself across a gamut of impulses and excitement that ultimately touch on the impending transformation of society itself.

III. Cultural Reification and the "Relief" of the Postmodern

All of this looks very different examined synchronically: in other words, the feeling that postmodern people have about the modern will now begin to tell us more about postmodernism itself than about the system it supplanted and overthrew. If modernism thought of itself as a prodigious revolution in cultural production, however, postmodernism thinks of itself as a renewal of production as such after a long period of ossification and dwelling among dead monuments. The very word *production* itself—a much-buffeted straw in the wind during the 1960s, but which tended then always to signal the most empty and abstract, ascetic-formalistic endeavors (such as Sollers's early "texts")—turns out now in hindsight to have meant something after all and to have signaled a genuine renewal in the thing it was supposed to signify.

I think we now have to talk about the *relief* of the postmodern generally, a thunderous unblocking of logjams and a release of new productivity that was somehow tensed up and frozen, locked like cramped muscles, at the latter end of the modern period. This release was something a good deal more momentous than a mere generational change (any number of generations having succeeded themselves during the gradually canonical reign of the modern proper), although it also did something to the collective sense of what "generations" were in the first place. One cannot too often symbolically underscore the moment (in most U.S. universities, the late 1950s or early 1960s) in which the modern "classics" entered the school system and the college reading lists (before that, we read Pound on our own, English departments only laboriously reaching Tennyson). This was a kind of revolution in its own way, with unexpected consequences, forcing the recognition of the modern texts at the same time that it defused them, like former radicals finally appointed to the cabinet.

For the other arts, however, canonization and the "corrupting" influence of success will clearly take very different forms. In architecture, for instance, it seems clear that the built equivalent of reception in the academy is the appropriation by the state of high modernist forms and methods, the readaptation by an expanded state bureaucracy (sometimes identified as that of the "welfare state" or social democracy) of Utopian forms now degraded into anonymous forms of large-scale housing and office construction. The modernist styles then become stamped with just such bureaucratic connotation, so that to break with it radically produces some feeling of "relief," even though what replaces it is neither Utopia nor democracy, but simply the private-corporate constructions of the post-welfare state postmodern. Overdetermination is present here to the degree that the literary canonization of the modern also expressed a prodigious bureaucratic expansion of the university system in the 1960s. Nor should one in either case underestimate the active pressures in such developments of popular demands (and demography) of a more truly democratic or "plebeian" kind. What we need to invent is a notion of "overdetermination in ambivalence" in which works become endowed with associations at one and the same time "plebeian" and "bureaucratic," with the not unexpected political confusion inherent in such ambivalence.

This is only a figure, however, for what needs to be talked about in a more general way and on a more abstract level—namely, reification itself. The word probably directs attention in the wrong direction for us today, since "the transformation of social relations into things" that it seems most insistently to designate has become a second nature. Meanwhile, the "things" in question have themselves changed beyond recognition, to the point where one might well find people arguing for the desirability of the thinglike in our amorphous day and age.[10] Postmodern "things" are in any case not the kind Marx had in mind, even the "cash nexus" in current banking practices is a good deal more glamorous than anything Carlyle can have "libidinally cathected."

The other definition of reification that has been important in recent years is the "effacement of the traces of production" from the object itself, from the commodity thereby produced. This sees the matter from the standpoint of the consumer: it suggests the kind of guilt people are freed from if they are able not to remember the work that went into their toys and furnishings. Indeed, the point of having your own object world, and walls and muffled distance or relative silence all around you, is to forget about all those innumerable others for a while; you don't want to have to think about Third World women every time you pull yourself up to your word processor, or all the other lower-class people with their lower-class lives when you decide to use or consume your other luxury products: it would be like having voices inside your head; indeed, it "violates" the intimate space of your privacy and your extended body. For a society that wants to forget about class, therefore, reification in this consumer-packaging sense is very functional indeed; consumerism as a culture involves much more than this, but this kind of "efface-ment" is surely the indispensable precondition on which all the rest can be constructed.

The reification of culture itself is evidently a somewhat different mat-ter, since those products are "signed"; nor, in consuming culture, do we particularly want, let alone need, to forget the human producer T. S. Eliot, or Margaret Mitchell or Toscanini or Jack Benny, or even Sam Goldwyn or Cecil B. deMille. The feature of reification I want to insist on in this realm of cultural products is what generates a radical separa-tion between consumers and producers. Specialization is too weak and non-dialectical a term for that, but it plays its part in developing and perpetuating a deep conviction within the consumer that the produc-tion of the product in question—attributable no doubt to other human beings in the generic sense—is nonetheless beyond anything you can imagine; it is not something the consumer or user has any social sympa-thy for whatsoever. In that respect, it is a little like the feeling nonintel-lectuals and lower-class people have always had about intellectuals and what they do: you see them doing it, and it doesn't look very compli-cated, but even with the best will in the world you don't quite get it, you don't see why people would want to do things like that, let alone trust yourself to form an idea of what it is they actually do. True Gramscian subalternity that: the deep sense of inferiority in the face of the cultural other, the implicit acknowledgment of their innate superiority, to which punctual rage or anti-intellectualism or working-class contempt and machismo is itself only a secondary reaction, a reaction to *my* inferior-ity first and foremost, before being transferred onto the intellectual. I want to suggest that something like this subalternity—Gunther Anders years ago in a somewhat different connection called it Promethean shame, a Promethean inferiority complex in front of the machine[11]—is what we now feel for culture more generally.

But this cultural posture is less dramatic than anti-intellectualism, because it relates to things rather than to people; and so we must try to lower the figural level. A Marxian social psychology must above all insist on the psychological concomitants of production itself. The reason production (and what can loosely be called the "economic") is philosophically prior to power (and what can loosely be called the "political") lies here, in the relationship between production and feelings of power in the first place; but it is something that it is preferable and more persuasive to say the other way round (not least because it helps us thereby evade humanist rhetoric): namely, by insisting on what happens to people when their relations to production are blocked, when they no longer have power over productive activity. Impotence is first and foremost that, the pall on the psyche, the gradual loss of interest in the self and the outside world, very much in formal analogy to Freud's description of mourning; the difference being that one recovers from mourning (Freud shows how), but that the condition of non-productivity, since it is an index of an objective situation that does not change, must be dealt with in another way, a way that, acknowledging its persistence and inevitability, disguises, represses, displaces, and sublimates a persistent and fundamental powerlessness. That other way is, of course, consumerism itself, as a compensation for an economic impotence which is also an utter lack of any political power: what is called voter apathy is mainly visible among those strata who lack the means to distract themselves by way of consumption. I want to add that the way in which (objectively, if you like) this analysis takes on the appearance of anthropology or social psychology either is itself to be reckoned back into the phenomenon we are describing: not merely is this anthropological or psychological appearance a function of a basic representational dilemma about late capitalism (which we will touch on below); it is also the result of the failure of our societies to achieve any kind of transparency; indeed it is virtually the same as that failure. In a transparent society in which our various positions in social production were clear to us and to everybody else—so that, like Malinowski's savages, we could take a stick and draw a diagram of the socioeconomic cosmology on the sand of the beach—it would not sound either psychological or anthropological to refer to what happens to people who have no say in their work: no Utopian or Nowhereon would think you were mobilizing hypotheses about the Unconscious or the libido, or foundationally presupposing a human essence or a human nature; perhaps it would sound more medical, as though you were talking about a broken leg or paralysis of the whole right side. At any rate, it is thus, as a fact, that I would like to talk about reification: in this sense of the way in which a product somehow shuts us out even from a sympathetic participation, by imagination, in its production. It comes before us, no questions asked, as something we could not begin to imagine doing for ourselves.

But this in no way means that we cannot consume the product in question, "derive enjoyment" from it, become addicted to it, etc. Indeed, consumption in the social sense is very specifically the word for what we in fact do to reified products of this kind, that occupy our minds and float above that deeper nihilistic void left in our being by the inability to control our own destiny.

But now I want to restrict this account once again, so that it can be understood more specifically in relationship to modernism itself, and what postmodernism meant "originally," when it freed itself from this last. I want to argue that the "great modernist works" in effect became reified in this sense, and not only by becoming school classics. Their distance from their readers as monuments and as the efforts of "genius" tended also to paralyze form production in general, to endow the practice of all the high-cultural arts with an alienating specialist or expert qualification that blocked the creative mind with awkward self-consciousness and intimidated fresh production in a profoundly modernist and self-validating way. It was only after Picasso that Picasso's remarkably unselfconscious improvisations became stamped as unique activities of modernist style and genius inaccessible to other people. Most of the modernist "classics," however, wanted to stand as figures for the unblocking of human energy; the contradiction of modernism lay in the way in which that universal value of human production could achieve figuration only by way of the unique and restricted signature of the modernist seer or prophet, thus slowly canceling itself out again for all but the disciples.

This is, then, the relief of the postmodern, in which the various modernist rituals were swept away and form production again became open to whoever cared to indulge it, but at its own price: namely, the preliminary destruction of modernist formal values (now considered "elitist"), along with a range of crucial related categories such as the work or the subject. "Text" is a relief after "work," but you must not try to outsmart it and use it to produce a work after all, under cover of textuality. A playfulness of form, the aleatory production of new ones or joyous cannibilization of the old, will not put you in so relaxed and receptive a disposition that, by happy accident, "great" or "significant" form will come into being anyhow. (In any case, it seems possible that the price of this new textual freedom is paid for by language and the linguistic arts, which retreat before the democracy of the visual and the aural.) The status of art (and also of culture) has had to be irrevocably modified in order to secure the new productivities; and it cannot be changed back at will.

IV. Groups and Representation

All of which is so much grist for the production of postmodernism's populist rhetoric, which is to say that we here touch the border between aesthetic analysis and ideology. As with so many populisms, this one is the locus for the most pernicious confusions about the matter, very precisely because its ambiguities are real and objective (or, as Mort Sahl observed about the Nixon-Kennedy election, "in my considered opinion, neither can win"). For everything that has been said in the preceding section suggests that the cultural and artistic dimension of postmodernism *is* popular (if not populist), and that it dismantles many of the barriers to cultural consumption that seemed implicit in modernism. What is misleading about this impression is, of course, the illusion of symmetry, since, during its own life span, modernism was not hegemonic and far from being a cultural dominant; it proposed an alternative, oppositional, and Utopian culture whose class base was problematic and whose "revolution" failed; or rather, if you prefer, when modernism (like the contemporary socialisms) finally did come to power, it had already outlived itself, and what resulted from this posthumous victory was called postmodernism instead.

But affirmations of popularity and appeals to the "people" are notoriously unreliable, since people will always be found out there who decline the characterization and deny any implication in the matter. Thus microgroups and "minorities," women as well as the internal Third World, and segments of the external one as well, frequently repudiate the very concept of a postmodernism as the universalizing cover story for what is essentially a much narrower class-cultural operation serving white and male-dominated elites in the advanced countries. This is clearly also true, and we will examine the class base and content of postmodernism later on. But it is no less true that the "micropolitics" that corresponds to the emergence of this whole range of small-group, nonclass political practices is a profoundly postmodern phenomenon, or else the word has no meaning whatsoever. In that sense, the foundational description and the "working ideology" of the new politics, as it is found in Chantal Mouffe and Ernesto Laclau's fundamental *Hegemony and Socialist Strategy*, is overtly postmodern and must be studied in the larger context we have proposed for this term. It is true that Laclau and Mouffe are less attentive to the tendency to differentiation and separatism, infinite fission and "nominalism," in small-group politics (it does not seem quite right to call it sectarianism any longer, but there is certainly a group parallel with the various existentialisms on the level of individual experience), for they see the passion for "equality" from which the small groups spring as the mechanism which will also forge them—by way of the "chain of equivalents," the expansive power of the equations of identity—into alliances and reunified Gramscian hegemonic blocs. What they retain of Marx is thus his diagnosis of the historical originality of *his own* time, as the moment in which the doctrine of social equality had become an irreversible social fact; but with the omission of Marx's causal qualification (that this social and ideological development is the consequence of the universalization of wage labor,[12] this view of history tends rapidly to transform itself into the more mythical vision of the radical "break" of modernity and the radical difference between Western and precapitalist, or hot and cold, societies.

The emergence of the "new social movements" is an extraordinary historical phenomenon that is mystified by the explanation so many postmodernist ideologues feel themselves able to propose; namely, that the new small groups arise in the void left by the disappearance of social classes and in the rubble of the political movements organized around those. How classes could be expected to disappear, save in the unique special-case scenario of socialism, has never been clear to me; but the global restructuration of production and the introduction of radically new technologies—that have flung workers in archaic factories out of work, displaced new kinds of industry to unexpected parts of the world, and recruited work forces different from the traditional ones in a variety of features, from gender to skill and nationality—explain why so many people have been willing to think so, at least for a time. Thus the new social movements and the newly emergent global proletariat both result from the prodigious expansion of capitalism in its third (or "multinational") stage; both are in that sense "postmodern," at least in terms of the account of postmodernism offered here. Meanwhile, it becomes a little clearer why the alternative view, that the small groups are, in fact, the *substitute* for a disappearing working class, makes the new micro-politics available for the more obscene celebrations of contemporary capitalist pluralism and democracy: the system congratulating itself for producing ever greater quantities of structurally unemployable subjects. What really needs to be explained here is not the ideological exploitation but rather the capacity of a postmodern public to conceive of two such radically incommensurable and contradictory representations all at once: the tendential immiseration of American society (filed away under the rubric of "drugs") and the self-congratulatory rhetoric of pluralism (generally activated in contact with the topic of socialist societies). Any adequate theory of the postmodern ought to register this historic progress in schizophrenic collective consciousness, and I will offer an explanation for it later on.

Pluralism is thus the ideology of groups, a set of phantasmic representations that triangulate three fundamental pseudoconcepts: democracy, the media, and the market. This ideology cannot, however, be adequately modeled and analyzed unless we realize that its conditions of possibility are real social changes (in which "groups" now play a more significant role), and without somehow marking and specifying the historical determinacy of the ideological concept of the group itself (quite different from that of Freud's or LeBon's period, for example, let alone the older revolutionary "mob"). The problem, as Marx put it, is that "the subject . . . is given, both in reality and in the mind, and that therefore the categories express forms of being, determinations of existence—and sometimes only individual aspects—of this particular society, of this subject, and that even from the scientific standpoint it therefore by no means begins at the moment when it is first discussed as such."[13]

The "reality" of groups then must be related to the institutional collectivization of contemporary life: this was, of course, one of Marx's fundamental prophecies, that within the "integument" of individual property relations (private ownership of the factory or enterprise), a whole new web of collective production relations was coming into being incommensurate with its antiquated shell, husk, or form. Like the three wishes in the fairy tale, or the devil's promises, this prognosis has been fully realized, with only the slightest of modifications that make it unrecognizable. We have touched briefly on property relations in the postmodern in a previous chapter; suffice it to say now that in itself, private property remains that dusty and drearily old-fashioned thing whose truth one used to glimpse when traveling in the older nation-states and observing, with Mr. Bloom's "grey horror" that sears the flesh, the hoariest antique forms of British commerce or French family firms (Dickens remaining the most precious imperishable afterimage of the juridical exfoliation of these entities, unimaginable crystalline growths like some cancerous Antarctica). "Immortality" and the joint-stock company do nothing to change this; but one has not grasped the spirit and the impulse of the imagination of the multinationals in postmodernism, which in new writing like cyberpunk determines an orgy of language and representation, an excess of representational consumption, if this heightened intensity is not grasped as sheer compensation, as a way of talking yourself into it and making, more than a virtue, a genuine pleasure and jouissance out of necessity, turning resignation into excitement and the baleful persistence of the past and its prose into a high and an addiction. This is surely the most crucial terrain of ideological struggle today, which has migrated from concepts to representations, and where the thrill of multinational business and the peculiar opulence of the yuppie life world has (for the mind's libidinal eye) an attraction far outweighing the nineteenth-century charm of the Hayek-Friedmann arguments about the market as such.

The other, social face of this tendential reality—the organization and collectivization of individuals after the long period of individualism, of social atomization and existential anomie—is perhaps better grasped by way of daily life; that is to say, by way of the new structures of oppositional groups and "new social movements" rather than in the workplace or the corporation, whose "organization men" and new white-collar conformism were already recorded by Whyte and C. Wright Mills in the 1950s, when they then served as topics for public discussion and "cultural critique." The process is, however, more visible, and more easily grasped as an objective historical tendency, when it is seen to affect rich and poor alike, indifferently, and on both sides of the political spectrum. And this is in turn more easily demonstrated by registering the disappearance, from postmodern society, of the older kinds of solitude: not only the pathetic misfits and victims of anomie (abundantly collected and catalogued from naturalism to Sherwood Anderson) no longer present in the nooks and crannies of a then more natural and capacious social order, but the solitary rebels and existential antiheroes who used to allow the "liberal imagination" to strike a blow at the "system" have also vanished, along with existentialism itself, and their former embodiments have become the "leaders" of various *groupuscules*. No current media topic illustrates this better than the "bag people" (also known, in media euphemism, as the "homeless"). No longer solitary freaks and eccentrics, they are a henceforth recognized and accredited sociological category, the object of the scrutiny and concern of the appropriate experts, and clearly potentially organizable when they are not in fact already organized in good postmodern fashion. This is the sense in which, even if Big Brother is not everywhere watching you, Language is; media and specialized or expert language that seeks tirelessly to classify and categorize, to transform the individual into the labeled group, and to constrict and expel the last spaces for what was in Wittgenstein or Heidegger, in existentialism or in traditional individualism, the unique and the unnameable, the mystical private property of the ineffable and the unspeakable horror of the incomparable. Everyone today is, if not organized, then at least organizable: and the ideological category that slowly moves into place to cover the results of such organization is the concept of the "group" (this last is sharply differentiated, in the political unconscious, from the concept of *class* on the one hand, but also from that of *status* on the other). What someone once said about Washington, D.C., that you only apparently met individuals there, who all eventually turned out to be lobbies in the end, is now true of the social life of advanced capitalism generally, except that everyone "represents" several groups all at once. This is the social reality that psychoanalytic currents on the left have analyzed in terms of "subject-positions," but in reality the latter can be grasped only as the forms of identity afforded by group adherence. Meanwhile, Marx's other insight, that the emergence of collective (universal or abstract) forms encourages the development of concrete historical and social thinking more vigorously than individual or individualistic forms did (which function to conceal the social), is also corroborated: thus we know at once, and reckon into our definition of the "bag people," that they are the consequence of the historical process of land speculation and gentrification at a very precise moment of the history of the postcontemporary city, while the "new social movements" themselves are immediately enabled by the expansion of the state sector in the 1960s and bear this causal origin within their consciousness as a badge of identity and a map of political strategy and struggle.

(It should be stressed, however, that something fundamental has been achieved by the now more widely shared awareness of the correlation between consciousness and group adherence: this is, indeed, something like the postmodern's version of that theory of ideology invented or discovered by Marx himself, which posited a formational relationship between consciousness and class adherence. The new or postmodern development, indeed, remains progressive to the degree to which it dispels any last illusions as to the autonomy of thought, even though the dissipation of those illusions may reveal a wholly positivist land-scape from which the negative has evaporated altogether, beneath the steady clarity of what has been identified as "cynical reason." In my view, the method whereby a healthy sociologization of the cultural and conceptual can be prevented from disintegrating into the more obscene consumerist pluralisms of late capitalism as such is by way of the same philosophical strategy adopted by Lukács for the devel-opment of class-ideological analysis—namely, to generalize its analy-sis of the constructive links between thought and a class or group *stand-point*, respectively, and to project a full-blown philosophical theory of the standpoint in which the generative production or transfer point between conceptuality and collective experience is brought to the foreground.)

What is sometimes now called "professionalism" is evidently a fur-ther intensification of this "new historical" sense of the relationship between group identity and history, which is also in some peculiar sense self-fulfilling. A historical examination of the disciplines, for example, undermines their claims to correspond to truth or to the struc-ture of reality, by betraying the opportunistic way in which they swiftly readapt to this or that current hot topic, for them perceived as an immediate problem or crisis (the topic of postmodernism is just such a crisis). Thus Lester Thurow's *Dangerous Currents* ends up portraying the economists as professionals who have had to scramble from one topical problem area to another in such a way that the field itself, as such, has seemed in the process to dissolve; meanwhile Stanley Aronowitz and his colleagues have discovered that (despite the lag in academic institutional arrangements and the persistence of the onto-logical illusion that the science departments, taken together, some-how model the physical world) virtually all research in the hard sci-ences today involves this or that form of physics, life sciences outside of molecular biology, for example, having thereby become as archaic as alchemy.[14]

It does no good, of course, to distinguish origins from validity and to insist patiently that the fact that something can be seen to have emerged historically is not an argument against its truth content (any more than the fall in its scholarly stock-exchange rating testifies to its essential falsity). Not only is history (and change) still strongly felt to be the opposite of nature and being, what seems to have human and social causes (very often economic ones) is felt to be the contrary of the structure of reality or the world. As a consequence, a kind of historical thinking develops that reads all that as a kind of self-reinforcing panic; and it suffices to mention the unmentionable—that all these sciences are in historical evolution—for the very rate of that historical modification to be intensified, as though to point out the absence of an ontological ground or foundation was suddenly to loose all the moorings that had traditionally held the disciplines in place. Now suddenly, in English departments, the canon, in the very middle of the debate on its existence, begins furiously to melt away, leaving a great rubble pile of mass culture and all kinds of other noncanonical and commercial literature behind it—a kind of "quiet revolution" even more alarming than those in Quebec and Spain where semifascist and clerical regimes, under the warming impact of consumer society, turned into swinging sixties-like social spaces overnight (something that now seems imminent in the Soviet Union as well and suddenly calls into question all our notions about the traditional, about social inertia, and about Edmund Burke's slow growth of social institutions). Above all, we begin to question the temporal dynamics of all that, which have either accelerated, or were always more rapid than we registered in an older mind's eye.

This is very precisely what has happened in the art world also, and it vindicates Bonito-Oliva's diagnosis[15] of the end of modernism as the end of the modernist developmental or historical paradigm, where each formal position built dialectically on the previous one and created a whole new kind of production in the empty spaces, or out of the contradictions. But this could be registered from the modernist perspective with a certain pathos: everything has been done; no more formal or stylistic invention is possible, art itself is over and to be replaced by criticism. From the postmodern side of the divide, it does not look like that, and the "end of history" here simply means that anything goes.

There remain then the groups themselves and the identities that had seemed to correspond to them. Just because economics, poverty, art, and scientific research have become "historical" in some new sense (which one had better call neohistorical), bag people, economists, artists, and scientists have not disappeared; rather, the nature of their group identity has been modified and become seemingly more questionable, like a choice of fashion. And indeed neohistory, having nowhere else to channel the increasingly swift currents of its Heracleitean stream, seems almost certain to turn to fashion and the market, that now being understood as a deeper ontological economic reality that is as mysterious and final as nature once was. Neohistorical explanation thus leaves the new groups in place, does away with ontological forms of truth, and pays lip service to some more secular, ultimately determining, instance by anchoring its findings in the market rather than in the modifications of capitalism. The return to history everywhere remarked today demands closer scrutiny in the light of this "historical" perspective—only it is not a return exactly, seeming rather to mean incorporating the "raw material" of history and leaving its function out, a kind of flattening and appropriation (in the sense in which it has lately been said that neo-expressionist German artists today are lucky to have had Hitler). Yet the most systemic and abstract analysis of this tendency—towards a collective organization that envelops business and its underclasses alike—assigns the ultimate systemic condition of possibility for all such group emergence (what used to be called its causalities) to the dynamics of late capitalism itself.

This is an objective dialectic that populists have often found repellent and which has often been more narrowly rehearsed in the form of the paradox or the paralogism: the emergent groups as so many new markets for new products, so many new interpellations for the advertising image itself. Is not the fast-food industry the unexpected solution—as with philosophy, its fulfillment and abolition all at once—to the debate on pay for housework? Are minority quotas not to be understood first and foremost as the allocation of segments of television time, and is not the production of the appropriate new group-specific products the truest recognition a business society can bring to its others? Finally, then, is not the very logic of capitalism itself ultimately as dependent on the equal right to consumption as it once was to the wage system or a uniform set of juridical categories applicable to everyone? Or, on the other hand, if individualism is really dead after all, is not late capitalism so hungry and thirsty for Luhmannian differentiation and the endless production and proliferation of new groups and neoethnicities of all kinds as to qualify it as the only truly "democratic" and certainly the only "pluralistic" mode of production?

Two positions must be distinguished here, which are both wrong. On the one hand, for a properly postmodern "cynical reason," and in the spirit of the preceding rhetorical questions, the new social movements are simply the result—the concomitants and the products—of capitalism itself in its final and most unfettered stage. On the other hand, for a radical-liberal populism such movements are always to be seen as the local victories and the painful achievements and conquests of small groups of people in struggle (who are themselves figures for class struggle in general, as that has determined all the institutions of history, very much including capitalism itself). In short, and no longer to put so fine a point on it, are the "new social movements" consequences and aftereffects of late capitalism? Are they new units generated by the system itself in its interminable inner self-differentiation and self-reproduction? Or are they very precisely new "agents of history" who spring into being in resistance to the system as forms of opposition to it, forcing it against the direction of its own internal logic into new reforms and internal modifications? But this is precisely a false opposition, about which it would be just as satisfactory to say that both positions are right; the crucial issue is the theoretical dilemma, replicated in both, of some seeming explanatory choice between the alternatives of agency and system. In reality, however, there is no such choice, and both explanations or models—absolutely inconsistent with each other—are also incommensurable with each other and must be rigorously separated at the same time that they are deployed simultaneously.

But perhaps the alternative of agency or system is just that old dilemma of Marxism—voluntarism versus determinism—wrapped up in new theoretical material. I think this is so, but the dilemma is not limited to Marxists; nor is its fatal reappearance particularly humiliating or shameful for the Marxian tradition, since the conceptual limits it betrays seem to be closer to Kantian limits on the human mind itself. But just as the identification of the base-superstructure dilemma with the old mind-body problem does not necessarily debunk or reduce the former, but rather restages the latter as a distorted and individualistic anticipation of what finally turns out to be a social and historical antinomy, so here also the identification of earlier precursive philosophical forms of the antinomy between voluntarism and determinism rewrites those genealogically as earlier versions of this. In Kant himself, clearly, such an "earlier version" is offered by the superposition and coexistence of the two parallel worlds of the noumenon and the phenomenon, which seem rigorously to occupy the same space, but of which (like waves or particles) only one can be "intended" by the mind's eye at any point. Freedom and causality then in Kant rehearse a dialectic altogether comparable to this one of agency and system, or—in its practical political or ideological form—voluntarism versus determinism. For the phenomenal world in Kant is "determined" at least to the degree that in it the laws of causality reign supreme and tolerate no exception. Nor would "freedom" be such an exception, exactly, since it evokes another intelligibility altogether and simply does not compute within the causal system, even as some inversion or negation of this last. Freedom, which equally characterizes the human and social world when its individuals are grasped as things in themselves (they cannot really be so grasped conceptually, but the Kantian resonances of Sartre's existential period give something of a feeling of what that would look like, even though the whole point of the noumenon is that it precisely cannot "look like" anything), in that sense can only be understood as an alternative code for the same realities that are also causal (in another world). Kant showed that we cannot hope to use these codes together or coordinate them in any meaningful way, and above all, that it would be vain (and metaphysical) to hammer them together into a "synthesis." He did not exactly suggest, I think, that we were thereby condemned to an alternation between them; but that would seem to be the only conclusion to draw.

An even earlier precursor of this Kantian version of what would seem to be the antinomy of historical change and collective praxis redirects our attention to a rather different feature of the dilemma, since this version—more actively ethical than Kant's (who simply presupposes the existence and possibility of a proper conduct)—seeks in some distress to reconcile "causality," or "determinism," with the very possibility of action itself. The predestination debate[16] is, of course, more dramatically contradictory than the later and more secular bourgeois and proletarian forms we have been considering in Kant and Marx; the awkwardness of its "solutions" are more embarrassing for the modern mind. Nonetheless, some conception of divine pansynchronism, of the providential anticipation or the thoroughgoing predestination of all the acts of history, is surely the first mystified form whereby people (in the "West") attempted to conceptualize the logic of history as a whole, and to formulate its dialectical interrelationship and its telos. To wonder, then, how the necessity of my future acts is to be squared with any active obligation on my part to struggle to make them come out right is to tap the same anxiety that will confront political activists later on when a doctrine of historical necessity and inevitability seems on the point of sapping their militant resolve. The equivalent of James Hogg's well-known reductio ad absurdum (in which one of the elect concludes that he is then free to commit any crime or enormity that passes through his head)[17] would then turn out to be—mutatis mutandis—the seemingly more respectable figure of the *Katheder-sozialist*, or perhaps the "renegades" and revisionists of the Second International.

Yet it seems possible that the ideologues of the predestination debate found a "solution" which on a little reflection is nowhere near as ludicrous as one might first presume, and furthermore proves to be genuinely dialectical or, at the very least, an admirably creative leap of the philosophical imagination. "The outward and visible signs of inward election": the formula has the merit of including and acknowledging a freedom that it outsmarts and outflanks at the same time. Its genuine conceptual rigor solves its problems by disqualifying it at the same time that it raises it to a higher level: your free choice of right action does not then qualify you for election or earn your right to salvation, but it is the latter's sign and external mark. Your freedom and praxis is thereby itself enveloped within the larger "deterministic" scheme, which foresees your capacity for just this agonizing encounter with free choice in the first place. The later distinction between individual and collective can then clarify this antiquated machinery of clarification, since it makes a little clearer how the very condition of possibility of individual commitment and action is given within the development of the collective itself. In that sense, there never is an alternative between voluntarism and determinism (which is exactly what the theologians sought to argue): your commitment to praxis is then not a disproof of the doctrine of objective circumstances (the situation being or not being "ripe") but, on the contrary, testifies to this last from the inside and confirms it, just as "infantile" or suicidal voluntarism confirms it the other way round, being itself fully as much a product of social circumstances as collective praxis. The distinction clearly solves nothing from the individual or existential point of view, for, like Hegel's "ruse of reason" or Adam Smith's "invisible hand" (not to speak of Mandeville's *Fable of the Bees*), the whole point is to follow one's nature and one's passion in the first place. The point where "determinism" or a collective logic of history spirals around those choices and passions and reincludes them at a higher level can be glimpsed when we reflect not merely that such passions and values are themselves social but that the very proclivity to be demoralized and discouraged by a logic of circumstances, the appropriation of that as an excuse and an alibi for passivity and for temporizing withdrawal, is also social and is thus factored into the larger perspective while still remaining a free choice in the individual sense. One's reaction to necessity, in other words, is itself an expression of freedom.

Meanwhile, the two versions we have examined, the theological and the dialectical, both seem to cheat on the present and its agonizing choices by shifting the perspective to the very ends of time: theology spreading everything forward from a beginning in which it is all foretold in the first place; the dialectic "winging its flight at dusk" and pronouncing on the historic necessity of what has already taken place (if it happened that way, it is because it had to happen that way). But what had to happen included all the forms of individual agency, very much including their convictions as to their own freedom and their own efficacity. It is a fable one can tell, the other way round, perhaps, about the Cuban Revolution, in which, notoriously, the old Cuban Communist party failed to participate until very late in the day, owing to its assessment of "objective historical possibility." One can then deduce a facile lesson about the debilitating effect of a belief in historical inevitability and the energizing capacities of certain voluntarisms. On a larger view, however, it has been argued that[18] whatever the immediate assessment and practical decision of the party in the fire of the event, its own work among Cuban workers in the previous decades played an incalculable part in an ultimate revolutionary victory for which it was not itself immediately responsible. The creation of a revolutionary culture and consciousness—along the lines of Marx's image of the "mole of history" —is no less a form of agency than the final struggle: but it is also itself part of the objective circumstances and the historical necessities that from a more immediate angle of praxis seem incompatible with action and agency in the first place.

Such "philosophical solutions," which proceed, as we have said, by a differentiation of incompatible codes and models (and which I have tried to reformulate in the doctrine of levels in *The Political Unconscious*), of course, themselves still lie in the phenomenal world and are thus susceptible to transformation into ideological alibis: all science is also necessarily ideology at one and the same time, insofar as we cannot but take the position of the individual subject on what vainly attempted to stand beyond the perspectives of individual subjectivity.

Nonetheless, the proposal is clearly immediately relevant to the issue of the "new social movements" and their relationship to capitalism insofar as it provides the simultaneous possibility of active political commitment along with disabused systemic realism and contemplation, and not some sterile choice between those two things.

Meanwhile, if we object that the philosophical dilemma or antinomy hereby evoked holds only for absolute change (or revolution), and that these problems disappear when the sights are lowered to punctual reforms and to the daily struggles of what we may metaphysically call a kind of local politics (where systemic perspectives no longer hold), we have of course located the crucial issue in the politics of the postmodern as well as the ultimate stake in the "totalization" debate. An older politics sought to coordinate local and global struggles, so to speak, and to endow the immediate local occasion for struggle with an allegorical value, namely that of representing the overall struggle itself and incarnating it in a here-and-now thereby transfigured. Politics works only when these two levels can be coordinated; they otherwise drift apart into a disembodied and easily bureaucratized abstract struggle for and around the state, on the one hand, and a properly interminable series of neighborhood issues on the other, whose "bad infinity" comes, in postmodernism, where it is the only form of politics left, to be invested with something of Nietzsche's social Darwinism and with the willed euphoria of some metaphysical permanent revolution. I think myself that that euphoria is a compensation formation, in a situation in which, for a time, genuine (or "totalizing") politics is no longer possible; it is necessary to add that what is lost in its absence, the global dimension, is very precisely the dimension of economics itself, or of the system, of private enterprise and the profit motive, which cannot be challenged on a local level. I believe that, en attendant, it will be politically productive, and will remain a modest form of genuine politics in its own right, to attend vigilantly to just such symptoms as the waning of the visibility of that global dimension, to the ideological resistance to the concept of totality, and to that epistemological razor of postmodern nominalism which shears away such apparent abstractions as the economic system and the social totality themselves, such that for an anticipation of the "concrete" is substituted the "merely particular," eclipsing the "general" (in the form of the mode of production itself).

That the "new social movements" are postmodern, insofar as they are effects and consequences of "late capitalism," is however virtually a tautology which has no evaluative function. What is sometimes characterized as a nostalgia for class politics of some older type is generally more likely to be simply a "nostalgia" for politics *tout court*: given the way in which periods of intense politization and subsequent periods of depolitization and withdrawal are modeled on the great economic rhythms of the boom and bust of the business cycle, to describe this feeling as "nostalgia" is about as adequate as to characterize the body's hunger, before dinner, as a "nostalgia for food."

V. The Anxiety of Utopia

Where one may be permitted to differ from the programmatic formulations of some of the ideologues of postmodern politics probably is to be located in the content rather than the form of the assertions. Laclau and Mouffe's exemplary description of the way in which alliance politics function—in the establishing of an axis of "equivalence" along which the parties line up—has nothing to do, as they themselves point out, with the content of the issues around which the equivalence is constructed. (They allow, for example, for the theoretical possibility, in a specific and unique conjecture, that "what occurs at *all* levels of society . . . [might be] absolutely determined by what happens at the level of the economy.")[19] Very often, obviously, the equivalence will be hammered together on nonclass issues such as abortion or nuclear energy. What those who are "nostalgic for class politics" assert in such circumstances is not that these alliances are "wrong," whatever that might mean, but that they are generally not as durable as those organized around class; or better still, that such alliances become more durable forces and movements by developing in the direction of class consciousness. As hapless postmodern standardbearers have occasionally accused me of "disavowing" the non-class-based movements and have recommended the Rainbow Coalition instead,[20] it ought to be noted here that the Jackson experience is exemplary in this respect, inasmuch as he rarely makes a speech in which working-class experience is not "constructed" as the mediation around which the equivalence of the coalition is to find its active cohesion. But this is very precisely what is meant by the rhetoric of class politics and the language of totalization, an operation which Jackson has virtually reinvented for our time in the political area.

As for "totalization" itself—evidently, for postmodernists, one of the most sordid residual vices to be eradicated from the populist health and fitness of the new era—individuals, like Humpty Dumpty, cannot make it mean what they want it to mean, but groups can, and in the face of current doxa ("'to totalize' does not just mean to unify, but rather means to unify with an eye to power and control; and as such, this term points to the hidden power relations behind our humanist and positivist systems of unifying disparate materials, be they aesthetic or scientific")[21] one can only patiently review the real history of the word—somewhat as one rescues the histories of minorities or underclasses that have fallen into oblivion—and then let it go at that.

The term—a Sartrean coinage linked to the project of the *Critique of Dialectical Reason*—should initially be sharply distinguished from that other stigmatized word, *totality*, to which I will return later on. Indeed, if the word *totality* sometimes seems to suggest that some privileged bird's-eye view of the whole is available, which is also the Truth, then the project of totalization implies exactly the opposite and takes as its premise the impossibility for individual and biological human subjects to conceive of such a position, let alone to adopt or achieve it. "From time to time," Sartre says somewhere, "you make a partial summing up." The summing up, from a perspective or point of view, as partial as it must be, marks the project of totalization as the response to nominalism (something I will discuss below, with particular reference to Sartre). What ought first to be evoked, in the totalizations of modernism and the "wars on totality" of the postmodern, is then very precisely that concrete social and historical situation itself, before we come to possible responses to it.

If the meaning of a word is its use, we can best grasp "totalization" in Sartre through its function—to envelope and find a least common denominator for the twin human activities of perception and action. A younger Sartre had already combined these activities by way of one of their dominant features, under the concept of negation and nihilation (*néantisation*) since for him both perception and action were forms through which the actually existing world was negated and made into something else (the complications involved in affirming this about perception—or cognition—are part of the burden of his great early book, *The Imaginary*, in which, for example, sense perception is characterized by the strong awareness that the color or texture is above all *not* me, *not* consciousness). "Nihilation" was then for the Sartre of *Being and Nothingness* already a totalizing concept, so to speak, since it aimed at uniting the twin realms of contemplation and action with a view towards dissolving the former into the latter. This was reinforced by the later proposed equivalent of "praxis," under which perception and thought are also subsumed (except for peculiarly specialized bourgeois attempts in both areas to escape that humiliating subsumption). A fading afterimage of Gestalt psychology will now be helpful in specifying the advantages of the new word "totalization" as an equivalent for "praxis" itself; it cannot be denied that the concept is designed in part to stress the unification inherent in human action; and the way in which what was formerly called negation can also be seen as the forging of a new situation—the unification of a construct, the interrelating of a new idea to the old ones, the active securing of a new perception, whether visual or auditory, its forced conversion into a new form. Totalizing, in Sartre, is, strictly speaking, that process whereby, actively impelled by the project, an agent negates the specific object or item and reincorporates it into the larger project-in-course. Philosophically, and barring some genuine mutation of the species, it is hard to see how human activity under the third, or postmodern, stage of capitalism could elude or evade this very general formula, although some of postmodernism's ideal images—schizophrenia above all—are clearly calculated to rebuke it and to stand as unassimilable and unsubsumable under it. As for "power," it is equally clear that praxis or totalization always aims at securing the fragile control or survival of an even more fragile subject within a world otherwise utterly independent and subject to no one's whims or desires. I suppose it can be argued that the disempowered do not want power, that "the Left wants to lose," as Baudrillard once put it, that in such a corrupt universe failure and weakness are more authentic than "projects" and "partial summings up" in the first place. I doubt if many people really feel this way, however; in order to be utterly admirable such an attitude would surely have to be absolutized to the point of Buddhism; at all events, this was equally obviously not the lesson the Jackson campaign had for us. As for all the scare images of 1984, they are even more ludicrous in the Gorbachev period than they were before; and it is, to say the least, a difficult and contradictory operation to proclaim the death of socialism and issue spine-chilling messages about its totalitarian bloodlust in one breath.

The hostility to the concept of "totalization" would thus seem to be most plausibly decoded as a systematic repudiation of notions and ideals of praxis as such, or of the collective project.[22] As for its apparent ideological cognate, the concept of "totality," we will see later on that it is to be grasped as one philosophical form of the notion of a "mode of production," a notion that it would seem equally strategic for the postmodern to evade or to exclude.

Yet some final word needs to be said about some of the more philosophic disguises of these disputes, in which "totality" and "totalization," indistinctly confounded, are taken as the signs, no longer even of a Stalinism of the mind so much as of a properly metaphysical survival, complete with illusions of truth, a baggage of first principles, a scholastic appetite for "system" in the conceptual sense, a yearning for closure and certainty, a belief in centeredness, a commitment to representation, and any number of other antiquated mindsets. It is curious that, simultaneously with the newfound pluralisms of late capitalism, but in the tangible decline of any active political praxis or resistance, such absolute formalisms should begin to make their way; they diagnose the survival of content within a given intellectual operation as the telltale mark of "belief" in some older sense, as the stain left behind it by the continuing existence of metaphysical axioms and illicit presuppositions, which have not yet, following the basic Enlightenment program, been expunged. It is clear (not least from its proximity to John Dewey and to a certain pragmatism) that Marxism itself must have much sympathy for the challenging of concealed presuppositions, which it, however, identifies as ideology, just as it unmasks the privileging of a given type of content as "reification." The dialectic is in any case not exactly a philosophy in that sense, but rather that peculiar other thing, a "unity of theory and practice." Its ideal (which famously involves the realization and the abolition of philosophy all at once) is not the invention of a better philosophy that—in opposition to all of Gödel's well-known laws of gravity—seeks to do without premises altogether, but rather the transformation of the natural and social world into a meaningful totality such that "totality" in the form of a philosophical system will no longer be required.

But there is an existential argument frequently concealed and presupposed within such now conventional anti-Utopian attitudes, which are triggered indifferently by a whole range of stigmatized terms—from "identity" as it is posited in the philosophy of the Frankfurt School all the way to the cognate language of "totalization" (Sartre) and "totality" (Lukács) already touched on here—and also, and not least, by the very language of Utopia itself, now generally recognized as a code word for the systemic transformation of contemporary society. This hidden argument posits the end or master term of all such themes as this or that variant of a still essentially Hegelian notion of "reconciliation" (Versöhnung): which is to say, the illusion of the possibility of some ultimate reunion between a subject and an object radically sundered or estranged from each other, or even (the term betraying its debt to schematic and potted accounts of Hegel in the manuals) to some new "synthesis" between them. "Reconciliation" in this sense, then, becomes assimilated to this or that illusion or metaphysic of "presence," or its equivalent in other postcontemporary philosophical codes.

Anti-Utopian thought therefore here involves a crucial mediation, which it does not always spell out. It argues that the social or collective illusion of Utopia, or of a radically different society, is flawed first and foremost because it is invested with a personal or existential illusion that is itself flawed from the outset. According to this deeper argument, it is because the metaphysics of identity are at work everywhere in private life that it can be projected onto politics and the social. Such reasoning, of course, implicit or explicit, betrays a very old middle-class notion of the collective and the political as unreal, as a space onto which subjective and private obsessions are noxiously projected. But this notion is itself the effect of the split between public and private existence in modern societies and can take familiar, low-level forms such as the characterization of the student movement in terms of Oedipal revolt. Contemporary anti-Utopian thought has, however, erected far more complex and interesting arguments on this seemingly tired and unpromising basis.

Meanwhile, the political sequels to this first move, which condemns political vision on the strength of existential illusion, require responses of a different type, which will not be spelled out here. Foremost of these conclusions is that Utopian thinking—although seemingly benign, if not altogether ineffectual—is in reality dangerous and leads among other things to Stalin's camps, to Pol Pot, and (freshly rediscovered during the bicentenary period) to the "massacres" of the French Revolution (which themselves lead us back immediately to the ever vital thought of Edmund Burke, who first warned us about the violence that was bound to emerge from the hubris of human attempts to tamper with and transform the organic fabric of the existing social order).

Yet a rather different "conclusion" often coexists with this one, and it is the libidinal fear or fantasy that Utopian society, the Utopian "reconciliation of subject and object," will somehow be a place of renunciation, of the simplification of life, of the obliteration of exciting urban difference and of the muting of sensory stimulus (fears of sexual repression and taboo are here explicitly deployed), a place, finally, of the return to simple "organic" village forms of "rural idiocy," from which everything interestingly complex about "Western civilization" has been amputated. This fear or anxiety about "Utopia" is a concrete ideological and psychological phenomenon that demands sociological investigation in its own right. As for its intellectual expression, however, the late Raymond Williams has succinctly disposed of it with the retort that socialism will not be simpler than capitalism, but much more complicated; and that to imagine the daily life and the organization of a society in which, for the first time in human history, human beings are fully in control of their own destinies makes demands on the mind which are forbiddingly difficult for subjects of the present "administered world" and often understandably frightening to them.

But to put it this way is also to recall that it is the socialist ideal which finally seeks to put an end to metaphysics, and to project the first elements of a vision of some achieved "human age," in which the "hidden hand" of God, nature, the market, traditional hierarchy, and charismatic leadership will definitely have been disposed of. Not the least contradiction of contemporary anti-Utopian positions, then, lies in the way in which what is (quite properly) identified as metaphysical in the existential illusions of reconciliation and presence is then "projected" onto a secular political ideal which in fact for the first time seeks to have done with metaphysical authority on the level of human society itself.

The philosophical content of anti-Utopian thought, however, is to be located in what we have called its intermediary step, namely, the conflation of "identity" with this or that form of dialectical "reconciliation," to which we now return. Ironically, the power of this moment of the argument is itself relatively dialectical, since what it generally stresses is not the immediate experience of reconciliation or of presence—for which few except mystics of various kinds would claim genuine existence—but rather the damage done by the illusion of its possible future existence, or, what amounts to the same thing, but its logical presupposition, its implication within our working concepts. Thus, to take this second danger first, concepts such as those of "subject" and "object" will be flawed by the way in which they seem to imply, and are thus logically founded on, a notion of the "reconciliation" of subject and object, which is illusory. Those who manipulate such "dialectical" concepts, therefore—whatever they go on to *say* about the concrete possibilities of reconciliation (and no reader of Adorno will find much reassurance along those lines)—nonetheless by logical implication perpetuate the hidden foundational "synthesis" in what then seems to work out into a virtually narrative or even historical pattern—a moment of "primal unity" before the separation of subject and object, and a moment of unity reinvented at the end of time when subject and object are once again "reconciled." A nostalgic-Utopian triad thus emerges which is handily identified as the Marxist "vision of history": a golden age before the fall, that is to say, before capitalist dissociation, which can optionally be positioned where you like, in primitive communism or tribal society, in the Greek or the Renaissance polis, in the agricultural commune of whatever national or cultural tradition before the emergence of state power; the "modern age" or in other words capitalism; and then whatever Utopian vision can be appealed to replace that. But the notion of a "fall" into civilization, the modern, the "dissociation of sensibility," is rather, unless I am mistaken, a feature of the right-wing critique of capitalism which preceded Marx, and of which T. S. Eliot's view of history is still the most familiar version for humanists; while the Marxian conception of a multiplicity of "modes of production" makes this nostalgic and triadic narrative relatively unthinkable.

In the case of Adorno and Horkheimer, for example, the peculiar originality of their conception of a "dialectic of enlightenment" is that it excludes any beginning or first term and specifically describes "enlightenment" as an "always-already" process whose structure lies very precisely in its generation of the illusion that what preceded it (which was also a form of enlightenment) was that "original" moment of myth, the archaic union with nature, which is the vocation of enlightenment "proper" to annul. If it is a matter of telling a historical story, therefore, we must read Adorno and Horkheimer as positing a narrative without a beginning in which the "fall," or dissociation, is always there already. If, however, we decide to reread their book as a diagnosis of the peculiarities and the structural limits and pathologies of historical vision or narrative itself, then we may conclude, in a somewhat different fashion, that the strange afterimage of "primal unity" always seems to be projected after the fact onto whatever present the historical eye fixes as its "inevitable" past, which vanishes without a trace when frontal vision is displaced onto it in turn.

Derrida's influential version of all this, which turns on Rousseau's own primordial version, is more subtle and complicated than the analysis outlined above, since he adds into the picture the very language used by the Utopianist to evoke a state by definition lacking in language itself. Here, conceptual confusion or philosophical error (matters of "consciousness" and thinking) have been displaced by the fatalities of sentence structures, which cannot be made to do what the Utopian "thinker" needs to have them do, namely, to secure something radically different from his own present of speaking and writing. Meanwhile, that "present" of speaking and writing being itself illusory (since sentences have to move in time according to the laws of the hermeneutic circle), it can scarcely be called upon to stage any adequate picture of a present or a presence elsewhere in "time." Derrida's conception of supplementarity has often been enlisted in the anti-Utopian arsenal of polemic weapons and arguments; it may now be preferable to see whether it cannot be read in a somewhat different way as an ensemble of consequences to be drawn about the sentence itself.

When projected back out of the linguistic realm onto the existential, however, in the form of a kind of Derridean "ideology," this position on "reconciliation" conflates with other versions into a kind of ethic of temporality best dramatized in an older Sartrean language (even though the Sartrean heritage of such thinking was obscured, not to say occulted, by the energetic break between emergent structuralism and Sartrean phenomenology). In *Being and Nothingness*, for example, "presence" or the reconciliation between subject and object is staged as the inescapable but impossible longing (of "being-for-itself" or consciousness) to incorporate the stable plenitude of the "being-in-itself" of things: what constitutes consciousness in the first place is just this longing to absorb "being" without actually becoming a thing outright, or, in other words, dying. All human temporality is driven by this mirage of the plenitude of subject-object reconciliation just out of reach before us: and the advantage of Sartre's phenomenological terminology is to enlarge this drama well beyond the merely epistemological or aesthetic and to show it at work fully as much in the interstices and micrologies of everyday life as in the grandest metaphysical stances and conflicts. Thus, the very drinking of a glass of water in thirst deploys a ghostly imminence of the plenitude of thirst quenched, which then recedes into the past without achieving realization.

This mirage of being, which also governs our ambitions and our tastes, our sexuality and our ways of handling other people, our leisure as well as our labor, then inspires a diagnosis and an ethic which can readily be translated into the "textual" or deconstructive ones: namely, the effort to imagine a way of living that could radically eschew these illusions, already designated as metaphysical in Sartre: a life in time capable of doing without the longing to become the "in-itself-for-itself" ("what the religions call God"), and this down to the very microstructure of our most minute gestures and feelings. This ethical ideal of anti-transcendent human existence (which Sartre calls "authenticity" and which his own fragmentary philosophical sequels were unable to work out fully in terms of purely individual existence) is surely one of the most glorious of all post-Nietzschean Enlightenment visions, which tracks religion, metaphysics, and transcendence into the most seemingly secular spaces and events of an only apparently "enlightened" modern world. It is much more closely related to the Derridean scrutiny of the metaphysical than to Adorno's conception of Enlightenment. The latter clearly admires Sartre but implacably repudiates the individual focus of existential thinking and analysis, for him inseparable from the work of his great political and philosophical adversary, Heidegger.

Yet what is worth asking today about this seemingly Utopian and unrealizable vision of an authentic or a "textualized" existence in full postmodernism is whether it has not already in some sense become socially realized, and whether it may not very precisely be one of the transformations of everyday life and of the psychic subject designated by the term postmodern. In that case, the critique of the metaphysical shadows and traces that persist within modernity paradoxically turns around into a replication of that very postmodern triumph over the metaphysical remnants of the modern, where to call for the shedding of any illusion about psychic identity or the centered subject, for the ethical ideal of good molecular "schizophrenic" living, and for the ruthless abandonment of the mirage of presence may turn out to be a description of the way we live now, rather than its rebuke or subversion. Adorno's life ended at the threshold of this "new world," which he envisioned only intermittently, and on the prophetic mode; but his position on the impossibility of transcendence and metaphysics is still instructive, if only to make it plain that the lament over the passing of these things need not be conservative or nostalgic: for he saw in the loss of philosophy's metaphysical and speculative vocation not a program for restoring the latter on the mode of "as if," but rather a supreme historical symptom of the technocratization of contemporary society.

There is, however, another conclusion to be drawn from this long excursus on the existential presuppositions of contemporary anti-Utopian thought, for it suggests that, rather than conflate the individual and existential metaphysics of presence, plenitude, or "reconciliation" with the political will to transform the social system itself, we must break the link between the two. The unexamined premise of this new conservatism was that the political vision of a radically different society was somehow a projection of the personal metaphysics of identity, and therefore must be renounced along with this last. Politically and ideologically, however, the situation is in fact reversed; and it is the power of the philosophical critique of existential metaphysics which is pressed into service in the project to dismantle political visions of social change (or in other words "Utopias"). But there is no reason to think that these two levels have anything in common; anti-Utopianism mainly affirms their "identity" without arguing it, and the Utopian ideal of a fully human and immensely more complex society than this one need not be invested with any of the longings and illusions unmasked by the existential critique. What ultimate anxieties such a society involves are materialist and biological, the deconcealment of human history as a dizzying sequence of dying generations and as a generalized demographic scandal for the mind: things Adorno consigns to the realm of natural rather than human history. But the foundational texts for that realm are neither Thomas More nor Dostoyevsky's "Grand Inquisitor," but probably something closer to Kafka's "Josephina the Mouse-Singer," or perhaps the classics of Buddhism.

VI. The Ideology of Difference

Thus the ideology of groups and difference does not really strike a blow, either philosophically or politically, against tyranny. But as Lynda Hutcheon suggests, its real target may lie elsewhere in that somewhat different thing (which, however, Toqueville still identified with "tyranny"), namely, consensus:

> What is important in all these internalized challenges to humanism is the interrogating of the notion of consensus. Whatever narratives or systems that once allowed us to think we could unproblematically and universally define public agreement have now been questioned by the acknowledgement of differences—in theory and in artistic practice. In its most extreme formulation, the result is that consensus becomes the illusion of consensus, whether it be defined in terms of minority (educated, sensitive, elitist) or mass (commercial, popular, conventional) culture, for both are manifestations of late capitalist, bourgeois, informational, postindustrial society, a society in which social reality is structured by discourses (in the plural)—or so postmodernism endeavors to teach.[23]

But if this is so, then a transfer of social and political targets has imperceptibly taken place, and for one mode of production another has been substituted. "Tyranny" meant the ancien régime; its modern analogue, "totalitarianism," intends socialism; but "consensus" now designates representative democracy, with its ballots and public opinion polls, and it is now this that, already objectively in crisis, finds itself politically challenged by the new social movements, none of which find the appeal to majority will and consensus particularly legitimate any longer, let alone satisfactory. What will concern us here for another moment is, on the one hand, the suitability of the general ideology or rhetoric of difference to articulate those concrete social struggles, and, on the other, the deeper implicit representation or ideological model of the social totality on which the logic of groups is based and which it perpetuates —a model which also involves, as has been suggested in an earlier chapter, a metaphorical exchange of energies with those other two characteristic postmodern systems (or representations!) which are the media and the market.

For the very concept of difference itself is booby-trapped; it is at least pseudodialectical, and its imperceptible alternation with its sometimes indistinguishable opposite number, Identity, is among the oldest language and thought games recorded in (several) philosophical traditions. (Is the difference between the Same and the Other the same as the difference between the Other and the Same, or is it different?) Much of what passes for a spirited defense of difference is, of course, simply liberal tolerance, a position whose offensive complacencies are well known but which has at least the merit of raising the embarrassing historical question of whether the tolerance of difference, as a social fact, is not the result of social homogenization and standardization and the obliteration of genuine social difference in the first place. The dialectic of neoethnicity, then, clearly belongs here, for there is a "difference," one would think, between one's being condemned to be identified as a member of a group and a more optional choice of the badge of group membership because its culture has become publicly valorized. Ethnicity in the postmodern, in other words—neo-ethnicity—is something of a yuppie phenomenon, and thereby without too many mediations a matter of fashion and the market. On the other hand, the acknowledgment of Difference can under those circumstances come as something of an offense as well, as the non-Jew who identifies Jews as such involuntarily triggers all the old signals of anti-Semitism in spite of himself. The mirage held out by the neoethnic groups—it was stronger in the sixties than it is today—is still the cultural envy of the achieved collective: the "groupie," something of a caricature of the class traitor, is one who casts his or her lot with a collective that is fantasized as being more strongly

cohesive and archaic than your own. The class content of the phenomenon persists, since it is a feature of the social dynamic of capitalism
(and perhaps of other modes of production) that in a first moment, and
before a reaction of panic whereby they pull back together, the ruling
class will be less cohesive socially and more given over to individualism and anomie than the subordinate ones, whom economic necessity
holds together. If the fundamental premise of any Marxian social psychology lies in the well-nigh ontological attraction and force of gravity
of the achieved collective as such,[24] then the envy and nostalgia of elites
for the realer people of the underclasses is at once given (and something
of the same effects can be distributed spatially, by imperialism and tourism, among the metropolis and the Third World). Nonetheless this particular appeal of ethnicity seems on the wane today, perhaps because
there are now too many groups, and because their affiliation to representation (most often of a media type) is clearer and undermines the
ontological satisfactions of the fiction in question.

On the other hand, if "difference" is a doubtful political slogan full of
inner slippages—for example, it quite properly prolongs the sixties
defense of what are sometimes horribly called "life-style issues," until
at the last minute veering around into a Cold War-type antisocialism,
—"differentiation," surely the fundamental sociological instrument for
grasping the postmodern (and the conceptual key to the ideology of
"difference" in the first place), is no less unreliable. This is then the
deeper paradox rehearsed by the attempt to grasp "postmodernism" in
the form of periodizing or totalizing abstraction; it lies in this seeming
contradiction between the attempt to unify a field and to posit the hidden identities that course through it and the logic of the very impulses
of this field, which postmodernist theory itself openly characterizes as
a logic of difference or differentiation. If what is historically unique
about the postmodern is thus acknowledged as sheer heteronomy and
the emergence of random and unrelated subsystems of all kinds, then,
or so the argument runs, there has to be something perverse about the
effort to grasp it as a unified system in the first place. The effort at
conceptual unification is, to say the least, strikingly inconsistent with
the spirit of postmodernism itself; perhaps, indeed, ought it not to be
unmasked as an attempt to "master" or "dominate" the postmodern, to
reduce and exclude its play of differences, and even to enforce some
new conceptual conformity over its pluralistic subjects? Yet, leaving the
gender of the verb out of it, we all do want to "master" history in whatever ways turn out to be possible: the escape from the nightmare of

history—the conquest by human beings of the otherwise seemingly blind and natural "laws" of socioeconomic fatality—remains the irreplaceable will of the Marxist heritage, whatever language it may be expressed in.

But the notion that there is something misguided and contradictory about a unified theory of differentiation also rests on a confusion between levels of abstraction: a system that constitutively produces differences remains a system; nor is the idea of such a system supposed to be in kind "like" the object it tries to theorize, any more than the concept of dog is supposed to bark or the concept of sugar to taste sweet. It is felt that something precious and existential, something fragile and unique about our own singularity, will be lost irretrievably when we find out that we are just like everybody else. In that case, so be it; we might as well know the worst; the objection is of course the primal form of existentialism (and phenomenology), and it is rather the emergence of such anxieties that needs first to be explained. Objections to the global concept of postmodernism in this sense seem to me to recapitulate, in other terms, the classical objections to the concept of capitalism itself—something scarcely surprising from our perspective here, which consistently affirms the identity of postmodernism with capitalism itself in its latest systematic mutation. For those objections turned essentially around one form or the other of the following paradox: namely that although the various precapitalist modes of production achieved their capacity to reproduce themselves through various forms of solidarity or collective cohesion, the logic of capital is, on the contrary, a dispersive and atomistic, "individualistic" one, an antisociety rather than a society, whose systematic structure, let alone its reproduction of itself, remains a mystery and a contradiction in terms. Leaving aside the answer to the conundrum (the market), what may be said is that this paradox is the originality of capitalism, and that the verbally contradictory formulas we necessarily encounter in defining it point beyond the words to the thing itself (and also give rise to that peculiar new invention, the dialectic). We will have occasion to return to problems of this kind in what follows: suffice it to say all this more crudely by pointing out that the very concept of differentiation itself (whose most elaborate development we owe to Niklas Luhmann[25]) is itself a systematic one; or, if you prefer, it turns the play of differences into a new kind of identity on a more abstract level.

All of which is further complicated by the intellectual and philosophical obligation to distinguish between inert or extrinsic difference and dialectical opposition or tension: a differentiation that produces the first kind of merely external difference disperses phenomena in a random and "heterogeneous" way (to use another term that is charged and valorized in postmodernism). But this kind of distinction (black is not white) is everything but "the same" as an opposition that depends on its opposite in its very being (black people are *not* white people) and must thus be analyzed in terms of a dialectical conceptuality in which the central notion of *contradiction*—which has no equivalent in analytic systems—still reigns supreme.

Philosophically, these paradoxes are virtually the central terrain of post-Marxism and the stage for its strategic regression to Kant and Kantianism. What is at stake here, as the work of the most brilliant of such thinkers, Lucio Colletti, emblematically testifies, is the rolling back of Hegel and Marx by way of the conceptual discrediting of contradiction and dialectical opposition. From the feeling—virtually universal in "Western Marxism"—that the dialectic was not likely to occur "in nature," and that Engels's illicit transformation of inert, external, natural, and physical differences (water is not an ice cube) into dialectical oppositions (the basis for much of "dialectical materialism") was philosophically shoddy and ideologically suspect, to the conviction that "dialectical oppositions" are not even "in society" and that the dialectic is itself a mystification—from the first of these positions to the second is not quite what you would call a "mere step," since it involves political apostasy and a deconversion in shame and betrayal; but it is surely the central philosophical step in what is called post-Marxism.

As always, however, we have every interest in separating out the levels and distinguishing from each other cognate topics that in the postmodern often seem generically to fold back into each other. For one thing, a very crucial feature of the topic of difference is foregrounded by the modernist version of it, which insisted on the radical break between the West and the rest, between the modern and the traditional, as we shall see later on (this is the feature according to which Marxism can be said itself to be one of the modernisms—perhaps the only one).

But we must also disentangle from the social version of group difference (as well as from the philosophical debates on the difference between contradiction and opposition) the reigning aesthetic and psychic (or psychoanalytic) forms of this topic, not least because any number of political category-mistakes can often be identified as illicit transfers from the aesthetic itself). The aesthetics of difference—what is often called textuality or textualization—foregrounds a perceptual modification in the apprehension of postmodern artifacts, which I have characterized, in the opening chapter by way of the slogan of "difference relates"; later on I will offer a further, spatial analysis of this new kind of perception. As for the psychic subject and its theories, this is the area colonized by the Deleuze-Guattari notion of the ideal schizophrenic—that psychic subject who "perceives" by way of difference and differentiation alone, if that is conceivable; of course, the conceiving of it is the construction of an ideal which is, so to speak, the ethical—not to say the political —task proposed by their *Anti-Oedipus*. I think one cannot too often emphasize the logical possibility, alongside both the old closed, centered subject of inner-directed individualism and the new non-subject of the fragmented or schizophrenic self, of a third term which would be very precisely the non-centered subject that is a part of an organic group or collective. Indeed, the final form of Sartre's theory of totalization emerges in the very attempt to theorize such a group and the subject-positions within it.) Meanwhile, although the theory and the rhetoric of multiple subject-positions is an attractive one, it should always be completed by an insistence on the way in which subject-positions do not come into being in a void but are themselves the interpellated roles offered by this or that already existing group. Whatever truce or alliance one wants to stage between one's various subject-positions, therefore (deliberately excluding the stigmatized possibility that one might try to unify them), what will ultimately be at stake is some more concrete truce or alliance between the various real social groups thereby entailed.

As for Althusser's influential but now somewhat outmoded model of "interpellation," what needs to be said is that it was already a group-oriented theory to begin with, since class as such can never be a mode of interpellation, but rather only race, gender, ethnic culture, and the like. (It is no accident that Althusser's examples are religious ones. Indeed, the deeper ground of rhetorics of difference can always be shown to involve fantasms of culture as such, in the anthropological sense, which are themselves authorized and legitimized by notions of religion, always and everywhere the ultimate "thought of the other.") It is only in the cinema (in Fellini's *I Vitelloni*, to be exact) that wealthy young ne'er-do-wells shout "down with the workers!" from the window of their speeding car at the road gangs outside. But it is in reality that group affiliation becomes a daily badge of shame and reproach of inferiority. Or perhaps this should be said in a more complicated way: namely, that class consciousness as such—something infrequently achieved and only laboriously conquered throughout social history—marks the moment in which the group in question masters the interpellative process in a new way (different from the usual reactive mode), such that it becomes, however momentarily, capable of *interpellating itself* and dictating the terms of its own specular image.

In what follows, however, I will not pursue these registers of the topic. Rather, I will concentrate on the complementary problem (which already anticipates that of cognitive mapping) of the potential representability of the new category of groups as compared to the older one of social classes. For the proposition that we now map or represent our social world to ourselves by way of the category of groups now sheds a somewhat different light on these various developments. Group representation is above all anthropomorphic and, unlike representation in terms of social classes, gives us to understand the social world as divided up and colonized down to the last segment by its collective actors and allegorical representatives, betokening a real world "as full as an egg," as Sartre used to say, and as human as Utopia (or as that "pure poetry" in which none of the remnants of matter or contingency slosh around in the bottom like dregs or stick out like sore thumbs—the plays of Racine, the novels of Henry James). Class categories are more material, more impure and scandalously mixed, in the way in which their determinants or definitional factors involve the production of objects and the relations determined by that, along with the forces of the respective machinery: we can thus see down through class categories to the rocky bottom of the stream. Meanwhile, classes are too large to figure as Utopias, as options you choose and identify with in phantasmatic ways. Besides the occasional stray fascism, the only Utopian gratification offered by the category of social class is the latter's abolition. But groups are small enough (at the limit, the famous "face-to-face" plaza or city-state) to allow for libidinal investment of a more narrative kind. Meanwhile, the externality carried around within the category of the "group" like a skeleton is not *production* but rather *institution*, already, as we shall see, a more suspicious and equally anthropomorphic category —whence the superior mobilizing force of groups over classes: one can come to love one's guild or fraternity and die for it, but the cathexis determined by the three-field rotational system or the universal lathe is probably of a somewhat different and less immediately politicizable type. Classes are few; they come into being by slow transformations in the mode of production; even emergent they seem perpetually at distance from themselves and have to work hard to be sure they really exist as such. Groups, on the other hand, seem to offer the gratifications of psychic identity (from nationalism to neoethnicity). Since they have become images, groups allow the amnesia of their own bloody pasts, of persecution and untouchability, and can now be consumed: this marks their relationship to the media, which are, as it were, their parliament and the space of their "representation," in the political fully as much as the semiotic sense.

The political horror of consensus—mistaken for a dread of "totalization"—is then simply the justified reluctance of groups that have conquered a certain pride in their own identity to be dictated to by what turn out to be simply other groups, since now everything in our social reality is a badge of group membership and connotes a specific bunch of people. The high-literary "canon," transformed into the class furniture of older white males of a certain distinctive class background, is only one example; the U.S. political party system is another, as are most of the other institutional habits of the superstate, with the signal exception of the media and the market, which, alone among what ought to be institutions, are somehow universal and thereby uniquely privileged in other ways that will be discussed in a moment. It is important, however, to grasp both the links and the differences between this personification of the institutions by group ideology and the older dialectical critique of the social and ideological function of institutions. That the former somehow grew out of the latter—by way of the black box of the 1960s—is likely enough; but on the other (Marxian) view, the class function of a given institution is mediated by the system as a whole, and thus only personalized in the crudest caricatural way (no one, as Marx never tired of saying, thinks all businessmen are individually wicked). Thus the newspaper plays an ideological role in our social order, but not because it is the plaything of a specific social group; for example, commentators, paparazzi, anchormen and -women, and the lords of Fleet Street are from a class perspective merely the class fractions determined by the institutional structure. But in postmodern group consciousness, newspapers and the news portions of the media generally somehow actually belong to what is now a new (and powerful) social unit in its own right, a collective actor on the historical scene, feared by politicians and tolerated by the "public," wearing some well-known faces and in its anthropomorphic structure virtually a human being in its own right (although without much depth, even as a narrative character). The sixties had already begun to think in these terms when it projected its struggle against the Vietnam War onto the authoritarian figures of Johnson and the generals, who were thought to be pursuing this war (it is true that

rational motives for it were not easy to deduce) out of sheerly patriar-
chal malignancy. But once the collective cast of characters gets fixed,
each acquires a representational semiautonomy, and it is not easy to
square the category of "media journalists," for example, with that more
functional older class one of ideologues of big business (or if you prefer
something more colorful, "lackeys of capitalism"), even though the great
media campaigns (the panic about small children being violated in day-
care centers, the assurances about the death of Marxism and socialism
everywhere, the "drug war," or the allegedly noxious effects of budget
deficits) sweep predictably across all the channels of diffusion with all
the regularity of metereological events or of the party directives in the
"socialist" countries.

The representational paradoxes involved in any narrative whose fundamental category is the postmodern "group" can then be articulated as
follows: since the ideology of groups comes into being simultaneously
with the well-known "death of the subject" (of which it is simply an
alternate version)—the psychoanalytic undermining of experiences of
personal identity, the aesthetic attack on originality, genius and modernist private style, the waning of "charisma" in the media age and of
"great men" in the age of feminism, the fragmentary, schizophrenic aesthetic alluded to above (which in reality begins with existentialism)
—the consequence will be that these new collective characters and representations that are groups cannot any longer, by definition, be subjects.
This is, of course, one of the things that problematize the visions of
history or "master narratives" of either bourgeois or socialist revolution
(as Lyotard has explained), for it is hard to imagine such a master narrative without a "subject of history."

Virtually Marx's first published essay, the "Critique of Hegel's Philosophy of Right. Introduction," in a remarkable philosophical leap discovered just such a new subject of history—the proletariat. Marx's
early format was then maintained for other such now marginal subjects
—blacks, women, the Third World, even, somewhat abusively, students
—in the rewriting of the doctrine of "radical chains" during the 1960s.
Now, however, in the pluralism of the collective groups, and no matter
how "radical" the immiseration or the marginalization of the group
in question, it can no longer fill that structural role, for the simple reason that the structure has been modified and the role suppressed. Historically, this is scarcely surprising, since the transitional nature of the
new global economy has not yet allowed its classes to form in any stable
way, let alone to acquire genuine class consciousness, so that the very

lively social struggles of the current period are largely dispersed and anarchic.

What is more surprising, and perhaps more immediately serious politically, is that the new representational models also foreclose and exclude any adequate representation of what used to be represented—however imperfectly—as a "ruling class." Several features necessary to such a representation are indeed missing, as we have already seen: the dissolution of any conception of production or of an economic infrastructure, and its replacement by the already anthropomorphic notion of an institution, means that no *functional* conception of a ruling group, let alone class, can be conceived. There are no levers for them to control and not much in the way of production for them to manage. Only the media and the market are visible as autonomous entities, and whatever falls outside them, and outside the apparatus of representation in general, will be covered by the amorphous term *power*, whose ubiquity—despite its singular ineptness for describing an increasingly "liberal" global reality —ought to inspire some deeper ideological suspicions.

This lack of functionality in our picture of the social groups, along with the breakdown of their capacity to constitute a subject or an agency, means that we tend to dissociate the acknowledgment of the individual existence of a group (pluralism as a value) from any attribution of a project that becomes registered not as a group but as a *conspiracy*, and thereby falls to another, different slot in the representational apparatus. Reagan's businessmen, for example, about whom by now just about virtually everybody is willing to admit the virtually immediate link between private gain and the most varied legislative program, are perceived —from that perspective—as a list of names in the newspaper, a local network of cronies that you could expand into a regional confraternity (southern California, the Sunbelt); what is most paradoxical, however, is the fact that thus perceived, they shed no discredit on business or businessmen at all. The taxonomy of groups is thus remarkably elastic ideologically and can differentiate in such a way as to preserve the innocence of the original collective, always provided that is secured from breaking that fundamental conceptual barrier or taboo which separates a group from a social class.

That the "new narratives" lack the allegorical capacity to map or model the system can also be seen when we turn to the managerial role of the business class and its command relationship to modifications in daily life. I believe that since we now grasp social reality synchronically—in its strongest sense, which has lately been revealed as that of a *spatial* system—changes and modifications in daily life must henceforth be deduced after the fact rather than experienced. Bertrand Russell once evoked a very postmodern temporality in which the world itself, in fact freshly created only a second ago, was carefully "antiqued" in advance and deliberately endowed with the artificial traces of deep wear and age and use, so that it seemed to carry a past and a tradition within itself intrinsically (just as its human subjects—as with *Bladerunner's* androids—were furnished with seemingly private stocks of personal memory images, like photograph albums of a spurious family and childhood). The discontinuing of traditional products on the market must now be reconstructed like a word on the tip of the tongue: in most cases the sheer absence of something is hard to recast in the form of an act or a decision to be explained and which can be supposed to imply an agent. The discussions in a boardroom are thus difficult to link up narratively to changes in daily life that are themselves only perceivable ex post facto, and not in the making. As for the future, it is equally absent from the synchronous mint world of the postmodern, whose entire system is, however—like the departure of the area's only major factory —subject to reshuffling without warning, like a deck of fortune-telling cards that are real. The impact of postmodern unemployment on postmodern time consciousness is bound to be considerable, but perhaps unexpectedly indirect: indexing versus catastrophe, the immediate modification of all the valences on the next rollover, as in automatically adjusting mortgage interest rates. Insurance companies—in many ways archaic holdovers from an older temporal (and realist or modernist) universe in which the "life destiny" was still a meaningful narrative category and the funeral home a very central place in the ethnic neighborhood—seem obnubilated with a spurious apotheosis in which to the naked eye they seem on the point of transmogrification into socialism (infrared photography, however, reveals a more humdrum business reality). A new kind of fear—rather than Lenin's famous bribes—now seals this system in, since you have a personal stake in its smooth and unobstructed reproduction, something beginning to happen so fast it is no longer visible. Nor is your fear, now systemic, visible, either, having been experientially repressed; the need to avoid evaluations of the system as a whole is now an integral part of its own internal organization as well as its various ideologies.

This is indeed another reason why the representation of "decision-making"—whether it be the old-fashioned realistic picture of the boardroom or some modern indirect and modernist approach by way of the problem of representing it in the first place—breaks off unceremoniously in the postmodern, which presupposes as its entry ticket a kind of blasé knowledge in advance of how the system functions. Adorno and Horkheimer's intuition of Hollywood was in this respect prophetic of the later system as a whole: "the truth that [movies and radio] are just business is made into an ideology in order to justify the rubbish they deliberately produce."[26] They had in mind the now classic Hollywood defense of mediocrity, not merely in terms of the general public's taste but in terms of their own function as a business selling products to a public with those tastes. As with all arguments from the "public," then, a seriality results in which the public becomes a phantasmatic other to every single one of its members, each of whom—whatever his or her reactions to this particular mediocre product—has also learned and interiorized the profit motive doctrine that excuses it on the grounds of the motivations of "everyone else." It is like left-handed people being forced to use tools made for right-handers: the knowledge is built into the consumption, which it discounts in advance. As Europeans, Adorno and Horkheimer were obviously scandalized by the openness and vulgarity with which the great movie magnates alluded to the business dimension of their operations and gloried in the profit motive shamelessly attached to each feature, whether modest or pretentious in its "artistic ambitions."

Our own mass culture today, in full postmodernism, naturally enough seems a good deal more sophisticated than the radio and the movies of the thirties and forties; the television public is presumably better educated and also has a good deal more experience of images than its parents had in the Eisenhower era. But I want to argue that if anything, Adorno and Horkheimer's intuition of the ideology of the thing is even more profoundly true today than it was then. For that very reason—its very universalization and interiorization—it is less visible as such and has been transformed into a veritable second nature. To try to represent and visualize the boardroom and the ruling class is uncool because it involves an old-fashioned commitment to content in a situation in which only form as such—that most formalistic of all types of law or regularity, the profit motive (which clearly outweighs even such more vivid ideological slogans as "efficiency")—counts, and in which the commitment to form, the tacit presupposition of the profit motive, is assumed in advance and not subject to reexamination or to thematization as such. This Occam's razor clearly shears away a great many henceforth metaphysical topics of conversation once indulged by earlier generations in a less purely functioning capitalist system, and can, indeed, be characterized as a certain end of idealism constitutive of the postmodern.

The formalism of the profit motive is then transmitted—but no longer in the cumbersome form of those religious doctrines whose role it supplants—to a kind of external nouveau riche public, which, from the age of the "organization men" of the 1950s to that of 1980s "yuppies," has grown ever less shameless in its pursuit of success, now reconceptualized as the "life-style" of a specific "group." But I also want to argue that it is no longer exactly profit as such that forms the ideal image of the process (money is merely the external sign of inward election, but fortune and "great wealth" are harder to represent, let alone libidinally to conceptualize, in an epoch in which numbers like billions and trillions are more frequently encountered). Rather, what is at stake is know-how and knowledge of the system itself: and this is no doubt the "moment of truth" in postindustrial theories of the new primacy of scientific knowledge over profit and production; only the knowledge is not particularly scientific, and "merely" involves initiation into the way the system functions. But now those in the know are too proud of their lesson and their know-how to tolerate any questions about why it should be like that, or even worth knowing in the first place. This is the insider cultural capital of the nouveaux riches which includes the etiquette and table manners of the system; along with cautionary anecdotes, your enthusiasm—fanned into a veritable frenzy in cultural spinoffs like the cyberpunk corporate fiction already mentioned—has more to do with having the knowledge of the system than it does with the system itself. The social climbing of the new yuppie in-group knowledge now spreads slowly downward, via the media, to the very zoning boundaries of the underclasses themselves; legitimacy, the legitimation of this particular social order, being secured in advance by a belief in the secrets of the corporate life-style that includes the profit motive as its unspoken "absolute presupposition," but which you can't learn and question all at once, any more than you can mentally redesign a sailboat you are doing your first sailing in. Lenin's theory of the bribery of advanced sectors of the working class thus needs to be replaced by a theory of status bribery and of the distribution of postmodern cultural badges, which is I suppose more or less what Bourdieu currently offers us—except that, as we have already seen, such concepts of "status," evolved for the postmodern group, need to be sharply distinguished from the traditional sociological theories in which the concept of status was an alternative to the concept of class (and in which, therefore, a certain structure of the feudal ancien regime was being played off against an awareness of the originality of bourgeois society).

But if yuppies can find some satisfaction in sheer know-how, the staff and maintenance personnel of the postmodern may not be so easy to please. For them, then, a certain synchronic blackmail is available which is historically and socially unique only in the way it is locked into time perception and simultaneously repressed (as though it was the most natural thing in the world). It's democratic too, and the entire upper level of management may have vanished without a trace the day before the plant itself shuts down. It is as though you were part of a computer game whose constellations are subject to change without notice and include you among their optional tokens: even good behavior may not be sufficient grounds nowadays for retaining a position or keeping a job.

For the foreigners, meanwhile, a third type of motivation, of a more religious type, is now again available, and what is here practiced with all the disinterested frenzy of drug addiction shows up on un-American television sets as a beneficent vision of the Utopia of the market; what we take for granted they still think is this year's latest model, confusing consumerism with consumption and getting the discount store mixed up with democracy. Driven out of the Third World by our own counter-insurgencies, and lured out of the Second by our media propaganda, the would-be immigrants (whether spiritual or material), not understanding how little they are wanted here, pursue a delirious vision of transubstantiation in which it is the world of the products that is desired, like a landscape, and no one of them in particular: products particularly obsessional like the word processor or the fax machine being themselves allegorical emblems of the whole, mesmerizing properly aesthetic postmodern structures in which the identity of the media and the market is perceptually reenacted, something like a high-tech special effects dramatization of the ontological proof.

The crucial nexus that demands investigation, then, is the way in which the very representation of the media itself manages to represent the market, and vice versa, while "democracy" (not generally in our system represented or indeed representable) steams off of each as a connotation and one of the more recognizable of the thirty-seven flavors.

We have already seen, indeed, how easy it is to slip from the market to the media about which the intervention in real politics must also be registered before the reappropriation of that intervention by the media's ideology can be observed.[27] That the media (save when carefully excluded, as in our invasion of Grenada, but even then they were in a

position to make noise about it had they wanted to) has a benign restrain-
ing influence on world torture and civic law enforcement and police
repression cannot be doubted, although the now global concern for the
national or governmental reputation is generally mediated by worry about
American funding, except where it turns out to be more lucrative to be
conquered by the United States in the first place. American television
reporting, whose specific version of preparing for the last war consists
in its (praiseworthy) determination not to humiliate itself again by covering for something like Vietnam in the future, can also be counted on
with unfailing reliability to reproduce the most tendentious Cold War
attitudes when it comes to socialism (as most recently in the networks'
truly obscene coverage of Gorbachev's 1989 visit to Cuba, where Fidel
was compared to Ferdinand Marcos!). As to a specific new or postmodern
media *politics*, it has also clearly long since come into being (sometimes in the form of so-called terrorism) as one of the rare weapons
available to powerless minorities or subgroups screened out and cen-
sored with the latest equipment. The world does seem at least relatively
less violent—however such a thing might be measured—than in Hitler's day, let alone in the nineteenth-century bourgeois nation-state or
under the feudal absolutism of the ancien régime (with its public exe-
cutions so dear to Foucault!). Nonetheless, and apart from the genesis
of genuinely high-tech instruments of torture as well, media politics
turns out not to be a substitute for politics as such, and the image
smuggled out or the leaked facts fall quickly into the sterile ground of
exhausted material and overly familiar punchlines, unless its implementation of politics by other means can also mobilize the ordinary
ones, support groups, popular pressure, alliances, and a certain healthy
identification of their own self-interest by oppressed groups in this particular "image of the other."

On the other hand, the end of "privacy" in all the sex-and-violence
senses, the prodigious enlargement of what we can still call a public
sphere, if we really mean all the senses of "public" by it, also results in
an enormous enlargement of the idea of rationality itself, in what we are
willing to "understand" (but not endorse), as what we can no longer
have removed from the visible record as "irrational" or incomprehensible, unmotivated, insane or sick.

It is finally necessary to add about the "media" that it also failed to
come into being; it did not, finally, become identical with its own "concept," as Hegel liked to say, and can thus be counted among the innumerable "unfinished projects" of the modern and the postmodern, to

use Habermas's polite phrase. What we have now, what we call "media" is not that, or not yet that, as might be demonstrated by one of its more revealing episodes. In modern North American history, of course, the assassination of John F. Kennedy was a unique event, not least because it was a unique collective (and media, communicational) experience, which trained people to read such events in a new way.

Yet it would be too simple to explain this extraordinary resonance on the basis of Kennedy's public position. Rather, there are grounds for thinking that his posthumous public meaning is better grasped the other way round, as the projection of a new collective experience of reception. It has often been pointed out, indeed, that Kennedy's personal popularity and prestige were at a particularly low ebb at the moment of his death; what is less often remarked is that this event was also something like the coming of age of the whole media culture that had been set in place in the late 1940s and the 1950s. Suddenly, and for a brief moment (which lasted, however, several long days), television showed what it could really do and what it really meant—a prodigious new display of synchronicity and a communicational situation that amounted to a dialectical leap over anything hitherto suspected. Later events of this kind were then recontained by sheer mechanical technique (as with the instant playbacks of the Reagan shooting or the *Challenger* disaster, which, borrowed from commercial sports, expertly emptied these events of their content). Yet this inaugural event (which may not even have had the emotional charge of Robert Kennedy's death, or that of Martin Luther King, Jr., or of Malcolm X.) gave what we call a Utopian glimpse into some collective communicational "festival" whose ultimate logic and promise is incompatible with our mode of production. The sixties, often taken as the moment of a paradigm shift toward the linguistic and the communicational, can also be said to begin with this death, not because of its loss or the dynamics of collective grief, but because it was the occasion (like May 1968 later on) for the shock of a communicational explosion, which could have no further consequences within this system but which scars the mind with the briefly glimpsed experience of radical difference, to which collective amnesia aimlessly returns in its later forgetfulness, imagining itself to be brooding over trauma where it is in fact seeking to produce a new idea of Utopia.

No wonder, then, that the small screen longs for yet another chance at rebirth by way of unexpected violence; no wonder also that its truncated afterlife is available for new semiotic combinations and prosthetic symbioses of all kinds, of which the marriage to the market has been the most elegant and socially successful.

VII. Demographies of the Postmodern

Media populism, however, suggests a deeper social determinant, at one and the same time more abstract and more concrete, and a feature whose essential materialism can be measured by its scandalousness for the mind, which avoids it or hides it away like plumbing. To speak, however, of the role of the media globally in terms of what is virtually a literal figure of enlightenment, that is, of the reduction of public state violence by means of the glare of worldwide information, is perhaps to get things backward. For the sense of epochal change can just as adequately be expressed in terms of some new self-consciousness of the world's peoples, after the great wave of decolonization and movements of national liberation in the 1960s and 1970s. The West thus has the impression that without much warning and unexpectedly it now confronts a range of genuine individual and collective subjects who were not there before, or not visible, or—using Kant's great concept—were still *minor* and under tutelage. Everything that is condescending about this very ethnocentric view of global reality (reflected in everything from the albums of stamp collectors all the way to the syllabi of courses on world literature in English) clearly falls back ignominiously on the viewer, but equally clearly does not diminish the interest of the "impression" itself. Here, for example, is a savage recapitulation of the matter by a radical writer, whom, as will be apparent in a moment, we have other reasons for quoting in this context: "Not so very long ago, the earth numbered two thousand million inhabitants: five hundred million *men* and one thousand five hundred million *natives*. The former had the Word; the others merely had use of it."[28] Sartre's figure mocks European racism at the same time that it grounds its objectivity as an ideological illusion in history (it is only *since* decolonization and its aftermath that the "natives" have turned out to be "human beings") and in a certain philosophy of the subject and of the recognition of the Other as a subject which he shares with Fanon, and which stresses not the inert fact of my existence as a subject but rather the active and energetic, violent, gesture whereby I compel *recognition* of my existence and my status as a human subject. The old Hegelian fable of the master and the slave—by now as familiar as Aesop—shows through this philosophy like an archetype, again demonstrating its reliability for what it

explains not of revolution itself or liberation but rather of their consequences: the emergence of new subjects; that is to say, new people, other
people, who were somehow not even there before, even though their
bodies and their lives filled the cities and certainly did not suddenly
materialize yesterday. Such media developments now seem to mobilize
what Habermas calls a "public sphere," as though those people were
not in it before, not visible, not public somehow, but have become so by
virtue of their new existence as recognized or acknowledged subjects.
So it was not just the extra cables and the klieg lights, the hand-carried
camera equipment, and the fortuitous presence of Western reporters in
"godforsaken" places, but rather some new visibility of the "others"
themselves, who occupy their own stage—a kind of center in its own
right—and compel attention by virtue of their voice and of the act of
speaking itself, which—far above and beyond Fanon's old punctual act
of physical violence—becomes for a language-conscious generation the
first primordial violent act by which you force yourself on another's
attention. *Que de royaumes nous ignorent!* Is this not simply a global
parochialism, thrust with astonishment into the teeming, humdrum daily
life of other places and other planets? Are these momentous discoveries
any more than global equivalents of the newfound liberal tolerance of
the post-1960s media, with its refurbished mailing lists of newly recognized and accredited minorities and neoethnicities? For, as has already
been suggested, the apparent celebration of Difference, whether here at
home or on the global scale, in reality conceals and presupposes a new
and more fundamental identity. Whatever the new liberal tolerance is, it
has little to do with the exotic range of the emblematic Family of Man
exhibit, in which the Western bourgeoisies were asked to show their
deeper human affinity with Bushmen and Hottentots, bare-breasted
island women and aboriginal craftsmen, and others of the anthropological type who are unlikely to visit you as tourists. These new others,
however, are at least as likely to visit us as are immigrants or *Gastarbeiter*;
to that degree they are more "like" us, or at least "the same" in all kinds
of new ways, which new internal social habits—the forced social and
political recognition of "minorities"—help us to acquire in our foreign
policy. This ideological experience may well be limited to First World
elites (although even if it was, it would still have dramatic and incalculable effects on everybody else): all the more reason to factor it into the
description of the postmodern, where it emerges—somewhat more
crudely (or *materialistically*, as I began to put it)—in the form of sheer
demography itself. There are more people now, and that "fact" has impli-

cations that transcend mere spatial discomfort and the prospect of the intermittent shortage in luxury goods.

We need to explore the possibility that there exists, in what quaintly used to be called the moral realm, something roughly equivalent to the dizziness of crowds for the individual body itself: the premonition that the more other people we recognize, even within the mind, the more peculiarly precarious becomes the status of our own hitherto unique and "incomparable" consciousness or "self." That does not change, of course, nor are we magically endowed with any greater sympathy (in the immemorial philosophical sense) with those increasingly numerous others, with whom, in fact, we can less and less individually sympathize. Rather, as with the undermining of a very fundamental kind of false consciousness or ideological self-deception, we are led to anticipate the imminent collapse of all our inward conceptual defense mechanisms, and in particular the rationalizations of privilege and the well-nigh natural formations (like extraordinary crystalline structures or coral formations excreted over millennia) of narcissism and self-love. That phobia is no doubt the fear of a fear, the sense of that approaching collapse, rather than the thing itself, the terror of anonymity imminent; and it can be called upon to explain political opinions and reactions, even though it is mostly handled by that form of repression which is oblivion and forgetfulness, a self-deception that does not want to know and tries to sink ever deeper into a willful involuntarity, a directed distraction. Such an existential hypothesis would go a long way toward documenting the status of demography as materialism, indeed as a new kind or dimension of materialism: neither that of the individual body (as in bourgeois mechanical materialism or positivism), for multiplied bodies, although they do not fuse together into some monstrous physical collective oversoul, reduce the precious individual corporality to something trivially biological or evolutionary; nor that of Marx's "real, concrete individuals" (those from whom in *The German Ideology* "we" famously "set out"), since they are still redolent of personal identities and names, and even workers in the mass do not seem demographic enough, threatening to lead on or lapse back into "humanism." Still, even Marx's concrete individuals offered a kind of materialism, in the strict sense not of some materialist system but of a mental operation of materialist reversal and demystification—alone the feature by which "materialism" as such can be identified. Marx's operation, however, as its immediate context (but also its conceptual shape and thrust) testifies, is directed against the idealisms of the various disciplines (not the "history of ideas" or ideology or the sciences, etc.—the great Hegelian continuities of forms and thoughts—but rather individual people in their swarming, far more synchronous, history). The materialist reversal inherent in demography[29] also flips over the rug of this still anthropomorphic history, but substitutes for it not so much statistical aggregates as the sheer being of natural history itself. It is not the content of the historical vision or paradigm thus substituted (itself always a representation and thus susceptible again to the framing and the domestication of the various ideologies, as is the reversal effect itself that confronts us starkly for the moment with a nonanthropomorphic, indeed a well-nigh in- or nonhuman, reality that we cannot conceptually assimilate. Demography, conceived as a dimension of materialism, would indeed go a long way toward stripping from this last its own representational and idealizable features (specifically those thematized around a "notion" of matter itself).

Few enough thinkers have credited this enlargement of the peopled universe with radical cultural effects, or have, for example, attributed the very stylization and "formidable erosion of contours" of the modern movement itself, as a movement toward a kind of universalism, to just such

> unresting preoccupation with the surprise of the gulf between each tiny occasion of the daily life and the vast stretches of time and place in which every individual plays his role.
>
> By that I mean the absurdity of any single person's claim to the importance of his saying: "I love!" . . . "I suffer!" when one thinks of the background of the billions who have lived and died, who are living and dying, and presumably will live and die.
>
> This was particularly developed in me by the almost accidental chance that having graduated from Yale in 1920, I was sent abroad to study archaeology at the American Academy in Rome. We even took field trips in those days and in a small way took part in diggings. When one has swung a pickaxe which will reveal the curve of a street four-thousand years covered over which was once an active, much traveled highway, you are never quite the same again. You look at Times Square as a place about which you imagine some day scholars saying: "There appears to have been some kind of public center here."[30]

This testimony, however, is still essentially a modernist one, which inflects the results and consequences of the demographic experience in the direction of abstraction and universalization, it is of a piece with the modernist disjunction of the sign from the referent, with a view towards constructing an "open work" which the multiple fragmented publics of the late nineteenth and early twentieth century imperialist states can freely recode and recontextualize. The formulation is polemically sharpened against the conquest of the unique furniture of the realist and naturalist stage, with its dating and its weather, its here-and-now anchored in the newspapers of empirical national time. But the subsequent postmodern reaction against this modernist abstraction and stylization—which were themselves determined by a revulsion with such bric-a-brac and with the ephemeral trappings of an unsubstantial individualism—marks a "return to the concrete" with a difference; its schizophrenic nominalism includes the rubble and the ruins of much of that—place, personal names, etc.—without the personal identity or the temporal and historical progression, the coherence of the situation and its logic (however desperate), that gave bourgeois realism its tension and its substance. Perhaps, indeed, we here observe the great philosophical and Hegelian logical triad—specificity, universality, individuality (or particularity)—in reverse, as though in history the concrete individual came first, then the repressive system, then the breakup into random empirical features.

At any rate, the dispersive impact of demography is another very different and perhaps more characteristically postmodern effect, felt first and foremost in our relationship to the human past. It would seem, according to some reports, that the quantities of human beings now alive today on earth (some five billion) is rapidly approaching the total number of hominids who have already lived and died on the planet since the beginning of the species. The present is thus like some new thriving and developing nation-state, whose numbers and prosperity make it an unexpected rival for the old traditional ones. As with bilingual speakers in the United States, one can at least predictively calculate the moment when it will overtake the past: that demographic moment is already at hand, as a rapidly approaching point in the not so distant future, and thereby to that degree already part of the present and the realities with which it must reckon. But if this is so, then the relationship of the postmodern to historical consciousness now takes on a very different appearance, and there is some justification, and a plausible argument to be made, for consigning the past to oblivion as we seem to be doing; now that we, the living, have the preponderance, the authority of the dead—hitherto based on sheer numbers—diminishes at a dizzying rate (along with all the other forms of authority and legitimacy). It used to be like an old family, old houses in an old village with only a few young people around, who had to sit in the darkened rooms at night and listen to the elders. But (with the few horrible exceptions we know) there has not been a major war for several generations or two: the curve of births rising sharply augments the proportion of teenagers to the rest of the population, marauding bands making noise in the street outside and leaving the old people to their television sets. If we outnumber the dead, in other words, we win; we are more successful merely by virtue of the fact of having been born (Beaumarchais's account of aristocratic privilege readapting unexpectedly to the generational luck of the yuppies).

What the past has to tell us is therefore little more than a matter of idle curiosity, and indeed our interest in it—fantastic genealogies, alternate histories!—comes to look a little like an in-group hobby or adoptive tourism, like the encyclopedic specialization in the late show or Pynchon's interest in Malta. The salute to non-great-power languages or extinct provincial traditions is, of course, politically correct and a cultural spinoff of the micropolitical rhetoric discussed earlier.

As far as I know, the only philosopher to have taken demography seriously, and to have produced concepts on the basis of an evidently idiosyncratic lived experience of it, was Jean-Paul Sartre, who wanted no children as a result, but whose other historic philosophical originality —to have made a philosophical problem out of that peculiar thing we all take for granted, namely, the existence of other people—may, in fact, turn out to be the consequence of this one, rather than the other way round. It would obviously have been more logical and Cartesian to proceed from the simpler issue—is this really an Other?—to the more complicated one (why are there so many of them?): but Sartre's characters seem to move from the multiple to the individual, in that strange experience it is permitted to call synchronicity:

> I hear the wind carrying a siren's call. I'm all alone. . . . At this very instant there are boats on the open sea that are echoing with music; lights are going on in all the cities of Europe; Communists and Nazis are fighting in the streets of Berlin, unemployed workers are pounding the pavement in New York, women, sitting in front of their mirrors, in a warm room, are putting shadow on their eyelids. And I'm here, in this empty street, and every shot that rings out of a window in Neukölln, every bloody gasp from wounded bodies being carried away, the most minute gestures of those women making

themselves up, syncopates each one of my footsteps, each heartbeat of my heart.[31]

This pseudoexperience, which must be marked as a fantasy and as a failure to achieve representation (by means of representation), is also a second-degree, reactive effort, an attempt to recuperate what lies beyond the reach of my own senses and life experience and, drawing that back inside, to become, if not self-sufficient, then at least protectively self-contained, like a hedgehog. It seems at the same time to be a relatively aimless and exploratory fantasy as well, as though the subject were afraid of forgetting something but could not quite imagine the consequences: Will I be punished if I forget all the others busy living simultaneously with me? What benefit could I possibly derive from doing so when it is in any case impossible to do the job right? Nor would the achievement of conscious synchronicity enhance my own immediate situation, since by definition the mind overleaps that toward others personally unknown to me (and therefore, in the detail of their existences, by definition unimaginable). The effort is thus voluntaristic, an assault of the will on what is "by definition" structurally impossible of achievement rather than something pragmatic and practical that seeks to augment my information about the here and now. The Sartrean character would seem to have launched a preemptive strike or probe: to imagine, mentally to encompass in advance, those numerical multitudes that, ignored, might otherwise ontologically overwhelm you.

The probe must also fail because, as Freud observed, there can be no meaningless invented numbers, and a psychoanalysis of Sartre (or of his characters) would presumably end up thematizing the content of the items willed to be random. Nor is the solitude of the imagining subject irrelevant (the lone siren triggers this "associative" project), nor, above all, the time itself, the historical moment in which the manifold from which this range of individual existences is to be culled at random is itself being unified—indeed, here it may be identified as what we now call *nominalism* as a personal and historical situation and dilemma. This is the sense in which, for all the web threads flung out beyond my "situation" into the unimaginable synchronicity of other people, Sartre is also (like Rousseau) the philosopher of small-group politics, the face-to-face event, which, no matter how large—the aerial shot of the plaza open into the crowded back streets of the polis itself— has to remain available to "live experience" (a less misleading expression than the rhetoric of the individual body and its senses, which evokes a rather different type of philosophy). What lies beyond that—as in social class itself—is somehow real but untrue, thinkable but unrepresentable, and thus doubtful and unverifiable for an existence philosophy that above all wants to avoid being cheated or shortchanged in its life experience. "Totalizing" does not imply a belief in the possibility of access to the totality, but rather a playing with the boundary itself, like a loose tooth, the comparison of notes and measurements that finally allows you to deduce the sound barrier itself, which, like the line between the analytic and the dialectic in Kant, can never be transgressed and somehow itself transcends experience. Yet that impossible experience that lies beyond it, the horror of multiplicity, is nothing more than sheer Number, which Sartre's philosophy alone in our century archaically reinvented for us, outdoing Heidegger's in its return to a well-nigh pre-Socratic primality. Too many people begin to cancel my own existence with their ontological weight; my personal life—the unique form of private property remaining to me—grows pale and dim like the Homeric ghosts, or like a piece of real estate whose value has been driven down to a worthless handful of crumpled bills. This now starts to become postmodern, however, in the planetary influence it exerts over temporal thoughts and the possibility of representing time. Sartre is still very much a modern, but it is instructive to observe the gravitational mass of sheer synchronic numbers bend back on temporal themes to warp them into the only "concept" that can now be squeezed out between history and demography, the only relevant spatio-temporal category that could also, in a pinch, be made to do double duty as an experience: namely, the concept of synchronicity itself, the ultimate limit of representation until you reach television, at which point all these unimaginably multiple bulbs light up again, the metaphysical problem they seemed to designate and to rehearse vanishes away, and postmodern global space replaces and annuls the Sartrean problematic of totalization. With this transformation also, as we have had occasion to see in so many other instances, the essential tension of the modern and the commitment to the impossible drama of representation also weaken and fade away. Global totality is now drawn back inside the monad, on flickering screens, and the "interior," once the heroic proving ground of existentialism and its anxieties, now becomes as self-sufficient as a light show or the inner life of a catatonic (while in the spatial world of real bodies the extraordinary demographic displacements of mass migrant workers and of global tourists invert this individual solipsism to a degree unparalleled in world history). The term *nominalism* can now also serve for this result, from which the universals have paled save for spasmodic intermittencies of a sublime or a new mathematical infinite; but in that case it would be a nominalism which is no longer conceived as a problem and thus has in the process lost its own proper name as well.

VIII. Spatial Historiographies

With this new experience of demography, however, and its unexpected consequences, we are back in the spatial itself (as well as in postmodernism as culture, as ideology and representation). The notion of a predominance of space in the postcontemporary era we owe to Henri Lefebvre[32] (to whom, however, the concept of a postmodern period or stage is alien: his experiential framework was essentially the modernization of France in the postwar, but above all in the Gaullist, era), and it has perplexed any number of readers who recall the Kantian conception of space and time as empty formal containers, as categories of experience so all-encompassing that they cannot themselves enter into the experiences of which they stand as the framework and the structurally enabling presupposition.

These wise restrictions, which include a salutary warning as to the essential impoverishment of the themes themselves, did not prevent the modernists from making much of time, whose empty coordinates they tried to conjure into the magical substance of an element, a veritable experiential stream. But why should landscape be any less dramatic than the Event? The premise, in any case, is that memory has been weakened in our time, and that the great rememberers are a virtually extinct species: for us, memory, when it is a strong experience and still able to testify to the reality of the past, only serves to annihilate time and that past along with it.

What Lefebvre wanted to stress, however, was the correlation between these hitherto universal and formal organizational categories—which for Kant presumably held good for all experience throughout human history—and the historical specificity and originality of the various modes of production, in each of which time and space are lived differently and distinctively (if that is indeed the way to put it and if, as against Kant, we are capable of any direct experience of space and time). Lefebvre's emphasis on space did more than correct a (modernist) imbalance; it also acknowledged the increasing share, in our life experience fully as much as in late capitalism itself, of the urban and the new globality of the system. In effect, Lefebvre called for a new kind of spatial imagination capable of confronting the past in a new way and reading its less tangible secrets off the template of its spatial structures —body, cosmos, city, as all those marked the more intangible organization of cultural and libidinal economies and linguistic forms. The proposal demands an imagination of radical difference, the projection of our own spatial organizations into the well-nigh science-fictional and exotic forms of alien modes of production. But for Lefebvre *all* modes of production are not merely organized spatially but also constitute distinctive modes of the "production of space"; postmodernism theory, however, infers a certain supplement of spatiality in the contemporary period and suggests that there is a way in which, even though other modes of production (or other moments of our own) are distinctively spatial, ours has been spatialized in a unique sense, such that space is for us an existential and cultural dominant, a thematized and foregrounded feature or structural principle standing in striking contrast to its relatively subordinate and secondary (though no doubt no less symptomatic) role in earlier modes of production.[33] So, even if everything is spatial, this postmodern reality here is somehow *more* spatial than everything else.

Why that should be so is easier to see than *how* it could be so. The predilection for space, among postmodernism's theorists, is, of course, easiest understood as a predictable (generational) reaction against the official and long since canonized rhetoric of temporality of the critics and theorists of high modernism, the reversal making for dramatic and visionary accounts of the new order and its new thrills. But the thematic axis was not an arbitrary or gratuitous one, and it can be explored, in turn, for its own conditions of possibility.

In my opinion, a closer new look at the modern would disclose the root of its distinctive experience of temporality in the modernization processes and dynamics of turn-of-the-century capitalism, with its glorious new machinery (celebrated by the futurists and so many others, but no less dramatically deplored and demonized by other writers we also call "modernists"), which has nonetheless not yet completely colonized the social space in which it is emergent. Arno Mayer has reminded us, with a salutary shock, of the persistence of the old regime[34] well up into the twentieth century, and the very partial nature of the "triumph of the bourgeoisie" or of industrial capitalism in the modernist period, still predominantly rural and at least statistically dominated by peasants and landlords with feudal habits, among which the occasional motorcar strikes a jarring but exciting note, along with intermittent electrification and even the sparse aviational pyrotechnics of World War

I. First and foremost of the great oppositions not yet overcome by capitalism in this period is therefore that between town and country, and the
subjects or citizens of the high-modern period are mostly people who
have lived in multiple worlds and multiple times—a medieval *pays* to
which they return on family vacations and an urban agglomeration
whose elites are, at least in most advanced countries, trying to "live
with their century" and to be as "absolutely modern" as they know how.
The very value of the New and of innovation (as these are reflected in
everything from First World hermetic forms to the great drama of Old
and New played out variously in the Third and Second World countries) clearly enough presupposes the exceptionality of what is felt to be
"modern"; while deep memory itself, which inscribes and scars the
differentiation of experience into time and evokes something like the
intermittencies of alternate worlds, would seem also to depend on
"uneven development" of an existential and psychic, fully as much as
on an economic, kind. Nature is related to memory not for metaphysical
reasons but because it throws up the concept and the image of an older
mode of agricultural production that you can repress, dimly remember,
or nostalgically recover in moments of danger and vulnerability.

Implicit in all this is the thud of the predictable second shoe, namely,
the effacement of Nature, and its precapitalist agricultures, from the
postmodern, the essential homogenization of a social space and experience now uniformly modernized and mechanized (where the generation gap passes between the models of the products rather than between
the ecologies of their users), and the triumphant achievement of the
kind of standardization and conformity feared and fantasized in the
1950s but now clearly no longer a problem for the people successfully
molded by it (and who can no longer even recognize or thematize it as
such). This is why we were led earlier to define *modernism* as the experience and the result of *incomplete* modernization, and to suggest that
the postmodern begins to make its appearance wherever the modernization process no longer has archaic features and obstacles to overcome
and has triumphantly implanted its own autonomous logic (for which,
of course, at that point the word *modernization* becomes a misnomer,
since everything is already "modern").

Memory, temporality, the very thrill of the "modern" itself, the New,
and innovation are thus all casualties of this process in which not only
Mayer's residual ancien régime is obliterated but even classical bourgeois culture of the belle epoque is liquidated. Akira Asada's proposition[35] is thus even more grimly profound than it is witty, that the usual

figuration for the stages of capitalism (early, mature, late or advanced) is a misnomer that ought to be reversed: the earliest years now being designated as senile capitalism because it is still the affair of boring traditionalists from an older world; mature or adult capitalism would then retain its characterization, in order to reflect the coming into their own of the great robber barons and adventurers; whereas our own, hitherto late, period can henceforth be known as "infantile capitalism," inasmuch as everyone has been born into it, takes it for granted, and has never known anything else, the friction, resistance, effort of the earlier moments having given way to the free play of automation and the malleable fungibility of multiple consumer publics and markets: roller skates and multinationals, word processors and overnight unfamiliar postmodern downtown high rises.

On this account, however, neither space nor time is "natural" in the sense in which it might be metaphysically presupposed (as ontology or human nature alike): both are the consequence and projected afterimages of a certain state or structure of production and appropriation, of the social organization of productivity. Thus, for the modern, we have read a certain temporality back off its characteristically uneven space; but the other direction can be no less productive, which leads to some more articulated sense of postmodern space by way of postmodern fantastic historiography, as that is found alike in wild imaginary genealogies and novels that shuffle historical figures and names like so many cards from a finite deck. If it makes sense to evoke a certain "return to storytelling" in the postmodern period, the "return" can at least be witnessed here in its full emergence (alongside which the emergence of narrative and narratology in postmodern theoretical production can also be identified as a cultural symptom of changes more basic than the mere discovery of a new theoretical truth). At that point, all the precursors fall into place in the new genealogy: the legendary generational strings of the writers of the Boom, like Asturias or García Márquez; the tedious autoreferential fabulations of the short-lived Anglo-American "new novel"; the discovery, by the professional historians, that "all is fiction" (see Nietzsche) and that there can never be a correct version; the end of "master narratives" in much the same sense, along with the recovery of alternate histories in the past (silenced groups, workers, women, minorities whose scanty records have been systematically burned or expunged out of everything but the police archives) at a moment when historical alternatives are in the process of disappearing, and if you want to have a history, there is henceforth only one to participate in.

In short, postmodern "fantastic historiography" takes up the slack of these historical "tendencies" and combines them into a genuine aesthetic that seems to know two variants or mirror spirals. In the one, you make up a chronicle (generational or genealogical) whose grotesque succession and unrealistic personnel, ironic and melodramatic destinies, and heartrending (and virtually cinematographic) missed opportunities mime real ones, or to be more precise about it, resemble the dynastic annals of small-power kingdoms and realms very far from our own parochial "tradition" (the secret history of the Mongols, for example, or well-nigh extinct Balkan languages which were once the dominant power in their little universe). Here, a semblance of historical verisimilitude is vibrated into multiple alternate patterns, as though the form or genre of historiography was retained (at least in its archaic versions) but now for some reason, far from projecting the constraints of the formulaic, seems to offer postmodern writers the most remarkable and untrammeled movement of invention. In this peculiar form and content—real sewer systems with imaginary crocodiles in them—the wildest Pynchonesque fantasies are somehow felt to be thought experiments of all the epistemological power and falsifiable authority of Einstein's fables, and in any case to convey the feel of the real past better than any of the "facts" themselves.

Such fabulations—not unexpectedly cheered on by a whole generation of ideologues complacently but with relish announcing the death of the referent, if not the end of history itself—also clearly enough show signs of that release and euphoria of the postmodern to which we have already referred, and for much the same reasons. These historical fantasies, unlike those of certain other epochs (as in the pseudo-Shakespearean historical romance of the early nineteenth century), do not aim essentially at the derealization of the past, the lightening of the burden of historical fact and necessity, its transformation into a costumed charade and misty revels without consequence and without irrevocability. Nor does postmodern fantastic historiography seek, as in naturalism, to diminish the grisly and deterministic historical event into the minute workings of natural law, viewed from the epicycle of Mercury and thus receivable with textbook stoic resignation of a force and concentration capable of reducing to a minimum the anguish of decision and converting the pessimisms of failure into the more gratifying and musical falling cadences of a Wagnerian-Schopenhauerian worldview. The new free play with the past, however—the delirious nonstop monologue of its postmodern revision into so many in-group narratives—is obviously equally allergic to the priorities and commitments, let alone the responsibilities, of the various tediously committed kinds of partisan history.

Nonetheless, these narratives can be seen as entertaining a more active relationship to praxis than has been suggested above or would be allowable under some more literal minded reflection theory of history: here the making up of unreal history is a substitute for the making of the real kind. It mimetically expresses the attempt to recover that power and praxis by way of the past and what must be called fancy rather than imagination. Fabulation—or if you prefer, mythomania and outright tall tales—is no doubt the symptom of social and historical impotence, of the blocking of possibilities that leaves little option but the imaginary. Yet its very invention and inventiveness endorses a creative freedom with respect to events it cannot control, by the sheer act of multiplying them; agency here steps out of the historical record itself into the process of devising it; and new multiple or alternate strings of events rattle the bars of the national tradition and the history manuals whose very constraints and necessities their parodic force indicts. Narrative invention here thus by way of its very implausibility becomes the figure of a larger possibility of praxis, its compensation but also its affirmation in the form of projection and mimetic reenactment.

The second form of postmodern historiographic narrative is in some ways the inverse of this one. Here, the purely fictional intent is underscored and reaffirmed in the production of imaginary people and events among whom from time to time real-life ones unexpectedly appear and disappear: Doctorow's practice in *Ragtime*, with its Morgans and Fords, its Houdinis and Thaws and Whites, was my earlier reference[36] and may be maintained here, where it is, however, characteristic of a whole range and variety of such collage effects, in which a newspaper figure is pasted onto a painted backdrop, or the tickertape of a set of statistics unrolls in the middle of a domestic romance. These effects are not mere replications of Dos Passos, who still respected categories of verisimilitude when it came to his world-historical individuals; nor does this kind of fictional history have anything to do with that other characteristic postmodern product I have called nostalgia film, in which the tone and style of a whole epoch becomes, in effect, the central character, the actant and the "world-historical individual" in its own right (with a significant diminution in the kind of wild imaginative energy manifested by both types of historiographic fantasies in question here).

What one can affirm about this second type (in which the well-known formula is returned to its upright position and the toads again become "real" while the gardens grow imaginary) is that it is very precisely a kind of spatial historiography which has unique things to tell us both about postmodern spatiality and about what happened to the postmodern sense of history in the first place.

Spatiality is here registered, as it were, in second-degree form, as the consequence of some prior specialization—a kind of intensified classification or compartmentalization which I am tempted to describe as a division of labor of the mind and its modes of scanning and mapping the realm. Classical psychic fragmentation—for example, the separation of imagination and knowledge—was always a consequence of the division of labor in the social world; now, however, it is the very rational or knowledge functions of the mind which become somehow internally segmented and assigned to different floors and different office buildings.

Thus, for example, we may imagine (in such a postmodern narrative) the visit of the great Prussian neoclassical architect Schinkel to the new industrial city of Manchester: the conceit is historically possible, and offers the relatively postmodern charm of an episode that falls through the cracks (did the young Stalin actually go to London once? how about Marx's incognito inspection of the American Civil War?): Do I wake or sleep? But what is fundamentally postmodern about this is the incongruence of romantic Germany, glowing from within with all the magic realism of Caspar David Friedrich encountering the misery and surplus labor of Engels's great nascent factory city. It is a comic-book juxtaposition, somewhat like a schoolboy exercise in which all kinds of disparate materials are put together in new ways. The visit also happened in reality, it turns out; but by now one is tempted to recall Adorno's wisecrack about something else, namely, that "even if it was a fact, it wouldn't be true." The postmodern flavor of the episode returns upon the "historical record" to derealize and denature it and endow it with something of the fantastic aura of a Gabriel García Márquez version of Latin American history, about which in any case Carpentier famously and pointedly observed that it was magic-realist (real-maravilloso) to begin with.[37] But the question now is whether all of what used to be called History has not become precisely that.

Those are, however, the cultural and ideological effects of the structure, whose conditions of possibility lie very precisely in our sense that each of the elements involved, and thus incongruously combined, belong to radically distinct and different registers: architecture and socialism, romantic art and the history of technology, politics and the imitation of antiquity. Even if these registers do oddly and dialectically coincide, as in the matter of urbanism, in which "Schinkel" is fully as much an encyclopedia entry as Engels's book on Manchester, our preconscious minds refuse to make or acknowledge the link, as those these cards came from different files.

The dissonance and incompatibility in fact have "literary" analogies, which it is very strange to rediscover here, in the area of social and historical reality itself. Indeed, this peculiar mismatch reminds one of nothing quite so much as of *generic* discordance, as when a writer or an orator misguidedly incorporates a text of an incompatible type or lapses into a different register of discourse. In literature, of course, the disappearance of genres as such, along with their conventions and the distinct reading rules they project, is a familiar story. It would now seem that, far from becoming extinct, the older genres, released like viruses from their traditional ecosystem, have now spread out and colonized reality itself, which we divide up and file away according to typological schemes which are no longer those of subject matter but for which the alternative topic of style seems somehow inadequate. Yet it is surely something like the "style" of the encyclopedia entry "Schinkel," which simply does not go with the style of "Engels," even though the computer would turn both of them up under the headings "German," "nineteenth century," and so forth. In other words, the two entries do not "go together" or match in the "real world," that is, the world of historical knowledge; but they do go together in that realm we have been characterizing as postmodern historiography (a cultural genre thus itself generically separated from the other one called historical knowledge), where it is very precisely their interesting dissonance and the garish magic realism of their unexpected juxtaposition which is the bonus of pleasure to be consumed.

It should not be thought that the postmodern narrative in any way overcomes or transcends the bizarre discursive separation at issue here: the latter is not at all to be grasped as a "contradiction" to which the postmodern collage affords a semblance of "resolution." The postmodern effect, on the contrary, ratifies the specializations and differentiations on which it is based: it presupposes them and thereby prolongs and perpetuates them (for if some genuinely unified field of knowledge emerged, where Schinkel and Engels lay down side by side like the lamb and the lion, so to speak, all postmodern incongruity would at once evaporate). The structure thus confirms the description of postmodernism as something for which the word *fragmentation* remains much too weak and primitive a term, and probably too "totalizing" as well, particularly since it is now no longer a matter of the breakup of some preexisting older organic totality, but rather the emergence of the multiple in new and unexpected ways, unrelated strings of events, types of discourse, modes of classification, and compartments of reality. This absolute and absolutely random pluralism—and perhaps it is the only referent for which that charged term should be reserved, a kind of reality-pluralism—a coexistence not even of multiple and alternate worlds so much as of unrelated fuzzy sets and semiautonomous subsystems whose overlap is perceptually maintained like hallucinogenic depth planes in a space of many dimensions is, of course, what is replicated by the rhetoric of decentering (and what informs official rhetorical and philo-sophical attacks on "totality"). This differentiation and specialization or semiautonomization of reality is then prior to what happens in the psyche—postmodern schizo-fragmentation as opposed to modern or modernist anxieties and hysterias—which takes the form of the world it models and seeks to reproduce in the form of experience as well as of concepts, with results as disastrous as those that would be encountered by a relatively simple natural organism given to mimetic camouflage and trying to approximate the op art laser dimensionality of a science-fictional environment of the far future. We have learned much from psychoanalysis, and most recently from the speculative mapping of frac-tured and multiple subject positions, but it would be a pity to attribute those to some unimaginably complex new internal human nature rather than to the social templates that project them: human nature, as Brecht showed us, being capable of an infinite variety of forms and adapta-tions, and along with it, the psyche itself.

Meanwhile, the distinct differential structures (formalized by Doctorow in the minor but extraordinarily symptomatic patterns of *Ragtime's* historiography) also go a long way toward justifying the earlier account of postmodern perception in terms of the slogan that "difference relates." The new modes of perception seem indeed to operate by way of the simultaneous preservation of just such incompatibles, a kind of incom-mensurability-vision that does not pull the eyes back into focus but provisionally entertains the tension of their multiple coordinates (so that, if you thought the dialectic had to do with producing new "syn-theses" of various preformed and prearranged "opposites" calculated to fit together effortlessly, then to be sure all this would be decidedly "postdialectical").

But it must also be considered a *spatial* phenomenon in the most fundamental sense since, whatever the provenance of the various items combined in their postmodern incompatability—whether they stem from different zones of time or from unrelated compartments of the social and material universe—it is their spatial separation that is strongly felt as such. Different moments in historical or existential time are here simply filed in different places; the attempt to combine them even locally does not slide up and down a temporal scale (except to the degree that the spatial character of these figures here comes due and presents its bill) but jumps back and forth across a game board that we conceptualize in terms of distance.

Thus the movement from one generic classification to another is radically discontinuous, like switching channels on a cable television set; and indeed it seems appropriate to characterize the strings of items and the compartments of genres of their typologization as so many "channels" into which the new reality is organized. Channel switching, so often taken by media theorists as the very epitome of a postmodern attention and perceptual apparatus, does indeed seem to offer a useful alternative to the psychoanalytic model of multiple subject positions evoked earlier, which can, of course, still be retained as an alternate code in the process of transcoding so profoundly characteristic of postmodern theory itself, and which can now itself be grasped as the theoretical equivalent of channel switching on the perceptual, cultural, and psychic levels. "We" thus turn out to be whatever we are in, confront, inhabit, or habitually move through, provided it is understood that under current conditions we are obliged to renegotiate all those spaces or channels back and forth ceaselessly in a single Joycean day. The literary representation of this new reality would thus seem to be Vargas Llosa's remarkable "memoir" of the old days of the radio serials in Latin America, La Tia Julia y el Scribidor, where the separate daytime programs slowly begin to infect each other and colonize their neighbors, amalgamating in the most alarming—but as we have just seen, the most archetypically postmodern—of ways: such interfection is then the very prototype of what we may call the postmodern mode of totalizing.

It also characterizes our contemporary mode of historical and political as such, and it will be by way of Lefebvre's conception of a new kind of spatial dialectic that we need to grasp the preceding structures as implying more than mere cultural or fictional patterns. For our comprehension of current events also takes place against the background of the compartmentalization of reality that has been evoked in grasping the peculiarities of postmodern writing. It was never easy to grasp the present as history, since virtually by definition the manuals all stopped and were printed a year or two earlier in time, but a politically conscious collectivity can keep itself up-to-date by a ceaseless multiple or hydra-headed scrutiny of and commentary on the latest unexpected peripety. Today, however, collectivity in that form has been drawn back inside the media, leaving us as individuals bereft even of the feeling of being alone and individual. The occasional flash of historical understanding that may strike the "current situation" will thus happen by the well-nigh postmodern (and spatial) mode of the recombination of separate columns in the newspaper:[38] and it is this spatial operation that we continue to call (using an older temporal language) historical thinking or analysis. The Alaska oil spill thus sits cheek by jowl with the latest Israeli bombing or search-and-destroy mission in southern Lebanon, or follows closely on its heels in the segmentation of television news. The two events activate altogether different and unrelated mental zones of reference and associative fields, not least because within the stereotypical planetarium of current "objective spirit," Alaska is on some other side of the physical and spiritual globe from the "war-torn Middle East." No introspective examination of our personal history, but no inspection of the various objective histories either (filed under Exxon, Alaska, Israel, Lebanon), would in itself be enough to disclose the dialectical interrelatedness of all these things, whose legendary Ur-episode can be found in the Suez War, which determined the building of larger and larger oil tankers to circumnavigate the Cape of Good Hope, on the one hand, with its sequel, on the other, in 1967, a sequel that fixed the political geography of the Middle East in violence and misery for more than a generation. What I want to argue is that the tracing of such common "origins" —henceforth evidently indispensable for what we normally think of as concrete historical understanding—is no longer exactly a temporal or a genealogical operation in the sense of older logics of historicity or causality. The "solution" to a juxtaposition—Alaska, Lebanon—that is not yet even a puzzle until it is solved—Nasser and Suez!—no longer opens up historiographic deep space or perspectival temporality of the type of a Michelet or a Spengler: it lights up like a nodal circuit in a slot machine (and thus foreshadows a computer-game historiography of the future even more alarming).

But if history has become spatial, so also has its repression and the ideological mechanisms whereby we avoid thinking historically (the Alaskan example, indeed, offers the blueprint of a kind of reading well calculated to allow you to ignore the spatially contiguous columns); but

I now mean a larger aesthetic of information in which the generic incompatibilities detected in postmodern fiction now comes into a different kind of force in postmodern reality, dictating a peculiar new decorum or high cool in which the obligation to disregard items classified in other columns or compartments opens up a means for constructing false consciousness which is tactically far more advanced than older and more primitive tactics of lying and repression and can do without the now cumbersome and Ptolemaic technologies of classical ideology. This is a new way of defusing information, making representations improbable, discrediting political positions and their organic "discourses," and, in short, effectively separating "the facts" from "the truth," as Adorno put it. The superiority of the new method lies in its capacity to coexist perfectly adequately with information and full knowledge, something already implicit in the separation of subsystems and topics in various unrelated parts of the mind, which can only be activated locally or contextually ("nominalistically") in distinct moments of time and by various unrelated subject positions, so that a stylistic taboo is here combined with the human characteristic of finitude ("I can only be in one place—one discourse!—at one time") to exclude not merely older kinds of syntheses but even the therapeutic estrangement effects that used to result from confronting one piece of evidence with a seemingly unconnected one—as in dramatic reconstructions of the crime where two witnesses are unexpectedly brought face to face.

"Postmodernism" is itself the prime example of the conceptuality that results from such a system, in which reality itself is organized a little like those networks of political cells whose members have only met their immediate opposite numbers. Within this "concept," then, that coexistence of distinct representations we already know, but whose unique operations we have not sufficiently admired, can be compared to schizophrenia, if this last is really what Pynchon tells us it is ("Day by day, Wendell is less himself and more generic. He enters a staff meeting and the room is suddenly full of people").[39] A roomful of people, indeed, solicit us in incompatible directions that we entertain all at once: one subject position assuring us of the remarkable new global elegance of its daily life and forms; another one marveling at the spread of democracy, with all those new "voices" sounding out of hitherto silent parts of the globe or inaudible class strata (just wait a while, they will be here, to join their voices to the rest); other more querulous and "realistic" tongues reminding us of the incompetences of late capitalism, with its delirious paper-money constructions rising out of sight, its Debt, the rapidity of the flight of factories matched only by the opening of new junk-food chains, the sheer immiseration of structural homelessness, let alone unemployment, and that well-known thing called urban "blight" or "decay" which the media wraps brightly up in drug melodramas and violence porn when it judges the theme perilously close to being threadbare. None of these voices can be said to contradict the others; not "discourses" but only propositions do that, and the identity of identity and nonidentity does not seem very satisfactory for this one, for which "coexistence" is too reassuring a term as well, implying some ultimate chance of intergalactic collision in which matter and antimatter might finally meet and shake hands. Even Brecht's modest hypothesis about Hollywood, that in it God economized and planned but the one establishment ("heaven: it serves the unprosperous and unsuccessful as hell"), is much too functional, even though the notion of a city, and of that particular city! does rise imperiously in the mind as one of the last few thinkable "representations": postmodernism is alive and well in boutiques and fashionable little restaurants (we are indeed told that nowadays the remodeling of restaurants makes up a significant bulk of the postmodern architect's commissions), while the other realities wander around outside in old cars or on foot. As an ideology which is also a reality, the "postmodern" cannot be disproved insofar as its fundamental feature is the radical separation of all the levels and voices whose recombination in their totality could alone disprove it.

IX. Decadence, Fundamentalism, and Hightech

The last desperate stages of hide-and-seek suggest some final logical closets in which History (unmasked as sheerly spatial in its diachronic costumes) might still be found, despite the grim silence, house-deep, that leads you to conclude it might have smothered to death in its gags. Might it not still be possible, however, to generate history out of the present itself and to endow today's fantasy projections and wish fulfillments with the force if not of a reality, then at least of what grounds and inaugurates realities, as Heidegger liked to say (*stiften*).

These projections run in opposite directions, even though they can both be detected in the most substantial corpus of such symptoms —contemporary science fiction. The directions I hesitate to characterize as our old friends past and future, but perhaps they are new and postmodern versions of those, in a situation in which neither past nor future has, as we have seen, much in the way of legal claims on our attention or responsibility. Decadence and high technology are indeed the occasions and the launchpads for such speculation, coming themselves in antithetical guises and modes.

For while high technology is omnipresent and unavoidable, particularly in its various religious forms, *decadence* compels by its absence, like a smell nobody mentions or a thought all the guests are visibly making an effort not to think. One would have thought that the world of headphones and Andy Warhol, of fundamentalism and AIDS, of exercise machines and MTV, yuppies and books on postmodernism, punk hairdos and fifties'-style crewcuts, the "loss of historicity" and the *éloge* of schizophrenia, the media and obsessions with calcium and cholesterol, the logic of "future shock" and the emergence of scientists and counterinsurgency strike forces as new types of social groups, would have all the qualifications to pass for ripely decadent in the eyes of any sensible Martian observer; but it is corny to say so, and one of the other tactical achievements of the postmodern discursive system lies in the relegation of the *laudator temporis acti* to the storeroom of no longer very plausible or believable literary characters. To be sure, where the former norm has become just another "life-style," the category of the eccentric loses its reason for being; but the moderns still had this concept, which they sometimes acted out in a way that in our time only Fellini's great *Satyricon* recaptures, in the guise of a "nostalgia film" about the late Roman Empire, with this signal difference: that the nostalgia may somehow be real, in which case it must be identified as a hitherto unknown and unclassified species of feeling altogether (unless the whole thing is simply a costume remake of *La Dolce Vita*; in which case Fellini is just another moralizer without interest, something his film disproves by triumphantly eschewing the narcissistic pathos of its contemporary counterpart). Fellini here manages to construct a time machine in which we can still seize a glimpse not of the world as lived by the decadent Romans of the silver age but of that of high Modernists (at least in their first, symbolist stage), who unlike us could still think the concept of decadence concretely and with Flaubertian force. Meanwhile, as Richard Gilman pertinently reminds us,[40] the Romans in question had no such concept, and unlike the character in the costume drama who announces that he is off for the Thirty Years' War, but like ourselves, the postmoderns, were very far from pinching themselves at every moment to remind themselves that they were living "in the Decadence."

Gilman goes on to tell us to stop using this noxious concept, unaware that everyone else has long since done so; but it still offers an interesting laboratory in which to observe the peculiar behavior of that phenomenon called "the sense of historical difference." The paradox in the conceptual problems rehearsed by Fellini's representation draws its paralogical motor force from the paradoxes of difference in the first place: the "decadents" being as different from us as in another sense they are somehow the same, and the vehicles for our disguised symbolic identification. But "decadence" in that sense and as a theme or ideologeme is not some mere room in the imaginary museum (housing a "culture," for example, more peculiar than that of the Polynesians); nor is it, as Gilman sometimes thinks, a "theory" that includes presuppositions about psychic and racial health or imbalance; it is a secondary spin-off of a whole theory of history, and a special-case subset of what the Germans call *Geschichtsphilosophie*. Unfortunately, therefore, one must start from that and work one's way down to Des Esseintes or Fellini's Romans; it is a task that involves some reflection on the specificity of "modern times" and on the way in which it defines itself by way of its own difference from the rest of history, something Latour has recently and conveniently rebaptized "the Great Divide" (as though there were not any number of those still around!), but what is also sometimes called "the West and the rest," otherwise known as Western Reason, Western metaphysics, or indeed (Latour's own special preoccupation) Science itself, about which it is unnecessary to specify that it is Western in the first place (except for readers of Joseph Needham or Lévi-Strauss). Latour has cooked up a wonderful table of the synonyms and disguises of this view of Western exceptionalism, in which a number of old Marxist friends will also be found:

> the modern world
> secularization
> rationalization
> anonymity
> disenchantment
> mercantilism
> optimization
> dehumanization
> mechanization
> westernization
> capitalism
> industrialization
> postindustrialization

technicalization
intellectualization
sterilization
objectivization
Americanization
scientization
consumer society
one-dimensional society
soulless society
modern madness
modern times
progress[41]

Clearly enough, Latour has telescoped several historical stages into these positions, something which only underscores the deeper continuity of the situations from which they spring and which they express; meanwhile the "complicity" of the Left and Marxism in the perpetuation of this myth of Western exceptionalism is here made perfectly clear for anyone who had forgotten the pages of *The Communist Manifesto* devoted to the celebration of the new and historically unique dynamics of capitalism itself. In my opinion, however, it is modernism itself (or rather "modernity"; unless in reality it be "modernization") that stands accused, the novelty rather lying in the association of Marxism with all that, as just another modernism.

In fact, the stages aspect of historical materialism can be reframed in an unconventional way that transforms the absolute break most often (and rightly) felt to be present in Marxism between capitalism (and socialism) and the so-called precapitalist modes of production. Indeed, in the tradition, a number of diversely accented breaks wander along the historical continuum, like a line of verse about which one hesitates as to its meter or relative freedom. Marxism indeed posits one kind of break between tribal societies (hunters and gatherers, primitive communism) and those later modes of production (including capitalism) which know state power (along with the surplus, writing, the division between mental and manual labor, and so forth). It posits another kind of break between precapitalist power societies and that very special dynamic of capitalism, with its infinite expansion ("both positing a limit *specific* to itself and on the other hand driving beyond *any* limit")[42] that may be said to reinvent history in a new way, and also to constitute an incomparable and hitherto novel form of social imperialism; this is, of course, the break Latour has in mind. Meanwhile, one must also presumaby posit a fundamental break between capitalism and socialism, in the sense in which this last reinvents, on a new and higher level, collective forms and experiences which make it rather more comparable to precapitalist social formations, and in that respect dissimilar from the atomic fragmentation and individualism of capitalism per se (even though, in a Hegelian move, socialism will also claim to retain the new richness of individual subjectivity developed under the market system). But this sequence, as thus traditionally presented and now that we are no longer quite so worried about its Darwinian overtones (unilinear evolution or multilinear evolution), still raises embarrassing questions which are not altogether dispelled by the dialectical notion that capitalism now inaugurates a new kind of global history, whose very logic is "totalizing" in the strict sense: with the result that, even if before there were histories —many of them, and unrelated—now there is tendentially only one, on an ever more homogeneous horizon, as far as the eye can see.

A careful reading of the *Manifesto*, however, suggests a somewhat different way of thinking about Marx's view of capitalism as a stage, for it can be grasped as a kind of enormous black box or "vanishing mediator," one extraordinarily complex and temporally distended and developed laboratory, through which precapitalist peoples must pass in order to be reprogrammed and retrained, transformed and developed, on their way to socialism. This reading (which, although structural, remains dialectical) now redistributes the features of radical difference of the older series; it excludes questions about what kind of society, collective character, and culture capitalism itself involves, since this last is now seen as a process rather than a stage in its own right; finally, it obligates us to reconsider the features attributed to postmodernism in a functional way, as new and intensified forms of a structural tendency Marx famously described in terms of separation and disjunction, reduction, disaggregation, divestment, and the like.

Returning to other varieties of the experience of modernity, however, we have already seen the way in which modernity is at least at one with the sense of difference and of impending change, whether in the imminence of the object world or the psyche itself:

Not I, not I, but the wind that blows through me!
A fine wind is blowing the new direction of Time.
If only I let it bear me, carry me, if only it carry me!
If only I am sensitive, subtle, oh delicate, a winged gift!

If only, most lovely of all, I yield myself and am borrowed
By the fine, fine wind that takes its course through the chaos of the
　world
Like a fine, an exquisite chisel, a wedge-blade inserted;
If only I am keen and hard like the sheer lip of a wedge
Driven by invisible blows,
The rock will split, we shall come at the wonder, we shall find the
　Hesperides.[43]

It is an existential imminence that is interchangeable with so many expressions of the sense of objective change that sweeps the modern, along with a disgust for the survivals of the old, and a feeling that besides being a release and a liberation, the New is also an obligation: something you must do to yourself to rise to the occasion and be worthy of the new world tendentially in emergence all around you. But that is a world whose telltale signals tend to be technological, even though its claims and demands are subjective and involve the obligation to produce new people, wholly new forms of subjectivity. It is also, as John Berger reminds us,[44] a world whose Utopian promise will be blasted by World War I, save in the now more directed and restricted channel of systemic change and social and political revolution as such, now historically epitomized in the Soviet revolution with its remarkable new *modernist* cultural effervescence. This is not the place to recommemorate that ferment, save to observe not only that it offers a fundamental structural distinction from the postmodern (in which, everything being new, or rather, nothing any longer being "old," the excitement of the matter is greatly and dialectically diminished), but also that the vantage point of the postmodern ought now to offer new perspectives on a henceforth classical modernist heritage. What it does seem minimally possible to affirm is that modernity is inseparable from that feeling of radical difference under discussion here: moderns feel themselves to be radically different kinds of people from those of older precapitalist traditions or those in colonial areas on the globe contemporaneous with modernism (and imperialism). What is offensive here for other societies and other cultures (and, it does not seem superfluous to add, for other races as well) will now be complicated by the way in which a whole range of other societies interiorize the dilemma and in their various ways live out the drama of Old and New with dramatic anxiety. But the perfection of the grand machinery of capitalism (including its industry) is surely not some personal merit in the white (and often Protestant) northern

Europeans; it is an accident of historical circumstances and structures (or conditions of possibility), about which it ought to be a tautology to add that in it "the educators" were by definition themselves already "reeducated," since among the other technologies capitalism produces and develops is also the human one: the production of "productive labor."

Nonetheless, even this description, which no longer involves any kind of Eurocentrism, posits and presupposes the absolute difference of capitalism itself. What one wants to observe, then, about a global post-modernism in which differences of that sort are theoretically repudiated is that its own condition of possibility posits the far greater *modernization* of other segments of the globe than was the case in the modern (or classical imperialist) era.

Whence, then, this strange inner shadow or opacity within the modern of the decadence itself? Why should proud modern—or modernist —people, at best merely apprehensive about their insufficient modernity, harbor this secret fantasy of languid, neurasthetic difference, with which they then go on to tax the more ancient provinces in their empire, not to speak of their own "most advanced" artists and cultural intellectuals? Decadence is clearly something which both resists modernity and comes after it, as a future destiny in which all the promises of the modern go slack and unravel. The concept fantasizes the return of all the weirdest religious sects and foods, after the triumph of the secular, of homo economicus and of utilitarianism: it is thus the ghost of the superstructure, of cultural autonomy itself, that haunts the omnipotence of the base. "Decadence" is thus in some way the very premonition of the postmodern itself, but under conditions that make it impossible to predict that aftermath with any sociological or cultural accuracy, thereby diverting the vague sense of a future into more fantastic forms, all borrowed from the misfits and eccentrics, the perverts and the Others, or aliens, of the present (modern) system. In history, finally, or rather in the historical unconscious, "decadence" comes before us as the ineradicable otherness of the past and of other modes of production —an otherness posited by capitalism as such, but which it now, as it were, tries on, as with old costumes, since these ancient decadents (who have no concept of decadence themselves) are the others of an other, the difference of a difference: they look at their own surroundings with our eyes, seeing nothing but what is morbidly exotic, but complicitous and finally infected by that, so that the roles slowly reverse and it is we moderns who become "decadent" against the backdrop of the more natural realities of the precapitalist landscape.

Where nature has vanished, however, and along with it the very "otherness" that one can find offensive in the hubris and the exceptionalist ideology of modernity, the concept of decadence must then itself fade away, no longer available for characterizing and expressing our reactions to the postmodern. What seems to persist, on the other hand, is the historiographic stage set of all those "ends of the world" that lent the decadent moment its peculiar resonance and, as it were, its silver note. Late capitalism is in that sense a misnomer, insofar as "late" now yields none of the fin-de-siècle or late-Roman overtones we associate with it, nor are its subjects fantasized as being faint and listless with too much experience and history, too much jouissance and too many rare and occult intellectual and scientific operations. We have all those things, indeed, but we jog afterward to refresh the constitution, while by the same token computers relieve us of the terrible obligation to distend the memory like a swollen bladder retaining all these encyclopedia references.

Nonetheless, the imagination of catastrophe still retains the forms of a near and a far future category; if the atomic exchange has grown distant, the greenhouse effect and ecological pollution are, by way of compensation, ever more vivid. What we need to ask is whether such anxieties and the narratives in which they are invested really "intend" the future (in Husserl's technical sense of posing a genuine object), or somehow convolute and return to feed on our own moment of time. The paradigmatic vision of all this, the Australian film *Road Warrior* (which seems to have inherited a local tradition deriving from *On the Beach* and from the geographical sense of being the last in line for the atomic cloud), depicts what the Russians call a "time of troubles," a breakdown of civilization and a universal anarchy and regression to barbarism, which, like the more facile jeremiads of the decadence itself, could simply be taken as an unoriginal comment on and satire of the current state of things, from the oil crisis to muggings and tattoo culture.

Freud has taught us, however, that the manifest totality of a fantasy or a dream (something we can enlarge to include the mesmerization of this kind of cultural artifact) is not a reliable guide, save by inversion and negation, to the meaning of the latent content: dreams of dead loved ones proving in reality to be happy wish fulfillments about something utterly unrelated. I once suggested[45] that there could be conceived a kind of structural implication much tighter and more logical than this, in which the morbid features of the manifest content played a more immediate and functional role in diverting us from whatever in the latent might offend our self-esteem (or our internalized role models). The occasion was a made-for-television science fiction film in which a group of spelunkers serendipitously avoided the universal catastrophe (resulting either from the noxious effluvia of meteors or some short-term poison gas cloud, I can't remember which). As a convenience to the filmmakers, however, the victims' bodies, along with all the other dead organic material, were volatilized on the spot, without leaving even so much as a little telltale pile of dust. The last people on earth, therefore, emerged into a forbidding landscape in which they could fill their car without charge from the gas pumps and take cans of food off the shelves in empty grocery stores; California, for them, was returned to the stage of a paradisal landscape free of overpopulation, while the survivors settled down to idyllic agricultural and communal existences, much like the (to me) Utopian outcomes of John Wyndham's various apocalypses. The show thus offered existential terror and melodramatic grief, backed with the very real advantages of a reduction in competition and a more humane way of life. I call this kind of film a Utopian wish fulfillment wrapped in dystopian wolf's clothing, and think it is only fair and prudent, as far as the nastier sides of human nature are concerned, to vigilantly scrutinize apparent nightmares of this kind for traces of that different and more egotistical drive toward individual and collective self-gratification that Freud found living on insatiably in our Unconscious.

Road Warrior, of course, has some other features that separate it from a simple-minded postatomic narrative (of the type of *A Boy and His Dog* or *Glenn and Rhonda*): in particular, its temporal perspective converts its near-future narrative into a far-future one, endowing the present with legendary dimensions of a well-nigh mythical or religious kind (something then completed and finished off, with all the *i*'s dotted and *t*'s crossed, in the rather more christological *Terminator*). But later, more urban fantasies give the game away; and it is not only the visual splendor of *Blade Runner* that suggests image consumption of a more familiar (but no less sumptuous and gratifying) type, which has little to do with futures fantasized or not, but everything to do with late capitalism and some of its favorite marketplaces.

In my opinion, what films like this "mean" (not, perhaps, the best word for it) is not the breakdown of high technology in a future time of troubles, but its conquest in the first place. As representations, such postmodern dystopian films seem to give us thoughts and hypotheses about the future; and the thoughts and hypotheses are surely plausible enough, except for what we may now call the Adorno principle, which is as instantly activated by the future as it is by actuality: namely that even if they turn out to be facts, they may not necessarily be true. But what such films actually give us to consume are not those flimsy prognoses and dystopian meteorological bulletins but rather high technology itself and its own special effects. J. G. Ballard, himself one of the greatest postcontemporary dystopians, has found a stunning formulation for such aesthetic projections: they have reached, he tells us, a level of technology advanced enough to depict advanced technology in decline. True high technology means achieving the capacity to show historicity of high tech itself: *Wesen ist was gewesen ist* (negation is determination); you can't say what a thing is until it turns into something else; not the end of art but the end of electricity, and all the computers breaking down. The thought gives new and exemplary meaning to a haunting moment in Renoir's *La Règle du jeu*, when, at the climax of the costume ball in the chateau, now infiltrated by skeletons waving their lamps and celebrating mortality to the tune of Saint-Saëns's *Danse macabre*, the fat lady pianist, hands in her lap, can be glimpsed staring with rapt melancholia at the skeletal autonomy of the keyboard itself, behind which the piano rolls have taken charge with a vengeance. It is a fable of the work of art at that particular stage of its mechanical reproducibility, gazing at its own alienated power with morbid fascination. The postmodern has, however, reached a later stage than that; unlike the delight of the modern in its projection of wonder-working machinery, its delight with the very breakdown of that machinery at the critical point is subject to the gravest misunderstanding if we do not realize that this is precisely how postmodern technology consumes and celebrates itself.

We must, therefore, posit a kind of supplementary bonus of pleasure in the surplus of the technological image itself: since here high technology is identifiable not only in the content (the ostensible future things filmed and then screened for a jaded public) but in the process itself, the nature of this stock and equipment, the qualities of the material image and the successfulness of the "special effects," which, as in the paradoxes of the "suspension of disbelief," are judged by way of the negation of the negation to be not unlifelike, and thenceforth evaluated according to the millions of dollars spent in their construction (it is indeed well known that today big box-office successes are mainly obtained by new and remarkable "special effects," while each of these new constructs is accompanied by a whole secondary publicity about its mode of manufacture, its engineers, its novelties, and so forth). "Special effects" are thus here a kind of crude and emblematic caricature of the deeper logic of all contemporary image production, in which it becomes an exceedingly subtle matter to distinguish between our attention to the content and our appreciation of the form. "Expensive form" —rather than the older "significant form"—that is surely now the watchword for these peculiar commodities, whose exchange value has in some complex supplementary spiral become a commodity in its own right. (This is a somewhat different—and more classical—way of talking about the kind of status connotation first anatomized by Veblen, then codified in academic sociology, and finally reinvented in rich new ways by Pierre Bourdieu in our own time: in a society with inwardly colllapsing hierarchies, the notion of status seems uncertain; but the universalization of the formal effects discussed above—what has been called a "high-tech bonus"—explains why such notions should again have become attractive.)

The abstraction of this process—in which commodification reaches new and second-degree levels and seems to propagate itself upon its earlier stages—suggests parallels with the credit system and the constructions of paper money in current stock-exchange practices. Meanwhile, if one does not want to lapse back into technological determinism, it would be necessary to examine the structure of the new technology for its capacity to sustain libidinal investment of this kind: a jubilation with the new prosthetic powers which distinguish themselves from the older machinery (combustion engine, electricity, etc.) by their non-anthropomorphic character and thus give rise to forms of idealism utterly different from the classical types. There may also be structural parallels to be established between these new "informational" machineries that are neither basely physical nor "spiritual" in any nineteeth-century sense, and language itself, whose model has become predominant in the postmodern period. On this view it would not be the informationality of the new technology that inspires a meditation on language and spurs people on to the construction of new ideologies centered on it, but rather the structural parallels themselves between two equally material phenomena which equally elude physical representation of the older type.

Meanwhile, as religion has always been one of the principles by which modernity has tried to recognize itself and to specify its own difference, it may not be inappropriate to inquire about its status under the new postmodern dispensation, in which—just as its well-known lack of historicity has apparently generated any number of "returns to history"—religious revivals also seem endemic, without one's often caring to take them at face value. In Weber already, however, religion was the mark of difference, at the same time that some religions seemed to have more affinities with a modernism on the point of eradicating them than others, of a tenaciously conservative mindset and an incorrigibly traditionalist stamp. For these last, indeed, it can just as easily be said that the modernist campaigns of laicization and enlightenment reinforced and strengthened them, as that they achieved a life- and object-world in which such religious traditionalisms were ever more bereft of legitimation. Yet in the gentler atmosphere of an uncontested postmodernism, more effortlessly secular than any modernism could have wished, such religious traditionalisms seem to have melted away without a trace, like the authoritarian clericalism of an older Quebec under the paradigmatic Quiet Revolution, while the wildest and most unexpected forms of what is now sometimes called "fundamentalism" flourish, virtually at random and seemingly obedient to other climacterics and ecological laws.

It would be abusive or sentimental to account for such new "religious" formations by way of an appeal to some universal human appetite for the spiritual, in a situation in which spirituality virtually by definition no longer exists: the definition in question is in fact that of postmodernism itself. One of postmodernism's ultimate achievements is the utter eradication of all the forms of what used to be called idealism, in bourgeois or even in precapitalist societies. This means, of course, in passing, that it is fruitless to worry about materialism either, which came into the world as idealism's therapy and corrective, and which no longer finds anything much to do; nor is it worth taxing the postmodernisms with "materialism" in the other, North American, and consumerist sense, since no contrasting conduct is any longer imaginable in a fully commodified world. The problems, meanwhile, that an older Marxian concept of ideology has had to confront in recent years surely arise from its affinity with the various forms of idealism it was wont to denounce, which are themselves extinct. As far as the religious fundamentalisms are concerned, Marvin Harris has devoted part of an incongruously passionate indictment of postmodern times[46] to a denunciation of the emphasis of the new fundamentalisms on success of whatever type (life, liberty, or the pursuit of happiness—mostly financial), reminding us that no previous human religion on earth has ever valorized such things, let alone promised them. But the more "fundamental" question seems to me to be the one about tradition and the past, and how the new religions compensate their irreplaceable absence in the depthlessness of the new social order.

For I take it as axiomatic that what is now called fundamentalism is also a postmodern phenomenon, whatever it would like to think it thinks about a purer and more authentic past. The Iranian revolution, which became Islamic and clerical, was certainly launched against the Shah as an agent of modernization—in this, it was as anti-modern as it is postmodern in its insistence on all the basic features of a modern industrialized and bureaucratic state. But the paradox of Freudian repetition would seem to hold inversely for traditionalism as a postmodern (or even a modern) program—just as with the one you cannot really have any "first" time, with the other one you cannot imagine any restoration that can really be considered traditional or authentic. Modernist restorations seem to have produced a modernist form of tradition that was more accurately filed under the varieties of the different fascisms; the postmodern sorts all seem to have much in common with what the Left calls "new social movements"; indeed, they constitute various forms and varieties of those, and not all are reactionary—witness liberation theology.

What makes it as difficult to discuss "religion" in postmodern terms as to locate cognate experiential concepts such as the "aesthetic" or the "political" is the problematization of notions of belief in a postmodern social universe, and the theoretical challenge to such peculiarly self-confirming irrational doctrines in the conceptual area, where it is as though the "otherness" inherent in the doctrine of belief as such marked it out for eradication. Belief (along with classical ideology) was of course always redolent of a rhetoric of depth, and gave itself out as peculiarly resistant to persuasion or reasoning; its ontological position in the intellectual realm masked, I think, the weirder and more basic feature of this pseudo-concept which was always to have been attributed to other people (even as a believer, "I" myself never really believe enough, or so Pascal tells us).[47]

The very concept of belief is then the casualty of a period in which otherness as such—valorized difference resulting in an exceptionalism of the present, with its subalternities of the past and of other cultures—is critically grasped as a cornerstone of the modern and as its most deeply cherished superstition about itself. The clear conscience of the postmodern in this respect has not, of course, been paid for by any principled abdication of the technological and scientific infrastructure on which modernity's claim to difference was based; rather, it has been bought on credit and concealed by the representational transformation of that infrastructure in which the word processor replaces the assembly line in the collective mind's eye.

Still, the religious postmodernisms constitute a rolling-back of the dearly bought and deeply felt modernist sense of social and cultural difference fully as considerable as the social and cultural ones; if "gender," bourgeois distinction, and Western scientific reasoning are forms of difference which our First World forebears considered to be unique achievements, but which we have inherited with no little disgust and set about dismantling, so also a religious modernism offers the spectacle of a theological hermeneutic of great refinement, endowed with elaborate and supple casuistries, which can have no great appeal in an age that despises hermeneutics as such and has little need for casuistry.

For theological modernism seems to share with the other modernisms their constitutive sense of that radical otherness or difference of the past that constitutes us as modern people: the sense that everyone who went before us was therefore not modern, but was traditional, and in that sense radically different in their ways of thinking and behaving. All the old worlds die and become radically other from us at the moment of the birth of true modernity. The moderns thus, with their religion of the new, believed that they were somehow distinct from all the other human beings who ever lived in the past—and also from those nonmodern human beings still alive in the present, such as colonial peoples, backward cultures, non-Western societies, and "undeveloped" enclaves. (For the postmodern, then, the break stands or falls with some putative opening onto these forms of psychic, social, and cultural otherness, which raises the issue of a political Third Worldism in a new way, as it does the breakdown of the Western "canon," and the possibility of some new reception of other, global cultures.)

The hermeneutic task of theological modernism emerges from the desperate requirement to preserve or rewrite the meaning of an ancient precapitalist text within a situation of triumphant modernization, which threatens scripture along with all the other relics of an agrarian past in full-scale liquidation. Peasants at the time of the English Revolution had a life experience of the land and the seasons that was probably not very different from that of the characters of the Old Testament (or of the New Testament either); it is no wonder it was still possible for them to stage their revolution in biblical terms and to conceptualize it in theological categories. That possibility no longer exists for a nineteenth-century bourgeoisie within a life-world of factories and artificial streetlights, railroad trains and contracts, representative political institutions and telegraphs: what can stories about pastoral peoples dressed up in exotic costumes possibly mean for such modern Western men and women? A modernist hermeneutic then intervenes to save the day: the biblical narratives, including the gospel itself, are no longer to be taken literally—that way Hollywood lies! They are to be taken figuratively or allegorically and thereby stripped of their archaic or exotic content and translated into existential or ontological experiences, whose essentially abstract language and figuration (anxiety, guilt, redemption, the "question of being") can now, much like the "open works" of aesthetic modernism, be offered to a differentiated public of Western city-dwellers to be recoded in terms of their own private situations. The central hermeneutic difficulty is then clearly posed by the anthropomorphism of the narrative character of a historical Jesus; only intense philosophical effort is capable of turning this character into this or that christological abstraction. As for the commandments and the ethical doctrine, casuistry has long since settled the matter; they also need no longer be taken literally, and confronted with properly modern forms of injustice, bureaucratic warfare, systemic or economic inequality, and so forth, modern theologians and churchmen can work up persuasive accommodations to the constraints of complex modern societies, and provide excellent reasons for bombing civilian populations or executing criminals which do not disqualify the executors from Christian status.

This, then, is the modernist situation in which someone like the North American "fundamentalist" theologian John Howard Yoder[48] can be considered not merely anti-modern but also postmodern, by virtue of his affirmation of the literal claim on us today, in a fully modernized society, of the teachings of Jesus as elaborated in Scripture, specifically including the reaffirmation of the Sixth Commandment. In a situation in which such doctrinal reaffirmation is not residual (as in the traditional ideology of social groups on the point of dissolution and rationalization, in the Weberian sense), but rather appears within the postmodern environment of completed modernization and rationalization, it may be considered (without any disrespect) to have a simulated relationship to the past rather than a commemorative one, and to share characteristics of other such postmodern historical simulations. In our own context here, the striking feature of such simulation is in effect the denial of any fundamental social or cultural difference between postmodern subjects of late capitalism and the Middle-Eastern subjects of the early Roman Empire: such fundamentalism thus absolutely refuses what

Latour calls the Great Divide, particularly insofar as belief in that distinction authorized and legitimated modernity in the first place, as an experience as well as an ideology.

The example of Yoder, a Mennonite pacifist whose arguments were marshalled in opposition to the Vietnam war, can also serve as a timely reminder that the qualification of "postmodernity" does not automatically carry with it any readymade value judgment: I will assume, indeed, that for any number of readers this particular expression of postmodern fundamentalism will (like liberation theology, in contemporary Roman Catholicism) be taken much more positively than politically more reactionary expressions of the same historical phenomenon, whether in the evangelicals or the "Islamic revolution" in Iran. Both these last are, however, small-group movements in an authentically postmodern sense;[49]indeed, the Iranian case poses the very interesting problem of how far a postmodern politics (including the most modern forms of media, such as the cassettes of the Ayatollah's speeches that were smuggled into the Shah's Iran) is consistent with the totalizing and modernist seizure of state power. The deeper theoretical problem raised by these forms of postmodern religion lies, however, in their distribution across the new world system to which the postmodern corresponds: there was never any problem of understanding how a modernism could come into being on the basis of a fundamental hostility towards and repudiation of modernization as such. Here, however, in a contemporary Third World within the postmodern system, one is tempted to adapt Jencks's formula and to speak of some "late anti-modernism," even though it was presumably the extension and fulfillment of the modernizing process that made the Iranian revolution (and also the CIA-organized antirevolutionary evangelical movements in Latin America) possible in the first place.

X. The Production of Theoretical Discourse

Throughout these pages I have insisted on a characterization of postmodern thought—for it turns out to be this that we used to call "theory" in the heroic discovery period of poststructuralism—in terms of the expressive peculiarities of its language rather than as mutations in thinking or consciousness as such (and, ineffable or linguistic by turns, it would finally have to be dramatized by some larger social-stylistic characterization of the type of the culture critique). An aesthetics of this new "theoretical discourse" would probably include the following features: it must not emit propositions, and it must not have the appearance of making primary statements or of having positive (or "affirmative") content. This reflects the widespread feeling that inasmuch as everything we utter is a moment in a larger chain or context, all statements that seem to be primary are in fact only links in some larger "text." (We think we're walking firmly on solid ground, but the planet is spinning in outer space.) This feeling also entails another one, which is perhaps only a temporal version of the preceding intuition; namely, that we can never go far enough back to make primary statements, that there are no conceptual (but only representational) beginnings, and that the doctrine of presuppositions or foundations is somehow intolerable as a testimony to the inadequacies of the human mind (which needs to be grounded on something, which in its turn proves to be nothing but fiction, religious belief, or, most intolerable of all, some philosophy of "as if"). Any number of other themes can be mobilized to enrich or inflect this one, such as the idea of nature and the natural as some ultimate content or referent, whose historical obliteration in a postnatural "human age" then centrally characterizes the postmodern as such. But the crucial feature of what we have called a theoretical aesthetic lies in its organization around this particular taboo, which excludes the philosophical proposition as such, and thereby statements about being as well as judgments of truth. The much-decried poststructural swerve away from truth judgments and categories—comprehensible enough as a social reaction to a world already overpopulated with such things—is thus a second-degree effect of a more primary requirement of language, which is no longer to frame utterances in such a way that those categories might be appropriate.

This is clearly a demanding aesthetic indeed, one in which the theorist walks a tightrope, the slightest lapse precipitating the sentences in question into the old-fashioned (system, ontology, metaphysics) or sheer opinion. What one then uses language for becomes an issue of life and death, particularly since the option of silence—a high-modernist one—is also excluded. My sense is that everyday garden-variety theoretical discourse pursues a task finally not very different from that of common-language philosophy (although it certainly does not look much like that!), namely, the exclusion of error by way of the vigilant tracking of ideological illusions (as those are vehiculated in language itself). Language can, in other words, no longer be true; but it can certainly be false; and the mission of theoretical discourse thus becomes a kind of search-and-destroy operation in which linguistic misconceptions are remorselessly identified and stigmatized, in the hopes that a theoretical discourse negative and critical enough will not itself become the target of such linguistic demystification in its turn. The hope is, of course, vain, insofar as, like it or not, every negative statement, every purely critical operation, can nonetheless generate the ideological illusion or mirage of a position, a system, a set of positive values in its own right.

This illusion is ultimately the object of the theoretical critique (which thus becomes a *bellum omnium contra omnes*), but the latter can equally well—and perhaps somewhat more productively—mount a vigilant guard over the structural incompleteness of the sentence itself, for which saying anything at all means leaving something else out. A permanent revolution can also be staged around those omissions; and the nature of the theoretical debates since the 1960s shows that the implacability of the older Marxian ideological quarrels was itself only a foreshadowing and a crude figure for the universalization of at least this specific conception of "ideology critique" that turns on the misleading connotation of terms, the imbalance of the presentation, and the metaphysical implications of the act of expression itself.

All of which clearly tends to reduce linguistic expression generally to a function of commentary, that is, of a permanently second-degree relationship to sentences that have already been formed. Commentary indeed makes up the special field of postmodern linguistic practice generally, and its originality, at least with respect to the pretensions and illusions of philosophy in the preceding period, of "bourgeois" philosophy, that with some secular pride and confidence set out to say what things really were after the long night of superstition and the sacred. Commentary, however, also—in that curious play of historical identity and difference mentioned above—now secures the kinship of the postmodern (at least in this respect) with other, hitherto more archaic, periods of thought and intellectual labor, as with the medieval copyists and scribes or the endless exegesis of the great Oriental philosophies and sacred texts.

But in this desperately repetitive situation (which is to philosophical thought what the return to the formulaic is to the ambitions of great bourgeois modern narrative), in which the essential is absent—the sacred text that might lend a certain motivation to this life sentence to the commentary form—a linguistic solution nonetheless remains, and it turns on what has hitherto been called transcoding. For alongside the perspective in which my language comments on that of another, there is a somewhat longer vista in which both languages derive from larger families that used to be called weltanschauungen, or worldviews, but which have today become recognized as "codes." Where I used to "believe" in a certain vision of the world, political philosophy, philosophical system, or religion as such, today I speak a specific idiolect or ideological code—the badge of group adherence, viewed from a different and more sociological perspective—which presents many of the features of an officially "foreign" language (I have to learn to speak it, for example; I can say some things more strongly in one foreign language than in another, and vice versa; there is no Ur- or ideal language of which the imperfect earthly ones, in their multiplicity, are so many refractions; syntax is more important than vocabulary, but most people think it is the other way round; my awareness of linguistic dynamics is the result of a new global system or a certain demographic "pluralism").

Under these circumstances, several new kinds of operations are possible. I can *transcode*; that is to say, I can set about measuring what is sayable and "thinkable" in each of these codes or idiolects and compare that to the conceptual possibilities of its competitors: this is, in my opinion, the most productive and responsible activity for students and theoretical or philosophical critics to pursue today, but it has the drawback of being retrospective and even potentially traditionalist or nostalgic, insofar as the proliferation of new codes is an endless process that at best cannibalizes the preceding ones and at worst consigns them to the historical dustheap.

There thereby emerges a somewhat different possibility, which has its kinship with this one: namely, what I will call the production of theoretical discourse par excellence, the activity of generating new codes, it being understood that in a situation in which new ways of thinking and new philosophical systems are by definition excluded, this activity is utterly nontraditional and demands the invention of new skills altogether.

New theoretical discourse is produced by the setting into active equivalence of two preexisting codes, which thereby, in a kind of molecular ion exchange, become a new one. What must be understood is that the new code (or metacode) can in no way be considered a synthesis between the previous pair: it is not here a question of the kinds of operations that went into the construction of classical philosophical systems. The older attempt at a Freudo-Marxism can indeed give a certain idea of the difficulties of yoking two thought systems together; these are difficulties that fall away, and reveal a strange new conceptual landscape, when it is rather a question of linking two sets of terms in such a way that each can express and indeed *interpret* the other (in the strong sense of Peirce's interpretant). This is, no doubt, in its conditions of possibility, related to the channel-switching characterized above, and dependent in much the same way on the mutual parceling out and colonization of "reality" by various language zones and codes; only here a more active consequence is drawn than in culture as such, and the relationship between two channels, so to speak, becomes a solution rather than a problem, being maximized into an instrument in its own right. Hegemony here means the possibility of recoding vast quantities of preexisting discourse (in other languages) into the new code; meanwhile, the two codes thus identified may be seen to have something of a base and superstructure relationship, not by way of any kind of ontological priority that one is assigned over the other (rather, the new structure serves to absorb and defuse the otherwise inevitable and "natural" questions of this kind about priority) but more particularly owing to the cultural or semiotic overtones of one of the codes as opposed to the other.

Thus, in what is virtually the paradigm gesture of the new production process, Jean Baudrillard links the formula for exchange and use value (rewritten as a fraction) with the fraction for the sign itself (signifier and signified), thereby inaugurating a semiotic chain reaction whose fallout seems to have continued to the present. His own act of equivalence was no doubt modeled on the genial intuition of the great predecessors in the launching of "structuralism" itself, most notably Lacan, whose identification of the semiotic fraction with the "fraction" produced by the bar separating conscious from unconscious is well known and even more influential. More recently, Bruno Latour has combined a semiotic code with a map of social and power relations to "transcode" the scientific fact and the scientific discovery itself. Nothing, indeed, prevents the enlargement of the chain of equations to further codes. Nor are these isolated examples, as we have seen above in the theoretical chapters. Instead, they are the most visible and dramatic, owing to the naked deployment of the semiotic code itself, last and most visible of the secular postmodern idiolects.

That specific ideological effects can be derived from the new mechanism is something I have tried to show above in the example of the popular current identification between the "market" and the "media." But any theory of the production of theoretical discourse (to which the present remarks are only prolegomena and notes) will need to develop further in two distinct directions. One involves the reordering of the semiotic equation—the transcoding of the two distinct conceptual terminologies, their projection onto an axis of equivalence (to use the Jakobsonian model of Laclau and Mouffe, who can in this respect be read as offering an exemplary formal description of the production of theoretical discourse)—into a hierarchical relationship or strong fraction (of the Lacanian type) which sorts itself out into something like our old friends base and superstructure, with this difference that in theoretical discourse it is always the superstructure that is determinate. That superstructure is also always itself in one way or another communicational or mediatic. The sparks struck by the "theoretical" setting of two codes in equivalence with each other always require one code to have its deeper affinities with the media itself (something I will illustrate more concretely in my concluding discussion of cognitive mapping, which can in this respect be grasped as a kind of reflexive form of "theoretical discourse").

The other proposition that demands exploration is the generation, from out of the transcoding process, of strange new ambivalent abstractions, which look like traditional philosophical universals but are in reality as specific or particular as the paper they are printed on, and tend to turn ceaselessly into each other (that is to say, into their own logical opposites). We have already confronted several such pairs of abstractions: in Identity and Difference themselves, but also in the peculiar postmodern or late capitalist indistinction between uniformity or standardization and differentiation, or between separation and unification (which in this particular mode of production turn out to be the same thing). For the most part, however, specific ideological mirages are produced, as it were, in spite of the apparatus rather than because of it. In the desperate flight from everything ontological or foundational about the old philosophical "system," a kind of antisubstantialist doctrine about sheer process is invoked, and a momentum develops—thought as operation rather than as conceptualization—that nonetheless yields the old illusion of system and ontology in the pauses between the operations and the reified appearance of discourse served up on the page. Reification, indeed, not to mention commodification, would offer another "code" in which to characterize the same general fate or destiny of theoretical discourse, as it finds itself thematized and transformed into someone's personal philosophy or system.

In reality, however, the process of ideological delegitimation is most often secured in a rather different way from this ceaseless discursive warfare that if anything perpetuates the rights of all the players. As with any other economy or logic, to the mechanisms that drive the process forward must be added mechanisms that prevent it from slackening or lapsing back into habits or procedures of the past. Transcoding and the production of theoretical discourse are a flight forward, as the French say, and their momentum is maintained by what burns all the bridges and makes retreat impossible, namely, the growing old of the codes, the planned obsolescence of all the older conceptual machinery. A remarkable observation by Richard Rorty, whose modest Socratic dryness wants to confuse us into taking it for common sense, will serve for this particular point of new departure. He is talking about the "originality" of Derrida (for whom we may, however, substitute any distinctive form of postmodern thought); the paradox lies in the difficulty of distinguishing what made up the new and the original, the innovative, in the modern system from a postmodern dispensation in which "originality" has become a suspect concept, but where many of the basic postmodern features—self-consciousness, antihumanism, decentering, reflexivity, textualization—look suspiciously indistinguishable from the old modern ones. "What's the difference?"—a deManian question to which Rorty now responds: "It is a mistake to think that Derrida, or anybody else, 'recognized' problems about the nature of textuality or writing which had been ignored by the tradition. What he did was to think up ways of speaking which made old ways of speaking optional, and thus more or less dubious."[50]

This can now be grasped as virtually the constitutive feature in what Stuart Hall calls the "discursive struggle" over the delegitimation of opposing ideologies (or "discourses"): worse than incorrect, immoral, evil, or dangerous, is the apprehension that a particular code is simply one code among others, and an "older" one that has thereby and virtually by definition become "optional." The strategy can be seen in addition to mobilize those fears about consensus described above. Indeed, if a code attempts to assert its nonoptionality—that is to say, its privileged authority as an articulation of something like a truth—it will be seen not merely as usurpatory and repressive but (since codes are now identified with groups, as the badge of their adherence and the content of their expression) as the illicit attempt of one group to lord it over all the others. But if, in the spirit of pluralism, it makes its autocritique and humbly admits its mere "optionality," the media excitement falls away, everyone loses interest, and the code in question, tail between its legs, can shortly be observed making for the exit from the public sphere or stage of that particular moment of History or discursive struggle.

In this particular case, the riddle—if everybody loses, who wins?

—can be clarified, if not solved, by the proposition that in fact, ideologies in the sense of codes and discursive systems are no longer particularly determinant. As with so much else, it is an old 1950s acquaintance, "the end of ideology," which has in the postmodern returned with a new and unexpected kind of plausibility. But ideology is now over, not because class struggle has ended and no one has anything class-ideological to fight about, but rather because the fate of "ideology" in this particular sense can be understood to mean that conscious ideologies and political opinions, particular thought systems along with the official philosophical ones which laid claim to a greater universality —the whole realm of consciousness, argument, and the very appearance of persuasion itself (or of reasoned dissent)—has ceased to be functional in perpetuating and reproducing the system. That classical ideology once did so, in the earlier stages of capitalism, can be measured by the significance of the intellectuals themselves—professors and journalists, ideologues of all kinds—who were assigned a strategic role in inventing forms of legitimation and legitimacy for the status quo and its tendencies. Then, ideology was something a little more significant than mere discourse, and ideas, although they determined nothing in the mode of the various idealistic theories of history, still furnished the principle "forms in which people became conscious of class conflict and fought it out" (Marx). Why this should have been so fundamentally modified, and the role of intellectuals so diminished in our own time, may have several explanations, all of which finally amount to the same thing. One may, on the one hand, impute a certain enfeeblement of the individual concepts and messages, information and discourses, to a density hitherto unimaginable; on the other hand, one may also wonder, with Adorno, whether "in our time the commodity has not become its own ideology"—that is to say, whether practices have not replaced ratiocination (or rationalization), and in particular whether the practice of consumption has not replaced the resolute taking of a stand and the full-throated endorsement of a political opinion. Here too, then, the media meets the market and joins hands upon the body of an older kind of intellectual culture.

It would be a waste of time to deplore it, but autopsies are the place in which new lessons about anatomy are learned. In the present instance, the ideological or discursive strategy Rorty laid his finger on may be grasped as an unexpected extension of Marx's fundamental figure for social development and dynamics (a figure that runs through the *Grundrisse*, connecting the 1844 manuscripts in an unbroken line to

Capital itself): that is the fundamental notion of *separation* (as when Marx describes the production of the proletariat in terms of their separation from the means of production—i.e., enclosure, the exclusion of the peasants from their land). There has not yet, I think, been a Marxism based on this particular figure,[51] although it is a cognate of other figures such as alienation, reification, and commodification, which have all given rise to specific ideological tendencies (not to say schools) within Marxism itself. But the logic of separation may have become even more relevant for our own period, and for the diagnosis of postmodernism, in which psychic fragmentation and the resistance to totalities, interrelation by way of difference and the schizophrenic present, and above all the systematic delegitimation described here, all in one way or another exemplify the proteiform nature and effects of this particular disjunctive process.

XI. How to Map a Totality

So at length we return to the matter of totality itself (which we have presumably already learned to distinguish from "totalization" as an operation), a topic that will also afford me the private satisfaction of showing how the analysis of postmodernism is not alien to my earlier work but rather a logical consequence of it,[52] something I want to rehearse again myself in terms of the notion of a "mode of production," to which my analysis of postmodernism claims to make a contribution. It is first worth observing, however, that my version of all this—which obviously (but perhaps I haven't said so often enough) owes a great debt to Baudrillard, as well as to the theorists to whom he is himself indebted (Marcuse, McLuhan, Henri Lefebvre, the situationists, Sahlins, etc., etc.)—took form in a relatively complicated conjuncture. It was not only the experience of new kinds of artistic production (particularly in the architectural area) that roused me from the canonical "dogmatic slumbers": I will want to make the point later on that as I use it, "postmodernism" is not an exclusively aesthetic or stylistic term. The conjuncture also offered the occasion for resolving a long-standing malaise with traditional economic schemas in the Marxist tradition, a discomfort felt by a certain number of us not in the area of social class, whose "disappearance" only true "free-floating intellectuals" could be capable of entertaining, but in the area of the media, whose shock-wave impact on Western Europe enabled the observer to take a little critical and perceptual distance from the gradual and seemingly natural mediatization of North American society in the 1960s. Lenin on imperialism did not quite seem to equal Lenin and the media; and it gradually seemed possible to take his lesson in a different way. For he set the example of identifying a new stage of capitalism that was not explicitly foreseen in Marx: the so-called monopoly stage, or the moment of classical imperialism. That could lead you to believe either that the new mutation had been named and formulated once and for all, or that one might be authorized to invent yet another one under certain circumstances. But Marxists were all the more unwilling to draw this second antithetical conclusion because in the meantime the new mediatic and informational social phenomena had been colonized (in our absence) by the Right, in a series of influential studies in which the first tentative Cold War notion of an "end of ideology" finally gave birth to the full-blown concept of a "postindustrial society" itself. Mandel's book *Late Capitalism* changed all that, and for the first time theorized a third stage of capitalism from a usably Marxian perspective. This is what made my own thoughts on "postmodernism" possible, and they are therefore to be understood as an attempt to theorize the specific logic of the cultural production of that third stage, and not as yet another disembodied culture critique or diagnosis of the spirit of the age.

It has not escaped anyone's attention that my approach to postmodernism is a "totalizing" one. The interesting question today is then not why I adopt this perspective, but why so many people are scandalized (or have learned to be scandalized) by it. In the old days, abstraction was surely one of the strategic ways in which phenomena, particularly historical phenomena, could be estranged and defamiliarized. When one is immersed in the immediate — the year-by-year experience of cultural and informational messages, of successive events, of urgent priorities — the abrupt distance afforded by an abstract concept, a more global characterization of the secret affinities between those apparently autonomous and unrelated domains, and of the rhythms and hidden sequences of things we normally remember only in isolation and one by one, is a unique resource, particularly since the history of the preceding few years is always what is least accessible to us. Historical reconstruction, then, the positing of global characterizations and hypotheses, the abstraction from the "blooming, buzzing confusion" of immediacy, was always a radical intervention in the here and now and the promise of resistance to its blind fatalities.

But one must acknowledge the representational problem, if only to separate it out from the other motives at work in the "war on totality." If historical abstraction—the notions of a mode of production, or of capitalism, fully as much as of postmodernism—is something not given in immediate experience, then it is pertinent to worry about the potential confusion of this concept with the thing itself, and about the possibility of taking its abstract "representation" for reality, of "believing" in the substantive existence of abstract entities such as Society or Class. Never mind that worrying about other people's errors, generally turns out to mean worrying about the errors of other intellectuals. In the long run there is probably no way of marking a representation so securely *as* representation that such optical illusions are permanently forestalled, any more than there is any way to ensure the resistance of a materialistic thought to idealistic recuperations or to ward off the reading of a deconstructive formulation in metaphysical terms. Permanent revolution in intellectual life and culture means both that impossibility and the necessity for a constant reinvention of precautions against what my tradition calls conceptual reification. The extraordinary fortunes of the concept of postmodernism are surely a case in point here, calculated to inspire those of us responsible for it with some misgivings. But what is needed is not the drawing of the line and the confession of excess ("dizzy with success," as Stalin once famously put it) but rather the renewal of historical analysis itself, and the tireless reexamination and diagnosis of the political and ideological functionality of the concept—the part it has suddenly come to play today in our imaginary resolutions of our real contradictions.

The deeper political motivation of the "war on totality" lies elsewhere, however, in a fear of Utopia that turns out to be none other than our old friend 1984, such that a Utopian and revolutionary politics, correctly associated with totalization and a certain "concept" of totality, is to be eschewed because it leads fatally to the Terror: a notion at least as old as Edmund Burke, but helpfully revived, after innumerable restatements during the Stalin period, by the Cambodian atrocities. Ideologically, this particular revival of Cold War rhetoric and stereotypes, launched in the de-Marxification of France in the 1970s, turns on a bizarre identification of Stalin's gulags with Hitler's extermination camps, (but see Arno Mayer's remarkable *Why Did the Heavens Not Darken?* for a definitive demonstration of the constitutive relationship between the "final solution" and Hitler's anticommunism[53]); what can be "postmodern" about these hoary nightmare images, except for the depolitization to which they invite us, is less clear. The history of the revolutionary convulsions in question can also be appealed to for a very different lesson; namely, that violence springs from counterrevolution first and foremost, indeed, that the most effective form of counterrevolution lies precisely in this transmission of violence to the revolutionary process itself. I doubt if the current state of alliance or micropolitics in the advanced countries supports such anxieties and fantasies; they would not, for me at least, constitute grounds for withdrawing support and solidarity from a potential revolution in South Africa, say. Finally, this general feeling that the revolutionary, Utopian, or totalizing impulse is somehow tainted from the outset and doomed to bloodshed by the very structure of its thoughts does strike one as idealistic, if not finally a replay of doctrines of original sin in their worst religious sense.

But the question of totalizing thought can also be staged in a different way, interrogating it not for its truth content or validity but rather for its historical conditions of possibility. This is then no longer to philosophize exactly, or, if you prefer, to philosophize on a *symptomal* level, in which we step back and estrange our immediate judgments on a given concept ("the most advanced postmodern thought teaches us not to deploy concepts of totality or periodization") by way of asking the question about the social determinants that enable or shut down thought. Does the current taboo or totality simply result from philosophical progress and increased self-consciousness? Is it because we have today attained a state of theoretical enlightenment and conceptual sophistication that permit us to avoid the grosser errors and blunders of the old-fashioned thinkers of the past (most notably Hegel)? That may be so, but it ignores Rorty's lesson and would also require some kind of historical justification in its own right (in which the invention of "materialism" would presumably intervene). This hubris of the present and of the living can be avoided by posing the issue in a somewhat different way: namely, why it is that "concepts of totality" have seemed necessary and unavoidable at certain historical moments and, on the contrary, noxious and unthinkable at others. This is an inquiry which, working its way back on the outside of our own thought and on the basis of what we can no longer (or not yet) think, cannot be philosophical in any positive sense (although Adorno attempted, in *Negative Dialectics*, to turn it into a genuine philosophy of a new kind); it would certainly lead us to the intensified sense that ours is a time of nominalism in a variety of senses (from culture to philosophical thought). Such nominalism would probably turn out to have several prehistories or overdeterminations: the moment of existentialism, for instance, in which some new social sense of isolated individuals (and of the horror of demography, as we have seen, particularly in Sartre) causes the older traditional "universals" to pale and lose their conceptual force and persuasiveness; the age-old tradition of Anglo-American empiricism as well, which emerges from this death of the concept with renewed force in a paradoxically "theoretical" and hyperintellectual age. There is, of course, a sense in which the slogan "postmodernism" means all this, too; but then in that case it is not the explanation but what remains to be explained.

Speculation and hypothetical analysis of this kind that bears on the weakening of general or universalizing concepts in the present is the correlative of an operation that can often look more reliable, namely, the analysis of moments in the past when such conceptuality seemed possible; indeed, those moments in which the emergence of general concepts can be observed have often seemed to be privileged ones. As far as the concept of totality is concerned, I am tempted to say about it what I once said about Althusser's notion of structure; namely, that the crucial point to be made is this: we can acknowledge the presence of such a concept, provided we understand that there is only one of them — something otherwise often known as a "mode of production." Althusserian "structure" is that, and so is "totality," at least as I use it. As for "totalizing" processes, that often means little more than the making of connections between various phenomena, a process which, as I suggested above, tends to be ever more spatial.

We must be grateful to Ronald L. Meek for writing the prehistory of the concept of a "mode of production" (as that will later be worked out in the writings of Morgan and Marx), which in the eighteenth century took the form of what Meek calls the "four stages theory." This theory came together in France and the Scottish Enlightenment, as the proposition that human cultures historically vary with their material or productive basis, which knows four essential transformations: hunting and gathering, pastoralism, agriculture, and commerce. What will then happen to this historical narrative, above all in the thought and work of Adam Smith, is that having now produced that object of study which is the specifically contemporary mode of production, or capitalism, the historical scaffolding of the precapitalist stages tends to fall away and lend both Smith's and Marx's models of capitalism a synchronic appearance. But Meek wants to argue[54] that the historical narrative was essential to the very possibility of thinking capitalism as a system, synchronic or not; and something like that will remain my own position with respect to that "stage" or moment of capitalism some of us now seem to be calling "postmodernism."

I am here, however, essentially concerned with the conditions of possibility of the concept of a "mode of production," that is to say, the characteristics of the historical and social situation which make it possible to articulate and formulate the concept of "totality" in the first place. I will suggest, in a general way, that thinking this particular new thought (or combining older thoughts in this new way) presupposes a particular kind of "uneven" development, such that distinct and coexisting modes of production are registered together in the life world of the thinker in question. Meek describes the preconditions for the production of this particular concept (in its original forms as a "four stages theory") as follows:

> My own feeling is that thinking of the type we are considering, which lays primary emphasis on the development of economic techniques and socio-economic relationships, is likely to be a function, first, of the rapidity of contemporary economic advance, and, second, of the facility with which a contrast can be observed between areas which are economically advancing and areas which are still in "lower" stages of development. In the 1750s and 60s, in cities like Glasgow and in areas such as the more advanced provinces in the north of France, the whole social life of the communities concerned was being rapidly and visibly transformed, and it was fairly obvious that this was happening as a result of profound changes taking place in economic techniques and basic socio-economic relationships. And the new forms of economic organisation which were emerging could be fairly easily compared and contrasted with the older forms of organisation which still existed, say, in the Scottish Highlands, or in the remainder of France—or among the Indian tribes in America. If changes in the mode of subexistence were playing such an important and "progressive" role in the development of contemporary society, it seemed a fair bet that they must also have done so in that of past society.[55]

This possibility of thinking the concept of a mode of production for the first time is sometimes loosely described as one of the newly emergent forms of historical consciousness, or historicity. It is not necessary, however, to have recourse to the philosophical discourse of consciousness as such, since what are being described might equally well be termed new discursive paradigms, and this more contemporary way of talking about conceptual emergence is reinforced, for literary readers, by the presence alongside this one of yet another new historical paradigm in the novels of Sir Walter Scott (as Lukács interprets them in *The Histori-*

cal Novel). The unevenness that allowed French thinkers (Turgot, but also Rousseau himself!) to conceptualize a "mode of production" probably had as much as anything else to do with the prerevolutionary situation in the France of that period in which feudal forms stood out ever more starkly in their distinctive difference against a whole, newly emergent bourgeois culture and class consciousness. Scotland is in many ways a more complex and interesting case, for, last of the emergent First World countries, or first of the Third World ones (to use Tom Nairn's provocative idea in The Break-up of Britain), Enlightenment Scotland was above all the space of a coexistence of radically distinct zones of production and culture: the archaic economy of the Highlanders and their clan system, the commercial vigor of the English "partner" over the border, on the eve of its industrial "takeoff." The brillance of Edinburgh was therefore not a matter of Gaelic genetic material but rather owing to the strategic yet ec-centric position of the Scottish metropolis and intellectuals with respect to this virtually synchronic coexistence of distinct modes of production, which it was uniquely the task of the Scottish Enlightenment to "think," or to conceptualize. Nor is this merely an economic matter. Scott, like Faulkner later on, inherited a social and historical raw material, a popular memory, in which the fiercest revolutions and civil and religious wars inscribed the coexistence of modes of production in vivid narrative form. The conditions of thinking a new reality and articulating a new paradigm for it therefore seem to demand a peculiar conjuncture and a certain strategic distance from that new reality, which tends to overwhelm those immersed in it (this would be something like an epistemological variant of the well-known "outsider" principle in scientific discovery).

All of which, however, has another secondary consequence of greater significance to us here that bears on the gradual repression of such conceptuality. If postmodernism, as an enlarged third stage of classical capitalism, is a purer and more homogeneous expression of classical capitalism, from which many of the hitherto surviving enclaves of socioeconomic difference have been effaced (by way of their colonization and absorption by the commodity form), then it makes sense to suggest that the waning of our sense of history, and more particularly our resistance to globalizing or totalizing concepts like that of the mode of production itself, are a function of precisely that universalization of capitalism. Where everything is henceforth systemic the very notion of a system seems to lose its reason for being, returning only by way of a "return of the repressed" in the more nightmarish forms of the "total system" fantasized by Weber or Foucault or the 1984 people.

But a mode of production is not a "total system" in that forbidding sense; it includes a variety of counterforces and new tendencies within itself, of "residual" as well as "emergent" forces, which it must attempt to manage or control (Gramsci's conception of hegemony). Were those heterogeneous forces not endowed with an effectivity of their own, the hegemonic project would be unnecessary. Thus, differences are presupposed by the model, something that would be sharply distinguished from another feature which complicates this one, namely, that capitalism also produces differences or differentiation as a function of its own internal logic. Finally, to recall our initial discussion of representation, it is clear that there is a *difference* between the concept and the thing, between this global and abstract model and our own individual social experience, from which it is meant to afford some explanatory distance but which it is scarcely designed to "replace."

A number of other reminders about the "proper use" of the mode of production model are also advisable: that what is called a "mode of production" is not a productionist model it always seems worth saying. What also seems worth saying is that it involves a variety of levels (or orders of abstraction) that must be respected if discussions about it are not to degenerate into random shouting matches. I proposed a very general picture of such levels in *The Political Unconscious*, and in particular the distinctions that have to be respected between an examination of historical events, an evocation of larger class and ideological conflicts and traditions, and an attention to impersonal socioeconomic patterning systems (of which the well-known thematics of reification and commodification are examples). The question of agency, which arises often in these pages, has to be mapped across these levels.

Featherstone,[56] for example, thinks that "postmodernism" is on my use a specifically cultural category. It is not, and for better and for worse it is designed to name a "mode of production" in which cultural production finds a specific functional place and whose symptomatology is in my work mainly drawn from culture (this is no doubt the source of the confusion). Featherstone therefore advises me to pay closer attention to the artists themselves and to their publics, as well as to the institutions which mediate and govern this newer kind of production. (Nor can I see why any of these topics should be excluded; they are very interesting matters indeed.) But it is hard to see how sociological inquiry at that level would become *explanatory*: rather, the phenomena he is concerned with tend at once to reform into their own semiautonomous sociological level, one which then requires a diachronic narrative. To say what the art market and the status of the artist or the consumer are now means saying what they were before this transformation, and even at some outside limit leaving a space open for some alternate configuration of such activities (as is the case, for example, in Cuba, where the art market, galleries, investments in painting, etc., do not exist).[57] Once you have written up that narrative, that series of local changes, then the whole thing gets added into the dossier as yet another space in which something like the postmodern "great transformation" can be read.

Indeed, although concrete social agents seem to make their appearance with Featherstone's proposals (postmodernists are then those artists or musicians, those gallery or museum officials or record company executives, those specific bourgeois or youth or working-class consumers), here too the requirement of differentiating levels of abstraction must be maintained. For one can also plausibly assert that "postmodernism" in the more limited sense of an ethos and a "life-style" (truly a contemptible expression, that) is the expression of the "consciousness" of a whole new class fraction that largely transcends the limits of the groups enumerated above. This larger and more abstract category has variously been labeled as a new petit bourgeoisie, a professional-managerial class, or more succinctly as "the yuppies" (each of these expressions smuggling in a little surplus of concrete social representation along with itself).[58]

This identification of the class content of postmodern culture does not at all imply that yuppies have become something like a new ruling class, merely that their cultural practices and values, their local ideologies, have articulated a useful dominant ideological and cultural paradigm for this stage of capital. It is indeed often the case that cultural forms prevalent in a particular period are not furnished by the principal agents of the social formation in question (businessmen who no doubt have something better to do with their time or are driven by psychological and ideological motive forces of a different type). What is essential is that the culture ideology in question articulate the world in the most useful way functionally, or in ways that can be functionally reappropriated. Why a certain class fraction should provide these ideological articulations is a historical question as intriguing as the question of the sudden dominance of a particular writer or a particular style. There can surely be no model or formula given in advance for these historical transactions; just as surely, however, we have not yet worked this out for what we now call postmodernism.

Meanwhile, another limitation of my own work on the subject (as formulated in the opening chapter of this book) now becomes clear; namely, that the tactical decision to stage the account in cultural terms has made for a relative absence of any identification of properly postmodern "ideologies," something I have tried partially to rectify in the subsequent chapter on the ideology of the market. But since I have been particularly interested in the formal matter of the new "theoretical discourse," and also because the paradoxical combination of global decentralization and small-group institutionalization has come to seem an important feature of the postmodern tendential structure, I have mainly singled out intellectual and social phenomena like "poststructuralism" and the "new social movements," thus giving the impression, against my own deepest political convictions, that all the "enemies" were on the left.

But what has been said about the class origins of postmodernism has as its consequence the requirement that we now specify another higher (or more abstract and global) kind of agency than any so far enumerated. This is, of course, multinational capital itself: it may as a process be described as some "nonhuman" logic of capital, and I would continue to defend the appropriateness of that language and that kind of description, in its own terms and on its own level. That this seemingly disembodied force is also an ensemble of human agents trained in specific ways and inventing original local tactics and practices according to the creativities of human freedom is also obvious, from a different perspective, to which one would only wish to add that for the agents of capital the old dictum holds: "people make their history, but not in circumstances of their own choosing." It is within the possibilities of late capitalism that people glimpse "the main chance," "go for it," make money, and reorganize firms in new ways (just like artists or generals, ideologists or gallery owners).

What I have tried to show here is that although my account of the postmodern may seem in the eyes of some of its readers and critics to "lack agency," it can be translated or transcoded into a narrative account in which agents of all sizes and dimensions are at work. The choice between these alternate descriptions—focalizations on distinct levels of abstraction—is a practical rather than a theoretical one. (It would, however, be desirable to link up this account of agency with that other very rich (psychoanalytic) tradition of psychic and ideological "subject positions.") If the objection arises that the descriptions of agency described above are merely alternative versions of the base-superstructure model—an economic base for postmodernism on the one account, a social or class base on this other—then so be it, provided we understand that "base and superstructure" is not really a model of anything, but rather a starting point and a problem, an imperative to make connections, something as undogmatic as a heuristic recommendation simultaneously to grasp culture (and theory) in and for itself, but also in relationship to its outside, its content, its context, and its space of intervention and effectivity. How one does that, however, is never given in advance, and while the descriptions and the analyses in this book seek to characterize and measure the space of ideological and theoretical struggle, I can imagine a whole range of very different practical conclusions and political recommendations being drawn from them.

Even as far as a cultural politics is concerned, at least two different kinds of strategy seem conceivable. The more properly postmodern political aesthetic—which would confront the structure of image society as such head-on and undermine it from within (in the postmodern, paradoxically, offensive has become at one with subversion, and, as with Proust's two ways, Gramsci's war of maneuver has turned out to be the same as his war of position after all)—might be termed the *homeopathic* strategy, most dramatically and paradigmatically exemplified in our time by Hans Haacke's installations, which turn institutional space inside out by drawing the museum in which they are technically contained into themselves, as part of their thematics and subject matter: invisible spiders, whose net contains their own containers and turns the private property of social space inside out like a glove. Formally, however, as was suggested earlier, Haacke, along with many other contemporary artists of whom the photographers and the videomakers seem the most political and the most innovative, seems intent on undermining the image by way of the image itself, and planning the implosion of the logic of the simulacrum by dint of every greater doses of simulcra.

In contrast, what I have called cognitive mapping may be identified as a more modernist strategy, which retains an impossible concept of totality whose representational failure seemed for the moment as useful and productive as its (inconceivable) success. The problem with this particular slogan clearly lay in its own (representational) accessibility. Since everyone knows what a map is, it would have been necessary to add that cognitive mapping cannot (at least in our time) involve anything so easy as a map; indeed, once you knew what "cognitive mapping" was driving at, you were to dismiss all figures of maps and mapping from your mind and try to imagine something else. But it may be more desirable to take a genealogical approach and show how mapping has ceased to be achievable by means of maps themselves. This involves the proposition (often reiterated in these pages) that the three historical stages of capital have each generated a type of space unique to it, even though these three stages of capitalist space are obviously far more profoundly interrelated than are the spaces of other modes of production. The three types of space I have in mind are all the result of discontinuous expansion of quantum leaps in the enlargement of capital, in the latter's penetration and colonization of hitherto uncommodified areas. A certain unifying and totalizing force is presupposed here—not the Hegelian Absolute Spirit, nor the party, nor Stalin, but simply capital itself; and it is at least certain that the notion of capital stands or falls with the notion of some unified logic of this social system itself.

The first of these three kinds of space is that of classical or market capitalism in terms of a logic of the grid, a reorganization of some older sacred and heterogeneous space into geometrical and Cartesian homogeneity, a space of infinite equivalence and extension of which you can find a kind of dramatic or emblematic shorthand representation in Foucault's book on prisons. The example, however, requires the warning that a Marxian view of such space grounds it in Taylorization and the labor process rather than in that shadowy and mythical entity Foucault called "power." The emergence of this kind of space will probably not involve problems of figuration so acute as those we will confront in the later stages of capitalism, since here, for the moment, we witness that familiar process long generally associated with the Enlightenment, namely, the desacralization of the world, the decoding and secularization of the older forms of the sacred or the transcendent, the slow colonization of use value by exchange value, the "realistic" demystification of the older kinds of transcendent narratives in novels like Don Quixote, the standardization of both subject and object, the denaturalization of desire and its ultimate displacement by commodification (or, in other words, "success") and so on.

The problems of figuration that concern us will only become visible in the next stage, the passage from market to monopoly capital, or what Lenin called the "stage of imperialism"; and they may be conveyed by way of a growing contradiction between lived experience and structure, or between a phenomenological description of the life of an individual and a more properly structural model of the conditions of existence of that experience. Too rapidly we can say that, while in older societies and perhaps even in the early stages of market capital, the immediate and limited experience of individuals is still able to encompass and coincide with the true economic and social form that governs that experience, in the next moment these two levels drift ever further apart and really begin to constitute themselves into that opposition the classical dialectic describes as *Wesen* and *Erscheinung*, essence and appearance, structure and lived experience.

At this point the phenomenological experience of the individual subject—traditionally, the supreme raw material of the work of art—becomes limited to a tiny corner of the social world, a fixed-camera view of a certain section of London or the countryside or whatever. But the truth of that experience no longer coincides with the place in which it takes place. The truth of that limited daily experience of London lies, rather, in India or Jamaica or Hong Kong; it is bound up with the whole colonial system of the British Empire that determines the very quality of the individual's subjective life. Yet those structural coordinates are no longer accessible to immediate lived experience and are often not even conceptualizable for most people.

There comes into being, then, a situation in which we can say that if individual experience is authentic, then it cannot be true; and that if a scientific or cognitive model of the same content is true, then it escapes individual experience. It is evident that this new situation poses tremendous and crippling problems for a work of art; and I have argued that it is as an attempt to square this circle and to invent new and elaborate formal strategies for overcoming this dilemma that modernism or, perhaps better, the various modernisms as such emerge: in forms that inscribe a new sense of the absent global colonial system on the very syntax of poetic language itself, a new play of absence and presence that at its most simplified will be haunted by the exotic and be tattooed with foreign place names, and at its most intense will involve the invention of remarkable new languages and forms.

At this point an essentially allegorical concept must be introduced—the "play of figuration"—in order to convey some sense that these new and enormous global realities are inaccessible to any individual subject or consciousness—not even to Hegel, let alone Cecil Rhodes or Queen Victoria—which is to say that those fundamental realities are somehow ultimately unrepresentable or, to use the Althusserian phrase, are something like an absent cause, one that can never emerge into the presence of perception. Yet this absent cause can find figures through which to express itself in distorted and symbolic ways: indeed, one of our basic tasks as critics of literature is to track down and make conceptually available the ultimate realities and experiences designated by those figures, which the reading mind inevitably tends to reify and to read as primary contents in their own right.

The relationship of the modernist moment to the great new global colonial network, can be illustrated by a simple but specialized example of a kind of figure specific to this historical situation. Toward the end of the nineteenth century, a wide range of writers began to invent forms to express what I will call "monadic relativism." In Gide and Conrad, in Fernando Pessoa, in Pirandello, in Ford, and to a lesser extent in Henry James, even very obliquely in Proust, what we begin to see is the sense that each consciousness is a closed world, so that a representation of the social totality now must take the (impossible) form of a coexistence of those sealed subjective worlds and their peculiar interaction, which is in reality a passage of ships in the night, a centrifugal movement of lines and planes that can never intersect. The literary value that emerges from this new formal practice is called "irony"; and its philosophical ideology often takes the form of a vulgar appropriation of Einstein's theory of relativity. In this context, what I want to suggest is that these forms, whose content is generally that of privatized middle-class life, nonetheless stand as symptoms and distorted expressions of the penetration even of middle-class lived experience by this strange new global relativity of the colonial network. The one is then the figure, however deformed and symbolically rewritten, of the latter; and I take it that this figural process will remain central in all later attempts to restructure the form of the work of art to accommodate content that must radically resist and escape artistic figuration.

If this is so for the age of imperialism, how much the more must it hold for our own movement, the moment of the multinational network, or what Mandel calls "late capitalism," a moment in which not merely the older city but even the nation-state itself has ceased to play a central functional and formal role in a process that has in a new quantum leap of capital prodigiously expanded beyond them, leaving them behind as ruined and archaic remains of earlier stages in the development of this mode of production.

The new space that thereby emerges involves the suppression of distance (in the sense of Benjamin's aura) and the relentless saturation of any remaining voids and empty places, to the point where the postmodern body—whether wandering through a postmodern hotel, locked into rock sound by means of headphones, or undergoing the multiple shocks and bombardments of the Vietnam War as Michael Herr conveys it to us—is now exposed to a perceptual barrage of immediacy from which all sheltering layers and intervening mediations have been removed. There are, of course, many other features of this space one would ideally want to comment on—most notably, Lefebvre's concept of abstract space as what is simultaneously homogeneous and fragmented—but the disorientation of the saturated space will be the most useful guiding thread in the present context.

I take such spatial peculiarities of postmodernism as symptoms and expressions of a new and historically original dilemma, one that involves our insertion as individual subjects into a multidimensional set of radically discontinuous realities, whose frames range from the still surviving spaces of bourgeois private life all the way to the unimaginable decentering of global capital itself. Not even Einsteinian relativity, or the multiple subjective worlds of the older modernists, is capable of giving any kind of adequate figuration to this process, which in lived experience makes itself felt by the so-called death of the subject, or, more exactly, the fragmented and schizophrenic decentering and dispersion of this last (which can no longer even serve the function of the Jamesian reverberator or "point of view"). But what is involved here is in reality practical politics: since the crisis of socialist internationalism, and the enormous strategic and tactical difficulties of coordinating local and grassroots of neighborhood political actions with national or international ones, such urgent political dilemmas are all immediately functions of the enormously complex new international space in question.

Let me illustrate this by way of a brief account of the greatest importance and suggestiveness (for problems of space and politics) a historical narrative of the single most significant political experience of the American 1960s. *Detroit: I Do Mind Dying*, by Marvin Surkin and Dan Georgakis[59] is a study of the rise and fall of the League of Black Revolutionary Workers in that city in the late 1960s. The political formation in question was able to conquer power in the workplace, particularly in the automobile factories; it drove a substantial wedge into the media and informational monopoly of the city by way of a student newspaper; it elected judges; and finally it came within a hair's breadth of electing the mayor and taking over the city power apparatus. This was, of course, a remarkable political achievement, characterized by an exceedingly sophisticated sense of the need for a multilevel strategy for revolution that involved initiatives on the distinct social levels of the labor process, the media and culture, the juridical apparatus, and electoral politics.

Yet it is equally clear—and far clearer in virtual triumphs of this kind than in the earlier stages of neighborhood politics—that such strategy is bound and shackled to the city form itself. Indeed, one of the enormous strengths of the superstate and its federal constitution lies in the evident discontinuities between city, state, and federal power: if you cannot make socialism in one country, how much more derisory, then, are the prospects for socialism in one city in the United States today?

But what would happen if you conquered a whole series of large key urban centers in succession? This is what the League of Black Revolutionary Workers began to think about; that is to say, they began to feel that their movement was a political model and ought to be generalizable. The problem that arises is spatial: how to develop a *national* political movement on the basis of a *city* strategy and politics. At any rate, the leadership of the league began to spread the word in other cities and traveled to Italy and Sweden to study workers' strategies there and to explain their own model; reciprocally, out-of-town politicos came to Detroit to investigate the new strategies. At this point it ought to be clear that we are in the middle of the problem of representation, not the least of it being signaled by the appearance of that ominous American word "leadership." In a more general way, however, these trips were more than networking, making contacts, spreading information: they raised the problem of how to represent a unique local model and experience to people in other situations. So it was logical for the league to make a film of their experience, and a very fine and exciting film it is.

Spatial discontinuities, however, are more devious and dialectical, and they are not overcome in any of the most obvious ways. Such discontinuities in fact returned on the Detroit experience as some ultimate limit before which it collapsed. What happened was that the jet-setting militants of the league had become media stars; not only were they becoming alienated from their local constituencies, but, worse than that, nobody stayed home to mind the store. Having acceded to a larger spatial plane, the base vanished under them; and with this the most successful social revolutionary experiment of that rich political decade in the United States came to a sadly undramatic end. I do not want to say that it left no traces behind, since a number of local gains remain, and in any case every rich political experiment continues to feed the tradition in underground ways. Most ironic in this context, however, is the very success of their failure: the representation—the model of this complex spatial dialectic—triumphantly survives in the form of a film and a book, but in the process of becoming an image and a spectacle, the referent seems to have disappeared, as so many people from Debord to Baudrillard always warned us it would.

The example may also serve to illustrate the proposition that successful spatial representation need not be some uplifting socialist-realist drama of revolutionary triumph but may be equally inscribed in a narrative of defeat, which sometimes, even more effectively, causes the whole architectonic of postmodern global space to rise up in ghostly profile behind itself, as some ultimate dialectical barrier or invisible limit. And the Detroit experience may now specify more concretely what is meant by the slogan of cognitive mapping, which can now be characterized as something of a synthesis between Althusser and Kevin Lynch. Lynch's classic work, *The Image of the City*, indeed spawned the whole low-level subdiscipline that today takes the phrase "cognitive mapping" as its own designation. His problematic, to be sure, remains locked within the limits of phenomenology, and his book can no doubt be subjected to many criticisms on its own terms (not the least of which is the absense of any conception of political agency or historical process). My use of the book will be emblematic or allegorical, since the mental map of city space explored by Lynch can be extrapolated to that mental map of the social and global totality we all carry around in our heads in variously garbled forms. Drawing on the downtowns of Boston, Jersey City, and Los Angeles, and by means of interviews and questionnaires in which subjects were asked to draw their city context from memory, Lynch suggests that urban alienation is directly proportional to the mental unmappability of local cityscapes. A city like Boston, then, with its monumental perspectives, its markers and statuary, its combination of grand but simple spatial forms, including dramatic boundaries such as the Charles River, not only allows people to have, in their imaginations, a generally successful and continuous location to the rest of the city, but gives them something of the freedom and aesthetic gratification of traditional city form.

I have always been struck by the way Lynch's conception of city experience—its dialectic between the here and now of immediate perception and the imaginative or imaginary sense of the city as an absent totality—presents something like a spatial analogue of Althusser's great formulation of ideology itself, as "the Imaginary representation of the subject's relationship to his or her Real conditions of existence." Whatever its defects and problems, this positive conception of ideology as a necessary function in any form of social life has the great merit of stressing the gap between the local positioning of the individual subject and the totality of class structures in which he or she is situated, a gap between phenomenological perception and a reality that transcends all individual thinking or experience; but which ideology, as such, attempts to span or coordinate, to map, by means of conscious and unconscious representations. The conception of cognitive mapping proposed here therefore involves an extrapolation of Lynch's spatial analysis to the realm of social structure, that is to say, in our historical moment, to the totality of class relations on a global (or should I say multinational) scale. Unfortunately, in hindsight, this strength of the formulation is also its fundamental weakness: the transfer of the visual map[60] from city to globe is so compelling that it ends up re-spatializing an operation we were supposed to think of in a different manner altogether. A new sense of global social structure was supposed to take on figuration and to displace the purely perceptual substitute of the geographical figure; cognitive mapping, which was meant to have a kind of oxymoronic value and to transcend the limits of mapping altogether, is, as a concept, drawn back by the force of gravity of the black hole of the map itself (one of the most powerful of all human conceptual instruments) and therein cancels out its own impossible originality. A secondary premise must, however, also be argued — namely, that the incapacity to map spatially is as crippling to political experience as the analogous incapacity to map spatially is for urban experience. It follows that an aesthetic of cognitive mapping in this sense is an integral part of any socialist political project.

What must be stressed methodologically, in the operation of mapping as it emerges from Georgakis and Surkin's interesting text (or from the only full-dress analysis of cognitive mapping at work in a cultural artifact that I have myself succeeded in completing) is that in the present world-system, a media term is always present to function as an *analogon* or material interpretant for this or that more directly representational social model. Something thereby emerges which looks like a new postmodern version of the base-and-superstructure formula, in which a representation of social relations as such now demands the mediation of this or that interposed communicational structure, from which it must be read off indirectly. In the film I myself studied (*Dog Day Afternoon*, 1975, directed by Sidney Lumet),[61] the possibility of a class figuration in the content (the sinking of the older middle-class strata into proletarianization or wage work, the emergence of a sham "new class" in the government bureaucracy) is projected out onto the world system on the one hand, and on the other articulated by the form of the star system proper, which interposes itself and is read as the *interpretant* of the content. The doctrine of the Sartrean *analogon* permitted a theorization of this indirection and its mechanisms: and showed how even representation itself needs a substitute or a *tenant-lieu*, a placeholder, and as it were a small-scale model of a radically different and more formal type for its completion. What now seems clear is that this kind of *triangulation* is historically specific and has its deeper relationship with the structural dilemmas posed by postmodernism as such. It also retroactively clarifies the provisional description of postmodern "theoretical discourse" offered above (and also rehearsed in the peculiar new ideological symbiosis, in the postmodern, between the media and the market). These are, then, not really theories, but rather themselves unconscious structures and so many afterimages and secondary effects of some properly postmodern cognitive mapping, whose indispensable media term now passes itself off as this or that philosophical reflection on language, communication, and the media, rather than the manipulation of its figure.

Saul Landau has observed of our current situation that there has never been a moment in the history of capitalism when this last enjoyed greater elbowroom and space for maneuver: all the threatening forces it generated against itself in the past — labor movements and insurgencies, mass socialist parties, even socialist states themselves — seem today in full disarray when not in one way or another effectively neutralized; for the moment, global capital seems able to follow its own nature and inclinations, without the traditional precautions. Here, then, we have yet another "definition" of postmodernism, and a useful one indeed, which only an ostrich will wish to accuse of "pessimism." The postmodern may well in that sense be little more than a transitional period between two stages of capitalism, in which the earlier forms of the economic are in the process of being restructured on a global scale, including the older forms of labor and its traditional organizational institutions and concepts. That a new international proletariat (taking forms we cannot yet imagine) will reemerge from this convulsive upheaval it needs no prophet to predict: we ourselves are still in the trough, however, and no one can say how long we still stay there.

This is the sense in which two seemingly different conclusions to my two historical essays on the current situation (one on the sixties[62] and the other the first chapter of this volume, on postmodernism) are in reality identical: in the second, I called for that "cognitive mapping" of a new and global type which has just been evoked here; in the first, I anticipated a process of proletarianization on a global scale. "Cognitive

mapping" was in reality nothing but a code word for "class consciousness" — only it proposed the need for class consciousness of a new and
hitherto undreamed of kind, while it also inflected the account in the
direction of that new spatiality implicit in the postmodern (which Ed
Soja's *Postmodern Geographies* now places on the agenda in so elo-
quent and timely a fashion). I occasionally get just as tired of the slogan
"postmodern" as anyone else, but when I am tempted to regret my complicity with it, to deplore its misuses and its notoriety, and to conclude
with some reluctance that it raises more problems than it solves, I find
myself pausing to wonder whether any other concept can dramatize the
issues in quite so effective and economical a fashion.

The rhetorical strategy of the preceding pages has involved an experiment, namely, the attempt to see whether by systematizing something
that is resolutely unsystematic, and historicizing something that is resolutely ahistorical, one couldn't outflank it and force a historical way at
least of thinking about that. "We have to name the system": this high
point of the sixties finds an unexpected revival in the postmodernism
debate.

Notes

Introduction

1 In William Gibson, *Mona Lisa Overdrive* (New York, 1988). This is the place to regret the absence from this book of a chapter on cyberpunk, henceforth, for many of us, the supreme *literary* expression if not of postmodernism, then of late capitalism itself.

2 Achille Bonito-Oliva, *The Italian Trans-avantgarde* (Milan, 1980).

3 Michael Speaks develops this point at some length in his dissertation, "Remodelling Postmodernism(s): Architecture, Philosophy, Literature."

4 Thus, Jost Hermand's exhaustive inventory of sixties culture, "Pop, oder die These vom Ende der Kunst" (in Stile, Ismen, Etikketen [Wiesbaden, 1978]), covers virtually all the *formal* innovations of the so-called postmodern in advance.

5 See *The Political Unconscious* (Princeton, 1981), pp. 95–98.

6 Cf. Jacques Derrida: "Each time I fall upon this expression 'late capitalism' in texts dealing with literature and philosophy, it is clear to me that a dogmatic or stereotyped statement has replaced analytical demonstration"; in "Some Questions and Responses," *The Linguistics of Writing*, Nigel Fabb, Derek Attridge, Alan Durant, and Colin MacCabe, eds. (New York, 1987), p. 254.

7 See my *Late Marxism: Adorno, or, the Persistence of the Dialectic* (London, 1990); the topic deserves extended study. So far I have only found passing references, except for Giacomo Marramao, "Political Economy and Critical Theory," *Telos* no. 24 (Summer 1974); and also Helmut Dubiel, *Theory and Politics* (Cambridge, Mass., 1985).

8 See Karl Marx, *The Grundrisse*, (in *Collected Works*, volume 28 [Moscow, 1986]), for example, pp. 66–67, 97–98, 451.

9 Accounts and versions increasingly abound, of which I will recommend: David Harvey, *The Condition of Postmodernity* (Oxford, 1989); Antonio Benitez Rojo, *La Isla que se repite* (Hanover, N.H., 1990); Edward Soja, *Postmodern Geographies* (London, 1989); Todd Gitlin, "Hip-Deep in Postmodernism," *New York Times Book Review*, Nov. 6, 1988; p. 1; and Steven Connor, *Postmodernist Culture* (Oxford, 1989).

10 In a related work (see note 7 above) I have "felt myself able," as Hayden White might put it, to adopt the German term *Spätmarxismus* for the kind of Marxism that might be appropriate for the new system's moment.

I The Cultural Logic of Late Capitalism

1 Robert Venturi and Denise Scott-Brown, *Learning from Las Vegas*, (Cambridge, Mass. 1972).

2 The originality of Charles Jencks's pathbreaking *Language of Post-Modern Architecture* (1977) lay in its well-nigh dialectical combination of postmodern architecture and a certain kind of semiotics, each being appealed to to justify the existence of the other.

Semiotics becomes appropriate as a mode of analysis of the newer architecture by virtue of the latter's populism, which does emit signs and messages to a spatial "reading public," unlike the monumentality of the high modern. Meanwhile, the newer architecture is itself thereby validated, insofar as it is accessible to semiotic analysis and thus proves to be an essentially aesthetic object (rather than the transaesthetic constructions of the high modern). Here, then, aesthetics reinforces an ideology of communication (about which more will be observed in the concluding chapter), and vice versa. Besides Jencks's many valuable contributions, see also Heinrich Klotz, *History of Postmodern Architecture* (Cambridge, Mass., 1988); Pier Paolo Portoghesi, *After Modern Architecture* (New York, 1982).

3 Heidegger, "The Origin of the Work of Art," in Albert Hofstadter and Richard Kuhns, eds. *Philosophies of Art and Beauty* (New York, 1964), p. 663.

4 Remo Ceserani, "Quelle scarpe di Andy Warhol," *Il Manifesto* (June 1989).

5 Ragna Stang, *Edvard Munch* (New York, 1979), p. 90.

6 This is the moment to confront a significant translation problem and to say why, in my opinion, the notion of a postmodern spatialization is not incompatible with Joseph Frank's influential attribution of an essentially "spatial form" to the high modern. In hindsight, what he describes is the vocation of the modern work to invent a kind of spatial mnemonics reminiscent of Frances Yates's *Art of Memory*—a "totalizing" construction in the stricter sense of the stigmatized, autonomous work, whereby the particular somehow includes a battery of re- and pre-tensions linking the sentence or the detail to the Idea of the total form itself. Adorno quotes a remark about Wagner by the conductor Alfred Lorenz in precisely this sense: "If you have completely mastered a major work in all its details, you sometimes experience moments in which your consciousness of time suddenly disappears and the entire work seems to be what one might call 'spatial,' that is, with everything present simultaneously in the mind with precision" (W. 36/33). But such mnemonic spatiality could never characterize postmodern texts, in which "totality" is eschewed virtually by definition. Frank's modernist spatial form is thus synedochic, whereas it is scarcely even a beginning to summon up the word *metonymic* for postmodernism's universal urbanization, let alone its nominalism of the here-and-now.

7 For further on the 50s, see chapter 9.

8 See also "Art Deco," in my *Signatures of the Visible* (Routledge, 1990).

9 "Ragtime," *American Review* no. 20 (April 1974): 1–20.

10 Linda Hutcheon, *A Poetics of Postmodernism* (1988), pp. 61–2.

11 Jean-Paul Sartre, "L'Etranger de Camus," in *Situations II* (Paris, Gallimard, 1948).

12 The basic reference, in which Lacan discusses Schreber, is "D'Une question préliminaire à tout traitement possible de la psychose," in *Écrits*, Alan Sheridan, trans. (New York, 1977), pp. 179–225. Most of us have received this classical view of psychosis by way of Deleuze and Guattari's *Anti-Oedipus*.

13 See my "Imaginary and Symbolic in Lacan," in *The Ideologies of Theory*, volume I (Minnesota, 1988), pp. 75–115.

14 Marguerite Séchehaye, *Autobiography of a Schizophrenic Girl*, G. Rubin-Rabson, trans. (New York, 1968), p. 19.

15 *Primer* (Berkeley, Calif., 1988).

16 Sartre, *What Is Literature?* (Cambridge, Mass., 1988).

17 Ernest Mandel, *Late Capitalism* (London, 1978), p. 118.

18 See, particularly on such motifs in Le Corbusier, Gert Kähler, *Architektur als*

Symbolverfall: Das Dampfermotiv in der Baukunst (Brunswick, 1981).

19 "To say that a structure of this type 'turns its back away' is surely an understatement, while to speak of its 'popular' character is to miss the point of its systematic segregation from the great Hispanic-Asian city outside (whose crowds prefer the open space of the old Plaza). Indeed, it is virtually to endorse the master illusion that Portman seeks to convey: that he has re-created within the precious spaces of his super-lobbies the genuine popular texture of city life.

"(In fact, Portman has only built large vivariums for the upper middle classes, protected by astonishingly complex security systems. Most of the new downtown centres might as well have been built on the third moon of Jupiter. Their fundamental logic is that of a claustrophobic space colony attempting to miniaturize nature within itself. Thus the Bonaventure reconstructs a nostalgic Southern California in aspic: orange trees, fountains, flowering vines, and clean air. Outside, in a smog-poisoned reality, vast mirrored surfaces reflect away not only the misery of the larger city, but also its irrepressible vibrancy and quest for authenticity including the most exciting neighbourhood mural movement in North America)." (Mike Davis, "Urban Renaissance and the Spirit of Postmodernism," *New Left Review* 151 [May-June 1985]: 112).

Davis imagines I am being complacent or corrupt about this bit of second-order urban renewal; his article is as full of useful urban information and analysis as it is of bad faith. Lessons in economics from someone who thinks sweatshops are "precapitalist" are not helpful; meanwhile it is unclear what mileage is to be gained by crediting our side ("the ghetto rebellions of the late 1960s") with the formative influence in bringing postmodernism into being (a hegemonic or "ruling class" style if there ever was one), let alone gentrification. The sequence is obviously the other way round: capital (and its multitudinous "penetrations") comes first, and only then can "resistance" to it develop, even though it might be pretty to think otherwise. ("The association of the workers as it appears in the factory is not posited by them but by capital. Their combination is not *their* being, but the being of capital. To the individual worker it appears fortuitous. He relates to his own association with other workers and to his cooperation with them as *alien*, as to modes of operation of capital," [Karl Marx, *Grundrisse, Collected Works*, volume 28 (New York, 1986), p. 505]).

Davis's reply is characteristic of some of the more "militant" sounds from the Left; right-wing reactions to my article generally take the form of aesthetic handwringing, and (for example) deplore my apparent identification of postmodern architecture generally with a figure like Portman, who is, as it were, the Coppola (if not the Harold Robbins) of the new downtowns.

20 Michael Herr, *Dispatches* (New York, 1978), pp. 8–9.

21 See my "Morality and Ethical Substance," in *The Ideologies of Theory*, volume I (Minneapolis, 1988).

22 Louis Althusser, "Ideological State Apparatuses," in *Lenin and Philosophy* (New York, 1972).

2 Theories of the Postmodern

1 The following analysis does not seem to me applicable to the work of the *boundary 2* group, who early on appropriated the term *postmodernism* in the rather differ-

ent sense of a critique of establishment "modernist" thought.

2   Written in spring 1982.

3   See his "Modernity—An Incomplete Project," in *The Anti-Aesthetic*, Hal Foster, ed. (Port Townsend, Wash., 1983), pp. 3–15.

4   The specific politics associated with the Greens would seem to constitute a reaction to this situation rather than an exception from it.

5   See J. F. Lyotard, "Answering the Question, What Is Postmodernism?" in *The Post-Modern Condition* (Minneapolis, 1984), pp. 71–82; the book itself focuses primarily on science and epistemology rather than on culture.

6   See, in particular, *Architecture and Utopia* (Cambridge, Mass., 1976) and, with Francesco Dal Co, *Modern Architecture* (New York, 1979) as well as my "Architecture and the Critique of Ideology," in *The Ideologies of Theory*, volume 2 (Minneapolis, 1988).

7   See chapter 1; my contribution to *The Anti-Aesthetic* is a fragment of this definitive version.

8   See, for example, Charles Jencks, *Late-Modern Architecture* (New York, 1980); Jencks here, however, shifts his usage of the term from the designations for a cultural dominant or period style to the name for one aesthetic movement among others.

9   See "The Existence of Italy" in *Signatures of The Visible* (New York, 1990).

3   Surrealism Without the Unconscious

1   Raymond Williams, *Television* (New York, 1975), p. 92. Readers of collections like E. Ann Kaplan's *Regarding Television*, American Film Institute Monograph no. 2 (Maryland: 1983), and John Hanhardt's *Video Culture: A Critical Investigation* (New York, 1986), may find such assertions astonishing. A frequent theme of these articles remains, however, the absence, tardiness, repression, or impossibility of video theory proper.

2   "Time, Work-discipline, and Industrial Capitalism," *Past and Present* 38 (1967).

3   This is a point I have tried to argue more generally about the relationship between the study of "high literature" (or rather, high modernism) and that of mass culture, in "Reification and Utopia in Mass Culture," (1977; reprinted in *Signatures of the Visible*, 1990).

4   I mean here essentially the *good* anonymity of handicraft work of the medieval kind, as opposed to the supreme demiurgic subjectivity or "genius" of the modern Master.

4   Special Equivalents in the World System

1   André Malraux, *Les Voix du silence* (Paris, 1963).

2   In their *Kafka: pour une littérature mineure* (Paris, 1975).

3   For a provocative reevaluation of this moment, see D. N. Rodowick, *The Crisis of Political Modernism* (Urbana, Ill., 1988).

4   Robin Evans, "Figures, Doors and Passages," *Architectural Design* (April 1978), pp. 267–78.

5   Modern science fiction has often been a laboratory for such language experiments, as in Ursula LeGuin's model of the social structure of a hermaphroditic species (for which she uses only the masculine gender), in *The Left Hand of Darkness* (New York, 1969), or Samuel R. Delany's elaborate "reply," in *Stars in My Pocket Like Grains of*

Sand (New York, 1984), in which (for sexually differentiated beings of our own type) the feminine pronoun is used universally for the psychic subject, while the masculine pronoun is restricted to a person who is the object of desire (of whatever physical sex).

6 Barbara Diamonstein, *American Architecture Now* (New York, 1980), p. 46.

7 Ibid., pp. 43–44.

8 Gavin Macrae-Gibson, *Secret Life of Buildings* (Cambridge: MIT Press, 1985); see also the useful review of criticisms and opinion about the house in Tod A. Marder's "The Gehry House," Tod A. Marder, ed., *The Critical Edge* (Cambridge, Mass., 1985).

9 Macrae-Gibson, *Secret Life of Buildings*, pp. 16–18.

10 Ibid., p. 2.

11 Ibid., p. 5.

12 Raw materials are also ways of evoking tools as such, and Gehry's biographers trace his fascination with both back to jobs in his grandfather's hardware store when he was young. (*FG*, p. 12). The only other generally late modern or postmodern work in which tools and materials are so insistently foregrounded is Claude Simon's *Leçon de choses*, (see chapter five, below) a conscious reply to "Marxism" and a work which, along with the Gehry house, raises the question of the comparative capacities of realism and postmodernism, respectively, to convey the reality and the being of labor and of what Heidegger called *das Gestell* (instrumentation).

13 Ibid., pp. 12, 14, 16.

14 The reference is to my analysis of Portman in "Postmodernism, Or, The Cultural Logic of Late Capitalism"; see above, chapter one.

15 Diamonstein, *American Architecture Now*, pp. 37, 40.

16 Ibid., p. 44.

17 The reference is to his novel *Now Wait for Last Year* (New York, 1966); see also chapter eight.

18 Henry Cobb, ed., *The Architecture of Frank Gehry* (New York, 1986), p. 12.

19 Macrae-Gibson, *Secret Life of Buildings*, p. 12.

20 Ibid., p. 27.

21 See, for the cognitive mapping of all this, Rayner Banham's beautiful *Los Angeles: The Architecture of Four Ecologies* (Harmondsworth, 1973).

5 Reading and the Division of Labor

1 Claude Simon, *Les Corps conducteurs* (Paris: Minuit, 1971), trans. Helen R. Lane as *The Conducting Bodies* (Viking, 1974), where the first number refers to the French original and the second to the English translation. Henceforth all references will be given in this dual form within the text with the designation CC.

2 Celia Britton, *Claude Simon: Writing the Visible* (Cambridge, 1987), p. 37. In addition to this fine study, to the Heath book referred to below, and to the classic analyses of Jean Ricardou, see Ralph Sarkonak, *Claude Simon: les carrefours du texte* (Toronto, 1986).

3 David Bordwell and Kristin Thompson offer a paradigmatic discussion of genre in *Classical Hollywood Cinema* (New York, 1985), p. 6.

4 Britton, chapter two.

5   Barthes was among others notoriously responsible for this view; Barthes's best-known essays on the *nouveau roman*, republished in *Critical Essays* (Evanston, Ill., 1972), are "Objective Literature," "Literal Literature," "There Is No Robbe-Grillet School," and "The Last Word on Robbe-Grillet?"

6   Alain Robbe-Grillet, *Dans le labyrinth* (Paris, 1959), pp. 45–46.

7   Claude Simon, *La Bataille de Pharsale* (Paris, 1969), p. 132; all further references in the text are given as *BP*.

8   For Foucault, nomination would seem to have essentially been an eighteenth-century or "classical" operation: "It is the name that organizes classical discourse . . ." (quoted in Stephen Heath, *The Nouveau Roman* [Philadelphia, 1972], p. 106). In that case, the inaugural chapter of Hegel's *Phenomenology* to which we are about to refer would mark the breakup of this episteme; in the present context, however, and in the hindsight afforded by the very emergence of the *nouveau roman* itself, this crisis would seem to be the beginning, rather than the end, of something (if only of the postmodern).

9   G. W. Hegel, *Phenomenology of Spirit*, Miller, trans., p. 66.

10   Ibid., pp. 60, 64.

11   Ibid., p. 60.

12   Niklas Luhmann, *The Differentiation of Society* (New York, 1982), pp. 230–31.

13   "Jean-Paul Sartre s'explique sur *Les Mots*," *Le Monde*, April 18, 1964, p. 13; for further on this, see Heath, p. 31.

14   "Sensible aux reproches formulés à l'encontre des écrivains qui négligent les 'grands problèmes,' l'auteur a essayé d'en aborder ici quelques-uns, tels ceux de l'habitat, du travail manuel, de la nourriture, du temps, de l'espace, de la nature, des loisirs, de l'instruction, du discours, de l'information, de l'adultère, de la destruction et de la reproduction des espèces humaines ou animales. Vaste programme que des milliers d'ouvrages emplissant des milliers de bibliothèques sont, apparemment, encore loin d'avoir épuisé.

   Sans prétendre apporter de justes réponses, ce petit travail n'a d'autre ambition que de contribuer, pour sa faible part et dans les limites du genre, à l'effort général."

15   Claude Simon, "Le roman mot a mot," *Nouveau roman: hier, aujourd'hui*, volume II: *Pratiques* (1972), pp. 73–97), where the Rauschenberg installation is invoked, and where Simon proposes a number of graphic representations (reminiscent of René Thom's catastrophe theory) for the narrative forms of several of his novels.

16   See the discussion of Adorno's *Aesthetic Theory* in my *Late Marxism: Adorno, or, The Persistence of the Dialectic* (London, 1990).

6   Utopianism After the End of Utopia

1   Page references are to J. G. Ballard, *Best Short Stories* (New York, 1985).

2   Berger, *The Look of Things* (New York, 1974), p. 161 (italics mine).

3   Georg Lukács, *History and Class Consciousness* (Cambridge, Mass., 1984), p. 186.

4   All page references in the text to Achille Bonito-Oliva's *The International Trans-avantgarde* (Milan, 1982), hereafter cited as *IT*.

5   Susan Sontag, *On Photography* (New York, 1977), p. 180.

6   J. G. Ballard, "The University of Death," in *Love and Napalm: Export U.S.A.* (American title of *The Atrocity Exhibition* [New York, 1972]), p. 27.

7   Ballard, *Best Short Stories*, p. 114.

8   See T. W. Adorno and Max Horkheimer, *Dialectic of Enlightenment* (New York, 1972), pp. 15ff.

7   Immanence and Nominalism in Postmodern Theoretical Discourse

1   Berkeley, Calif., 1987. All further references in the text are given as *GS*.

2   In W. J. T. Mitchell, ed., *Against Theory* (Chicago, 1985), pp. 11–28. The second installment of this article (on Derrida and Gadamer) appeared in *Critical Inquiry*. References in the text are to the former and are designated *AT*.

3   Stephen Greenblatt, *Renaissance Self-Fashioning* (Chicago, 1980), p. 256.

4   T. W. Adorno, *Negative Dialektik*, (Frankfurt, 1982), pp. 362–369.

5   Karl Marx, "The Civil War in France," in the *Collected Works*, vol. II (New York, 1933), p. 504.

6   Baudrillard's word for it.

7   Susan Sontag, *On Photography* (New York, 1977), p. 180.

8   But see chapter eight, below.

9   The reader of this particular book probably does not need to be told that a construction like "the cultural logic of the market (circa 1910)" has different methodological and historical implications from one like "the logic of naturalism."

10   Gertrude Stein, *Four in America* (New Haven, 1947), p. vii.

11   See *Allegories of Reading* (New Haven, 1979), p. ix. All further references to this work in the text are given as *AR*.

12   Paul de Man, *The Rhetoric of Romanticism* (New York, 1984), p. vii.

13   Jean-Jacques Rousseau, *The First and Second Discourses*, Roger D. Masters, ed. (New York, 1964), p. 103. All further references to this work are given in the text as *RSD*.

14   J. M. D. Meiklejohn. See, for example, *The Critique of Pure Reason* (Chicago, 1952), p. 180A. Meiklejohn's English expression translates Kant's original word *aufheben*, which was to know a spectacular augmentation of fortune in the next decades.

15   See Jean-Paul Sartre's *Search for a Method* (New York, 1968), chapter three.

16   As far as the dialectic as a language experiment is concerned, I have always felt that the following remark, in the *Émile* (Paris, 1859), p. 101, note 1, contained some essential hints as to its reason for being:

"I have often reflected, in the course of writing, how impossible it is, in a long work, always to confer the same meaning on the same words. No language is rich enough to furnish as many terms, turns of phrase, or sentence-types, as our ideas have modifications. Splendid but unpractical is the method that consists in defining all the terms and ceaselessly substituting the definition for the term thereby defined; for how can this avoid circularity? Definitions could be good only if we did not need words to achieve them. Despite all this, I am convinced we can be clear, even in our linguistic poverty, not by always trying to give the same meanings to the same words, but by so proceeding that every time we use a word its provisional acceptance be adequately determined by the ideas connected with it, and that each period in which the word in question appears stands, as it were, as its definition. Thus I sometimes say that children are incapable of reasoning, and sometimes have them reason with some acuity. I do not thereby, I believe, contradict myself in my ideas, but I am unable to dissent from the proposition that I often contradict myself in my expressions."

17 Karl Marx, *Capital*, volume 1, Ben Fowkes, trans. (London: Penguin-NLB, 1976), p. 139. All further references are given in the text as *MC*.

18 The four stages are outlined in *Capital*, volume 1, book 1, part 1, chapter 1, section 3.

19 Gayatri Spivak, *In Other Worlds* (New York, 1987), p. 154.

20 Ibid., p. 154.

21 Denis Diderot, *Le Rêve de d'Alembert*, volume 17 of *Oeuvres complètes* (Paris, 1987), p. 128.

22 Kant, *Critique of Pure Reason*, part 1, chapter 3, section 6, p. 187.

23 Stanley Cavell, *The World Viewed* (Cambridge, Mass., 1979).

24 For more on nominalism, see my *Late Marxism: Adorno, or, the Persistence of the Dialectic* (London, 1990).

25 It will be remembered that the eudaimonic (pleasure-pain) plays the same kind of linking-separating role in Kant: "It was possible to effect this verification of moral principles as principles of a pure reason quite well, and with sufficient certainty, by a single appeal to the judgment of common sense, for this reason, that anything empirical which might slip into our maxim as a determining principle of the will can be detected at once by the feeling of pleasure or pain which necessarily attaches to it as exciting desire; whereas pure practical reason positively refuses to admit this feeling into its principle as a condition (*Critique of Practical Reason*, Thomas Kingsmill Abbott, trans. [Chicago, 1952], part 1, book 1, chapter 3, p. 330.

26 See his interesting remarks on de Man, in Geoffrey Galt Harpham, *The Ascetic Imperative in Culture and Criticism* (Chicago, 1987), pp. 266–68.

27 I realize as I write this that I have no idea how Paul himself actually felt about music; a certain satiric contempt, however, is not at all incompatible with a certain vicarious appreciation, as in Musil's portrait of his Nietzschean music enthusiasts:
    "Every time when he arrived they were playing the piano. They took it as a matter of course not to notice him until they had got to the end. This time it was Beethoven's *Hymn to Joy*; the millions sank, as Nietzsche describes it, into the dust in awe, the hostile frontiers dissolved, the gospel of universal harmony reconciled and united those who had been separated. The two of them had forgotten how to walk and talk and were about to soar up, dancing, into the ether. Their faces were flushed, their bodies hunched, and their heads bobbed and jerked up and down, while splayed claws battered at the rearing bulk of sound. Something immeasurable was happening. A dimly outlined balloon filled with hot emotion was being blown up to bursting-point, and from the excited fingertips, from the nervous wrinkling of the foreheads and the twitchings of the bodies, ever more and more feeling radiated into the monstrous private upheaval." (*The Man Without Qualities*, trans. E. Wilkins and E. Kaiser [London, 1979], vol. 1, p. 50.)

28 A recent assessment of Henrik de Man can be found in Lutz Niethammer, *Posthistorie: ist die Geschichte zu Ende?* (Hamburg, 1989), pp. 104–15.

29 See in particular Victor Farias, *Heidegger et le fascisme* (Paris: Verdier, 1987); and Hugo Ott, *Martin Heidegger unterwegs sur Biographie* (Frankfurt: Campus, 1988).

30 See Edouard Colinet, "Paul de Man and the Cercle du Libre Examen," in *Responses: On Paul de Man's Wartime Journalism*, Werner Hamacher, Neil Hertz, and Thomas

Keenan, eds. (Lincoln, Nebraska, 1989), pp. 426–37, especially p. 431.

31   See Pierre Bourdieu's *Ontologie politique de Martin Heidegger* (Paris, 1988); and also J. Habermas, *The Philosophical Discourse of Modernity* (Cambridge, Mass., 1987).

32   "Les Juifs dans la litterature actuelle," *Le Soir*, March 4, 1941, in *Paul de Man, Wartime Journalism, 1939–1943* (Lincoln, Nebraska, 1988), p. 45. The concluding flourish, on sending the Jews off to an island somewhere, is obviously in hindsight ominous indeed, but refers to the so-called Madagascar "solution," discussed until the war with Britain closed the sea lanes. See Arno Mayer, *Why Did the Heavens Not Darken?* (New York, 1988).

33   Compare the role of irony in Venturi, particularly in his *Complexity and Contradiction* (New York, 1966) but also in *Learning from Las Vegas* (Cambridge, Mass., 1972). One of the motifs in the present book has been the survival of just such residual modernist values into full postmodernism.

8   Postmodernism and the Market

1   Marx and Engels, *Collected Works*, volume 28 (New York, 1987), p. 180.

2   "Only two paths stand open to mental research: aesthetics, and also political economy." Stéphane Mallarmé, "Magie," in *Variations sur un sujet*, in *Oeuvres complètes* (Paris, 1945), p. 399. The phrase, which I used as an epigraph to *Marxism and Form*, emerges from a complex mediation on poetry, politics, economics, and class written in 1895 at the very dawn of high modernism itself.

3   Norman P. Barry, *On Classical Liberalism and Libertarianism* (New York, 1987), p. 13.

4   Ibid., p. 194.

5   Gary Becker, *An Economic Approach to Human Behavior* (Chicago, 1976), p. 14.

6   Ibid., p. 217.

7   Ibid., p. 141.

8   Barry, *On Classical Liberalism*, p. 30.

9   Marx and Engels, *Collected Works*, vol. 28, pp. 131–32.

10   Milton Friedman, *Capitalism and Democracy* (Chicago, 1962), p. 39.

11   See Albert O. Hirschman, *The Passions and the Interests* (Princeton, 1977), part 1.

12   "Periodizing the Sixties," in *The Ideologies of Theory* (Minneapolis, 1988), vol. 2, pp. 178–208.

13   T. W. Adorno and Max Horkheimer, *Dialectic of Enlightenment*, John Cumming, trans. (New York, 1972), pp. 161–67.

14   See Jane Feuer, "Reading *Dynasty*: Television and Reception Theory," *South Atlantic Quarterly* 88, no. 2 (September 1989): 443–60.

15   Guy Debord, *The Society of the Spectacle* (Detroit, 1977), chapter 1.

16   See Barry, *On Classical Liberalism*, pp. 193–96.

10   Conclusion

1   See "Marxism and Historicism," *The Ideologies of Theory*, volume II (Minneapolis, 1988), pp. 148–77.

2   Nathalie Sarraute, "Flaubert the Precursor," in *The Age of Suspicion*, Maria Jolas, trans. (New York, 1963); Colin MacCabe, *James Joyce and the Revolution of the Word*

(London, 1979); and my three essays on Rimbaud, Stevens, and the literature of imperialism, "Rimbaud and the Spatial Text," in *Rewriting Literary History*, Tak-Wai Wong and M. A. Abbas, eds. (Hong Kong, 1984), pp. 66–88; "Wallace Stevens," in *New Orleans Review* 11, no. 1 (1984): pp. 10–19; "Modernism & Imperialism," in *Nationalism, Colonialism & Literature*, no. 14, (Field Day Pamphlet, Derry, Ireland, 1988), pp. 5–25.

3 I am indebted to Jonathan Dollimore for instructions as to the proper use of this term. As for the time-consciousness of the postmodern, John Barrell has said it all, speaking of postmodern decorators for whom "to modernise was the same thing as to antiquate," "Gone to Earth," *London Review of Books*, March 30, 1989, p. 13.

4 But see on the term, Matei Calinescu, *Five Faces of Modernity* (Durham, N.C., 1987) and also Peter Burger, *Prosa der Moderne* (Frankfurt, 1988) and Antoine Compagnon, *Les cinq paradoxes de la modernité* (Paris, 1990).

5 See, for example, Pierre Bourdieu, *L'Ontologie politique de Martin Heidegger* (Paris, 1988), and Anna-Maria Boschetti, *The Intellectual Enterprise: Sartre and "Les Temps modernes"* (Evanston, Ill., 1988).

6 In much the same way, Gertrude Stein imagines Henry James as a "great general" in *Four in America* (New Haven, 1947).

7 See Ernst Bloch, "Nonsynchronism and Dialectics," *New German Critique* no. 11 (Spring 1977), pp. 22–38.

8 See Perry Anderson, "Modernism and Revolution," *New Left Review* no. 144 (March-April 1984), pp. 95–113.

9 In John Berger, *Ways of Seeing*, chapter on Cubism (New York, 1977).

10 Even though a whole neo-classical politics, from Hulme and imagism on, did just that in the 1910s.

11 In his *Antiquiertheir des Menschen* (Munich, 1956).

12 For Marx, equality—or the demand for it—is the result of the equivalences instituted by wage labor, whence the suggestiveness of this remark: "The capitalist epoch is therefore characterized by the fact that labour-power, in the eyes of the worker himself, takes on the form of a commodity which is his property; his labour consequently takes on the form of wage-labour. On the other hand, it is only from this moment that the commodity-form of the products of labour becomes universal." *Capital*, volume I, Ben Fowkes, trans. (Harmondsworth, 1976), note 4, p. 274.

13 Karl Marx, *Grundrisse*, in *Collected Works*, vol. 28 (Moscow, 1986), p. 43.

14 Lester C. Thurow, *Dangerous Currents: The Stc'e of Economics* (New York, 1983); see also Stanley Aronowitz, *Science and Technology and the Future of Work* (Minneapolis, forthcoming).

15 Achille Bonita-Oliva, *The Italian Trans-avantgarde* (Milan, 1980).

16 Its relevance is historically sharpened if, with Weber, we grasp it as a unique theoretical event in some fashion coordinated with that equally unique historical event which is the emergence of capitalism (and of the "West"). See section viii of this chapter.

17 James Hogg, *The Memoirs and Confessions of a Justified Sinner* (1824; reprint: London, 1924).

18 I am indebted to John Beverley for this insight.

19 Ernesto Laclau and Chantal Mouffe, *Hegemony and Socialist Strategy* (London, 1985), p. 77.

20 See *Postmodernism/Jameson/Critique*, Douglas Kellner, ed. (Washington, D.C., 1989),

pp. 324ff. Portions of this conclusion were originally published as a reply to the various critiques contained in this volume and republished separately in *New Left Review* no. 176 (July/August 1989): 31–45.

21 Lynda Hutcheon, *A Poetics of Postmodernism* (New York, 1988), p. xi.

22 To which it only remains to add the obvious paradox that Sartre's *Critique* is also in fact not only very much a theory of groups, but also one which, unfinished as it is, seems relatively uncomfortable with the larger category of social class as such.

23 Hutcheon, *Politics of Postmodernism*, p. 7.

24 Jean-Paul Sartre, *Search for Method* (New York, 1968): "What did begin to change me was the *reality* of Marxism, the heavy presence on my horizon of the masses of workers, an enormous somber body which lived Marxism, which practiced it, and which at distance exercized an irresistible attraction on petty bourgeois intellectuals," p. 18.

25 Niklas Luhmann, *The Differentiation of Society* (New York, 1982).

26 T. W. Adorno and Max Horkheimer, *Dialectic of Enlightenment*, J. Cumming, trans. (New York, 1972), p. 121.

27 But see chapter eight.

28 Jean-Paul Sartre, "Preface," to Frantz Fanon, *The Wretched of the Earth*, Constance Farringon, trans. (New York, 1963), p. 7.

29 We owe a pathbreaking reintroduction of the demographic question into the Marxist problematic (so long intimidated by the example of Marx's own attacks on Malthus) to a now-classical study by Wally Seccombe, "Marxism and Demography," in *New Left Review* no. 137 (January-February 1983): 22–47. See also my discussion of Adorno's idea of natural history in *Late Marxism: Adorno, or, the Persistence of the Dialectic* (London, 1990).

30 Interview with Thornton Wilder, *Paris Review* no. 15 (1957): 51.

31 Jean-Paul Sartre, *La Nausée*, in *Oeuvres romanesques* (Paris, 1981), p. 67.

32 See above all *La Production de l'espace* (Paris, 1974), available at last in an English translation by Donald Nicholson-Smith (Blackwell, 1991).

33 For a valuable survey of contemporary theories of space, see Ed Soja's *Postmodern Geographies* (London, 1989).

34 See the eponymous book (New York, 1981).

35 In *Postmodernism and Japan*, Masao Miyoshi and Harry Harootunian, eds. (Durham, N.C., 1989), p. 274.

36 See chapter 1 of this book.

37 Alejo Carpentier, "Prologo" to *El Reino de este mundo* (Santiago, 1971).

38 Indeed, a postmodern Dickens swims into view when we recall (as Jonathan Arac has done for me) Walter Bagehot's comment on him: "London is like a newspaper. Everything is there, and everything is disconnected" (*Literary Studies* [London, 1898], p. 176).

39 *The Crying of Lot 49* (New York, 1982), p. 104.

40 Richard Gilman, *Decadence* (New York, 1979).

41 Bruno Latour, *The Pasteurization of France* (Cambridge, Mass., 1988), p. 207.

42 *Grundrisse*, p. 350.

43 D. H. Lawrence, "Song of a Man Who Has Come Through," *Complete Poems* (New York, 1964), p. 250.

44 See note 8, above.

45 See my "Metacommentary," in *The Ideologies of Theory*, volume I (Minneapolis, 1988), pp. 3–16.

46 Marvin Harris, *America Now* (New York, 1981).

47 For an anthropological deconstruction of the concept of belief, see Rodney Needham, *Belief, Language and Experience* (Oxford, 1972).

48 John Howard Yoder, *The Politics of Jesus* (Grand Rapids, Mich., 1972).

49 Gulles Kepel's account of Islamic fundamentalism, in *Muslim Extremism in Egypt: The Pharoah and the Prophet*, trans. J. Rothschild (Berkeley, Calif., 1986), suggests a good many parallels with North American black movements in the sixties. See also Bruce Lawrence, *The Defenders of God* (San Francisco, 1989).

50 Quoted in Hutcheon, p. 14.

51 But see the insistence on dispersal in Sartre's *Critique*.

52 Something demonstrated by Douglas Kellner in his introduction to *Postmodernism/Jameson/Critique*. Again, the text here follows the critiques contained in that volume.

53 New York, 1988.

54 Ronald L. Meek, *Social Science and the Ignoble Savage* (Cambridge, 1976), pp. 219, 221.

55 Ibid., pp. 127–28.

56 In *Postmodernism/Jameson/Critique*, pp. 134ff.

57 On this, see the interesting research of Adelaïde San Juan.

58 Of the meager analytical literature on "yuppies," Fred Pfeil's "Making Flippy Floppy: Postmodernism and the Baby Boom PMC," *The Year Left* (1985), pp. 268–95, can be recommended; see also the literature on the so-called "professional-managerial class," in particular Pat Walker, ed., *Between Labor and Capital* (Boston, 1979).

59 Dan Georgakis and Marvin Surkin, *Detroit, I Do Mind Dying* (New York, 1975).

60 Baudrillard quite properly reminds us—but he has used it so often that the reminder has something of the same effect as kicking the ladder out from under himself—that in the postmodern such essentially transcoded objects or symbiotic constructions as the famous Borges map (that always springs to mind on such occasions) or the images of Magritte cannot be used as figures or allegories for anything; and in the high theory of the postmodern they have all the vulgarity and lack of "distinction" of Escher prints on the walls of middlebrow college students. "If we were able to take as the finest allegory of simulation the Borges tale where the cartographers of the Empire draw up a map so detailed that it ends up exactly covering the territory (but where, with the decline of the Empire this map becomes frayed and finally ruined, a few shreds still discernible in the deserts—the metaphysical beauty of this ruined abstraction, bearing witness to an imperial pride and rotting like a carcass, returning to the substance of the soil, rather as an aging double ends up being confused with the real thing), this fable would then have come full circle for us, and now has nothing but the discreet charm of second-order simulacra. . . . The territory no longer precedes the map, nor survives it. Henceforth, it is the map that precedes the territory . . ." ("Simulacra and Simulations," Jean Baudrillard, *Selected Writings*, (Polity, 1988), p. 166).

61 "Class and Allegory in Contemporary Mass Culture: *Dog Day Afternoon* as a Political Film," in my *Signatures of the Visible* (New York, 1991).

62 See "Periodizing the Sixties," in my *The Ideologies of Theory*, vol. II, pp. 178–208.

Index

Illustration Credits

Vincent Van Gogh, "A Pair of Boots," The Baltimore Museum of Art: The Cone Collection, formed by Dr. Claribel Cone and Miss Etta Cone of Baltimore, Maryland, BMA 1950.302

Andy Warhol, "Diamond Dust Shoes," 1980. Copyright, The Estate and Foundation of Andy Warhol, 1989. Reproduced courtesy of ARS, N.Y.

René Magritte, "Le modèl rouge," Charly Herscovici/Art Resource, N.Y. Reproduced courtesy of ARS, N.Y.

Edvard Munch: "The Scream," photo and reproduction rights courtesy of Nasjonalgalleriet, Oslo.

Duane Hanson, "Museum Guard" and "Tourist II," Hokin Gallery, Bay Harbor Islands, Florida—Courtesy of Dorothy Berenson Blau.

Diego Rivera, "Man at the Crossroads," Reproduced courtesy of the Museo del Palacio de Bellas Artes, Mexico City, Mexico.

Oliver Wasow, "#146" from the "Utopia Post Utopia" catalog. Reproduced courtesy of Josh Baer Gallery.

Frank Gehry house, Photo by Tim Street-Porter. Reproduced courtesy ESTO Photographics.

Kitchen photo: Photographer unknown. Side view, Photographer unknown. Exploded view —Reproduced courtesy of Frank O. Gehry & Associates, Santa Monica, California.

Andrey Tarkovsky, from *Nostalgia*, "The Russian house inside the Italian cathedral." Photo courtesy of the British Film Institute. Reproduced courtesy of Grange Communications.

Walker Evans, "Floyd Burroughs' Work Shoes," Hale County, Alabama, 1936. Reproduced courtesy of the Library of Congress.

Wells Fargo Court (Skidmore, Owings and Merrill). Photo by Arthur Denner. Reproduced courtesy of the photographer.

The Westin Bonaventure, photo courtesy The Westin Bonaventure, Los Angeles, California.

The Westin Bonaventure (interior), photo courtesy of Nakashima Tschoegl & Associates, Inc.

Le Corbusier, "Unite d'Habitation" credit, Biraudon/Art Resource, N.Y. Reproduced courtesy of ARS, N.Y.

AlienNATION, Photos courtesy of Video Data Bank, Distributors, 280 S. Columbus, Chicago, Illinois, 60603

Robert Gober, "Untitled Installation." Photos courtesy of the artist and Paula Cooper Gallery.

Nam June Paik, "T.V. Clock." Collection: The artist. Exhibition: Nam June Paik, April 30-June 27, 1982. Photography (not artwork) © 1982 by Peter Moore. Reproduced courtesy of The Whitney Museum of American Art, New York.

Nam June Paik, "T.V. Garden," Collection: The artist. Plants donated by Kenneth J. West Plants, Inc., New York City. Exhibition: April 30-June 27, 1982. Photography (not artwork) © 1982 by Peter Moore. Reproduced courtesy of The Whitney Museum of American Art, New York.

David Salle, "Wild Locusts Ride," "75 by 104½" (2) acrylic, oil/canvas, fabric, 1985. Private Collection. Reproduced courtesy of Mary Boone Gallery, N.Y.

The Author

Fredric Jameson is William A. Lane, Jr.,
Professor of Comparative Literature and Director
of the Graduate Program in Literature and the
Duke Center for Critical Theory, Duke University.
He is the author of numerous books and is the
coeditor, with Stanley Fish, of the series, Post-
Contemporary Interventions.